RAV DOVBER PINSON

לבי ער

Purim

UNMASKING THE MYSTERIES

Volume 1

IYYUN PUBLISHING

Published by IYYUN Publishing
650 Sackett Street
Brooklyn, NY 11217

http:/www.iyyun.com

Iyyun Publishing books may be purchased for educational, business or sales promotional use. For information please contact: contact@IYYUN.com

Editor: R. Pinson

Editor: Mattisyahu Brown

Cover and book design: RP Design and Development

pb ISBN 979-8-9919640-4-3

Pinson, DovBer 1971-
PURIM : Unmasking the Mysteries Volume 1

ב"ה

לכי ער

RAV DOVBER PINSON

Purim

UNMASKING THE MYSTERIES

—— Volume 1 ——

Dedicated to our Children
in Gratitude:

אברהם קלמן שיחי'
Avraham Kalman Rosen שיחי'

משה צבי שיחי'
Moshe Tzvi Rosen שיחי'

and
יוסף דובער שיחי'
Yosef Dovber Rosen שיחי'

May you be blessed with
infinite joy and joy in the Infinite.
May Hashem bless you with wisdom,
Deveikus, good health, abundance,
and beautiful Jewish homes.

Ze'ev and Rivkah Rosen
שיחי'

Opening

Following *the destruction of the First Beis haMikdash over two and a half millennia ago,* Jewish history unfolds as a profound narrative of resilience amid adversity. This saga recounts not only a struggle for survival through exile, forced migrations, and persecution but also a remarkable story of miraculous triumph and extraordinary endurance.

Throughout the ages, the Jewish People has faced numerous adversities, often personified by figures like Haman (the villain in the Purim story), among others who sought to annihilate or humiliate us. Yet, seemingly against all odds, our collective spirit endures and shows itself to be Eternal. Though at times physically battered and emotionally scarred, *K'neses Yisrael* / the community of Israel consistently reawakens, ultimately rising to the top, thriving in every society, and excelling in every field possible, when given the opportunity. Our collective story is a testament to the strength, perseverance, and unwavering hope, which define our experience throughout history. This extraordinary saga is a testament to the *Nitzchiyus* / eternality of our People.

Not only was our nation exiled from our homeland for thousands of years, but it was also expelled, humiliated, and persecuted for much of that time. For this nation to survive, flourish, and ascend to great heights wherever it goes is nothing short of miraculous. It is beyond logic. It is a historical unfolding that is, in a sense, more profound than the Splitting of the Sea (Ya'avetz, *Siddur Sulam Beis Keil*, Hakdamah. See also *Chovos haLevavos*, Sha'ar haBechinah, 5. *Tzeidah LaDerech*, 4, Klal 7, 1).

The mighty empires of Greece, Assyria, Babylon, Persia, and Rome, once towering in their grandeur, their armies vast, their dominion unchallenged, have crumbled into dust, their echoes fading into the corridors of history. Yet, a small and scattered people, exiled and without a kingdom, without legions or fortresses, endures. Against all odds, we have withstood the tides of time, defying the very 'rules' of history. Our survival is not merely remarkable; it is arguably the greatest miracle ever witnessed by the world as a whole.

Countless tyrants, Pharaohs, Hamans, and their like, have risen up with a singular, burning mission: to erase the Jewish People from existence, Heaven forbid. Yet, we endure. Empires have crumbled, oppressors have faded into oblivion, but Am Yisrael remains, an unbreakable thread woven through the fabric of time.

Ironically, the very first known mention of the Jewish People outside of the Torah appears on the Merneptah Stele, unearthed in Thebes and dated to 1007 BCE:

Canaan has been plundered into every sort of woe,
Ashkelon has been overcome,
Gezer has been captured,
Yanoam has made nonexistent,
Israel is laid waste, his seed is not.

These hieroglyphics proclaim our annihilation, yet it was not we who vanished, but those who sought our end. They stand as a silent witness to history's greatest paradox: those who rise to destroy us are themselves lost to time, while we, against all odds, endure. Here we stand, alive, unwavering, our roots deep and unshaken, our branches reaching ever higher. We have not only survived but flourished, blossoming with a strength that defies the very words etched in stone. Those who sought our end are but whispers of the past, while we endure, proud and ever-renewing.

Salvation, whether in full or in part, has always found its way to us. It has taken countless forms across the tapestry of our history, each one another miracle in the face of potential annihilation.

Yet, for some reason which needs to be explored, among all the stories of peril and survival, the tale that unfolded in ancient Persia is singled out. The Purim narrative has been chosen to be commemorated each year as a holiday, a Yom Tov for all generations, and for eternity.

There is only one Purim in the year (though in many communities throughout history, "small Purims" were observed to mark local acts of salvation), the question is why? Why is this story, in particular, so unique? What elevates it above the rest, qualifying it as a celebration for all time, for the entire Jewish People, for all generations?

Moreover, one might wonder how a story from thousands of years ago can hold any true relevance in our lives today. What does the Purim story have to offer us in the present? Why is it so crucial to remember, and how does this ancient tale resonate with our current circumstances and our personal journey through life? What timeless lessons does it carry, speaking to the struggles and triumphs that we face even currently?

All these questions will be addressed. For now, suffice it to say that Purim is, as are all *Yamim Tovim* / holy days, not mere 'remembrances of things past' or nostalgic commemorations; rather, they are celebrations of events that continuously recur, including in the present. Yamim Tovim are vibrant celebrations that reveal timeless truths and Divine intervention, which affect all of Klal Yisrael today, and shape each of our individual lives, as well.

We do not celebrate history as 'his-story', someone else's story, from the past. For us, history is actually 'meta-history', sacred moments of the past that are deeply felt in the present because their message transcends time.

Events such as the Purim story are not merely historical; they are part of an unfolding narrative, a living story that began in the past but continues to shape our present and guide our future. Each retelling of this story is not just a remembrance, but a 're-living' that connects us today to the Divine revelation that was first revealed then.

Torah-based holidays, and even those instituted by the Rabbis, were established only when the Sages perceived that these events were not essentially isolated moments in history, but depictions of eternal truths, moments whose echoes reverberate throughout all time. They recognized that these celebrations were not just memories, but living, breathing experiences that continue to shape the fabric of existence. For example, a miracle that occurred physically on a certain date in the past may continue to unfold in the present on a metaphysical level, and most vividly on that same date on the calendar.

Through our remembrance and celebration of Purim, the miracle that gave rise to the story is, in a sense, rekindled, and it reoccurs for us. As *Megilas Esther* / 'The Scroll of Esther' states, these days are נזכרים ונעשים / "remembered and performed." Through 'remembering' and commemorating these days, they are actually being 're-performed' and reenacted in the present.

As we remember the story of Purim, we tap into a boundless reservoir of spiritual energy that flows abundantly on the day those events took place. Not only that, but the same Divine force that animated the miracles of the past flows through us each year with greater power than ever before. As our Sages teach, "Matters of holiness always increase." Each year, the relevance and transformative potential of each Yom Tov intensifies, infusing us with a deeper connection to the miracles of our shared history.

Yom Tov literally means 'a good day'. On each Yom Tov, whoever engages with it is gifted with an outpouring of blessings from the Ultimate Source of Goodness. The day is 'good' not simply on its own, but rather because Divine goodness is flowing so abundantly and accessibly. The Heavens open, and any soul can drink deeply from this well of Divine favor, delighting in the superabundant goodness, blessing, insight, joy, and potential for personal and communal miracles.

Each year, as the sacred days of Yom Tov return in the cycle of time, we ascend yet another rung on the infinite ladder of spiritual growth. A deeper truth unveils itself, a hidden reality awakens. Time does not merely revolve in a circle; it surges forward, ascending ever higher. It is not only cyclical but progressive, spiraling upward.

Each year, as we traverse the same sacred moments of the past, we do so from a loftier vantage point. As we enter Purim once more, activating its remembrance and joy and performing its unique *Mitzvos* / Torah-infused actions, we are transported to the point in time when the miracle first unfolded. And there, as we tap into the source that gave rise to the original miracle, the light of Purim is reawakened in the present moment with an even brighter, deeper light.

Both Chanukah and Purim are unique in that, at the conclusion of the Yom Tov, no *Havdalah* / ritual of separating from the Yom Tov is performed. On a basic level, this is because they are Rabbinically-instituted Yamim Tovim without Shabbos-like restraints on mundane 'work'. On a more profound level, it is because the spiritual light of these days does not fade when the day ends. The Light of Purim is not confined to a day on the calendar; rather, it continues to pour out its grace, permeating and transforming every day and time. Through celebrating Purim, we participate in weaving its light into the fabric of our days, illuminating our entire year. At least subtly, every day becomes Purim, every moment infused with its elation, its revelation, and boundless elevation.

Chapter 1

The History & Story of Purim

In the years between the destruction of the First Beis haMikdash and the rebuilding of the Second, at the conclusion of the 70 years of the Babylonian exile, the Jewish People were nearly annihilated by means of a plan devised by a wicked Persian minister who had gained the consent of the foolish yet powerful ruler.

At that juncture of history, the mighty ruler of Persia was King Achashverosh / Ahasuerus. Perhaps this is the Persian ruler historically called Khshayarsha and known to the Greeks, who did not have a '*sh*' sound, as Xerxes. The Greeks probably also added '-es' as the end of the name, to turn it into a more Greek-sounding name, similar to how they turned Moshe's name into *Mos-es* when the Torah was translated into Greek.

After the Babylonians, led by Nebuchadnezzar, exiled the Jewish People from *Eretz Yisrael* / Israel, the Babylonians were defeated by King Darius of Media and later King Cyrus of Persia. Cyrus's successor, and the one who unified the kingdom, was Achashverosh. Achashverosh married Vashti, the daughter of Belsatzar and granddaughter of Nebuchadnezzar. Achashverosh ruled over one hundred and twenty-seven provinces and was considered the supreme ruler and king of the ancient world.

As the Purim story begins, King Achashverosh is entertaining his guests at a royal birthday feast (*Medrash Abba Guriyon*, Parsha 1) in the capital city of *Shushan* / Susa. While displaying his wealth and riches, the king desires to show off his wife Vashti, and demands that she appear "with her crown," that is, undressed, wearing *only* her crown.

This is poetic justice, as Chazal (*Megilah*, 12b) explain, since Vashti had wished to humiliate Jewish women by gathering them on Shabbos and making them undress and work for her ('Work' can also be a euphemism: *Sotah*, 36b).

Vashti refuses to obey this shameful demand and chooses not to appear. Angered, the king asks his advisors what to do. The court minister Memuchan, who is actually Haman, suggests that the king dethrone Queen Vashti, so that her refusal should not influence women throughout the kingdom to refuse to do the bidding of their husbands. He also offers that the king should go ahead and find himself a better woman for his wife, hoping the king would choose his own daughter to be queen (*Medrash Esther*, 4:6).

In order to find a new queen, a proclamation goes out that there will be a competition, and all eligible women are forcibly gathered to the king's harem in order to participate. The one chosen from among the hundreds, if not thousands, of participants, is called Esther. Esther's Hebrew name is Hadassah, the cousin and adopted daughter (or perhaps wife: *Megilah*, 13a) of the court Jew, Mordechai (The name Mordechai may be related to the Persian name Marduk, as his name was actually P'sachya: *Shekalim*, 5: 1. *Maharasha, Chulin*, 139b). Following Mordechai's advice, Esther does not reveal her nationality to the king. Achashverosh loves Esther more than all the other women of his harem and makes her the primary Queen of Persia.

Some time later, by 'chance', Mordechai overhears two conspirators, servants of the king, planning to overthrow Achashverosh by poisoning him. Apparently, they felt overworked ever since the king married his new wife (*Megilah*, 13b). Mordechai immediately reports the conspiracy to Esther, who in turn reports it to the King, in the name of Mordechai. The king's life is saved, and Mordechai's heroic act is recorded in the official Book of Remembrances.

During Esther's reign, the king's prime minister is a devilish and power-hungry individual named Haman. He craves honor and becomes angry when Mordechai the Jew, who resolutely keeps the commandment to bow only in front of the Creator, does not bow before him as the king has ordered. Haman seeks his annihilation, along with that of the entire Jewish community, whom he represents. Haman easily (*Megilah*, 14a) convinces King Achashverosh that the Jews do not respect the royal decrees, and that he should worry about them rebelling. In an unfortunately familiar line of reasoning, Haman tells the king, "There is a certain people scattered and dispersed among the peoples in all the provinces of your realm. Their laws are different from those of every other people, and they do not observe the king's laws; therefore, it is not befitting for the king to tolerate them." The Megilah narrates, "Accordingly, written instructions were dispatched by couriers to all the king's provinces to destroy, massacre, and exterminate all the Jews, young and old, children and women, on a single day, on the thirteenth day of the twelfth month, that is, the month of Adar, and to plunder their possessions."

Before presenting his plan to the king, to determine the date to implement his plan of annihilation, Haman throws a lottery as a form of 'divination'. "In the first month (Nisan)… a lot was cast before Haman concerning every day and every month, (until it fell on) the twelfth month, that is, the month of Adar."

Haman casts the lots during the Thirteenth of Nisan, and he does so "day to day, month to month." What does this mean? First, he casts lots to determine the day of the month that would be best to implement his evil plan, and afterward, he casts lots for the month itself. As Haman's intention is to take immediate revenge on the nation of Mordechai, he begins by casting the lot regarding the fourteenth of a month, hoping that he could implement the plan on the following day, the Fourteenth of Nissan. The answer the lot gives him is negative. He then casts it for the fifteenth and sixteenth of a month, yet each time the lot comes up negative, pushing the date further, delaying it until past the end of the month. He then begins casting lots for the first of a month, hoping that the first of the month of Iyyar will be chosen, but again, the day is pushed off, and it continues to be pushed off until finally a lot falls on the thirteenth. Now he knows that the 13th day of a certain month will be auspicious for his evil plan, but he still needs to confirm the month.

Haman begins casting the lot to determine the auspicious month. He starts with Nissan, realizing that perhaps the 13th of Nissan, that very day, would be chosen, and he could start right away. Not only does the lot not fall on Nissan, but the lot continues to reject each month until it finally affirms the last month of the year. With chagrin, Haman sets the date for the 13th of Adar, a full eleven months into the future. This is a hidden miracle, as, with Hashem's help, the Jewish People will have ample time to avert the decree (Malbim).

When Mordechai hears of the devastating decree, he tears his garment, puts on sackcloth and ashes, and begins to cry to Hashem for salvation. He then sends a message to Esther, pleading with her to save the Jewish People by speaking to the king. After being convinced, Esther requests that Mordechai gather all the Jews to fast with her for three successive days and pray for her success. On the third day, Esther risks her life by appearing before the king without being summoned. When the king breaks his protocol and accepts Ester's approach, she asks only that he attend a party in her chambers. Her invitation is for the king and his trusted prime minister, Haman.

During this party, Achashverosh turns to Esther and says, 'Tell me your request (the reason for your urgent appearance), and I will give it to you, and tell me your desires and I will fulfill them

— anything, even up to half of my kingdom.' Esther responds, 'If you really want to fulfill my desire, then please come back, you and Haman, tomorrow, for another party. There, I will tell you.'

Haman leaves the feast in great spirits, pleased that the king and queen are giving him exclusive invitations. When he sees that Mordechai still does not bow to him, however, he is filled with anger. When he gets home, he tells his wife Zeresh about his glorious day with the king and queen, but then adds, 'But all of this is worthless when Mordechai does not respect me and bow down.' Zeresh and his friends advise him to build a gallows fifty feet high and tell the king to hang Mordechai on it. He is thrilled by the idea. He takes a plank of wood that was plundered from the *Kodesh haKodashim* / Holy of Holies (*Pirkei d'Rebbe Eliezer*, Chap 50. *Medrash Talpiyos*, Achashverosh. This means Haman was aiming to tap into the highest realm of Transcendence. The Rokeach, in *Hilchos Purim*, brings another oral tradition that Haman takes the plank from the Ark of Noach), and sets it up as a gallows to hang Mordechai.

That night, on the eve of the invitation for the second party, Achashverosh could not sleep. Perhaps he was ruminating about Esther and Haman possibly becoming too close to each other, as she has been unexplainably inviting Haman to the parties (*Megilah*, 15b). As he is tossing and turning, he orders that the Book of Remembrances be read to him. When the tale of Mordechai and the two conspirators is recounted, he recalls that he never rewarded Mordechai appropriately for saving his life. He summons Haman to advise him on how to reward an upright and noble person. Without knowing to whom the king is referring, but arrogantly assuming that it must be to himself, Haman suggests that this noble man be honored by dressing him in the royal garments, putting him in the royal chariot, and escorting him through the streets with the proclamation, "Thus shall be done to the man whom the king desires to honor!" To his shock, the king orders him to do what he just suggested to Mordechai, and that he himself should walk in front of the chariot and declare to the citizens of Persia, "Thus shall be done to the man whom the king desires to honor!"

Greatly humiliated and mortified, Haman returns home. When his wife hears what has occurred, she meekly tells him that, in this case, he has no chance to stand up against Mordechai.

In this humiliated condition, Haman makes his way to Esther's second party. As the wine is served and Achashverosh is in a happy mood, he again asks Esther what she desires. At this moment, Esther surprises both men by revealing her Jewish identity and Haman's malicious plans to destroy her people. Achashverosh is furious. Following the suggestion by Charvona, a eunuch attending to the king, Haman is made a victim of his own plot; he is sentenced to death by hanging on the gallows that he himself built, while Mordechai inherits Haman's position and possessions as the new prime minister.

As the wicked Haman's decree is still in effect, Esther requests that the king annul it. Achashverosh tells Esther and Mordechai to write up a new decree, and they do so, giving the Jews permission to gather on the Thirteenth day of Adar to defend themselves against their enemies, against those who would attack them. On that day, many battles were fought between the Jews and those who desired to implement Haman's evil decree. Now a united and empowered people, the Jews are victorious.

On the following day, the Fourteenth of Adar, a day of feasting and rejoicing, is established as a day celebrating their salvation. In the capital, the walled city of Shushan, the battles extend for an additional day, and so their victory celebration is held on the Fifteenth. From then on, Purim is celebrated as a day when the Jews were spared, and the day set for their demise was transformed into a festival of happiness, unity, and sharing.

"Mordechai recorded these events, and he sent dispatches to all the Jews throughout the provinces of King Achashverosh, near and far, charging them to observe celebrations on the fourteenth and fifteenth days of Adar,* every year. They were to observe them as days of feasting and merrymaking, and as an occasion for sending gifts to one another and presents to the poor... For that reason, these days were named 'Purim', after Pur (the lot)."

This is the core narrative.

---

* To this day, cities that were without encircling walls in times of Yehoshua / Joshua celebrate Purim on the Fourteenth of Adar, while cities, such as Shushan, that did have walls in the times of Yehoshua celebrate "Shushan Purim" on the Fifteenth of Adar.

Chapter 2

FOUNDATION:
THE UNIQUENESS OF PURIM
The Questions

efore delving into the laws, customs, and deeper significance of Purim, twenty-one fundamental and often perplexing differences between Purim and all other *Yamim Tovim* / Holidays will be highlighted. These distinctions hold the key to understanding the essence of this extraordinary day. As the journey through this book unfolds, each piece of the puzzle will fall into place, revealing with clarity why Purim stands apart, imbued with its own unique character and profound qualities.

QUESTION 1:

All Yamim Tovim, Holidays, have a Hebrew name. *Pesach* / 'Pass-Over', Rosh Hashanah / 'Head of the Year', even Chanukah, as in *Chanu Chaf-Hei* / 'They rested on the twenty-fifth (day of the month)', are Hebrew phrases which give meaning to the Yom Tov. Yet, *Purim* is not Hebrew, but a Persian word for 'lots', *Pur* in the singular. Why is Purim distinct in this way?

QUESTION 2:

All Yamim Tovim are named for the *Nes*, the miracle they represent, and which we celebrate. For example, Pesach relives the miracle when death 'passed over' our doors. The Yom Tov of Sukkos relives (according to one opinion) the miraculous 'booths' of the Clouds of Glory that enveloped us when we left Egypt. A stark contrast, Purim is named after the lottery that Haman drew, which was part of the plot to annihilate the Jewish People. Why do we refer to Purim using the term for the instrument of the evil plot, rather than a term for the miracle? Even if the evil decree must be referenced, it would seem a better name might be 'the Yom Tov of *Nahafoch-Hu*' / "It (the evil decree) was Reversed."

QUESTION 3:

The other Yamim Tovim are celebrated for open and revealed miracles that occurred for us, such as the Ten Plagues and the splitting of the sea during Pesach, and the miracle of the burning oil on Chanukah. The Purim story, however, has no such revealed miracles; it is, rather, a series of natural events and 'coincidences' that came together to create a very unexpected positive outcome. In the language of the Sages, the summation of the entire story of the Megilah is "There was once a foolish king who killed his wife at the advice of his friend, and then killed his friend at the advice of his wife" (הרג אשתו בשביל אוהבו ואחר כך הרג אוהבו בשביל אשתו: *Medrash Rabbah*, Esther. *Yalkut Shimoni*, Esther, 1045). What is the significance of miracles that are so vested within the natural world that they appear to be mere coincidences?

QUESTION 4:

The two major Yamim Tovim that are given to us in the Torah are Pesach and Sukkos (the third *Regel* / major Holiday, Shavuos, is a culmination of Pesach). Both of these begin on the fifteenth day of the month when there is a full moon, whereas Purim begins, for those in the Diaspora and those living in unwalled cities in *Eretz Yisrael* / Israel, on the fourteenth of the month, when the moon is almost, but not quite complete (Note Ma'amar *Basi I'Gani*, 5724). Why this distinction?

QUESTION 5:

Every other Yom Tov is celebrated on the same calendar day by every person, regardless of their location. Purim is celebrated on two different days, depending on a person's location. Virtually everywhere in the Diaspora, it is celebrated on the Fourteenth of

Adar, while within ancient walled cities in Eretz Yisrael, it is celebrated on the Fifteenth of Adar.* It is highly unusual for there to be a Yom Tov that some people celebrate on one day and others on another day.

Even more perplexing is the fact that the salvation of Klal Yisrael in the Purim story began with the call, לך כנוס את־כל־היהודים / "Go, gather all the Jews" (*Esther*, 4:16). In this way, 'Jewish unity' was clearly the key to redemption, and this was a direct counter to Haman's accusation, ישנו עם־אחד מפוזר ומפורד בין העמים / "There is a certain people, scattered and divided among the nations" (*Esther*, 3:8). While Haman's claim highlighted our disunity, Esther's response called forth a deep, national unity. How is it, then, that some of Klal Yisrael celebrate Purim on the Fourteenth of Adar, while others on the fifteenth? This seems to reinforce a sense of separation and fragmentation within Klal Yisrael. It would seem that a commemoration of unity should be expressed through a single, unified celebration on a single day.

QUESTION 6:

The Mitzvos of every Yom Tov are performed on the day itself. Matzah is eaten as a positive Mitzvah ("You shall…") only on Pesach. Eating meals in a Sukkah is only applicable within the actual days of Sukkos. The definitive Mitzvah of Purim, reading the

---

* Technically, any walled city from the times of Yehoshua, during the first entry of the Klal Yisrael / the Jewish People, even outside of Eretz Yisrael, needs to keep Purim on the Fifteenth of Adar. Many cities are discussed as possibilities, such as Sidon and Damascus. However, the only city in the world that is universally accepted and which therefore celebrates *only* on the Fifteenth, is Yerushalayim / Jerusalem.

Megilah, can, under certain pressing circumstances, be read even three days before the Yom Tov (from the eleventh of the month). In extreme cases of need, one can fulfill his or her obligation in this Mitzvah from the beginning of the month of Adar, almost two weeks before the Yom Tov begins (*Yerushalmi*, Megilah, 1). A parallel to this would be eating Matzah before Pesach and sitting in a Sukkah before Sukkos, but these acts would be meaningless in terms of the valid performance of a Mitzvah. Why is Purim different?

QUESTION 7:

The main protagonists and heroic figures of all other Yamim Tov are male. For example, Moshe is the protagonist in the story of the Exodus from Egypt, celebrated on Pesach. On Shavuos, Moshe is the main receiver of the Torah, and on Sukkos, he is leading our journeys through the Desert. On Chanukah, we are led by Mattisyahu and his sons. However, the greatest protagonist and hero in the Purim story is Queen Esther. Why is Purim distinct in that it has a feminine heroine? (Note, all men who are connected with a major redemption have the letter Mem at the beginning of their name: Moshe, Mattisyahu, Mordechai, and Mashiach (and Mashiach's given name, according to various sources in Chazal, will be Menachem). Mem is generally a 'masculine' letter… ללמדך שעיקר המ"ם הוא זכר: *Sefer haBahir*, 85).

QUESTION 8:

All of the books of *Tanach* / 'Torah, Prophets and Writings' that have passages defining the Yamim Tovim have titles referencing their male authors, such as 'Toras Moshe', Megilas Eicha (of

Yirmiyahu), and Megilas Antiyochos. Purim is the exception; the Megilah for Purim is known as Megilas *Esther* (In fact, it was Esther who pushed the Sages to write the scroll... שלחה להם אסתר לחכמים כתבוני לדורות / "Esther sent word to the Sages: 'Write (for) me (this narrative) for future generations (and canonize the scroll as part of the Torah)'": *Megilah*, 7a).

QUESTION 9:

On the other Yamim Tov, women are for the most part exempt from the obligation to perform the Yom Tov's special Mitzvos, as women are exempt from time-bound Mitzvos. On Purim (and Chanukah), women are just as obligated as men are to perform the Mitzvos of the day. We need to ask why.

QUESTION 10:

The Yamim Tovim all mark the beginnings of new cycles, be they monthly or yearly cycles. For instance, the Yamim Tovim of Tishrei begin the new year, and Pesach begins a new cycle of months. Purim alone is an 'end' Yom Tov, celebrated in the twelfth month of the monthly cycle, meaning at the end of the year as counted from Nissan, as well as the end of a six month period of "winter" (The holy days occurring in the "summer," Nissan though Elul, have a different inner character and theme from those from occurring in the "winter," Tishrei through Adar: see *The Spiral of Time: Unravelling the Yearly Cycle*, Chap. 1). Either way, no other Yom Tov occurs this 'late' in a cycle.

QUESTION 11:

Although Purim is the 'final' Yom Tov in the 'year of months' (counting from Nissan), and the middle month in the 'year of days' (counting from Tishrei), Purim is also a beginning of sorts. "All the Yamim Tovim of the year will be nullified (meaning 'superfluous') in the World to Come, besides Purim." In this way, Purim is eternal and the foundational Yom Tov of the future, the 'beginning', as it were, of the World to Come. This is another distinctive quality of Purim (שכל המועדים עתידים בטלים, וימי הפורים אינם בטלים לעולם: *Medrash*, Mishlei, 9:1. A similar (although not an exact) idea is expressed in the Rambam, *Hilchos Megilah v'Chanukah*, 2:18, based on the *Yerushalmi*, Megilah, 1:5: אף מגילת אסתר כל ספרי הנביאים וכל הכתובים. Here are the words of the Rambam: והלכות אינן עתידין ליבטל עתידין לבטל לימות המשיח חוץ ממגלת אסתר והרי היא קימת כחמשה חמשי תורה וכהלכות של תורה שבעל פה שאינן בטלין לעולם. ואף על פי שכל זכרון הצרות יבטל... ימי הפורים לא יבטלו / "All the books of the Prophets and all the Holy Writings will be nullified in the Messianic era, with the exception of *Megilas Esther*. It will continue to exist, as will the Five Books of the Torah and the Halachos of the Oral Law, which will never be nullified. Although all memories of the difficulties endured by our people will be nullified...the celebration of the days of Purim will not be nullified").

QUESTION 12:

Another difference between Purim and all other Yamim Tovim is in their meta-historical spiritual roots. "'And they stood under the Mount (Sinai)...' This teaches that the Holy One, blessed be He, overturned the mountain upon them like an inverted cask, and said to them, 'If you accept the Torah, good; if not, here will be your burial.' Yet even so, they re-accepted it in the days of Achashverosh, and did so with love" (*Shabbos*, 88a). We embraced the Torah once more, and not from fear, rather from devotion; not under compulsion, but with willing love. So, whereas the other Yamim Tovim are rooted in the first acceptance of Torah at Sinai, when our obligation was first sealed, Purim is also rooted in the re-acceptance of Torah during the time of Mordechai and Esther.

QUESTION 13:

While the other Yamim Tovim are related to Moshe, as Moshe received the Torah from Sinai, Purim is more closely related to his 'successor', Yehoshua. The cities in Eretz Yisrael (and theoretically any ancient walled city) that were walled in during the time of Yehoshua's conquest of Eretz Yisrael celebrate Purim on the fifteenth day of the month, whereas all other locations celebrate on the fourteenth day. So there is an intrinsic connection between Purim and Yehoshua. What is the meaning of, and reason for, this connection? (The Mishnah says, כרכין המוקפין חומה מימות יהושע בן נון / "(Purim is celebrated on the Fifteenth of Adar in) walled cities that were already walled in the time of Yeshoshua": *Megilah*, 1:1. Yet, there is also the opinion that they are כרכין המוקפין חומה מימות אחשורוש קורין בחמשה עשר / "walled cities that were walled in the time of Achashverosh": *Megilah*, 2b. This opinion is straightforward, as any city during the Purim story that was walled, similar to Shushan, celebrates as they did in Shushan, on the Fifteenth. What is the connection between Yehoshua and Purim, besides the fact (see *Bartenura*, ad loc.) that we want to remember Eretz Yisrael and that Yeshoshua was the first one to wage battle against Amalek, as the commentators write: *Orchos Chayim*, Hilchos Megilah, 8. Chida, *Birkei Yoseph*, Orach Chayim, Siman 688:2).

QUESTION 14:

The events that we celebrate on the other Yamim Tovim all oc-curred either in Eretz Yisrael (such as the Chanukah story), or as Klal Yisrael was traveling out of Egypt and slavery toward Eretz Yisrael (such as Pesach and Sukkos). Purim celebrates events that happened outside of Eretz Yisrael, in Persia (it is called נס שבחוצה לארץ / "a miracle in the diaspora": *Megilah*, 14a). What is the significance of this?

QUESTION 15:

The other major Yom Tov instituted by our Sages is Chanukah, which celebrates events that occurred when the Beis haMikdash in Eretz Yisrael was standing. Purim occurred when there was no Beis haMikdash, as it was between the times of the First and Sec-ond Temples. What does this difference mean?

QUESTION 16:

On the other Yamim Tovim, 'mundane' activities, such as writ-ing or lighting a flame, are prohibited. On Purim (and Chanukah), all work is allowed (מלאכה לא קבילו עלייהו / "They did not accept upon them-selves (laws regarding) doing work": *Megilah*, 5b). What does the allowance of mundane activities represent?

QUESTION 17:

Every other Yom Tov comes with a directive to be aware of and understand a certain principle. We sit in a Sukka, "So that we shall know that Hashem sat us in Sukkos when we left *Mitzrayim / Egypt*," and we eat Matzah on Pesach to become aware that we went out of Mitzrayim. *Da'as* / awareness is an essential part of these Yamim Tovim. Purim is the opposite; the objective of the day is to reach a point of *Lo Yada* / not knowing, beyond Da'as. Why?

The question here is not merely 'why' such drinking is prescribed, but how it is even possible. How *can* a person drink to the point of *Lo Yada* / "not knowing the difference between 'cursed is Haman' and 'blessed is Mordechai,'" when the very essence of Purim is the clear recognition that Haman *is* cursed and Mordechai *is* blessed? After all, the entire celebration rests on that distinction, from the downfall of Haman and the elevation of Mordechai, to the nullification of the decree and the revelation of the miracle. If a person begins to drink while conscious of this distinction, how exactly do they arrive at a state in which blessing and curse are no longer differentiated?

This question echoes a parallel idea regarding Bedikas Chametz. One of the reasons we search our home for Chametz before Pesach is the concern that, if our living space remains unexamined, we might later find Chametz on Pesach and come to eat it. However, if one was not able to perform the search, one still needs to check for the Chametz on Pesach (*Pesachim*, 10b: לא בדק בארבעה עשר יבדוק בתוך המועד). This is because when a person's entire intention is to eliminate Chametz, there is no concern that the search itself will lead to eating it (הוא עצמו מחזר עליו לשורפו, מיכל קאכיל מיניה). The mindset itself safeguards the act; one never reaches a point beyond knowing the difference between 'prohibited is Chametz and commanded is Matzah.' The same principle applies to drinking on Purim. If one begins with full focus on the difference between the cursed Haman and the blessed Mordechai, even intending to "blot out the name of Haman," it is debatable if drinking could lead to a state of "not knowing" (Ma'amar of Purim 5717. *Toras Menachem*, p. 149. This is especially true from the perspective that the Torah prohibits harming oneself, including by drinking until one loses consciousness or is drunk to the point of cognitive impairment).

QUESTION 18:

On the Yamim Tovim that are *Kodesh* / holy, our Sages direct us to drink wine, yet there is a specific measurement of wine. On Pesach, we must drink four cups of wine, and we should endeavor to drink more than the minimum (a cheek full), and at least most of the cup (Even if a bit of a headache may follow: *Nedarim*, 49b. *Yerushalmi*, Pesachim, 10:1. *Beis Yoseph*, Orach Chayim, 472:15). Yet, our Sages do not encourage us to become drunk. When a person is drunk, they are considered less *Kodesh* / holy, and more *Chol* / mundane (In the language of Rashi, עבודה שאתה עובד בשכרות קרויה חול / "If a Cohen performs an Avodah in the Beis haMikdash (Holiness) when he is drunk, he is (nonetheless) considered as Chol": *Zevachim*, 17b). Nevertheless, on Purim we are specifically instructed to drink without measure, or at least until we are no longer aware of the difference between "Blessed is Mordechai and cursed is Haman." What is unique about Purim that encourages us to drink until we are beyond the limitations of Da'as?

QUESTION 19:

On Chanukah, the other *Yom Tov mi-d'Rabanan* / festival enacted by our Sages, we are not given a specific Mitzvah to have feasts, yet on Purim, there is a specific Mitzvah to eat a lavish meal in order to feel joy in the body. Purim has a special emphasis on the body. Why is this?

QUESTION 20:

The dress code for all the Yamim Tovim is 'respectable attire'. In contrast, Purim is a day in which children, and some adults, dress up in costumes and 'silly' or unusual get-ups (Although the Maharil writes, and the Rama quotes, יש נהגו ללבוש בגדי שבת ויום טוב בפורים וכן נכון / "On Purim, our custom is to dress in our Shabbos and Yom Tov garments, and to do so is appropriate": *Orach Chayim*, 695:2). Why this strange behavior? Perhaps it is for the purpose of merriment and joy, but why only on Purim? One can experience a deep lightness on Purim; some can even take this into a carnivalistic state (*l'Havdil* / 'distinguish this' from authentic holiness), albeit very serious and holy as well, but why the lightness?

QUESTION 21:

On all the other Yamim Tovim there is a Mitzvah to be *b'Simchah* / joyful, and on Sukkos (*Zeman Simchaseinu* / the Season of Our Joy) there is *Simchah Yeseira* / additional joy (אף על פי שכל המועדות מצוה לשמח בהן. בחג הסכות היתה במקדש יום שמחה יתרה :Rambam, *Hilchos Shofar, Sukkah,*

8:12). Yet, Purim is a day of unlimited Simchah, and as a result, the entire month is transformed into a time of joy: "When Adar enters we increase in joy," thus on every progressive day of Adar we are to enter Adar with greater joy. Why is Purim more joyful than any other Yom Tov, including Sukkos?

These are twenty-one out of the many other elements that make Purim unique among Yamim Tovim. Throughout this text, all these questions will be explored, and eventually, a comprehensive understanding of the delightful uniqueness of Purim will (G-d willing) emerge and become revealed.

Chapter 3

FOUNDATION:

The Characters of the Story & What They Represent

hroughout these chapters, we will journey through the Purim story, exploring each of its central figures, not only as they appear in the simple reading of the Megilah but also through the deeper spiritual qualities they embody.

The characters of the Megilah are more than just historical figures. They are archetypes, living portraits of fundamental traits that exist within us all. Although they walked this earth in a specific time and place, like all personalities in the Torah, they transcend their own stories. They are luminous reflections of the inner forces that shape the human experience, each one personifying a particular quality in its most vivid and essential form.

Some five hundred years ago, the brilliant young sage Rebbe Moshe Isserles, "the Rama," unveiled a hidden dimension of the Purim story. In a short yet profound work called *Mechir Yayin*, he revealed that the characters of the Megilah are not just figures of the past but voices within us, the forces that shape our inner world. Mordechai stands as the Yetzer Tov, the soul's voice of truth and righteousness, while Haman embodies the Yetzer haRa, the seductive pull of ego and destruction. Queen Esther is the Neshamah, the hidden yet radiant essence of the soul, and Vashti is the fleeting reign of superficiality, indulgence, and pride.

Similarly, in the pages that follow, we will journey deeper into the Megilah's timeless wisdom, uncovering how these characters are not only reflections of our inner struggles but also cosmic forces woven into the fabric of existence. We will explore their interplay, their battles, and ultimately, how we can emerge victorious — not just in the story of Purim, but in the story of our own lives.

When we read the Megilah and celebrate Purim, we are, of course, not simply reminiscing about the past. As explained in the Opening, we are reliving history in order to gain a deeper understanding of our own life as a present-day Megilah narrative. "Anyone who reads the Megilah backwards (from the end to the beginning), has not fulfilled his obligation" (*Mishnah*, Megilah, 2:1). The Baal Shem Tov explains that this refers not only to reading the Megilah in reverse order, but to reading the story as if it belongs to the past alone.

If you 'read' or understand the Megilah as merely a record of an event that happened to others in another time, you are reading it 'backwards', and you have not fulfilled your obligation. You need to read the Megilah as *your* story, as what is happening to you right now. The miracles, the struggles, and the hidden hand of destiny are not distant memories, but living truths woven into our present lives. Esther's courage, Mordechai's faith, the triumph of light over darkness — all of these are within us.

The following are short descriptions of each of the main characters of the Megilah and what they represent for us.

1. KING ACHASHVEROSH

King Achashverosh is the most impartial figure in the entire Purim story. He is an empty vessel swayed by the voices around him. At the counsel of his advisor Haman, he executes his queen. At the counsel of his queen, Esther, he executes his advisor Haman. He has no opinions, no convictions of his own, only the sheer, unbounded authority of a ruler whose decree is absolute. Yet, he is more than a human caricature. He is a reflection of Melech haOlam, the King of the World, and more specifically, the *Ohr haSovev Kol Almin* / 'Surrounding Divine Light' that transcends the details of Creation, beyond duality, judgment, and binary categories. Achashverosh wears a crown, itself symbolizing this *Makif* / Surrounding Divine Light in which all possibilities exist at once, where reality simply *is*, untouched by man-made definitions and perspectives.

Achashverosh's reign stretches "from Hodu to Kush." In Hebrew, *Hodu* means 'gratitude' and 'radiance', while *Kush* signifies 'darkness'. This means he is a ruler who embraces both light and shadow, who holds within him the entirety of existence, the brilliant and the blurred, the beautiful and the blemished, the revealed and the concealed. He represents a force that transcends distinctions, encompassing all within its boundless expanse (*Ohr haTorah*, Megilas Esther, p. 3).

While the name Achashverosh is actually just a Hebrew pronunciation of his Persian name, our Sages tease out many interpretations of what the name means in proper Hebrew (*Megilah*, 11a). Among these interpretations is that the name contains the words *Rosh* / head, and *Ach* / woe, and so it means, "Everyone who recalled him said, 'Woe upon his head!'" Alternatively, the last syllable can be read as *Rash* / poor, and thus "The name alludes to the fact that everyone became poor in his days." The Rikanti writes that the name Achashverosh is an abbreviation for *Achris Ve'reishis Shelo* / "The end and the beginning are His" (Rikanti, Parshas Vayeitzei. Rama, *Mechir Yayin*. See also Rebbe Meir Papirush, *Meoros Nasan*, Meorei Ohr, Ma'areches Aleph, 182. *Kehilas Yaakov*, Ma'areches Aleph).

'Holding the beginning and the end' represents a transcendent level of Divinity that includes and embraces all of time, and all experiential beginnings and endings, elevations and descents.

2. VASHTI

Before Esther came on the scene, Vashti was queen, draped in allure, the face of the kingdom's indulgence. Her very name whispers of the Hebrew word *Shtei* / two, division, duality; this suggests a duality and division between how things appear and what they really are. She embodies the world's outer beauty, the tempting glimmer of the material, seductive pull of the surface that masks the depths beneath. She is the *Kelipas Nogah* / the husk that shines, the illusion of radiance that obscures the true light within. Vashti is not merely a person; she is a force, the outer shell of existence, the veil that conceals the essence.

If Esther is 'the hidden one' (as will be explained), Vashti is the garment that covers it. Vashti is the façade, the dazzling exterior, the illusion that there is nothing beyond what the eye can see. When the king summons her to appear without any garments, she refuses, not out of modesty, but because she cannot exist without her exterior appearance. She is nothing but garments. Without her coverings, she vanishes, exposed as emptiness.

Vashti only masquerades as 'substantial', just like the external world does, the realm of excess, arrogance, and fleeting beauty, the world that glitters with promise but is hollow at its core. She thrives in the domain of vanity, where what something *seems* to be matters more than what it *is*. She is the mirage that entices, the outer layer that deceives, the temptation that draws one away from deeper truths. But illusions cannot stand forever. The time comes when the veil is lifted, the mask falls, and Vashti, the queen of superficiality, is cast away. This makes way for the emergence of Esther, the queen of mystery and depth, of hidden Oneness.

3. ESTHER

Esther's Hebrew name is Hadassah (*Megilah*, 13a), while Esther is her Persian name, from the word *Istahar* / 'Star', Venus or Moon in Persian (הדסה שמה, ולמה נקראת אסתר שהיו אומות העולם קורין אותה על שום אסתהר / "Hadassah was her real name. Why then was she called Esther? The nations of the world named her after Istahar, Venus (or Astarte)": *Megilah*, ibid., Rashi (moon). See also Maharsha, *Chulin*, 139b). In Hebrew, the name *Esther* means 'hidden' or concealment (*Haster Astir: Chulin*, 139b). Thus, not only does Esther hide her identity as a Jew (ולמה נקראת שמה אסתר על שם שהיתה מסתרת דבריה), she also changes her name to one that in her native language means 'hidden'. This is a double concealment.

Hadassah means myrtle, a plant of quiet resilience, fragrant yet unassuming. But to the outside world, her Persian name Istahar identifies her with a star or celestial body that shines yet remains distant, is luminous yet veiled in mystery. However, this Persian name's Hebrew meaning, *Hester* / hiddenness, implies that her Persian name itself is a mask, a second layer of secrecy. She is hidden within her hiddenness, a presence wrapped in mystery, an unknown story that will be revealed only when the time is right. She represents the world of the concealed, the mystery within, the quiet depth of inwardness, the ever-pure soul. She dwells in the realm of *Malchus* / Sovereignty, the feminine quality of receptivity, the vessel that holds everything yet claims nothing of its own (*Meorei Ohr*, Ma'areches Aleph, 144. *Ohr haTorah*, Megilas Esther, Vayehi Omein).

Malchus is also called *Ayin* / 'nothingness'; Malchus has "nothing of its own," for it is the unitary space in which all things are contained. This space itself is not a 'thing' per se; it has no fixed form.

It is said of Esther, כי אין לה אב ואם / *Ki Ein (Ayin) Lah Av va'Eim* / "For she had neither father nor mother." She has no earthly source because she comes from אין / *Ayin*, untethered to earthly forms and external appearances, unattached to that which defines others.

Paradoxically, it is from this very state of Ayin that she is rooted in the highest *Ani* / 'I', the ultimate 'Self', the Divine Source, the true *Yesh* / existence of *Keser* / Divine Crown, which transcends relative existence (Esther is Malchus of Beriah, *ibid.*, or Malchus of Atzilus: Rebbe Rashab, 5679, *Vayehi Omein*. Yet she is also Atik (Keser) of Beriah: *Ohr haTorah*, Megilas Esther, 92a. See *Likutei Sichos*, Purim, p. 148, Note 73).

On another level of 'Ayin', Esther is not just an individual; she is the embodiment of Kneses Yisrael, the collective soul of the Jewish People. She moves unseen through the corridors of power, yet she is the force that shapes destiny. She speaks softly, yet her words turn the wheels of history. She is the hidden thread that holds the tapestry together, the concealed light waiting to be revealed.

4. HAMAN

Haman, too, is more than a historical individual; he is an embodiment of Amalek, the destructive force of cold indifference, the philosophy that denies meaning, the shadow that mocks purpose. Amalek is the prototypical enemy of humanity, and the essential weapon that he wields is seeding doubt, a sense of randomness, and depicting the world as a chilling place where nothing is sacred and everything is arbitrary. This 'demonic' power functions beneath the realm of free choice, where distinctions between good and evil dissolve, and where morality is stripped of its absolutes, reduced to mere constructs.

Haman does not simply desire power; he is intoxicated by it. He thrives in a world where there are no guiding principles, no *Emes* / higher truth, and no real definitions of *Tov v'Ra* / good and evil, only the shifting tides of dominance and submission. He craves the collapse of decency, the unraveling of values, the nihilistic sense that nothing is inherently just or unjust, that all is a game of power dictated by those strong enough to impose their will. His worldview is one of chaos, without cause and effect or connection between action and reaction, only raw, untamed force. His arrogance is boundless because he believes in nothing beyond himself. He is the force that declares that there is no order, no Divine guiding hand, no purpose in the rise and fall of nations and individuals. Everything, in his eyes, is mere chance, a lottery, and power belongs only to those ruthless enough to seize it.

Yet, Haman is not merely an opportunist; he is rooted in something far more primal. The Sages trace his origins back to the Garden of Eden, before *Bechirah* / the choice between good and evil became part of human destiny (*Chulin*, 139b). He is an echo of that primordial state, the Fiftieth Gate, the place where all possibilities exist without differentiation, where the lines between light and darkness blur into uncertainty. Haman is the Safek, the great question mark, the force that breeds doubt and confusion. He is the venom of Amalek, the cooling of passion, the cold severance connection, the whisper that nothing truly matters. He stands in stark contrast to Esther and Mordechai, who affirm that history has meaning, that choices matter, that good and evil are not illusions but realities woven into the fabric of existence.

5. MORDECHAI

Mordechai's essence is hidden within his name, a name that, like Esther's, is not of Hebrew origin, yet carries within it a profound secret. Our Sages (*Chulin*, 139b) reveal that his name stems from *Mira Dachya* / flowing myrrh, a fragrant and precious spice (מרדכי מן התורה מנין דכתיב מר דרור ומתרגמינן מירא דכיא). This connection is not incidental, for Mordechai is deeply connected to the sense of smell, the one sense that remains untouched by the event of the Tree of Knowledge. When Adam and Chavah partook of the forbidden fruit, they engaged all their senses: they saw, they touched, they tasted, and they heard. Only their sense of smell was untainted. Thus, scent can still connect us to an untouched, pure realm beyond fragmentation and duality. Mordechai, too, is rooted in this space beyond not only the Tree of Knowledge of Good and Evil, but beyond the binary version of reality itself, a realm of absolute light and goodness without an opposite.

While Haman is linked to the chaotic space where good and evil blur, where morality is stripped of meaning and power dictates all, Mordechai is connected to something higher still. He is not merely 'beyond good and evil'; he is beyond the construct of 'beyond good and evil'. He dwells in the space of *Keser Kol haKesarim* / the Crown of all Crowns, the hidden source of Divine Will. In this space, goodness is not 'chosen' for its utility, nor for its superiority over evil. Here, goodness simply *is*, because it is the Will of the Creator. Here, goodness is not an intellectual decision or a moral calculation, but a simple, absolute truth.

Even within his name, Mordechai, this truth is encoded. The *MoR* of **Mor**dechai also spells *RoM* / exalted. He is not merely a force within the world; he is a beacon from above, an exalted light that shines even within the darkest of times. Unlike the realm of Daas, where good and evil must be weighed and chosen, Mordechai is rooted in a realm beyond the mind, the 'crown' above the head, where no such choice is necessary. And yet, Mordechai's power is not only in his loftiness, but in his 'reach', his ability to touch and transform the lowest depths. *Mor* / myrrh, the fragrant substance that his name alludes to, is derived from the congealed blood of a non-Kosher animal (see *Tur*, Orach Chayim, Siman 216). It begins as something impure, seemingly unfit for holiness. Yet, through a process of transformation, it becomes a 'spice' of great value, used in the service of Hashem. This is the essence of Mordechai's mission: to take the Mor, the bitter and unrefined, and elevate it to Rom, the exalted, to reveal within the depths of exile the hidden light that never fades. For even when the Divine Presence seems to slumber, even when the world is shrouded in uncertainty, there is a light that never ceases to shine. This is the light of Mordechai, the radiance of Chochmah, the wisdom that exists in all times, in all realities, whispering that beyond the veils of concealment, beyond the shifting tides of history, goodness is not a choice, nor a construct, nor an outcome. It simply is the only truth, because that is the will of Hashem (Mordechai is *Yesod* / the aspect of *Abba* / Chochmah that 'reaches' down into Creation: *Pri Eitz Chayim*, Sh'ar 19, 5. He is the pure Ohr, in which even the *Kli* / vessel is Light: *Likutei Sichos*, Purim, p. 144).

Chapter 4

THE CONTEXT OF PURIM:
Purim & the Month of Adar

"*For Haman…had plotted to destroy the Jewish People, and had cast a pur (lottery) to terrify and destroy them; but when she (Esther) appeared before the King, he commanded…that the evil scheme which he (Haman) had devised against the Jews, should recoil upon his own head…*" (*Esther*, 9:24-25).

In the sacred dance of time, each month in the calendar carries its own spiritual melody, a unique resonance that shapes the narratives and celebrations within it. Sefer Yetzirah, among other texts, reveals the unique qualities, themes, and spiritual practices corresponding to each of the twelve months of the year. Delving more deeply into the inner aspects of Adar will help us crack the code of Purim and reveal the mystery of the Yom Tov of Purim.

Every Yom Tov has both a narrative, the miracle that happened, and a seasonal context, the time of year when the miracle happened. In a sense, it is the seasonal metaphysical climate that is expressed in the physical climate as well, the underlying context that gives rise to the narrative and the miracle. The spiritual matrix of Adar gives rise to the day of Purim.

THE CONTEXT OF THE MONTH
GIVES RISE TO THE MIRACLE OF THE MONTH

Purim arises from the context of the month of Adar, as each month carries within it a unique spiritual essence, and the Yom Tov of that month emerges from its essence.

Take, for example, the first and primary Yom Tov in the Torah, Pesach, which occurs in Nisan. In Nisan, we do not commemorate our redemption only because we happened to leave Egypt in Nisan. We left Egypt in Nisan because Nisan is inherently a month of Geulah, of breaking free from constriction, of redemption. The Medrash teaches that long before the Exodus from Egypt, קבע בו ראש חודש של גאולה / "He designated for them a Rosh Chodesh for Geulah" (*Medrash Rabbah,* Shemos, 15:11). Similarly, in the month of Kislev, the Yom Tov of Chanukah reveals the Divine Light and flow that has always been present, from the beginning of time, a light that shines even within the deepest darkness. In this way, we celebrate Chanukah in Kislev because the miracles of Chanukah needed to happen in this month of the darkest, longest, coldest nights. Before the miracles happened, Kislev was already holding that hidden light of trust and 'illumination within darkness'.

In Adar, the miracle of Purim did not invent the Divine Light masked within the workings of nature; it simply unveiled what was always there: that even the most natural, unmiraculous events are orchestrated by Divine providence.

This reframes our understanding: we do not celebrate these Yamim Tovim just because of the stories that occurred. Rather, the stories occurred because the Divine Light of the Yom Tov was already pulsing within the month, waiting to be revealed. The historical events were simply the breaking of a resistance, the opening that allowed that light to flow into the world. The story is not the cause of the light; rather, the story is a manifestation of the shattering of a blockage that allows the pre-existing light of the month to be seen in our world.

Every Yom Tov is the expression of a deep, timeless reality and light that is, and always was, there. The story is just the key that opens the door. This also explains how the *Avos* / Patriarchs were able to celebrate the Yamim Tovim long before the events that occurred for their great, great, great-grandchildren. They were attuned to the spiritual currents of time. They did need the story to break open any resistance, as their souls could already sense and receive the light directly.

So let us delve into the context of the holy month of Adar, which gave, and gives, rise to the most magical of holy days, the festive Yom Tov of Purim.

THE LETTER-COMBINATION OF THE MONTH

There are four letters in the Name of Hashem: Yud, Hei, Vav, and Hei. Yud and Vav, which are graphically a point (Yud) and a line (Vav), are both 'giver' or masculine letters. The letter Hei is graphically more expansive, and is a 'receiver' or feminine letter. Each month of the year has an inner light refracted as a different sequence of these four letters. The sequence corresponding to the month of Adar is Hei-Hei-Yud-Vav.

This is, in a sense, an inverse image of the Name of Hashem. In the pattern of the normal spelling, there is first a 'giver' (Yud), then a 'receiver' (Hei), then another 'giver' (Vav), and then another receiver (Hei). In Adar's sequence, first come both of the 'receiver' letters, followed by two of the 'giver' letters.

In the cosmic dance of Creator and Creation, Hashem is the masculine Giver of Life, the all-bestowing Source, while *Klal Yisrael* / the Community of Israel and the Creation embody the feminine recipients of this vitality. However, the month of Adar, and the festival of Purim in particular, symbolize a profound shift from this top-down dynamic. During this time, there is a transition from the overtly 'masculine' paradigm of Divine revelation descending from Above to the more feminine paradigm of innovation emerging from Below. This shift underscores the empowerment of the created, highlighting the active role of human initiative and creativity in manifesting Divine will and bringing hidden potentials to fruition.

Purim occurred after the destruction of the First Beis haMikdash, toward the end of the Prophetic era. It is thus the first Yom Tov that was initiated by us, the people, not technically instituted from Above through prophetic revelation. In this sense, it could be called the first Rabbinic Yom Tov. And what's more, it was initiated by Queen Esther, embodying the feminine paradigm. It was Esther herself who suggested that the miracle of Purim be written as a scroll and celebrated each year (שלחה להם אסתר לחכמים קבעוני לדורות / "Esther sent to the Sages: 'Establish me (my celebration; my breakthrough) for future generations'": *Megilah*, 7a). It was Esther who specifically requested that the observance of Purim and the Megilah reading be instituted as an ordinance for all time. This was radically innovative.

As the Age of Prophecy was waning and the echoes of the First Beis haMikdash were fading, a remarkable transformation unfolded within our spiritual landscape. This period marked the emergence of a novel mode of connection with *HaKadosh Baruch Hu* / the Holy One, characterized by a shift from the masculine paradigm of Divine revelation descending from Above to Below, to a more feminine paradigm of innovation arising from Below to Above. This created a type of Divine connection whereby light was drawn from darkness, and revelation emerged through dedicated toil and exertion. This signaled the maturation of our relationship with Hashem. Revelation was no longer a monologue, from top-down, but more a dialogue that required the full presence and participation of both parties, wherein both the Divine and humanity actively engaged.

This reversal of 'Above to Below' and 'Giver to receiver' also reminds us of when Haman's destructive decree was reversed. Although the day of Purim was supposed to be when we would meet our end and demise, we came out on top. The day was transformed into a joyful festival of giving gifts.

Prophecy is direct, a clear revelation of light. Prophecy is similar to walking into a room and turning on the lights, and everything immediately becomes illuminated (*Moreh Nevuchim*, Hakdamah). It is an 'Above to Below' paradigm. During the luminous Era of Prophecy, the Torah was unveiled through the sacred writings of the *Tanach* / "Torah, Prophets and Writings," offering direct channels of Divine wisdom. In the same vein, during the times of the First Beis haMikdash, miracles manifested openly, descending from the heavens into our earthly realm, exemplifying an 'Above to Below' paradigm (*Yuma*, 21b. Note, *Avos*, 5:5).

Torah is Divine Light (אורה זו תורה, וכן הוא אומר: כי נר מצוה ותורה אור: *Megilah*, 16b, quoting *Mishlei*, 6:23), and Torah is one (תורה אחת: *Bamidbar*, 15:29). Even physical light is an expression of 'oneness'; there is no material division within light itself, only in the medium through which the light manifests or shines. Indeed, there is a manifestation of the Divine Light that illuminates the darkness, which is the 'revelation' of Torah she-b'Kesav, and there is a manifestation of the Divine Light that emerges *from* the darkness, which is the 'innovation' of Torah She-b'Al Peh.

As the age of prophecy drew to a close, the dynamic between the Divine and humanity underwent a profound transformation. The cessation of direct revelation marked the end of a monologue and heralded the beginning of an interactive dialogue. This new era saw the emergence of *Torah She-b'Al Peh* / the Oral Torah, which unfolds through human endeavor, intellectual struggle, questions, and innovative solutions. It is a 'from Below to Above' dynamic; it comes from within 'darkness' which is usually relegated to a lower, secondary status. Yet in this month, the dynamic is unexpectedly reversed, and the Oral Torah 'gives' to the Written Torah: the 'lower' letters Hei and Hei precede the 'higher' letters Yud and Vav. The Megilah, written by human beings without even the help of revealed 'prophecy', as it were, is accepted as a part of Tanach.

This dynamic needs to be explored in greater detail. As we engage with Torah She-b'Al Peh, we participate in a dance of questions and answers, tensions and resolutions, exiles and redemptions. Through this rigorous process of inquiry and contemplation, the light of certainty emerges from the darkness of doubt, and understanding is forged through the crucible of challenge.

LIGHT FROM DARKNESS

Our Sages interpret the Pasuk, verse, במחשכים הושיבני כמתי עולם / "He placed me in darkness, like those long dead" (*Eichah*, 3:6): "This refers to the *Talmud Bavli* / Babylon Talmud (*Sanhedrin*, 24a). In fact, the Sages of Bavel themselves live in 'darkness' and are likened to 'darkness' (*Zevachim*, 60b. Ritva, *Yuma*, 57a). This is understood on a deeper level to imply that they reveal a light that comes *from* the darkness, specifically. This is a type of learning where wisdom and clarity, light and resolution, are derived from the darkness of not-knowing and doubt, the dynamic tension of questioning and debate. Regarding this, our Sages teach (*Tanchuma*, Noach 3) that Torah She-b'Al Peh is "difficult to learn and in the learning of it there is considerable anguish, comparable to darkness itself, as it is said, העם ההלכים בחשך ראו אור גדול / 'The people that walked in darkness have seen a great light' (*Yeshayahu*, 9:1). The people referred to in this Pasuk are the masters of the Talmud, who beheld a great light when the Holy One, blessed be He, enlightened them as to what is prohibited and permitted, pure and impure."

At Mount Sinai, the Torah says, "And they stood under the Mount." Said Rav Avdimi... "This teaches that the Holy One, blessed be He, overturned the Mountain upon them like an (inverted) cask, and said to them, 'If you accept the Torah, good; if not, here shall be your burial.' Rav Acha...observed: 'This furnishes a strong protest against the Torah!' Said Rava, אף על פי כן קבלוה בימי אחשורוש / 'Yet even so, they re-accepted it in the days of Achashverosh... they consciously confirmed what they had already taken upon themselves through coercion at Sinai'" (*Shabbos*, 88a).

Purim is the culmination of the receiving of the Torah. Originally, at Mount Sinai, Klal Yisrael was 'forced' to accept the Torah. The Mountain "suspended overhead" is a metaphor for an overwhelming encounter with the Divine that compelled them to simply surrender their free choice and passively accept what was being given (as the Maharal explains, *Gur Aryeh*, Shemos, 19:17). Our initial acceptance at Mount Sinai was more a surrender of our will than a voluntary choice. During the events of Purim, however, we willingly accepted the Torah with love (Tosefos, *Shabbos*, ad loc.), rather than out of fear. This completed and crowned the process that began at Sinai, for we could only fully and unanimously accept the Torah through our own free will, our own volition, and not under duress or external imposition from Above. In fact, we accepted the Torah so 'internally' that we even accepted our own experience as described in the Megilah as part of Torah, and therefore welcomed Purim as a Yom Tov. What was originally given from Above was now fully internalized below. Our own experience was thus 'Divinized'.

What inspired Klal Yisrael to embrace the Torah with love, transforming their initial acceptance under pressure into a heartfelt choice? The Ohr haChayim haKadosh, writes (*Shemos*, 19:5) that they did this because שראו פעולת חכם לחיים אשר עשו להם מרדכי ואסתר חזרו לקבל ברצון לקיים כל דבר אשר יחדשו ויתקנו עליהם חכמיהם אחר אשר ראו מה גדלו מעשה הצדיקים שזולתם לא היה נשאר רושם משונאיהם של ישראל / " Upon witnessing the life-saving actions of Mordechai and Esther, the Sages, representing the Jewish People, willingly reaffirmed their commitment to uphold all future enactments and ordinances instituted by their sages, having seen the greatness of the deeds performed by these righteous individuals. For without them, G-d forbid, the Jewish People would have been erased." In other words, they recognized the power of the Sages, the power of Torah She-b'Al Peh, the full potential of humanity, and the ultimate role of Creation.

Purim signifies a pivotal moment in our spiritual journey, marking the revelation of the *Torah She-b'Al Peh* / Oral Torah,* and completing the cycle of Torah transmission. Purim completes not only the process of Matan Torah, but it also completes, in a way, the *Torah she-b'Kesav* / the Written Teachings.

Each letter possesses a numerical value in a system known as Gematria. The word תורה / *Torah* comprises the letters Tav/400 (ת), Vav/6 (ו), and Reish/200 (ר) and Hei/5 (ה), which add up to 611. Similarly, the word בעל-פה / *b'Al-Peh* / oral is numerically 187, and the word בכתב / in writing, totals 424. When we combine the values of *b'Al-Peh* (187) to *b'Kesav* (424), their sum is 611, mirroring

---

* This is why Purim is particularly connected with Yehoshua, as the Mishnah (*Megilah*, 1:1) teaches, כרכין המוקפין חומה מימות יהושע בן נון / "Cities that have been surrounded by a wall since the days of Yehoshua bin Nun, read the Megilah on the Fifteenth of Adar." Yehoshua, in comparison to Moshe, the giver of Torah, is Torah She-b'Al Peh. And Purim is all about Torah She-b'Al Peh.

the numerical value of Torah. This numerical harmony illustrates that the Torah's completeness is achieved when both its written and oral dimensions are fully revealed and embraced, a marriage of Above with below and below with Above and a dialogue between Heaven and earth, and earth and Heaven. Thus, Purim not only commemorates a historical deliverance but also symbolizes the completion and perfection of the Torah, achieved through the intertwining of its written and oral traditions.

The events of the Purim story occurred during the time of the *Anshei K'neses haGedolah* / Men of the Great Assembly. This was an assemblage of a remarkable group of one hundred and twenty men composed of about eighty-five rabbinic sages and thirty-five prophets. This esteemed assembly spontaneously emerged in the aftermath of the destruction of the First Beis haMikdash, extending into the early period of the Second Beis haMikdash. They served as a vital bridge across the divide of this transitional age, leading Klal Yisrael from the prophetic era, where Hashem spoke directly to us, into the era of the Sages, where Hashem communicates through us. They were the bridge across the chasm of this transitional age, guiding us forward into a new world and a new paradigm. The Mishnah in *Avos* (1:1) that speaks of the transmission of Torah says, משה קיבל תורה מסיני ומסרה ליהושע, ויהושע לזקנים, וזקנים לנביאים, ונביאים מסרוה לאנשי כנסת הגדולה / "Moshe received the Torah from Sinai and *transmitted* it to Yehoshua, Yehoshua to the Elders, the Elders to the Prophets, and the Prophets *transmitted* it to the Men of the Great Assembly." The first stage of transmission begins with Moshe and ushers in the Age of the Prophets, continuing until the *Nevi'im* / Prophets. This is the first mention of the word *u–Mesarah* / transmitted, above. The second use of the word comes in a new form: *Mesaruha.* It indicates a new kind of transmission, occurring between the Prophets and the Men of the Great Assembly. This is the shift from the written Torah, the Torah of the Prophets, to Torah She-b'Al Peh, the Torah of the Sages.

The Pasuk says, על־פי התורה אשר יורוך ועל־המשפט אשר־יאמרו לך תעשה לא תסור מן־הדבר אשר־יגידו לך ימין ושמאל / "You shall act in accordance with the instructions given you and the ruling handed down to you; you must not deviate from the verdict that they announce to you either to the right or to the left" (*Devarim*, 17:11). This refers to the *Beis Din haGadol* / the Great court of Yerushalayim, otherwise known as the Sanhedrin. Regarding this, Rashi writes, "Even if he (the judge of the Great Court) tells you of the right that it is the left, or about the left that it is the right (you must obey him)." (Sifri, *Devarim*, 154. Although, see *Yerushalmi*, Horayos, 1:1: "...Until they tell you, that right is right and left is left"). The Ramban, in his commentary, elaborates upon Rashi's teaching, stating: "The purport thereof is that even if you think in your heart that they are mistaken, and the matter is simple in your eyes just as you know the difference between your right hand and your left hand, you must still do as they command you. You are not to say: 'How can I (permit myself to) eat this real forbidden fat, or execute this innocent man?' Instead, you are to say, 'Hashem Who enjoined the commandments commanded that I perform all His commandments in accordance with all that they (who stand before Him in the place that He shall choose) teach me to do. He gave me the Torah as taught by them, even if they were to err.' ...Now the need for this commandment is very great, for the Torah was given to us in written form, and it is known that not all opinions concur on newly arising matters. Disagreements would thus increase, and the *one Torah* would become many Torahs. Torah, therefore, defined the law that we are to obey the Great Court that stands before Hashem (the Sanhedrin in Yerushalayim) in whatever they tell us with respect to the interpretation of the Torah, whether they received its interpretation by means of a witness of a witness (all the way back) until Moshe, (who heard it) from the Mouth of the Almighty, or whether they said so based on the implication of the Torah or its intent. For it was subject to their judgment that Hashem gave them the Torah even if it (the judgment) appears to you to exchange right for left" (Although, even if you yourself were a sage in the times of the Sanhedrin, you would need to go and present your case in front of them, and if they ruled against you, you would have to submit to their ruling. In other words, if one studies Torah, and their own reasoning may yield an understanding that seems fully rational and correct, if the Sanhedrin rules otherwise, it is their ruling that determines the will of Hashem at that moment: Ramban, *Sefer haMitzvos*, Shoresh Aleph. *Chinuch*, Mitzvah, 496. Ran, *Sanhedrin*, 85a, in the name of the Ramban).

In other words, the transmission of Torah to and through the Sages is so flawless that the Sages do not merely function as interpreters of the Torah; they become, in effect, conduits, or even 'creators' of its truth. The rulings of the Sages are not only binding, they 'retroactively' define what Torah itself is. If they declare that "the right is left and the left is right," then reality itself, in the framework of Torah, aligns with their declaration, and it becomes the truth. The Sages are not simply revealing an already-fixed truth, but through their own initiative and innovation, they establish the revealed will of the Divine in the world (Even if the Sanhedrin errs, the error itself becomes binding (see *Horayos*, in the beginning): until they themselves recognize and correct it on their own, no external body or individual can override them).

Torah She-b'Al Peh begins to emerge and take shape during this transformative historical era, unfolding specifically beyond and 'outside' the borders of the Holy Land, Eretz Yisrael (in Bavel, with the Sages of the Gemara). It is, perhaps, for this reason that Megilas Esther (8:17) tells us, ורבים מעמי הארץ מתיהדים / "…and many of the peoples of the Land converted and became Jews" (Rashi, ad loc.).

Torah She-b'Al Peh has a special connection with *Gerim* / converts (*Pri Tzadik*, Yisro). Converts represent the Below, so to speak, those who are on the 'outside' but through their own volition enter into the 'inside'. Often, they represent individuals who have grappled with feelings of uncertainty or a sense of not belonging, or belonging elsewhere. Yet, through their own perseverance, determination, and unwavering conviction, they transcend these challenges and, by their own efforts, forge a profound connection with the Holy One Above. In this way, the first translation of the Torah, a form of Torah She-b'Al Peh as it is an interpretative translation, was crafted by Unkolus the convert. The great Rebbe Akiva, who is the embodiment of Torah She-b'Al Peh (*Sanhedrin*, 86a, Rashi), was the child of converts (Rambam, *Hakdamah l'Mishneh Torah*). This phenomenon, beginning with Yisro the convert, underscores the profound connection between converts and the Oral Torah tradition, the Torah She-b'Al Peh.

Parenthetically, as we draw ever closer to the final Geulah, the ultimate redemption and the coming of Mashiach, a time when the world below will be fully revealed as one with the Above, we witness an inspiring proliferation of *Geirei Tzedek* / holy and righteous converts. These individuals who have 'returned' from the outside to enter into Klal Yisrael.

The first revealing of Torah She-b'Al Peh within the Torah itself is with the *Parsha* / Torah portion of Yisro, in which Moshe's father-in-law Yisro, a person on the 'outside' of Klal Yisrael, comes to meet Moshe in the Desert (either before or after, *Zevachim*, 116a. *Zohar* 2, 67b-68a). With his own intuition and intellectual understanding, he suggests a new system of courts to Moshe, and this is accepted by Hashem, human insight becoming part of Torah. In fact, he is called "Yisro" (Rashi, *Shemos*, 18:1) because he *Yeser* / adds a Parsha to the Torah (The core letters of Yisro's name are Reish, Vav, Tav, which are the same letters in the name of the other famous convert, Ruth. In numerical value, *Ruth* equals 606, and with the addition of 7, for the Seven Noachide Laws, they equal 613, the number of Mitzvos in the Torah. 606 is also the value of the filling letters of the Name 'Ado-noi': *Sha'ar haPesukim*, Esther. The Name of Divine concealment, Ado-noi, is connected with Purim, as will be explored in connection with the idea of Torah She-b'Al Peh). Yisro, too, is a convert and thus inherently connected with Torah She-b'Al Peh.

The Written Torah is fixed and unchanging, not subject to human modification. Yet, alongside the written dimension of Torah, we were given an oral dimension, with a sacred task of delving into its depths, expanding upon its principles, and uncovering its endless wisdom. This is the essence of the Oral Torah — an ever-evolving, dynamic tradition in which Klal Yisrael continuously engages, applying its timeless truths to new circumstances and making them ever-relevant. Through our intellectual efforts, we are called to be *Mechadeshim* / 'innovators', revealers of fresh insights that are nonetheless consistent with Torah and the transmission of the Sages. Purim is therefore when we, the 'Below', finally became full partners and collaborators in the development and articulation of the Torah that was revealed to us from 'Above'. In fact, the Yom

Tov of Purim is itself one of the great innovations that were meant to be initiated after the original giving of the Torah at Mount Sinai (מצות העתידות להתחדש כגון מקרא מגילה / "Mitzvos that were to be initiated in the future, for example, the Megilah reading": *Shavuos*, 39a. ומה שהסופרים עתידין לחדש ומאי ניהו מקרא מגילה / "…and what the Scribes were destined to innovate in the future. And what is this? It is the Megilah reading": *Megilah*, 19b. The *Yerushalmi* writes that there were eighty-five elders, among them prophets, who were worried about 'adding' the Yom Tov of Purim, as it might be a prohibition of *Bal Tosif* / "Do not add to the Torah": שמונים וחמשה זקנים ומהם שלשים וכמה נביאים היו מצטערין על הדבר הזה. אמרו. כתוב אלה המצות אשר צוה י את משה שנצטוינו מפי משה. כך אמר לנו משה. אין נביא אחר עתיד לחדש לכם דבר מעתה. ומרדכי ואסתר מבקשים לחדש לנו דבה לא חזו משם נושאים ונותנין [בדבר] עד שהאיר הקדוש ברוך הוא את עיניהם ומצאו אותה כתובה בתורה ובנביאים ובכתובים / "Eighty-five elders, and among them prophets, were worried about this matter. They said, It is written: 'These are the commandments which Hashem commanded to Moshe.' 'These are the commandments which we were commanded by Moshe, saying…' So, did Moshe not say to us, 'No other prophet will reveal to you anything afterwards,' (but) Mordechai and Esther want to introduce something new? They did not move from there but discussed (the matter) until the Holy One, praise to Him, illuminated their eyes and they found it (Purim) (already) written in the Torah, Prophets, and Kesuvim": *Yerushalmi*, Megilah, 1:5. Although, of course, the *Ko'ach* / power for the Below to rise up and reveal the Divine Presence in the world was given at Sinai, as until Sinai the world existed merely because of the Chesed from Above, but now it rested upon our acceptance of the Torah: *Pesachim*, 118a. Similarly, it was at Mount Sinai that the Ko'ach for the Below to reveal the *Ein Sof* / Infinite Light of Hashem through Torah was also given to Klal Yisrael: Alter Rebbe, *Torah Ohr*, Yisro, *Zechor Es Yom haShabbos*. See also *Yerushalmi*, Rosh Hashanah, 1:3. *Likutei Moharan*, Kama, 34. *Da'as Tevunos*, 158).

Our Sages teach, "Even what a proficient pupil is destined to *Mechadesh* / innovate (*Megilah*, 19b) was already said to Moshe at Sinai" (*Yerushalmi*, Pe'ah, 2:4). This statement means that although there are *Chidushim* / innovations of applying and understanding Torah which are unfolded in the Torah She-b'Al Peh and elucidated through the minds of our Sages, the foundation of these is always the Torah revealed at Mount Sinai. "Hashem revealed to Moshe at Sinai the general principles" (*Medrash Rabbah*, Shemos, 41:6), and the Sages throughout the generations extrapolated and unpacked the details and implications hidden in these principles. Our Sages faithfully revealed how all the details of their teachings were ultimately given by the One Shepherd, by the One G-d through the one Moshe (*Chagigah*, 3b).

At first glance, this idea seems self-contradictory. For if something was said to Moshe at Sinai, then it was not innovated by a student in the future, since it had already been taught to Moshe at Sinai. And if it was truly innovative later by a sage or student, then it seemingly could not have been said to Moshe at Sinai? This question only arises from the perspective of created beings, who are limited within the boundaries of time, within which the revelation of Matan Torah (the Giving of the Torah) took place first, and only afterwards, over the course of generations, the Sages have come to explain its inner secrets and to reveal the details of the Oral Torah. According to this view, these later innovations are not truly new, but rather are explanations and revelations of content that was already given at Sinai in foundational form.

However, on a higher level, these are in fact genuine innovations, and *were* nonetheless said at Sinai, even though this is something that appears impossible according to our human comprehension. For something can be new and also have existed beforehand, since the concept of time is not uniform or identical in all realms.

The power to resolve this seeming contradiction, to be within time and also beyond it, is due to the fact that both the Torah and the Jewish People actually existed prior to the creation of the world. That is to say, they are rooted beyond the limitations of created time, and their existence is eternal. Both are embedded in the very Essence of the Creator, blessed be He.

Even before the world was created, Torah and Yisrael existed, even before Hashem created the concept and constraints of time. For their root lies in the Divine Essence itself, and in fact, Yisrael precedes even the Torah (see *Tanna d'Vei Eliyahu Rabbah*, Chap. 14; also see *Medrash Rabbah*, Bereishis 1:4. *Zohar* 2, p.119b. The Rebbe Maharash, *Mayim Rabim*).

According to this, the innovations of the Sages (represented by the receptive letter Hei in the Name of Hashem), even when spoken many generations after Matan Torah, still have their source in the very Essence of the Giver of the Torah (represented by the letter Yud in the Name of Hashem) in eternity. When things that are beyond time enter into time, it is possible for something to be newly revealed within a later historical time period, and yet also to have been revealed already at the time of Matan Torah.

TORAH SHE-B'AL PEH
AND THE LETTER COMBINATION OF ADAR

To review, the sequence of the Divine Name corresponding to the month of Adar is Hei-Hei-Yud-Vav, and this arrangement represents a reversal of the usual flow of Light from Above to Below.

In the regular order of the Name (Yud-Hei-Vav-Hei), the Yud bestows Light upon the receptive upper Hei, and the Vav transmits it to the receptive lower Hei. This pattern expresses the descent of Divine wisdom, from Above to Below, the flow of Torah from the Yud, symbolizing Sinai and revelation, to the final Hei, representing us. This pattern also represents the Era of Prophecy in general, when Divine wisdom was solely manifested directly from Above.

In the subsequent era of the Sages, of which our current era is an extension, the lower Hei, the realm of human understanding, receives Divine wisdom from the Yud. Yet now, the lower Hei ascends toward the Yud and unites with it. Thus, as the Yud continuously unveils itself to the Hei, it also illuminates and reveals what has ascended, matured, and been made manifest through the awakening of the lower Hei.

In this way, there emerges a continuous reciprocal movement, a living dialogue, between the Above and the Below: revelation inspires innovation, and innovation ascends to the source of revelation. Thus, what originates below becomes woven, 'retroactively', into the original Divine flow from Above, and then is revealed to the Below.

To explore this dynamic more deeply:

The Zohar (3:73a) teaches that three knots are interconnected: Hashem, the Torah, and the People of Israel ("Hashem, Torah, and (Klal) Yisrael are one," is quoted frequently in Chasidus in the name of the Zohar, and it also appears in many sources, such as the *Nefesh haChayim* and the *Ramchal*. However, while it is not actually stated in this exact form anywhere in Zohar, the closest approximation is indeed found in the Zohar, *ibid.*). At first glance, it might seem that only two knots are needed to link three elements in a rope. However, these three knots form a triangular structure rather than a linear connection, symbolizing a deeper, cyclical relationship, a never-ending cycle: 1) Hashem is linked with the Torah, 2) the Torah is linked with Klal Yisrael, and 3) Klal Yisrael is linked with Hashem.

In essence, the process of revelation begins with Hashem, the Source of all Life, who imparts the Divine wisdom into and is the Torah, and then the Torah is revealed to Klal Yisrael. This forms the first two knots, a direct transmission from Hashem to the Torah, and from the Torah to Klal Yisrael. On its own, this would represent a linear chain, where each step flows naturally to the next. However, a third knot connects Klal Yisrael directly back to Hashem, completing a cycle. Klal Yisrael receives the Torah from Hashem, and begins to unfold innovations within that Torah, until the Torah is called *Toraso* / "*his* (the person's) Torah" (כי אם בתורת ה' / חפצו ובתורתו יהגה יומם ולילה / "In the Torah of Hashem is his desire, and in *his* [the person's 'own'] Torah he meditates day and night": *Tehilim*, 1:2. *Avodah Zarah*, 19a. *Kidushin*, 32b). Then, because Klal Yisrael is eternally bound to Hashem beyond time and space, these new insights 'retroactively' affect Hashem's original revelation of the 'past', of *His* Torah.

Even before the world was created, before Hashem created the constraints of time, both Torah and Yisrael already existed, for their root lies in the Divine Essence itself. Moreover, Yisrael precedes even the Torah (see *Tanna d'Vei Eliyahu Rabbah*, Chap. 14; also see *Medrash Rabbah*, Bereishis, 1:4. *Zohar* 2, p.119b. The Rebbe Maharash, *Mayim Rabim*). Thus, the new insights that Klal Yisrael 'births' within time are connected to the Essential realm beyond time, and affect Hashem's original revelation within time. As Klal Yisrael brings forth new Chidushim and connects them back to Hashem, the process of revelation extends beyond time. The new insights revealed thousands of years later are retroactively integrated into the original giving of the Torah at Sinai; hence, the paradoxical statement, "Even what a proficient pupil is destined to *Mechadesh* / innovate (in the future) was *already* said to Moshe at Sinai (in the past)."

In this vibrant cycle, there is a constant dance of revelation and innovation. As Klal Yisrael connects with HaKadosh Baruch Hu, who transcends time and space, each new insight, each novel understanding, is not merely a new revelation in Torah She-b'Al Peh, but a profound unfolding of what was always there. The *Chidush* / innovation, though 'new', is seamlessly woven into the fabric of the original, retroactively part of the Torah's original revelation at Mount Sinai.

Each knot perpetuates this continuous cycle, in which revelation and innovation continuously magnify each other, becoming more and more vibrant, alive, profound, relevant, and redemptive, as past and present loop together in sacred revelation. Through this connection to Hashem, the Infinite One, all that is revealed is both timeless and ever-new, a cycle that never ceases, forever renewing and deepening the revealed unity between Hashem, the Torah, and Klal Yisrael.

Three millennia after the revelation at Mount Sinai, Klal Yisrael continues to innovate Torah teachings in direct linkage with the Infinite Creator, and the Creator continues to 'retroactively' reveal these innovations as His own words spoken to Moshe at Mount

Sinai. This speaks of a perspective of timelessness or eternity; true innovations spoken thousands of years 'after' the giving of the Torah are rooted in the Timeless Eternal One, the Giver of Torah. Insofar as Torah and Klal Yisrael are linked with the Timeless Eternal One, both have an inherent aspect of timeless eternality within themselves, and they exist 'prior' to Creation or 'beyond'. Purim is the first major innovation of this kind. It is a new Yom Tov, established in later generations, and yet, it was also revealed at Mount Sinai. This means that the Hei (the Sages) rose up and aroused the Yud (the Giver of the Torah) through the awakening of Purim. And then the Yud revealed the concept of Purim retroactively, back at Mount Sinai.

Purim is unique in that it is a new Yom Tov, written by human hands and included as part of the *Kisvei haKodesh* / Holy Writings (*Kesuvim*), a canonized book of Tanach, the Written Torah. Esther (the lower Hei) gave birth to a higher understanding (the upper Hei) and requested of the Sages to write this miracle for all generations and as an eternal remembrance. This arousal from 'below' rose up to the Giver of the Torah, who transcends time (the Yud), and retroactively became included in the revelation (Vav) of Torah at Mount Sinai, the Torah of Hashem.

THE LETTER OF THE MONTH: KUF

The alphabetical letter corresponding to the month of Adar is the letter Kuf (ק). Our Sages teach that this letter represents *Kedushah* / holiness (*Shabbos*, 104a). Kedushah is the power of being set apart, elevated beyond the ordinary flow of life. Kedushah means to be dedicated, distinguished, and reserved for a higher purpose.

This is why the bond of marriage is called *Kidushin*. In that sacred moment under the Chupah, the groom declares to his bride: "You are *Mekudeshes Li* / holy to me," meaning: you are, *Meyuchedes Li* / מיוחדת לי / dedicated, set apart, singular, and special to me (*Kidushin*, 2b). In that instant, she becomes forbidden to all others, דאסר לה אכולי עלמא כהקדש / forbidden to anyone else like a consecrated item (*ibid.*); there is now an exclusive sacred relationship.

We, too, having entered a marriage with HaKadosh Baruch Hu, became a *Goy Kadosh* / holy nation by entering into such a covenant, and we are *Mekudeshes*, sanctified, chosen, and cherished (*Tanya*, 46). We stood beneath the mountain at Sinai like a bride beneath her canopy, and entered into an eternal covenant with the Divine. We became a *Goy Kadosh* / holy nation, bound in loyalty and monogamously dedicated to Hashem alone. Our relationship with HaKadosh Baruch Hu is not casual or ordinary; it is a bond of devotion, of intimacy, of exclusivity. We are His, and He is ours, forever dedicated, forever beloved.

Yet, the very same letter Kuf (ק), which speaks of Kedushah, also whispers of its 'opposite', for Kuf shares its name with Kof, a monkey, a creature that can 'mimic' a human being. Where Kedushah is authentic and exalted, the Kof suggests lightness, laughter, but also mockery and pretending. The Zohar (*Zohar* 2, 148b) deepens this mystery, teaching that Kuf symbolizes 'imitation' and even deceptive appearances. It is linked to *Sheker* / falsehood, and deliberate distortion of reality (*Zohar* 1, 2.2, see also *Shabbos*, 104a, regarding the letters of the word *Sheker*). The letter Kuf is even associated with Gehinom, a world of illusion and distance from the Divine (*Zohar* 2, 155a), a realm of 'the other side', or that which opposes holiness (*Zohar* 3, 180b).

The very shape of the Kuf tells its story. It imitates or 'mocks' the letter Hei (ה), the sacred letter through which Hashem formed this world (*Menachos*, 29b). Both Hei and Kuf are unique in their design, comprised of two distinct brush strokes, unlike all other letters, fashioned from a single substance (כל אות צריכה להיות גולם אחד / "Every letter needs to be of one substance… besides the letters Hei and Kuf. …And if the left leg of a ה or ק touch the roof of the letter, the (entire) Sefer Torah is *Pasul* / not Kosher": *Shabbos*, 104a. Tur and Mechaber, *Shulchan Aruch*, Orach Chayim, 36. Rosh, *Sefer Torah*, *Teshuvos haRashba*, and the Ramban and the Ran writing on the Gemara in Shabbos. Yet, the Rivash rules that בדיעבד / "after-the-fact," if the left leg of the Kuf touches the roof (top line), the Sefer Torah is Kosher, as suggested from *Menachos*, 29b. *Teshuvos haRivash*, Teshuvah 120. The Tashbetz also rules that it is Kosher: *Teshuvos haTashbetz*, Part 1:50-51). But look closely: while the Hei stands complete and elevated, its lines contained within the baseline (ה), the Kuf's left leg reaches downward, slipping beneath the line (ק), anchoring itself deeply into the ground. In this way, Kuf is a fragile echo of the Hei, a counterfeit shadow reaching into and pushing beneath the surface.

Let us now try to understand how the same letter Kuf holds within it two opposite worlds. How can it stand for Kedushah, truth, and sacredness, and yet also for mockery, imitation, and falsehood? How can one letter belong both to the side of light and to 'the other side', the realm of concealment and illusion? And more deeply still, what secret does this hold for the month of Adar and the Yom Tov of Purim?

Kuf associated with the monkey evokes images of playfulness, imitation, lightness, and laughter. In fact, *Sechok* / laughter is the 'sense' of the month, as explained in Sefer Yetzira. At first glance, laughter seems to belong to the realm of the frivolous: untethered, fleeting, even mocking. It can appear as something disconnected from the sacredness of life, a force that dissolves meaning rather than deepens it. Indeed, laughter without roots can easily slip into cynicism, irony, and despair.

Yet the laughter of Adar, the laughter that redeems and transforms, is of an entirely different kind. It is laughter with roots, as the letter Kuf is deeply anchored in the ground. It rises not from emptiness, but from fullness; not from detachment, but from deep anchoring in life's ultimate truths. Holy laughter is born from a soul so grounded in faith, so secure in its connection to the Source, that it becomes free; free to play, free to dance, free to shatter rigid forms and fixed definitions of reality (Dovid haMelech is called 'the Jester of the King Above': *Zohar* 2, p. 107a. Thus he was able to take himself lightly *before* Hashem and dance wildly.... דוד מפזז ומכרכר לפני ה' / "Dovid was leaping and whirling before Hashem": *Shmuel* 2, 6:16. Indeed, "Whoever holds himself proud, giving himself honor, and acts haughtily in such situations, is a sinner and a fool... because there is no greatness or honor other than celebrating *before* Hashem]": Rambam, *Hilchos Sukah, Lulav,* 8:15: Indeed, we are always 'before Hashem').

This laughter does not mock life; it liberates it. It loosens the chains of rote mindless living, of hardened identity, of smallness and fear. It reminds us that the world is not as fixed as we think, that reality itself is porous, alive, and an expression of the Divine Aliveness.

As such, the quality of the letter Kuf, the monkey, the mimic, the playful trickster, which is deeply rooted, becomes not a force of mockery but of renewal. It holds the paradox of sacred mischief, so to speak: at once grounded and free, serious and lighthearted, certain and questioning, holy and playful.

This is the laughter of Adar, the laughter that heals, that uplifts, that opens us to the infinite possibilities of life lived in the presence of the Divine.

It is true that this playful energy, this *mockery of the mundane*, has a power to free us. Indeed, it can shake us loose from narrow thinking, expand our sense of what is possible, and dissolve the false seriousness with which we often approach life. It allows us to laugh at our limitations, to step beyond the smallness of ego, and glimpse a reality more fluid, more alive. But like all medicines, this too requires discernment. For when untethered from conscious intention, when not rooted in holiness, laughter can turn destructive. A person deeply attuned to spirit, to beauty, to the living pulse beneath the surface of things, to a type of laughter and mockery of the trivial and mundane, may begin to feel alienated from the ordinary world. The mundane, with its dole routines, its narrow structures, its seeming emptiness, can feel unbearably shallow. And when this disillusionment festers without grounding, it easily devolves into despair, apathy, and the hollow laughter of cynicism.

Cynical laughter is a laughter that drains life of meaning, a laughter of nothingness. It is a humor that mocks all things equally, because nothing is seen as truly valuable, sacred, or dedicated. Much of contemporary humor arises from this place, a humor born not of freedom but of numbness; not of joy but of resignation.

But Adar teaches us another way: laughter of Kedushah. The letter Kuf, with its playful, monkey-like quality, reminds us that laughter can be both expansive and deeply anchored, both light and deeply rooted. This is not the laughter that escapes life, but the laughter that sanctifies it.

Rooted laughter does not mock what is sacred; it arises from it. It is not the laughter of emptiness, but the laughter of fullness, of a heart so grounded in truth that it can afford to be light. It is a laughter that lifts us without disconnecting us; that frees us without hollowing us out.

This is the deeper work of Adar: to hold the paradox. To drink, to dance, to laugh while remaining rooted in purpose, in dedication, in Kedushah. It is to be fluid without being lost, to be light without becoming weightless, to transcend the self, not by erasing it, but by anchoring it in something larger than itself.

Holy laughter is thus the bridge between heaven and earth, between form and formlessness, between I and Thou. It teaches us that joy is not an escape from reality; it is the deepest way of being *within* it.

HIDING REVEALS MORE DEEPLY

On the 'playful' day of Purim, it was once customary to light a bonfire inside a pit, and children would amuse themselves by leaping over the bonfire (Rashi, *Sanhedrin*, 64b. Perhaps this practice was borrowed from the local Persian culture). Today, this playfulness is expressed in the custom of dressing up in costumes, as mentioned by the Rama in Shulchan Aruch. Obscuring your identity or playfully imitating others represents hiding your superficial identity with the intention of revealing your true self. Paradoxically, the veiling of one layer of self allows for the unveiling of a deeper layer that lies beyond appearances and externality. When the conditions are right, to conceal is to reveal.

Additionally, Kuf represents earthly kingship, whereas Hei represents *Malchus* / Divine Kingship. It may seem that the earthly plane is ruled by randomness, chaos, mockery, and the obscuration of Hashem's Malchus. However, Purim teaches us that despite these appearances, Hashem actually reveals Divine Malchus, kingship, rulership, at all times. Purim shows us a way to see the miraculous within nature and mundane history, to see that everything in this world imitates and mimics what is present and occurring in the World Above. Ultimately, Purim demonstrates that the hiding of Hashem's Infinite Light, and the concealing of miracles and prophecy, actually allows for an even deeper revelation, a revelation (*Kiviyachol* / so to speak) of the *Etzem* / Essence of Hashem, beyond all attributes. Purim teaches us that despite these appearances, Hashem can reveal the ever-existing Divine kingship, at any time. To see the miraculous within earthly history, we must see that everything in this world imitates what is in the World Above.

Dressing in costume, hiding their identity behind masks, or playfully imitating others. When your earthly identity is altered, it can be easier to reveal who you truly are.

SENSE OF THE MONTH

According to Sefer Yetzirah, the sense connected with the month of Adar is *S'chok* / laughter and merriment. This is a laughter that is not merely a reaction; rather, a type of laughter that is a refined and elevated human capacity. Among all the senses and experiences that fill our lives, seeing, hearing, walking, eating, and sleeping, laughter stands apart. The animal world shares many of our basic instincts and functions, but the ability to laugh, truly laugh, belongs to the human soul alone (Rebbe Yehoshua Ibn Shuaiv, *Derashos Al haTorah*, Parshas Vayikra. Ya'avetz, *Mitpachas Sefarim*, 8:8. Gra, *Sefer Yetzirah*, 5:2). Only human beings have a sense of irony, meaning, not non-slapstick humor.

Not only is humor uniquely human, especially humor that rises above the slapstick and the superficial, but it is also deeply personal, even intimate. What we laugh at reveals something about who we are. Humor is like a fingerprint of who we are, subtle, particular, and shaped by our inner world. Different people laugh at different things; what delights one heart may leave another unmoved. The jokes we tell, the stories that make us smile, the things we find absurd or funny, all of these quietly trace the contours of our identity, and perhaps our upbringing, and the culture we come from.

"A person's true character is revealed in three things: בכוסו / in his cup; how he behaves when he drinks; and בכיסו / in his pocket; how he handles his money; and בכעסו / in his anger; how he responds when provoked. And some say, also בשחקו / in his laughter" (*Eiruvin*, 65b).

You can tell more about a person from their sense of humor than from almost anything else. For in laughter, the guard drops. The mask softens. The polished self that is often present to the world gives way, if only for a moment, and the real self is shown. In these unguarded moments of laughter, you catch a glimpse of the individual beneath the surface, beyond the roles played, beyond the persona carefully crafted for the eyes of others. Laughter reveals the truths of the individual, their innocence, their way of seeing the world, their inner softness or sharpness, their dreams, or their wounds. To know what makes someone laugh is to know something essential about who they are, not just what they think is funny, but who they are, how they carry wonder, how they hold contradictions, and how they connect to life.

As explored, there is healthy, productive, holy laughter, and there is negative, superficial, and cynical laughter. Cynical or superficial laughter not only expresses but reinforces the misperception that life is meaningless or fundamentally alienating. This is similar to how laughing when we are scared or embarrassed reinforces those reactions and perceptions. Cynical laughter and mockery often just masks our fears, embarrassments, or discomforts. Rather than healing, it hides. Rather than connecting, it isolates. This kind of laughter does not just reflect a sense of meaninglessness; it deepens it. Over time, it can leave us feeling empty, disconnected, and even depressed, as it merely reinforces the illusion that life is random, absurd, and not worth anything.

Positive laughter, by contrast, expresses and releases us. It helps us rise above narrowness, releasing us from rigid, trivial, and boxed-in ways of thinking. This kind of laughter is expansive; it opens the heart, uplifts the mind, and reminds us that, from a higher perspective, even the contradictions of life make sense.

As such, we need to continually evaluate our laughter. Are we expanding and growing from our laughter, or does it reinforce in us a sense of meaninglessness, purposelessness, and cynicism?

After laughing, do we feel slightly depressed or light and released? Lighter or heavier? When you laugh, does it shake you free and open you up to new possibilities, or does it create more uncertainties? Does the laughter lift us toward joy or sink us into doubt and more confusion? Does it emerge from awe and wonder, or from mockery and dismissal? Do we laugh at the expense of others, or in celebration of the unexpected brilliance hidden in life? Does it pull us down and leave us feeling empty, or does it uplift and empower us? Does our laughter build bridges or burn them?

BETWEEN COMEDY AND TRAGEDY: RELEASING OR SHATTERING PERCEPTION

There is often only a fine thread separating comedy from tragedy. At times, they are deeply intertwined, almost like two sides of the same mystery, flickering back and forth in the same moment. What causes one person to laugh may bring another to tears. And sometimes, we ourselves laugh until we cry, or find ourselves laughing in the midst of sorrow, regret, or grief.

This interplay is not accidental. It speaks to the deeper nature of how we experience reality. The human mind is exquisitely attuned to patterns. We observe the world through a sequence of moments, one image after another, one sound followed by the next. Our thoughts are trained to march in lines: logic, cause and effect, order. We grow up believing that life operates by these same orderly and understandable principles: eat well and you will be healthy, work hard and you will succeed, study and you will grow wise. This linear thinking offers a sense of safety, but it also sets us up for shock. Because life is not always linear. It does not always obey the rules we expect.

When something shatters those patterns, when the unlikely or inexplicable appears, it short-circuits the brain's usual way of making sense. A healthy person falls ill without warning. A fortune is made without effort. A tragedy strikes despite all precautions. In those moments, the rational mind falters. Its circuits overload, and what emerges in its place is often laughter or tears.

Tears of laughter and tears of sorrow often flow from the same hidden spring, a place beyond the mind's grasp, known in Chasidic thought as *Mosros haMochin* / overflow of the intellect. This is the space where the mind, faced with something it cannot fully comprehend, digest, or contain, spills over into emotion. When reality suddenly diverges from what we expect, when there is a striking gap between cause and effect, between what 'should be' and what is, the mind is momentarily disarmed. Logic falters. Proportion is disrupted, and in that moment of cognitive suspension, something deeper breaks through. Whether we burst into uncontrollable laughter or are overcome with tears, the source is the same: a sudden encounter with something that transcends our mental frameworks. Both are expressions of the same phenomenon, the individual responding to what the mind cannot tolerate.

Incongruity, the clash between what we expect and what actually unfolds, is at the heart of both comedy and tragedy. Both draw their power from this tension between the imagined and the real. We expect the young to live, and when they do not, the heart breaks; this is tragedy. We expect a chair to hold its occupant, and when it collapses, we laugh; this is comedy. Yet, despite their shared root, comedy and tragedy diverge sharply. Tragedy *shatters* our sense of how things ought to be. It confronts us with a reality that feels unjust, disproportionate, or cruel. In its wake, we feel broken, destabilized, or lost. It forces us to face the limitations of our understanding, and often, the pain of powerlessness.

Comedy, by contrast, offers a gentler transcendence. While it too disrupts our expectations, yet instead of breaking us, it releases us. The laughter invites us to loosen our grip on our rigid ways of thinking, to laugh at the absurdity of our assumptions, and in doing so, to rise above them. Laughter, in its purest form, is a soft undoing, a joyful surrender of control that opens the heart and expands the mind.

Comedy does not unhinge us; rather, it unbinds us. It does not break the soul, but gently lifts it. Where tragedy may leave us closed, aching, and grasping for meaning, comedy leaves us open, receptive, and breathing more freely. Comedy reminds us that the deepest truths and most wondrous miracles often do not emerge from the realm of the expected, but rather from the moment we release our expectations entirely, and in that release, make space for the Infinite One to enter.

In Hebrew, the word for laughter is שחוק / S'chok. This word has a numerical value of 414, the same as the term, אור אין סוף / Ohr Ein Sof / Infinite Light (The Tzemach Tzedek, Ohr haTorah, Beha'alosecha, p. 331a. Or שחוק / S'chok is twice the word אור / Ohr: Arizal, Sha'ar haMitzvos, Vayelech).

Through positive and holy laughter, we rise above the narrowness of conventional thought and the heaviness of the world's seemingly rigid forms. The veil of triviality and superficiality begins to dissolve, and in its place, the Infinite Light of Hashem shines through.

What once felt dense or limiting is released in a burst of joy, dissolving into spaciousness, freedom, and Divine Presence. When we glimpse the comedy within life's contradictions, we pierce the shell of rote awareness and self-serious posturing. We step beyond the confines of habit and ego, and in that moment of laughter, pure, unforced, unguarded, we touch Infinity.

Even on a practical level, a well-placed holy joke or lighthearted gesture can shake a person free from narrowness of mind, from the inability to think with clarity, and can open them to broader horizons. Through healthy and uplifting laughter, one can break out of smallness and constriction, and the mind is freed to rise toward deeper, higher, and more refined ways of thought. Chazal tell us that Rabbah, מקמי דפתח להו לרבנן אמר מילתא דבדיחותא ובדחו רבנן / "before beginning to teach, would say a humorous word, and the Sages would laugh. Only afterwards would he sit in reverence and begin the discourse" (*Shabbos*, 30b. *Pesachim*, 117a. The Alter Rebbe cites this Gemara in the name of Rava, *Tanya*, 7. Indeed, it is Rava who said, *Yuma*, 76b: "Wine and fragrance make one wise." And Rava is the one who says, "Is that to say that if the righteous enjoyed two worlds, it would be awful for them?" *Horayos*, 10b. Both Rabbah and Rava, whose very names mean "great" and "expansive," are intrinsically connected with the path of expansiveness in Avodas Hashem, Divine service).

The Rambam explains that this practice is fitting for every teacher (*Shemona Perakim*, 5). One who seeks to impart wisdom, or to clarify a matter of understanding to someone searching for fresh insight or answers to doubts, should begin with a touch of humor. A teacher of Torah must carry himself with dignity and seriousness so that his words will be received with the proper weight and be heeded

(Rambam, *Hilchos Talmud Torah*, 4:5). Yet a light remark at the outset, if it does not undermine the gravity of the teaching, can awaken the listener from intellectual slumber and open the mind to something new and creative. Laughter stirs the person, loosens rigid patterns of thought, and creates space for the teaching to enter more deeply.

When a person is caught in depression or despair, they are under the dominance of the element of earth, whose downward pull mirrors the heaviness of hopelessness. When the mind is locked into a fixed pattern of thought, unable to move beyond it, this is a sign of an excess of earth, weighing down the spirit and stifling the power of renewal and imagination. The mind, trapped in a single groove of thought, cannot move; the imagination feels sealed. It is a sign of too much earth, of spirit weighed down. To be lifted, one must call forth the element of wind, the ruach, a breath of freshness, movement, and renewal (*Bnei Yissaschar*, Sivan, 2:3). The return of the spirit in strength restores freshness and vitality, and this renewal can be brought about through the power of laughter.

This laughter is the essence of the month of Adar, the Divine *Shefa* / flow of reversal, of joyful unpredictability, of Divine laughter echoing through the universe. It is this quality that gave rise to the miracle of Purim, a moment in history that reads like the greatest cosmic joke, a Divine twist so unexpected that it can only be met with awe and laughter.

At the heart of Purim lies a profound incongruity: the Jewish People stood on the brink of annihilation under the decree of Haman, in the royal court of Achashverosh. All seemed lost, G-d forbid. The narrative pointed clearly in one direction: tragedy, devastation, an end. And yet, in a stunning turn of events, the exact opposite occurred. *VeNahafoch Hu* / "And it was turned upside down." The decree was overturned, sorrow transformed into joy, mourning into celebration, darkness into radiant light.

This is not merely a historical footnote that happened once, but rather it is a revelation of the inner pulse of this month. The power of Adar is the power to invert reality, to upend expectations in the most redemptive way possible. It is the month where the masks come off not to reveal more certainty, but to uncover a deeper truth: that beyond all human logic, there is Divine orchestration, often hidden in irony, reversal, and paradox.

As explored earlier, laughter arises when our usual ways of understanding collapse in the face of something greater. So too, the miracle of Purim reveals that when things seem most opaque, most constrained, the seeds of redemption are already being sown. Just as the Torah, from the Purim story forward, rises "from Below to Above," from the hidden to the revealed, so too the salvation of Purim arose not through open miracles, but from within the concealed, through a chain of natural events infused with divine irony and hidden light.

Purim teaches us to embrace the unexpected, to find the sacred in surprise, and to trust that even when the story seems to be heading toward despair, the Author has a deeper ending in store. In this month, we are invited to let go of rigid expectations, to laugh with the Divine, and to awaken to the possibility that what we fear may become the very soil from which our greatest joy will grow.

ASTROLOGICAL SIGN OF THE MONTH

Adar has 'strong' Mazal, a strong astrological positive influence. Adar is a time of בריא מזליה / *Bari Mazalei* / strong Mazal (*Ta'anis*, 29b). It is a month of *Hatzlachah* / success, and *Tov* / goodness (*Aruch haShulchan*, Orach Chayim, 686:6). The particular astrological influence of this month is *Dagim* / fish or Pisces (see also Rashi, *Baba Metziya*, 106b), a symbol associated with blessing, abundance, and hidden good.

While the month of Adar is associated with a strong and positive astrological influence, it is important to understand what that means in a Torah framework. The constellations themselves do not possess inherent power. Rather, their formations serve as an external expression of the way the Creator interacts with the world at a given moment. The inner Divine Will, the *P'nim* / inside, is reflected in the outer configuration, the *Panim* / face of creation. Just as a face reflects the inner emotional state of a person, so too the alignment of the celestial spheres reflects the Divine interaction with creation at this very moment in time.

Moreover, these influences are not deterministic. Astrology is not fate and inevitability. These cosmic alignments may set a certain context or atmosphere, but they do not dictate our destiny. We are never bound by the stars. The human soul, a direct spark of the Divine, has the power to transcend all external influences, whether they are astrological, psychological, physical, or circumstantial.

No matter the challenges or the conditions we are born into, be it upbringing, environment, or financial status, we are always endowed with the ability to choose freely. We can either live as the effect of our circumstances or rise to become the cause of what comes next. In doing so, we do not just react to life; we become active co-creators of it.

The zodiac sign associated with the month of Adar is *Dagim* / Fish, corresponding to Pisces. This astrological symbol of fish is reflected in the Yom Tov of Purim, and the Yom Tov that defines the month of Adar. Unlike land animals, which are visible and exposed, fish dwell beneath the surface, hidden from view. This quality of hiddenness mirrors the nature of the Purim miracle, a salvation that unfolded not through open wonders but through a tapestry of seemingly natural events. The miracle was concealed within the flow of history.

The natural lightness and fluidity of fish is reflected in their effortless, frictionless movement through water, a graceful dance that hints at a deeper lightness of being. This quality is intimately connected with laughter and playfulness, themes that shine brightly in the month of Adar. This lightness connected with laughter and playfulness, is found with the Livyasan, the great and the primordial fish: "There is Livyasan whom You have formed to laugh with" (*Tehilim*, 104:26), and Chazal, our Sages tell us that Hashem 'laughs' and 'plays' with this great fish every day (*Avodah Zarah*, 3b. *Baba Basra*, 74b. See also *Machshevos Charutz*, 13). Adar is the month of laughter, not just joy, but the kind that bursts forth from the incongruity of life turned inside out. Adar is a time when the unexpected becomes reality, when what once seemed certain is reversed in the most redemptive and transformative way. The spiritual power of Adar lies in its ability to invert reality, to upend expectations, the month of great turnarounds, and therefore the month of laughter.

TRIBE OF THE MONTH

There are twelve tribes of Israel, each *Sheivet* / tribe correspond-ing to another month of the year. The month of Adar is aligned with the tribe of Naftali. In his blessing, Yaakov describes his son Naftali as an *Ayala Shelucha* / swift and graceful deer (*Bereishis*, 49:21). This imagery captures not only physical speed, but a deeper quality of inner agility. As Rashi (and the Ramban) explains, the tribe of Naf-tali embodied a natural alacrity, a lightness of being.

This swiftness is not merely about physical motion; rather, it also represents a type of inner movement and a power to adapt, to stay emotionally and mentally fluid, to move through life with resilience rather than getting stuck. This inner mobility is at the very core of Adar's essence, and it is this quality that underlies the radical, unexpected reversals woven into the story of Purim, where everything shifted very quickly.

BODY PART OF THE MONTH

The organ associated with the month of Adar is the *Techol* / spleen. In the Gemara (*Berachos*, 61b), the spleen is linked to laughter, while the Zohar (*Tikunei Zohar*, Tikun 48) teaches that it is the seat of *Atzvus* / melancholy and sadness. This paradox points to a deeper truth: laughter can be two-faced (*Pri Tzadik,* Bamidbar, Rosh Chodesh Sivan). The laughter that is only skin deep, a brittle mirth, born of cynicism or escape, that often leaves the soul feeling emptier, more forlorn than before. Such laughter is like a fleeting shadow, mo-mentarily lifting the weight of being, yet, when it passes, leaving us only more aware of our sorrow.

A craving for surface-level joy, seeking delight in outer substances, like wine, which our Sages (*Sanhedrin*, 70a) note can stir a 'temporary gladness', often reveals a deeper ache within. It is the echo of an emptiness, a silent yearning masked by laughter and intoxication. Yet such joy, stimulated from the outside, cannot sustain the soul. It lifts for a moment, only to leave the spirit heavier than before. Cynical laughter, too, is a hollow mirth. It wears the mask of wit but hides a heart that no longer believes. The more one leans into cynicism, the more one begins to feel that nothing is sacred, that everything is a joke with no punchline. This erosion of meaning, this spiritual anarchy, leads, inevitably, to despair. And despair, when left unattended, settles into depression.

Deep, pure, holy laughter is not born of mockery or escape, but of awe, of Yirah. It arises in the stillness that follows a sudden shift in perspective, when meaning turns inside out and reveals a deeper, hidden light. In that moment of incongruity, when the heart is startled by wonder, the mind pauses, and the soul exhales.

This laughter is not an evasion but a revelation, flowing from the mystery itself, from the sacred space of not-knowing, where certainties dissolve and the Infinite peeks through the cracks. In that Divine, Infinite space, where anything and everything becomes possible, laughter is no longer a reaction, but a release. A letting go into the vastness of the Infinite. A song of the soul remembering its freedom.

NAME OF THE MONTH

Each one of the twelve months of the year has a distinct name, and every name has a meaning. According to our Sages, the current names we have for the months were carried back with us upon our return from the Babylonian Exile, and they can, in fact be traced to ancient Babylonian or Akkadian names (*Yerushalmi*, Rosh Hashanah, 1:2, *Medrash Rabbah*, Bereishis, 48:9. Tosefos, *Rosh Hashanah* 7a. *Even Ezra, Chizkuni*, Shemos, 12:2. *Bnei Yissaschar*, Nisan, Ma'amar 1:6). In the times before the Babylonian Exile, each month was commonly known by its corresponding number in the sequence of the year. For example, the month of Av was called the Fifth Month, and Cheshvan was known as the Eighth Month, and therefore, our month, Adar, was simply referred to as the Twelfth Month.

Even though the origin of most month names come from Babylon, there are various months whose names do appear in *Tanach* / Torah, Prophets and Writings, such as the months of Nisan (*Esther*, 8:9), Teves (*ibid.*, 2:16), Elul (*Nechemya*, 6:5), Kislev (*ibid.*, 1:1), and Adar (*Esther*, 3:7).

Though the names of the months originate in Babylonian or Akkadian tongues, our Sages, with their deep attunement to sacred meaning, reinterpreted them through the lens of *Lashon haKodesh* / holy language, Hebrew. They unveiled within each name layers of significance, discovering hidden meaning and light beneath foreign syllables (*Pesikta Zutresa, Bo*, 12:2. *Medrash Lekach Tov*, Shemos 12:2. *Berachos*, 56a. In the words of the Ya'avetz, *Lechem Nikudim*, Avos, 2:14: וכן הוא מנהג ארמיים ועברייים שמות ופעלים יוניות ממלות לגזור ז"ל החכמים). Nothing is mere coincidence or happenstance; to the contrary, everything is layered with meaning. This is certainly the case with something so significant as the names of the months in a Torah-year. In this way, what was once 'external' became 'internal', what was once 'borrowed' became our own.

The word *Adar* comes from the word *Adir*, meaning strong, solid, firm, noble, or certain, as in *Adir baMarom Hashem* / "Mighty on high is the Creator" (*Tehilim*, 93:4).

Adar / *Adir*, say our Sages, has בריא מזליה / *Bari Mazal* / 'mighty' Mazal, meaning that it brings one good fortune. Therefore, if you have litigation, you should arrange for it to occur in the month of Adar (*Ta'anis*, 29b. *Aruch haShulchan*, Orach Chayim, 686:6). Elsewhere, Chazal tell us, "He who desires his property to be preserved should plant therein an Adar (read as *Eder*) tree" (*Beitzah*, 15b). Planting and taking root are generally connected with the entire month of Adar, as the letter of the month, Kuf, is also associated with rootedness. Moreover, it appears that there is special value in planting on the day of Purim itself (*Megilah*, 5a).

In a leap year, when there are two Adars in the calendar, the first month of Adar is considered to have very strong Mazal, while the second month of Adar is said to be a month without Mazal. This is interpreted to mean 'beyond Mazal', meaning 'stronger than strong', and bringing good fortune that is from a world that is beyond good fortune (*Chizkuni*, Shemos 17:9. *Rabbeinu Ephrayim*, ad loc. *Ya'aros Devash*, 1, Derush 3. *Devash l'Phi*, 20:16. Others write the opposite, that the second Adar has the strong Mazal and the first Adar has "no Mazal": *Levush*, Orach Chayim, 685).

Adar is also derived from the Hebrew root words *Dar* / 'to dwell' (referencing space), or *Dor* / 'generation' (referencing time). Each of these interpretive etymologies suggests a powerful permanence and sense of rootedness and continuity. However, the word *Adar* also paradoxically communicates a sense of transience and fluidity. The word *Adar* is connected with the (Aramaic / Talmudic) word *Idra* (אדרא) / fish bone (*Shabbos*, 67a), the astrological sign of the month is fish, which also represents fluidity and easy, frictionless movement.

So what is beyond *Mazal* / good fortune and yet, paradoxically, contains strong Mazal? What, on the one hand, suggests rootedness, planting a tree, dwelling, generations, and yet also suggests free flowing, laughter, and fluidity?

The letters of the name *Adar* are an acronym for **Reisha D'Lo Is'yada**, 'the Unknowable Head' or 'the head that does not know', usually called by its acronym, *RaDL"A* (herein called *Radla*). This refers to a level of reality within the Sephirah of Keser of Atzilus ('Crown of Nearness'), the deepest level within the Divine Self, so to speak; the highest of the three levels within Keser. This level is so deep and hidden, it cannot be known by any being, even by Itself, so to speak. It is as if the Everpresence is hiding from Itself. Within this space of utter paradox, even the most destructive, negative plot (to annihilate the Jewish People) can be reversed and revealed as the greatest good. This is 'goodness beyond goodness'.

To grasp the sublime concept of Radla, a metaphor drawn from the human form is given. The body is composed of diverging aspects, a right and a left side. The right side embodies the quality of Chesed, the flowing impulse of generosity, giving, and outward expansion. The left side channels Gevurah, the measured strength of restraint, restriction, and inward focus. These opposing forces, though distinct, are essential to a balanced vitality. Above them both rests the head, the brain, centered and elevated. The brain transcends division, integrating and harmonizing the varied impulses and parts of the body. Yet even the head, the brain, is not the highest point, as within the brain itself, there are the right and left hemispheres. Hovering above the brain is the Keser, the crown, the vertex. A crown is not simply above the 'brain', it represents a realm that transcends even the loftiest faculties of thought, intention, and perception. The crown of the head, so to speak, embraces the totality of the human being: not only the right and left sides of the body, but also the full spectrum of emotional polarity, Chesed and Gevurah, expansion and contraction, as well as the dual hemispheres of the mind. The so-called 'crown of the head' surrounds, includes, and harmonizes all dimensions, all layers, all opposites within the human being.

Similarly, the level of Keser represents a transcendent dynamism, a meta-reality that transcends and yet includes all opposites. Keser is not limited by form or definition, and thus it can hold paradox without conflict, impossibility without rupture. Within Keser, the irreconcilable becomes harmonized, not through resolution but through a higher inclusion. This is the secret of Radla. It is the concealed root of all emergence, the hidden source from which all potential flows, the space where all things begin yet nothing is fixed. It is the womb of all possibilities, where every contradiction is not dissolved, but embraced in unity.

Haman sought to access the most transcendent stratum of reality, the realm of Keser, the concealed world of Radla, the plane beyond thought and discernment, where opposites coexist in silent tension, such as kindness and severity, light and darkness, good and evil. From this sublime and mysterious dimension, where all dualities dissolve into pure potential, Haman attempted to draw down the energy of destruction and annihilation.

A descendant of Amalek and its very embodiment, Haman thrived in the murky realms of confusion, those liminal spaces where clarity is eclipsed and uncertainty reigns. *Amalek* shares the same numerical value as *Safek* / doubt, and indeed, Haman sought to tap into that cosmic domain where nothing is certain, where truth is veiled in obscurity.

This is the reason why, to choose the date when to kill the Jewish People, he throws a lottery, a ritual act aligned with his philosophy of randomness and cosmic indifference. In doing so, Haman attempts to align himself with that primordial realm beyond reason, beyond structure, the place of *not-knowing*, the place where distinctions blur. And from that place, he felt he could draw down the power to destroy good people, to create evil in a place of goodness, and he could even approach the king and tell him that it is *Tov* / good to destroy Klal Yisrael. It is a grotesque parody of language, using the term *Tov* to justify evil, and yet the king accepts Haman's plan.

But what Haman failed to grasp, and what lay far beyond his reach and perception, was the hidden truth of Klal Yisrael's soul, that it is rooted not in the outer shell of Keser, but in its innermost essence, the Keser Kol haKesarim, the Crown of all Crowns. This level transcends even the 'Transcendent'. It lies beyond the Makifim, beyond even the Infinite Light, and is bound to *Atzmus* / the very Essence of the Creator. Haman believed he could manipulate the mystery of Keser, playing with uncertainty, doubt, and the shadows of non-knowing. But he only touched the outer periphery, the dim aura which is beyond good and evil. He did not know that the soul of Israel is anchored in the deepest point of Divine Will, a place where good is not an option, but the essential pulse of existence itself.

Within Atzmus, Essence beyond all measure and attribute, Hashem chooses the souls of the righteous over the unrighteous. Yet this choosing does not emerge from calculation of merit, nor from righteousness as a qualifier. It is not that the righteousness of the soul compels or colors this choice, for nothing compels Atzmus. Rather, the choice itself flows from the innermost delight and desire of the Divine. It is a choice born not of reason, but of *Ta'anug Pnimi* / inner pleasure; pure, free, and essential. Hashem chooses Klal Yisrael not because they are righteous, but because choosing them is embedded in the delight of Hashem's Essence.

Because the soul of Klal Yisrael is rooted in Atzmus, it was through this deep connection that the redemption of Purim was awakened. Mordechai was connected with, and drew strength from, the sublime realm of Keser Kol haKesarim, this most transcendent Will of Hashem. Esther, the faithful 'receiver' is the embodiment of Malchus, the vessel, channeling this highest Light into the world (hence, she is both Ayin and Ani). When Mordechai hears of the terrible decree, he tears his garments, dons sackcloth and ashes, and pours out his heart in prayer, beseeching Heaven for mercy. Esther, upon hearing of the decree, declares, "Go, gather all the Jews in Shushan, and fast on my behalf... Then I will go to the king (and beseech the actual King)." Mordechai turns 'Upward' in prayer; Esther draws that prayer 'downward' into concrete action. She channels his cry into practical tasks.

Indeed, through Mordechai's unwavering stand and steadfast faith, and Esther's silent courage, the people were stirred to reconnect with their innermost truth, to cleave to Hashem not out of fear, but out of deep connection. This awakening touched the level of Keser Kol haKesarim and from that sacred place, the miracle was born, and thus, the evil decree was not merely reversed, it was transformed to good; darkness gave way to light, sorrow to joy, and mourning to celebration.

Now we can begin to understand the profound duality of the month of Adar, and the immense spiritual power it contains. Adar embodies a paradox: it is a month of deep rootedness and ground-edness, and at the very same time, it flows with laughter, lightness, and unbounded movement. It both anchors and dances.

This dual nature arises because Adar is intimately connected with the deepest levels of Keser, the superconscious crown, the source of will and delight. Keser transcends all binaries, encompassing and harmonizing opposites. Keser is the place where stillness and motion coexist, where concealment and revelation intertwine, where joy is born not from certainty, but from the mystery itself. And yet, within this space of highest paradox, where nothing is fixed and everything flows, there is still choice. A Divine choice. A holy, deliberate turning toward life, toward goodness, toward the elevation of sparks hidden in the mundane.

As such, Adar becomes the sacred matrix from which Purim emerges, a womb of wonder, a vessel brimming with the hidden light of Keser Kol haKesarim. Once Purim is born from within it, every day of Adar glimmers with its joy, sparkles with its laughter, and carries the scent of redemption. Indeed, the holiness of Purim is not bound by a single day, and under certain circumstances, the soul of its celebration, the Megilah reading, can actually be on any day in the month of Adar (*Yerushalmi*, Megilah, 1:1. כל החודש כשר לקריאת המגילה: Shulchan Aruch, Orach Chayim, 688: 7. The Rama writes, והכי נהוג). For in truth, the light of Purim saturates the month of Adar just as the essence of Adar finds its fullest expression in Purim. One flows into the other until the boundary between day and month dissolves, and what remains is a sacred season of reversal, of joy, of hidden light made manifest.

CHAPTER 5

EXPLORING THE OUTER MEANING
of the
Name, Date, Laws & Customs
OF PURIM

THE NAME 'PURIM'

The story of Purim is truly a remarkable tale. In all aspects, it is a fantastic and intriguing narrative; a story of life and death, of hate and love, of power and corruption, of goodness and cruelty, of beauty and ugliness, and ultimately of a strange twist of events which leads to the downfall of the wicked and the rise of the righteous and a complete reversal of the assumed order.

Simply, the overarching theme of the story is a tale of persecution and salvation, a story that is all too familiar in the annals of Jewish history. It appears that every generation has their own Purim, their own story of survival and deliverance. In times gone by, communities and even individuals saved from impending persecution would celebrate their own salvation on the auspicious day of Purim. Purim has become the day to commemorate all salvations, and the embodiment of all physical redemptions.

There have been countless religious persecutions when local authorities desired hegemony and outlawed the practices of *Yidishkeit* / Judaism. For example, in the Chanukah story, the Greeks desired to eradicate Jewish practices. In other instances, there were physical threats, such as in the Purim story. Haman's decree was to literally annihilate the entire Jewish population that lived within the far-reaching grip of the Persian Empire, with the possible ominous result that other minor kingdoms would follow the same course. The deliverance was that the Jews were not harmed. Haman's plot was foiled, and a complete reversal of events occurred. What the wicked Haman desired to do was done to him, and Mordechai, the paragon of goodness and righteousness, was promoted in his stead.

The name *Purim*, as the Megilah tells us, is derived from the word *Pur*, meaning 'lot'. It is a Persian, and more precisely Akkadian, term referencing the lots that Haman cast to determine the most opportune day to carry out his sinister plan. As it is written, "Therefore they called these days 'Purim', after the name *Pur*" (*Esther*, 9:26). At first glance, this choice of name is deeply unsettling. Why name a day of salvation and joy after the instrument of our intended destruction? The very word *Pur* recalls Haman's cruel scheme, the ominous casting of lots that sealed a decree of annihilation. The word *Pur* evokes fear, vulnerability, and the darkness that hovered over an entire nation. Why then preserve this painful memory in the very name of the Yom Tov? Why immortalize the shadow instead of the light?

THE DATE

The reason this date was chosen as the day of celebration is that the month of Adar is the month that Haman chose via the throwing of the lot for the annihilation of the Jewish People. On the Thirteenth of Adar, they battled their enemies to save their own lives. On the following day, the Fourteenth of Adar, they celebrated their survival, and so do we celebrate on that date. In the capital city of Shushan, which was a walled city (*Megilah*, 2b), the battle raged for an extra day, and so the people in Shushan celebrated on the fifteenth of the month.

Seven out of every nineteen-year cycle are leap years, which contain an additional month of Adar. The prevailing opinion is that Purim is celebrated in the second month, one month prior to Pesach (It is nonetheless recommended to add a sense of celebration during the first month of Adar). The reason the second month was chosen was "to draw close one redemption to the next" (מסמך גאולה לגאולה :*Megilah*, 6b). That is, we want to juxtapose the redemption of Purim with the redemption from Egypt, the latter being the cause and inspiration of all subsequent redemptions.

Yet the fact that some celebrate Purim on the Fourteenth of Adar and others on the Fifteenth is puzzling and a rare phenomenon. No other Yom Tov is observed in such a manner, with one community rejoicing on one day and another on a different day, and besides, distinguishing between days and communities seems counter to the theme of Purim, the idea of unity. This distinction, unlike any other in the calendar of sacred times, invites deeper reflection. Why should a single miracle be commemorated on two separate days? What mystery lies in this unusual divergence of celebration?

THE MITZVOS / SACRED PRACTICES OF PURIM

A Yom Tov, literally 'a good day', is far more than a day of celebration; it is an extraordinary point in time that commemorates a redemptive event from our past, whose spiritual power remains alive and accessible on that day each year. Each Yom Tov is a portal into a distinct dimension of truth, a vital teaching for both our collective history and our personal journey. Pesach, for instance, is the celebration of our liberation from slavery, both literal, historical and internal, personal. Pesach teaches us that no bondage is permanent, that we can break free from whatever constrains us. Chanukah embodies spiritual illumination and resistance, the triumph of light over darkness, our collective resilience in the face of cultural and spiritual oppression. Purim, more than any other Yom Tov, speaks to the core of existential survival.* Purim recounts and relives the story of our people on the brink of annihilation, saved not through open miracles, but rather through a hidden orchestration of Divine Providence. The decree was real, the danger palpable, yet through an unexpected reversal, life triumphed over death. Purim is thus not only about survival, but about trivial, the ability to flourish even after being shadowed by doom.

---

*The Levush writes that the miracle of Purim is more connected with the body, yet Rebbe Yehoshua Ibn Shuaiv (Talmid of the Rashba) writes that there were in fact three types of persecution: religious persecution, the threat of physical annihilation, and financial persecution. Correspondingly, the Mitzvah of reading the Megilah is connected with religious persecution. Feasting is connected with physical annihilation, and giving gifts to each other and to the poor corresponds to financial persecution: *Derashos Al haTorah*, Tetzaveh.

As with all Yamim Tovim, in order to access the deeper energy and inherent quality of the day, we must do more than simply remember; we must participate. Each Yom Tov calls us to specific Mitzvos, sacred practices that open us to its Light. These actions on Purim, reading the Megilah, sharing gifts, giving to the needy, feasting with joy, are the spiritual tools that shift our consciousness, attune us to the essence of the day, and allow us to be transformed by its power.

There are four fundamental Mitzvos connected with Purim, and that need to be carried out during the course of the Yom Tov: reading the *Megilah* / Scroll of Esther, *Mishloach Manos* / sending two foods to a friend, *Matanos laEvyonim* / giving gifts to the poor, and *Seudas Purim* / the Purim feast, which includes festivity and rejoicing throughout the day. There are another three Mitzvos or practices connected with Purim: the special Torah reading that is read in the morning, the addition of the *Al haNisim* liturgy in our *Davening* / prayers and *Benching* / Grace after Meals, and the prohibition to fast or mourn on Purim. These three Mitzvos are not particular to Purim; rather, they are found in other Yamim Tovim as well. Here we will touch upon the specific Mitzvos related to Purim exclusively, or the ones that, with regards to Purim, assume a distinct 'Purim' twist.

MEGILAH READING

Here are the basics regarding reading the Megilah. The Megilah is read from an actual scroll on Purim eve and then again the next day, on the day of Purim (*Megilah*, 4a). Every word must be clearly pronounced and appropriately heard.

Since the Mitzvah is to "read the Megilah," how do we fulfill our obligation when someone else reads it for us? It seems we can only be passive listeners or active readers. In the legal codes, the question is debated whether the listeners also have to stand during the blessings. One principle is שומע כעונה / *Shomeah ke'Oneh* / "listening is like responding," which means that listening and answering the blessings from the reader is as if the members of the congregation are themselves like the reader. If so, they too need to stand as the reader needs to stand. An opposing principle is simply that the obligation to read the Megilah is fulfilled by the mere act of listening, and it is not that the listeners are like the actual reader. If this is the case, perhaps the listeners do not need to stand with the reader. According to most opinions, although the actual listening can be done standing or sitting, the listeners should stand during the recitation of the initial blessings (There are two ways to understand the principle of שומע כעונה / *Shomeah ke'Oneh* / listening is like responding" (*Sukkah*, 38b). Either it means that the listener fulfills his obligation by merely listening, or it means that the mouth of the reader is like the mouth of the listener: *Chazon Ish*, Orach Chayim, Siman 29. When the Alter Rebbe writes the *Halacha* / law regarding this principle, he writes, שפיו כפיהם / "The mouth of the person saying the blessing is like the mouth of the people hearing the blessing": *Shulchan Aruch*, Alter Rebbe, Orach Chayim, 213:6. The Mordechai writes, regarding hearing the Shofar, שומע כתוקע / "the person hearing the Shofar is like the blower": *Rosh Hashanah* 4, Siman 721).

Preferably, the Megilah is read in *Shul* / synagogue, or a place where many congregate. This is in accordance to the Torah principle of ברב־עם הדרת־מלך / *b'Rov Am Hadras Melech* / "The glory of the king is served among the many" (*Mishlei*, 14:28. *Ritva*, Megilah, 5a: ומשום ברוב עם הדרת מלך). The presence of a larger crowd not only magnifies the honor due to the King, but it also serves to enhance the *Pirsu-mei Nisa* / publicizing of the miracle, which is a central purpose of the Megilah reading. As Chazal teach, the more 'public' the reading, the greater the revelation of the miracle (דבעינן פרסום ניסא: Rashi, *ibid.* Ritva, *ibid.*: דרוב עם כל מאי דאיפשר משום פרסומי ניסא). That said, the Mitzvah can still be fulfilled privately, with a blessing, if circumstances prevent a communal gathering, when a larger group is unavailable, or it is impractical to gather (*Megilah*, ibid.).

During the reading, the listeners ought to pay close attention to what is being read. Over the past several centuries, a fascinating custom has taken root: the practice of 'blotting out the name of the wicked Haman' during the reading. This tradition is based on the Pasuk, "The name of the wicked shall be erased" (*Mishlei*, 10:7), and it reflects a deep desire to actively participate in the spiritual erasure of evil.

Interestingly, the original custom appears to have been somewhat different. As cited by the Rama (*Orach Chayim*, 690:17, and earlier by *Shibolei haLeket*, 200:3), children would engage in this symbolic act outside of the formal Megilah reading. "They would inscribe Haman's name on pieces of wood or stone, or fashion his image upon them, and then strike them together to symbolically fulfill the commandment, "You shall surely blot out the memory of Amalek" (*Devarim*, 25:19), and the teaching of "The name of the wicked shall be erased" (Rama, *ibid.*). Over time, this practice evolved, and what began as a general Purim activity for children became integrated into the Megilah reading itself (*ibid. Avudraham*, Purim. Although, see *Magen Avraham*, ibid., 19. *Sefer Maharil*, Minhagim, Purim. Perhaps the Maharil reserved this practice for the children). Either way, today, it is customary that whenever the name of Haman is mentioned during the Megilah reading, some form of noise is made, as an audible protest against evil and a symbolic act of erasure. Some people customarily shout, others clap their hands, and the more Kabbalistic custom is to stamp one's feet (*Ben Ish Chai*. The Rebbe tapped his feet. The *Shibolei haLeket*, 200:3, brings down a custom to stamp the feet: ומכין ברגליהן), as the negative force connected with Haman is Amalek and Amalek is associated with the heel, the Eikev, the lowest point of the body, symbolic of spiritual concealment and stubbornness. Of course, perhaps the most widespread and beloved tradition is the use of the Gragger, the classic Purim noisemaker that fills the room with joyful clamor. Some make noise at every mention of Haman's name, while others reserve it only for mentions that include a title or descriptor, such as Haman *ben Hamdasa* / 'the son of Hamdasa' or Haman *haRasha* / 'the wicked'. Whatever the variation, the intention remains the same: to blot out the name and influence of evil, and to actively participate in the triumph of light over darkness.

Throughout the Megilah reading, there are select *Pesukim* / verses that are recited aloud by the entire congregation. These moments of communal participation serve multiple purposes. Beyond the specific reasoning behind each individual Pasuk, and aside from the joy and energy they bring to the experience, these interludes share a deeper, unifying purpose: to ensure attentiveness. By interspersing the reading with moments of vocal engagement, the practice gently pulls the listener back into focus. These shared recitations act as spiritual signposts, inviting the audience not merely to hear, but to actively listen. This is especially true for younger children, who are often brought to hear the Megilah as part of their early Torah education. As the Levush notes, these communally recited

Pesukim help keep them (and maybe some adults) from drifting into sleepiness or distraction. The collective voice of the congregation keeps even the youngest listeners alert and connected. In this way, the recitation becomes not only a reading but a shared experience of presence, joy, and mindful participation.

Reading or listening to the Megilah is not merely a recounting of an ancient story; it is also a way of offering praise and thanks for the miracles of the day. Simply recounting the miracle is the highest praise, expressing gratitude for the miracles in our collective past and individual present.

On all Yamim Tovim, the Hallel prayer is recited, yet Purim is unique in that Hallel is omitted. The Sages offer various reasons. One is that the redemption of Purim was incomplete, as we still remained under foreign dominion, still in exile. In Hallel we recite, "Sing praise, O servants of Hashem," but throughout the Purim story and afterward, we were still technically the servants of Achashverosh. Another explanation is that the miracle occurred outside of Eretz Yisrael, and thus, some say, it lacked the full sanctity to warrant the recitation of Hallel in its formal sense. Yet Rav Nachman teaches (*Megilah*, 14a), קריינתה זו הלילא / "the reading itself is the Hallel." The Megilah is thus not just a story, it is a song. In fact, the Me'iri suggests that if one does not have access to a Megilah, he should recite the traditional Hallel verses, complete with a blessing (See *Shu"T Chasam Sofer*, Orach Chayim, Siman 192).

MISHLOCH MANOS: OFFERING FOODS TO FRIENDS

Over the course of the day of Purim, we send Mishloach Manos to our friends. These gifts should include at least two different types of ready-to-eat foods. The foods must be immediately edible; for example, raw meat or unbaked cookie dough would not fulfill this requirement. Traditionally, these food gifts are given to at least two different individuals, spreading the spirit of friendship and unity throughout the day.

Here is a sampling of some commonly discussed questions and Halachic debates surrounding the Mitzvah of Mishloach Manos. One frequently asked question is whether a man may send Mishloach Manos to a woman, or a woman to a man. Also, since the Megilah itself defines the Mitzvah of giving Mishloach Manos as *l'Re'ehu* / "to one's friend," can a student send gifts to their teacher and fulfill the obligation? Your 'teacher' is not your 'friend'. On the other hand, perhaps the word 'friend' is a generic term the Torah uses for any person, such, *V'Ahavta l'Re'acha* / "Love your 'friend' as yourself" which clearly does not only mean your actual friends, but any of your 'fellows', and ultimately any fellow human being (Shu't *Mahari Asad*, 204. *Mekor Ne'eman*, (Mazuz), 3, p. 167).

Another discussion centers on the wording of the commandment in the Megilah: "To enjoin upon them…to send Mishloach Manos to one another" (*Esther*, 9:21-22). Does this imply that our gifts must be delivered through a *Shliach* / messenger, or is it equally valid for the sender to hand over the gift personally? (See *Binyan Tziyon*, 44. *Mishnah Berurah*, Siman 695: 18. Shu't *Mahari Asad*, 27. *Shu'T Tzitz Eliezer* 9, 33. Note the language of the Rambam versus the language of Rashi with regard to exchanging meals or portions of food. Rambam speaks about "sending" food… ואם אין לו מחליף עם חברו זה שולח לזה סעדתו וזה שולח לזה סעדתו: Rambam, *Hilchos Megilah*, 2:15. Rashi does not speak about 'sending food', rather eating at each other's home. He writes, מחלפי סעודתייהו זה אוכל עם זה בפורים של שנה זו ובשניה זו סועד חברו עמו: Rashi, *Megilah*, 7b).

If a messenger is required, could a child serve in that role? While certain obligations require an adult to act as a legal agent, there is general agreement that in the case of Mishloach Manos even a child, especially one's own child, can serve as a valid messenger and agent (נפקא מיני' היכא שהקפידה תורה שהבע"ד בעצמו יעשה אלא שאנו אומרים שלוחו הוה כמו' עצמו. לזה בעי' דין שליחות דאל"ה לא הוה כמותו אבל היכי שאמרה תורה שישלח שליח כגון משלוח מנות זה סגי' אפי' ע"י קוף וכל הפסולים והבן זה כי כבר טעו בו גדולים וטובים ממני: *Chasam Sofer*, Gittin, 22b).

In fact, many authorities hold that it is preferable to fulfill this Mitzvah through a messenger. That said, if one chooses to deliver the Mishloach Manos personally, the obligation is still fulfilled (*Eishel Avraham*, 695. *Kaf haChayim*, ibid., 41: ולי נראה דאין יכול לדקדק מזה דוקא ע"י שליח דהרי מצינו בתורה בכמה מקומות לשין משלוח ואינו ע"י שליח). This aligns with the broader principle of "The Mitzvah lies with the person himself more than with his agent" (*Kidushin*, 41a).

There are also subtle and philosophical debates surrounding the Mitzvah of Mishloach Manos that invite us to look more deeply at the essence of 'giving'. Is the Mitzvah fulfilled through the act and intention of the giver, or is it only complete when the recipient has received and benefited from what was given? Consider a scenario: you send Mishloach Manos to a friend, but they refuse to accept the gift, saying they do not need it. Have you fulfilled the Mitzvah? What if you send it, but it gets lost or stolen on the way and never arrives? If the package is mailed on Purim but does not reach the recipient until after Purim, is the Mitzvah considered fulfilled because the sending took place on Purim? Conversely, what if it was sent before Purim but only arrived on the day itself; have you done the Mitzvah, since the recipient received it on Purim, or maybe not, as you did not perform the act on Purim? (This is debated among the Poskim, see, for example, *Birkei Yoseph,* Orach Chayim, 694:10. Shu't *Mahari Asad,* 207).

The answer may depend on the deeper purpose behind the Mitzvah. Is the root of Mishloach Manos to cultivate friendship and unity (*Manos Levi* on *Esther,* 9:19)? If so, perhaps the act of sending itself, even if declined or delayed, expresses that intent and thus fulfills the Mitzvah. Or is the goal more practical, to ensure that each person has food for their Purim Seudah, festive meal? (*Terumas haDeshen,* Teshuva 111, note *Megilah,* 7b: אביי בר אבין ורבי חנינא בר אבין מחלפי סעודתייהו להדדי. The Rambam writes, "If one does not have the means to send presents of food to a friend, one should exchange one's meal with him, each one sending the other what they had prepared for the Purim feast and in this way fulfill the Mitzvah of sending presents of food to one's friends": *Hilchos Megilah,* 2:15). If that is the case, then if the gift never reaches the recipient or is unusable for the meal, the Mitzvah may not have been fulfilled (see *Shu'T Chasam Sofer,* Orach Chayim, Siman 196).

This also raises another nuance: what if you send the gift anonymously, instructing the messenger not to reveal your identity? If the Mitzvah is about deepening personal connection and goodwill, anonymity undermines that goal. But if the purpose is simply to provide for another's meal, the identity of the giver may not be relevant.

Another interesting question arises when considering how Mishloach Manos is given and to whom. Suppose two people join together to send a package of Mishloach Manos to a third person, with each contributor providing only one food item. From the perspective of the recipient, it seems the Mitzvah has been fulfilled, as he indeed received two food items, as required. But if we focus on the *giver*, no single individual has personally given two items to another person. In that case, can we still say the Mitzvah has been properly fulfilled?

Conversely, what if one person sends a package containing two food items, but addresses it jointly to two people, to be shared between them? Here, the giver has indeed sent two food items, but not to one individual. Instead, the recipients only possess a *portion* of the two foods, each in partnership. On one hand, one might argue that the Mitzvah has been fulfilled, since both individuals received and benefited from the gift. But on the other hand, since neither individual received both items in full, perhaps the requirement of "sending portions to a friend" has not been satisfied, as no single friend received a complete, two-item gift.

Another question that can be raised is the following. Say, for example, if someone sent a chicken as Mishloach Manos, and the recipient ate it, only to later discover that the chicken was a *Treifa*, having been injured prior to ritual slaughter and therefore not Kosher, would the sender still have fulfilled the Mitzvah of Mishloach Manos? On one hand, the recipient did eat it and derived benefit from it; yet on the other hand, since it was not Kosher, perhaps it is considered as though nothing of value was truly given (נסתפקתי

מי ששלח לחבירו בשביל מנות תרנגולת טריפה והוא לא ידע ואכלו ואח"כ ביום פורים עצמו נודע לו שהיתה טריפה אם יצא ידי חובת מנות אם לא. *Ba'er Heitev*, Orach Chayim, 696:7. Note the argument between the S'ma and Shach regarding if someone sells his friend forbidden food, that is prohibited by the Torah and does so by mistake, does he still have to pay him back, if he ate it, since he did not really sell him anything.

:דאין אכילת האוכל מיחשב לו הנאה ואדרבה צער הוא לו שעבר על איסורא דאורייתא אף שהיה שוגג S'ma, Choshen Mishpat, 234:4. Shach, Yoreh De'ah, 119:25: דוקא כשידוע שהיה יודע See also Birkei .שהם דברים האסורים ומכרן במזיד קנסינן ליה הא לאו הכי לא דאפשר שוגג היה Yoseph, Orach Chayim, 695:7, where this debate regarding Mishloach Manos is tied to another argument between the Rambam and Ra'avad regarding Chazaka).

Another question: 'Can one fulfill the two Mitzvos of Mishloach Manos and Matanos laEvyonim through a single act of giving?' Say a person sends food to a poor friend with the intention of it being the Mitzvah of Mishloach Manos, or gives food to two poor people intending Mishloach Manos, would these also count toward the obligation of Matanos laEvyonim, since the recipients are poor? Or would it not suffice, because of the principle of אין עושין מצוות חבילות חבילות / "One should not combine multiple Mitzvos into a single act?" On the other hand, perhaps this principle does not apply in this case, and one could indeed fulfill both obligations at once, as perhaps this principle only applies when one performs two distinct Mitzvos simultaneously. Moreover, does this principle apply when one performs a single act while having in mind two separate Mitzvos? (see S'dei Chemed, Ma'areches 1, 19. Shu'T Kesav Sofer, Orach Chayim, Siman 139. Shu'T Chazon Ovadia, Dalet Kosos b'Yayin Shel Shevi'is, 8. p. 57)

These are just a few of the nuanced questions and debates that arise, reminding us that even a Mitzvah which appears simple and straightforward on the surface holds within it layers of meaning, and invites deeper exploration. What seems clear at first glance often conceals a richness that reveals itself only through thoughtful reflection and learning. In the following chapter, this Mitzvah, along with the other Mitzvos of Purim, will be explored through a Penimiyus / deeper lens, uncovering the inner dimensions and spiritual significance that lie beneath the surface of this Mitzvah.

MATANOS LAEVYONIM:
GIVING GIFTS TO THE POOR

Matanos laEvyonim, giving of gifts or money to the poor, is one of the most cherished Mitzvos of Purim. While we are obligated to care for those in need throughout the year, Purim brings with it a unique and elevated form of charity and giving. On this day, we are not merely encouraged but required to actively seek out at least two individuals in need and give to each one meaningful gifts or monetary offerings (plural). Though the Mitzvah is to give to two, the more the merrier, certainly when a poor person asks, we should give and give with a smile. Purim is a time of open-hearted generosity, guided by the principle "whoever stretches out a hand we give him." There is a double meaning to this, first of all to give anyone who asks, but also not to attempt to determine whether or not the hand that asks is really poor. Whoever reaches out to ask is given, for the very act of extending one's hand is itself a sign of need. If a person is willing to make themselves vulnerable and ask for help, then in some way, whether materially, emotionally, or mentally, they are lacking. On Purim, we honor them with open hands and open hearts.

This Mitzvah holds a special place in the heart of Purim. While all the Mitzvos of the day are precious, Chazal emphasize that giving generously to the poor is even more praiseworthy than sending numerous gifts to friends or preparing an extravagant Purim feast. As the Rambam writes: "It is preferable for a person to be more generous in giving to the poor than to be lavish in his Purim meal or in sending portions to friends. For there is no greater and more splendid happiness than to gladden the hearts of the poor, the orphans, the widows, and the converts. One who brings happiness to the hearts of these unfortunate individuals resembles the Divine Presence" (Rambam, *Hilchos Megilah*, 2:17).

This Mitzvah, like the broader Mitzvah of *Tzedakah* / charity, is deeply recipient-centered; the act is only complete when the poor person *receives* the gift. In fact, some early Rishonim (such as the Rashba) explain that this is why no blessing is recited before giving charity: because if the recipient refuses, the Mitzvah remains incomplete, and any blessing recited would have been said in vain. As such, it is not enough to intend to give; we must ensure that the giving lands, that it reaches its destination, and uplifts the one in need. (The Rambam differentiates holy joy from 'the joy of the stomach' by whether you are feeding yourself and your own family, or also actually feeding the poor and the destitute. "A person who locks the gates of his courtyard and eats and drinks with his children and his wife, without feeding the poor and the embittered, is (not indulging in) rejoicing associated with a Mitzvah, but rather the rejoicing of his gut": *Hilchos Yom Tov*, 6:18).

Besides the reason of giving to the poor as part of the Mitzvah of Tzedakah, on Purim, there is an additional reason to give Matanos laEvyonim, and that is for the purpose of *Simchah* / joy and friendship (*Ritva*, Baba Metziya, 78b˙).

---

* The Rambam writes, מוטב לאדם להרבות במתנות אביונים מלהרבות בסעדתו ובשלוח מנות לרעיו שאין / שם שמחה גדולה ומפארה אלא לשמח לב עניים ויתומים ואלמנות וגרים "It is preferable for a person to be more liberal with his Matanos laEvyonim than to increase (the luxuries) of his Purim feast and the Mishloach Manos for his friends. For there is no greater and more splendid happiness than to gladden the hearts of the poor, the orphans, the widows, and the converts": *Hilchos Megilah*, 2:17. This clearly means that Matanos laEvyonim is not just an act of Tzedakah, but also to enhance Simchah of the poor. Yet, from a closer reading of the Rambam, it seems that all three Mitzvos of Seudas Purim, Matanos laEvyonim, and Mishloach Manos are connected with Simchah; it is just that אין שם שמחה גדולה ומפארה / אלא לשמח לב עניים "There is no greater and more splendid happiness than to gladden the

We uplift not just through sustenance, but through connection, reminding every soul, especially those in hardship, that they are seen, valued, and not alone.

The Yerushalmi teaches a beautiful law unique to Purim: אין מדקדקין במעות פורים אלא כל מי שפושט ידו ליטול נותנים לו / "On Purim, we do not scrutinize the one who asks; rather, whoever extends their hand is given" (*Yerushalmi, Megilah*, 1:4. Rambam, *Hilchos Megilah* 2:16. Rama, *Orach Chayim* 694:3). On the surface, this teaches us about the *giver*, that on Purim, we are not to judge or question. We do not ask whether the person is truly in need, whether they deserve the help; we simply give, freely and joyfully, to all who reach out. But there is a deeper layer here as well: this principle also speaks to all of us, who receive our sustenance and help from the Creator, 'Above'. We must be *Poshet Yad* / 'extend our hand' to Hashem. Purim is an invitation to ask, to express our needs and vulnerability, and to open our hand to receive.

Hashem fulfills His own Mitzvos; on Purim, He too gives freely and joyfully to all who reach out to Him.* The only question is, will we be humble enough to ask? This Divine invitation applies not

---

hearts of the poor." In other words, all three Mitzvos are to create Simchah, but Matanos laEvyonim is the greater joy: The Rebbe, *Likutei Sichos*, 16, p. 365.

* On Yom Kippur, we declare, אתה נותן יד לפושעים, וימינך פשוטה לקבל שבים / "You extend a (left) hand even to those who have strayed, and Your right hand is outstretched to receive those who return." Yom Kippur reveals a profound truth: no matter how distant a person may feel, Hashem is never distant from them. Hashem's hand is already extended, waiting for the moment we choose to turn back. Purim is like Yom Kippur, yet the path is different. On Yom Kippur, we approach Hashem through awe, tears, and humility; on Purim, we approach Hashem through joy, celebration, and expansiveness of heart. And just as on Yom Kippur, so too on Purim — when we reach upward, Hashem's ימין פשוטה, His right hand is already stretched out toward us. This is especially true on Purim, when our turning is infused with joy and love.

only to *Gashmiyus* / material needs, but also to *Ruchniyus* / spiritual needs. Purim is a day of extraordinary Divine generosity, when all gates are open, but we must do our part, articulate what we need, and stretch out our hearts with our hands and say, "I am in need. I am open. I am ready." We need to open ourselves, to admit our lack and our longings, and in that moment of courageous honesty, make ourselves vessels for the endless blessings from on High that Purim is waiting to pour forth.

SEUDAS PURIM: THE FESTIVE MEAL

Toward the close of Purim day, in the afternoon, we begin the joyous Seudah, the festive Purim meal. Following *Minchah* / afternoon prayers, it is customary to wash our hands for bread and partake of a full meal, including at least one cooked dish. This meal is a profound expression of the spirit of the day.

Purim is a Yom Tov deeply rooted in the physical dimension. Haman's decree was not aimed at the Jewish soul but at their physical existence; it was a threat of total annihilation. As such, when the decree was overturned and our survival assured, the celebration was not abstract or 'spiritual', rather it was embodied, tangible, and joyful, in line with the principle of *Midah K'neged Midah* / measure for measure. Since the threat was physical, the salvation was physical, and so too is the celebration physical.

We eat, drink, and rejoice, not in indulgence, but in sanctified delight. The body is invited to join the soul in expressing gratitude and joy. Chazal tell us that part of the reason and root of the negative decree came through a physical lapse: the Jewish People had partaken in Achashverosh's non-Kosher, indulgent feast (מפני שנהנו

אשר נגזר מיתה מחמת עון אכילה / "The decree of death" : מסעודתו של אותו רשע .Megilah, 12a אשר נגזר מיתה מחמת עון אכילה
arose because of the sin of eating": *Shaloh haKadosh*, Torah Sh'be'Kesav, Mish-
patim, Torah Ohr, 120). And so, the rectification also comes through
a physical Purim Seudah. But this time, the meal is elevated; it
becomes a vessel for connection, unity, and the transformation of
the mundane into the holy, a place where body and soul, physicality
and spirituality, are united in joy.

Throughout the Megilah, meals play a central role, from the he-
donistic feast of Achashverosh to Esther's carefully orchestrated
banquets. Indeed, at Achashverosh's feast, the Jews compromised
their values and spiritual identity, losing their Divine protection
and becoming vulnerable to Haman's decree. And yet, something
remarkable unfolds within that same feast. At the very scene of
their spiritual descent, Vashti was removed from her throne. This
paved the way for Esther to replace her as queen, which set the
stage for the salvation of the Jewish People. In other words, within
their potential downfall lay the hidden seed of their redemption.
The place of failure became the very soil in which deliverance blos-
somed.

This captures one of the deepest themes of Purim, that even in
our moments of darkness, of misjudgment or transgression, Hashem's love remains. Even when we falter, the Master of the Universe
is already planting the beginnings of our *Teshuvah* / return. Within
the very act that made us vulnerable, in the place of our transgression and fall, Hashem is present and quietly preparing the kernels
of our redemption.

Purim teaches us that no exile is too far away, no mistake too
deep. The Divine is present even in our concealment, gently weav-

ing redemption into the very threads of our brokenness. This is the miracle of *VeNahafoch Hu* / 'and it was overturned'; not only was the decree reversed, but its very context was turned upside down, for within the descent, the ascent had already begun.

DRINKING WINE

"A person is obligated to drink on Purim until he does not know to differentiate between 'Cursed is Haman' and 'Blessed is Mordechai'" (*Megilah*, 7b).

The miracle of Purim is deeply intertwined with the theme of wine and feasting. It was during a wine-laden banquet that Queen Vashti was banished, setting the stage for Esther to rise to royalty. And it was at the wine-filled feasts of Esther that Haman was exposed and ultimately brought to justice. In remembrance of these pivotal moments, we too partake in wine on Purim, more than we might on any other day, echoing the pattern of the original events, yet doing so as a Mitzvah, transforming them into Kedushah (see Rebbe Yehoshua Ibn Shuaiv, *Derashos al haTorah*, Tetzaveh).

Unlike on other Yamim Tovim, where the Mitzvah is to rejoice, and the meal or wine serves as a means to achieve that joy, on Purim, the *Seudah* / festive meal itself, and the wine we drink during it, is a *central* Mitzvah of the day. The Seudah is not merely a path *to* joy, but an embodiment of joy. As such, we must take care to ensure that our Seudah is indeed celebratory, alive with sacred joy and Kedushah.

There is an obligation on Purim to partake in wine, and according to many opinions, this is to be done specifically during the

Seudah, the festive meal itself. The Rambam writes, "What is the nature of the obligation of this feast? A person should eat meat and prepare as festive a meal as his means allow. He should drink wine until he becomes intoxicated and falls asleep in his drunkenness" (*Hilchos Megilah*, 2:15. See also *Kaf haChayim*, 695:16. Given this, some authorities suggest that one should recite *Birchas haMazon* / the Grace After Meals, before becoming too intoxicated to do so properly. Others propose that one should complete the meal, recite the blessings, and only afterward indulge more freely in wine, fulfilling the Mitzvah in its fullest joy: *Magen Avraham*, Orach Chayim, 695:9. See also *Yesod Shoresh HaAvoda*, Sha'ar 12:6-7).

Our Sages explain that since the miracles of Purim unfolded in the context of wine-filled feasts, Vashti's downfall, Esther's rise, and Haman's unraveling all taking place around banquets, the Mitzvah to drink wine on Purim is instituted to reflect this theme. We drink until we reach a state where the boundaries of 'knowing' blur, where we no longer distinguish between "Cursed is Haman" and "Blessed is Mordechai" (*Megilah*, 7b. *Bi'ur Halachah*, 695:2: וא"ת האיך יחייבו חז"ל מה שנזכר בתורה ובנביאים בכמה מקומות השיכרות למכשול גדול וי"ל מפני שכל הניסים שנעשו לישראל בימי משתה אחשורוש היו ע"י). Obviously, this is not a call to reckless intoxication, but rather to enter a consciousness beyond human logic, a place of deep, paradoxical joy, where Divine Providence is felt even in the hidden, unexpected and unknown.

There is considerable debate among the early Rishonim, the post-Talmudic sages, regarding the precise meaning and practical application of the obligation to drink on Purim. Some authorities, such as the Ran and Rabbeinu Ephrayim (on *Megilah*, 7b), cited an incident recorded in the Gemara where excessive drinking led to near-tragedy, only averted by a miracle. Based on this story, they concluded that the original enactment was effectively set aside, and the practice of intoxication on Purim was no longer encouraged, even in the times of the Gemara.

Nevertheless, the majority of authorities maintain that the Mitzvah remains in effect. According to the Rambam (*Hilchos Megilah,* 2:15), the Mitzvah is to drink wine "until one becomes intoxicated and falls asleep" / עד שישתכר וירדם בשכרותו. The Rama (*Orach Chayim,* 695) adds that some interpret the obligation more leniently: one need not become fully intoxicated, but rather should drink more than usual, enough to become drowsy and fall asleep. In sleep, one naturally reaches a state of Lo Yada, where one can no longer distinguish between "Cursed is Haman" and "Blessed is Mordechai." (וי"א דא"צ להשתכר כל כך אלא שישתה יותר מלימודו ויישן ומתוך שישן אינו יודע בין ארור המן לברוך מרדכי). In this view, the goal is not excessive intoxication at all, but rather reaching a place of mental suspension, in which distinctions blur and the paradoxes of Purim are internalized (And perhaps the fulfilment of the obligation lies specifically in the act of sleeping, and drinking is used just to get you to the state where you fall asleep. Alternatively, sleeping is at least *part* of the Mitzvah of Lo Yada).

Other interpretations offer fascinating insights into what Lo Yada might mean. Some suggest that the Mitzvah is to drink just enough so that one cannot calculate the *Gematriyos* / numerical values of "Cursed is Haman" and "Blessed is Mordechai," both of which share the same gematria: 502 (*HaAgudah,* Megilah 6. *Rabbeinu Yerucham. Avudraham,* Purim. See also *Elyah Rabbah. Darkei Moshe. Bach, Magen Avraham, Ba'eir Heitiv,* ad loc.).

Others posit that the Mitzvah is to drink until one can no longer recite the entire poetic refrain of "Cursed is Haman, Blessed is

Mordechai" by heart without error (*Tosefos*, quoting the *Yerushalmi*, ad loc. *Chasam Sofer*, Megilah, 7a, in the name of Rebbe Nasan Adler. The Mitzvah is to be *Besumei* / light-headed and tipsy, not *Shikur* / drunk. We are not supposed to get Shikur on Purim; rather, we are to reach a point of Bisumei: see *KolBo*, Hilchos Purim, Siman 45. *Orchos Chayim*, Purim, Os 38. See also: Arizal, *Pri Eitz Chayim*, Sha'ar haPurim, Sod Mordechai v'Esther 6. *Shaloh haKadosh*, Torah Sh'beksav, Shuvavim Tat, Parshas Zachor. Chidah, *Moreh b'Etzba*, Os 307. *Yesod Shoresh haAvoda*, Sha'ar 12:7).

It is brought in the name of the Chacham Tzvi (See also *Shu"t Divrei Yatziv*, Vol. 2, Siman 297, quoting Rebbe Chayim of Tzanz) that whenever use use the term *Chayav*, such as in the statement *Chayav Adam l'Besumei* / "A person is obligated dto become intoxicated" (מיחייב איניש לבסומי בפוריא), it implies a level of commitment that reaches all the way to *Mesiras Nefesh* / self-sacrifice. This idea is echoed in the traditions regarding the Vilna Gaon, the Gra, who would drink heavily on Purim, to the point of personal risk and even danger. He did so not out of indulgence of course, but out of Mesiras Nefesh for the Mitzvah, understanding that the word *Chayav* carries with it a profound spiritual demand, a call to give oneself over fully to the Mitzvah, even if it involves stepping beyond the bounds of comfort or control (Although it should go without saying that the Torah never instructs us to step beyond our boundaries of physical and spiritual health. If drinking is possibly dangerous or detrimental to a person, or to others around them, they *must* take another path to Lo Yada.)

In this light, *Chayav* does not indicate merely a Halachic obligation; it is a spiritual calling. On Purim, a day of hidden light and radical inversion, we are called to go beyond, to surrender, to transcend, and perhaps even, in a deeply elevated way, to offer our

Da'as, our conscious knowing, as a form of Mesiras Nefesh (*Korban Nesanel* on the Rosh, Megilah, Os 10. See also: *Aruch haShulchan*, 695:5, who writes that when it says you need to drink עד דלא ידע / until a point (of not knowing), it is עד ולא עד בכלל / 'up to, but not including, Lo Yada. In other words, he rules that one should drink enough to become tipsy, but *not* to the point of genuine confusion between blessing and curse. The Yad Ephrayim holds the same, as does the Sefas Emes. Rebbe Yisrael Salanter offers a different perspective: he teaches that the Mitzvah of עד דלא ידע is not a *Shiur* / measure requiring a certain amount of drinking, but rather a *threshold*. Once a person drinks enough that they genuinely can no longer distinguish between blessing and curse, they are considered to have moved beyond Da'as, beyond conscious mind, and are therefore exempt from further *Chiyuv* / obligation to drink. In this way, the objective would be to get to a place beyond the world of duality, beyond *needing to be commanded* to do what is right, just, and holy. אבל השביעי רשות מעלמא דחירות שלמעלה מבחינת ההשתלשלות לכך אין חובה לאכול מיכלא דמהימנותא הנ"ל רק רשות בבחינת חירות העליון וכו :Siddur, Alter Rebbe, *Siddur Im Dach*, Sh'ar Chag haMatzos, p. 286).

Another issue raised regarding drinking on Purim to the point of Lo Yada, where one no longer discerns between "Cursed is Haman" and "Blessed is Mordechai," is whether or not the Mitzvah is specifically to drink wine, to the exclusion of all other intoxicating beverages.

Is the focus on wine due to the idea that wine inherently increases Simchah, joy (*Tanya Rabasi*, Siman 41. *Levush*, 695. אין שמחה אלא ביין / "There is no Simchah (today, when there are no offerings) except with wine": *Pesachim*, 109a)? Or is the Mitzvah to drink wine based on the fact that the miracle of Purim happened through wine feasts (*Avudraham*, Purim. Maharam m'Rotenberg, *Sha'arei Teshuvos*, 272)? One of the early Rishonim, the Rokeach, writes (*Hilchos Purim*) that *Yayin* / wine has a numerical value of 70, as Chazal highlight elsewhere, and there are numerous allusions throughout the Megilah to the number 70, weaving a deeper symbolic resonance between wine and the Purim story. It seems clear that the Rokeach considers the Mitzvah to be performed with wine specifically, not just any intoxicating beverage. (The Rambam writes to drink wine. *Hilchos Chanukah, Megilah,* 2:15. Fom Rashi it seems that the Mitzvah is specifically wine. לאבסומי: להשתכר ביין. *Megilah,* 7b. Although see, Rashi, *Baba Metziyah,* 66b).

Alternatively, perhaps the Mitzvah is not about wine per se at all. Rather, the goal is reaching a state of Lo Yada, transcending Da'as and rational consciousness. In this view, one could theoretically fulfill the Mitzvah by drinking other strong beverages, such as vodka (See *Nimukei Orach Chayim,* 695:4. See also *Yesod Shoresh haAvodah,* Sha'ar 12:7. *Kaf haChayim,* Siman 688, Os 45).

Another quality of wine (although it may be true with all intoxicating beverages) is expressed by our Sages: "When wine enters, secrets are revealed" (*Eiruvin,* 65a). Based on this, perhaps we drink wine on Purim because the miracle was a *hidden* miracle, a "secret" veiled within the fabric of nature. By drinking, we symbolically draw forth what is concealed, and we unveil the *Ohr haGanuz* / hidden light, the secret soul of reality itself, revealing that beneath the garments of the everyday world shines an endless, Divine wonder.

On a simple, experiential level, having an extra drink lowers one's guard, softens defenses, and gently peels back the layers of the assumed self, the external persona, the 'mask' that we present to the world.

In this softened state, one's inner world begins to emerge. Not always, and not for everyone, is this unveiling of the inner 'secret' entirely good; the secrets of the human heart are not always pure, and sometimes great darkness lurks there. But on Purim, the inner secret which will be revealed through a couple of drinks will surely be the more spiritual and transcendent dimensions of self, the layers that lie deep beyond all the dirt, hurt and chaos, mishaps and transgressions of the surface world. On this day, it is not the dirt that rises to the surface, but the hidden gem that lies beneath any dirt, the soul itself, a pure spark of the Divine, holy, luminous, and whole, untouched by the dust of outer layers, shining forth in its eternal beauty.

Purim has the power to draw forth the hidden treasure, the spark of transcendence buried beneath layers of dirt: habit, fear, and ego. For some, these inner gems gleam just beneath the surface; for others, it may be more deeply hidden, under the strata of piles of confusion and pain, but it is always there. And on this day, through joy and spiritual abandon, it rises up and becomes revealed. When a person drinks on Purim with intention, with presence and inner alignment, and sheds the outer shell, the superficial identity, what is revealed is the deeper, truer self. The soul shines through, unmasked, unbridled, untethered, radiating pure, unbroken light, no longer eclipsed by the layers of dirt, of fear, ego, or pretense, but soaring freely in the open air of beautiful joy.

MASKS

Though not a Mitzvah, one of the beloved customs of Purim, especially cherished by children and the young at heart, is the tradition of dressing up in costumes and hiding behind masks. There is even a tradition that the Rama himself, the great Sixteenth Century Polish scholar and the accepted *Posek* / 'Halachic decider' of all Ashkenazi world Jewry, would dress up in different, poor garments and go to peoples homes and remind them to Daven Ma'ariv, to pray the evening service (R. Akiva Schlesinger, *Lev haIvri*, 1, p. 8. Note, *Likutei Sichos* 39, p. 282. Although, generally, as the Rama writes, יש נהגו ללבוש בגדי שבת ויום טוב בפורים וכן נכון. מהרי"ל: Orach Chayim, 695:2).

As colorful, humorous, and joyful as wearing costumes has become,* the origin of the practice seems to have its roots in a more tender purpose: the Mitzvah on Purim to give gifts to the poor. To preserve their dignity, the impoverished were to disguise themselves on Purim (and perhaps also on Chanukah), covering their faces so as not to be recognized when collecting alms. In this way, charity could be given to anyone who needed it without calculation, and without shame or embarrassment. Over time, this compassionate custom evolved into the widespread Purim tradition we know today, in which people in general join in the fun of masking and hiding, enhancing the joy of the day.

Besides the compassionate origin of Purim costumes, and beyond the celebrative function they have today, dressing up is firmly connected with the essence of the day. At its heart, Purim cele-

---

* See *Darkei Moshe*, Orach Chayim, 696:5. *Teshuvas Mahari Mintz*, 17. It appears that there was once a frivolous custom to cross-dress on Chanukah as well, although in *Sefer haMaskil* (nephew of the Rosh), Hilchos Chanukah, this practice is strongly condemned. Yet, with regards to Purim the MaHari Mintz and the Rama, *ibid.*, do allow this practice: ה"נ בנדון דידן שמתנכרין בפרצופין לשם שמחת פורים. These are the words of the Rama: מה שנהגו ללבוש פרצופים. ליכא למיחש לאיסור לא ילבש בפורים וגבר לובש שמלת אשה ואשה כלי גבר אין איסור בדבר מאחר שאין מכוונין אלא לשמחה בעלמא. וכן בלבישת כלאים דרבנן וי"א דאסור אבל המנהג כסברא הראשונה. Although see *Bach*, Yoreh De'ah, 192:5. *Birkei Yoseph*, Orach Chayim, 696:13.

brates a miracle concealed within the 'garments' of nature. A simple reading of the Megilah might suggest a tale of random events and unpredictable turns, a series of chance encounters and fortunate coincidences. Yet, upon deeper reflection, we realize that every twist, every turn, was guided by an Invisible Hand. The miracle of Purim is a divine orchestration, like a puzzle whose scattered pieces somehow fall perfectly into place. To tangibly enact this truth, the custom arose to enclothe and conceal our outward self in a way that hints at the mystery that lies beneath appearances. Doing so celebrates the wondrous secret that even when hidden, the Divine is Everpresent.

Haman's decree was not aimed at an abstract people, but at Jews who openly identified with their Jewishness. Surely, if the Jews had been willing to forsake their Jewish identity (G-d forbid) to blend in and disappear as a unique people, Haman would have been content to let them live. This was long before the modern era of antisemitism, where the very essence of being Jewish is targeted, regardless of the level of faith or practice. Purim, then, becomes a time of reaffirming our true and inner identity. We play with our outer forms, dressing up, masking ourselves, stepping into roles, but it is precisely through this playful concealment that we reveal something deeper.

When we put on a mask, we show that our external image, the face that we present to the world, is only a 'garment'. Beneath the mask, beneath the surface self, our soul, the eternal Jewish essence, is always present, and it remains forever unchanged, unscathed, unsullied.

Purim invites us to rejoice not merely in how we appear, but in who we are within, in the unbreakable bond between the Jew and Hashem, a bond that no mask, no exile, no decree, and no hate, can ever sever.

HAMANTASCHEN

Concealment, as a theme, is also reflected in a traditional Purim delicacy, Hamantaschen, also called in Hebrew *Oznei Haman* / 'Haman's ears'.

This tri-cornered pastry was traditionally filled with poppy seeds, though today the fillings range widely, from apricot jam to chocolate, and beyond.

The exact origin of this custom is uncertain, but references to eating such pastries date back at least to the late 16th century. Over time, the Hamantash has become one of the most beloved symbols of Purim. Perhaps the origin of its name is German. In German, as in Yiddish (its linguistic cousin), the word *Tasch* means a pocket or pouch, and *Mohn* means poppy seeds. Thus, a pastry filled with poppy seeds was called a *Mohntasch*, plural, *Mohntaschen*.

It is possible that Jewish communities adopted the German pastry and imbued it with meaning and the spirit of Purim: just as the dough encloses or 'hides' the filling, the miracle was enclosed and hidden within the natural order. If so, the word *Mohn* was replaced with *Haman*, transforming it into Haman-Tash, a pocket of Haman.

Now that the word *Hamantash* is part of the Jewish vernacular, assimilated within a sacred tongue, we can also now read the word

Hamantash as if it were a Hebrew word. In this way, *Haman-Tash* can be understood as "Haman has become weakened" (שת / *tash* means to weaken or diminish). As such, the very act of eating the Hamantash becomes a symbolic act of 'consuming' or destroying Haman in a triumph of good over evil. Eating Hamantachen is thus a sweet reminder of the story of Purim, and in a mystical sense, a symbolic destruction of Haman and his ancestor, the evil Amalek.

REVELRY

Humor, by nature, arises from the unexpected, from the surprise of a sudden reversal, a twist that defies anticipation. Purim evokes great cosmic laughter through the great reversal, in which the lot cast for destruction became a cause of life and jubilation. Haman chose the month of Adar for his decree, seeing it as a time of misfortune, the month of Moshe Rabbeinu's passing. Yet hidden (from Haman) within that same month, on that very day, was Moshe's birth, a deeper life force that would undo the decree and bring about our redemption.

Intrinsic to the spirit of Purim is good, holy fun, but not frivolity, recklessness, or callousness, G-d forbid, and certainly, not mocking or shaming others or oneself (although one may mock idolaters: *Sanhedrin*, 63:2; *Orchos Tzadikim*, 21, hence mocking Haman and the like). However, if lightheartedly, one could dress up as a caricature of oneself, to laugh at one's own self-image. If it is not from self-ridicule or embarrassment, the ability to laugh at your own surface image could help you loosen any rigid sense of self-importance.

In the old country, and in vibrant enclaves of Jewish life even today, a Purim *Shpiel* / comedic play could be performed. In it, whimsical and fantastical Torah insights could be shared with wit and laughter.

Purim is a day when joy overflows into every corner of life. We go from friend to friend, sharing baskets of delights. Some don colorful costumes, and most people get a bit tipsy, but through it all, we never forget those in need, always remember the less fortunate, and keep our hands open to the poor.

CHAPTER 6

EXPLORING THE INNER MEANING
OF THE NAME, DATE & THE LAWS
AND CUSTOMS OF PURIM

THE NAME 'PURIM'

N*ames, what we call things, are often assumed to reflect the in-ner* properties or essential realities of the objects or concepts they describe. We naturally speculate that this is even more true with ideas than with physical objects. After all, there may be no intrinsic 'chairness' in the word *chair* any more than in the word *table*; yet, somehow, we call a chair by one name and a table by another. When it comes to concepts, however, we intuitively expect a deeper correspondence. But even here, there is a certain level of arbitrariness in language, very little connection between words and the realities they are meant to represent (Ran, *Nedarim,*

2a. See also Rashba, *ad loc. Biur Halacha,* Orach Chayim, Siman 62. Maharal, *Chidushei Agados,* Sotah, 33a). However, in Lashon haKodesh, the Holy Tongue, Hebrew, the names of things are intrinsically bound to the essence of what they describe (*Tanya,* Sha'ar haYichud ve-haEmunah, 1).

In *Lashon haKodesh,* the letters themselves are the "building blocks of Creation," channels through which Divine Life Force flows into the world. When something is labeled in Hebrew, it is actually brought into being; its inner reality is revealed through the sacred sequence of letters. Each letter carries spiritual flow; each word forms a conduit for the light and life of the thing it names. In this way, Hebrew names for things are precise maps of spiritual identity, keys to unlocking the hidden essence woven into the fabric of existence. The name of something is a window into its 'soul'.

When it comes to the Yamim Tovim, the name captures its innermost essence and the very heart of the day. Take, for example, *Pesach,* which recalls the moment when Hashem "passed over" the homes of the Jewish People, sparing them during the Plague of the Firstborn. *Shavuos* / 'Weeks' reminds us of the seven weeks we counted in eager anticipation of the Giving of the Torah at Mount Sinai. Following this pattern, we would expect that the name Purim similarly encapsulates the core miracle and spirit of the day. Yet at first glance, it seems puzzling: How does the name *Purim* / 'Lots' reflect the depth of the miracle or the essence of the Yom Tov?

At first glance, the origin of the name *Purim* seems almost incidental: in the narrative of the Megilah, Haman cast a *Pur* / lottery to determine the most auspicious date for his diabolical plan to annihilate, G-d forbid, the Jewish People. The lot fell on the Thirteenth of Adar. Yet it would seem puzzling if a minor and perhaps even inconsequential detail became the name of the Yom Tov.

Moreover, why name the Yom Tov after a moment of threat rather than after the miracle of salvation? Unlike other Yamim Tovim, which are named for their redemptive essence — Pesach, Chanukah, Sukkos — Purim appears to draw its name from the darkness, not the light. It references the plot, not the redemption. Why should we immortalize the casting of lots, a sinister act, and referencing an illusory sense of randomness, chaos, and concealment of the Divine Presence? (Perhaps a better name would have been Chanu/Yud/Dalet/ they rested on the fourteenth, as the *Kedushas Levi* suggests. Kedusha Rishona).

Even more perplexing is the choice of language. *Pur* is not in fact Hebrew, but Persian. If the essence of the day centers on the idea of a lottery, why not call the Yom Tov *Goral*, the Hebrew word for lot?

Indeed, some early scholars, such as the Radak, Rebbe David Kimchi, proposed that *Pur* is not actually Persian, but from the Hebrew root *Porer* / to crumble or dissolve, pointing to the crumbling of Haman's decree. Yet most commentators, and the Pasuk in the Megilah itself, state that *Purim* is named after the Pur, the lot: "Therefore they called these days 'Purim', from the term *Pur*" (*Esther*, 9:26). Thus, we are left with the enigma: the name of this most joyous and transformative Yom Tov is in a foreign lexicon, and worse, from a moment of danger rather than deliverance. What truth lies hidden in the Pur that reveals the secret of Purim itself?

Let us understand this by going to the root and the deeper essence of the issue. The story of Purim clearly pits the hero Mordechai, embodying all goodness and *Kedushah* / holiness, against the villain Haman, embodying all negativity and *Kelipah* / unholiness. As Torah figures, these are also eternal prototypes, archetypes of great historical, symbolic, communal, and personal value. Each sought to accomplish the diametric opposite: one desired redemption, the other, destruction.

We need to ask: from where does Haman draw such diabolical, destructive power, for if the Creator is the Source of all existence and the Essence of all goodness and truth, then how can evil take root at all? While human beings are granted a degree of free will, and thus evils committed are ultimately their responsibility, this only shifts the question to 'What is the source of free will?'

Where does the capacity to choose originate? What aspect of the Divine interface with Creation allows for the possibility of genuine choice, so real that a person could choose to bring about the suffering, devastation, and destruction of others, and even the world itself? This mystery lies at the heart of the human condition and reveals profound truths about the nature of Divine concealment and revelation.

To begin to understand this mystery, we must first clarify the nature of the Divine relationship with Creation, how the Creator interacts with this world, and allows space for human agency and the perpetuation of evil.

A powerful parallel is drawn between the human soul and the Divine Light invested in Creation. Just as the soul both permeates and transcends the body, so too the Divine light both animates and surrounds all existence (see *Berachos*, 10a). There are two modes of Divine influence: *Ohr Penimi* / the inner, measured light that fills and shapes Creation, and *Ohr Makif* / the encompassing light that transcends and encircles all. The first is the energy manifested as immanent and all pervasive, the second is energy expressed as a transcendent power unrelated or uninterested with the details of Creation. Ohr Penimi is also referred to as *Memaleh Kol Almin* / the light that fills all worlds, and Ohr Makif is *Sovev Kol Almin* / the light that surrounds all worlds. Memaleh represents the Divine flow that enters into the vessels of Creation, customizing itself to each creature's capacity, nurturing and sustaining the intricacies of existence. Sovev is not absorbed or grasped by the created world; it is a transcendent radiance that remains beyond, hovering above all, unaffected by causes and effects.

The realm of order, structure, and moral consequence is the domain of Memaleh. In this orderly reality, cause and effect prevail: righteousness begets goodness, and negativity invites breakdown. In the Memaleh world, everything is properly defined and appropriately placed. The order of the universe and the vitality that prods organisms toward their advancement and towards more intricate measures of complexity and diversity is Memaleh at work. But the power of Sovev does not enter into the specifics of existence; it births existence itself, as a generality. Sovev is the light that allows for existence to emerge in the first place. It is the source of substance before form, potential before actualization.

Memaleh gives form and function, distinguishing one creature from another, a tree form a blade of grass, a star from a grain of sand. But Sovev is what allows something to exist at all, before it becomes this or that. It's difficult to fathom substance without form, yet in the process of creation, first there emerges out of Divine nothingness a created 'reality' of something, a something that is not yet individuated and particularized, and then later on this substance takes on form, as in a tree and not a blade of grass.

Speaking of the primordial light of Sovev, a Chasidic sage once said in Yiddish, *Dort vu eidelkeit iz kein kli nit, iz groobkeit kein setira nit /* "Where refinement is not a vessel, coarseness is not a contradiction." In other words, from the perspective of Sovev, distinctions dissolve. It is a plane beyond opposites, where light and darkness, good and evil, high and low, have no meaning. From this lofty vantage, evil can be tolerated, not because it is desirable, but because it simply does not contradict the nature of that transcendent Light, the Light that is beyond the binary.

In a world of order, in a universe of cause and affect, righteousness breeds goodness and negativity generates destruction. Haman, the archetype of evil, the embodiment of Kelipah, understood consciously, subconsciously, or super-consciously, that to go through with his diabolical scheme, he needed not only physical prowess but meta-physical prowess as well.

Haman intuitively knew that if he wished to unleash true destruction, he could not rely on the ordered world of Memaleh. In the realm of inner light, where merit and meaning guide destiny, he could not prevail. So he sought to access the detached, transcendent plane of Sovev, a space beyond judgment, beyond morality, beyond good or evil, beyond consequence.

From this detached paradigm, even the righteous can suffer, and nothing needs to follow a deterministic inevitability of cause and effect. It is a world where everything is equal, and nothing matters more than the other. And this is why Haman cast a Pur. A lottery by nature transcends reason; it does not follow logic or order. It is blind to virtue or vice. Every outcome is equally likely, every participant equally poised to win or lose. A lot is cast precisely when no clear decision can be made, when one desires to invoke a force that lies beyond knowing.

When Haman wished to dedicate a date to the annihilation of Klal Yisrael, he cast a lot and let *it* choose. "In the first month... a Pur, which means 'lot', was cast before Haman concerning every day and every month, (until it fell on) the twelfth month, that is, the month of Adar" (*Esther*, 3:7). He chose to employ a tool of randomness and unpredictability, the power of Keser of Sovev, the possibility of all possibilities, to establish his plan, as the lottery could fall on any date within any month.

By using a lottery, he was as if he was saying, 'I surrender my free choice in thinking that I know what the best possible outcome is, and enter into a place of uncertainty and doubt, in order to let the "random" movement of the dice dictate an outcome. I am hereby asking for "chance" to take over.' The Hebrew word for lot is *Goral*, which has a numerical value of 239 (Gimel/3, Vav/6, Reish/200, Lamed/30). With the *Kolel* / the addition of 1 for the word itself, the number comes to 240. This is the same value as the word *Safek* / doubt, uncertainty. A Goral comes from *Makom haSafek* / the realm of doubt. Haman (again, whether consciously or subconsciously) wished to connect to this Divine space of 'doubt' and 'unknown' in order to activate the Kelipah or 'dark side' of Keser and Radla (as will be explored), and from there draw down havoc and destruction.

Chazal equate Haman with the primordial *Nachash* / Snake (*Medrash Rabbah*, Bamidbar, 14:12. *Nachash* begins with the letter Nun, which has a numerical value of 50. The other letters in *Nachash* spell *Chush* / sense. The word says, 'The snake has a sense for [the power of] 50'). The Snake represents the blurring of good and evil, a desire that is rooted beyond knowing, distinction, and a paradigm of good and evil. Hashem tells Adam and Eve, "The day you eat from the Tree of Knowledge you will die" (*Bereishis*, 3:1), and the snake argues, If you eat from that tree, "Your eyes will open, and you will be G-d-like," meaning that it will be *good* for you. Haman, as well, says, "If it is *good* for the king, he should write (a decree) to kill..." in a similar blurring of good and evil.

משרש נחש יצא צפע / "From the source of the snake sprouts an asp" (*Yeshayahu*, 14:29). The word צפע / asp in numerical value is 240, which is the same value as the word *Safek* / doubt. Safek is sourced in the Snake; the Snake functions in a world of uncertainty, a blurring of what is good and what is evil. The Snake wants Adam and Chavah to eat from the Tree of Knowledge and enter into that world of doubt and distortion of moral clarity. In fact, for this reason, many later Chasidic Rebbes call the Tree of Knowledge אילנא דספיקא / "the Tree of Doubt." Haman embodies crippling doubt, and like a spiritual asp, aspires to harness the Divine source of doubt, the source of the Snake, which is the Tree of Doubt.

Haman wishes to commit arguably the greatest evil, killing innocent men, women, and children. Yet when he speaks to the king he deliberately blurs the lines: "If it is *good* for the king, he should write to *kill*...." The king agrees: "Do what is *good* in your eyes" (*Esther*, 3:9-11). The word "good" is used here in the most perverse manner, as if there is something good, or even profitable, in committing genocide against an innocent people (not to mention that this particular people has the potential to activate the Light of the Torah, uplifting and benefitting all of Creation).

Fascinatingly, in the first part of the Megilah, where it speaks of the evil decree to annihilate (*Chalilah* / G-d forbid) Klal Yisrael, the word "good" appears 16 times, but not once does the word *Ra* / bad or evil appear. In the system of Gematria called *Mispar Katan Mispari*, the digits of the number 16 are added together to equal 7. Seven symbolizes our world of good and bad, which was created in six days plus Shabbos. In his twisted imagination, Haman wished to hang Mordechai, his arch-enemy, and so he erected a "tree," a wooden gallows of 50 *Amos* / cubits. This is the number that symbolizes transcendence of the world of seven, beyond the world of good and evil. The fullness of seven is 7 x 7 (49), and to take a step beyond 49 is to enter into the realm of 50, a realm beyond Creation, the realm of Sovev.

Haman built a gallows that would evoke the power of the *Sha'ar haNun* / the Fiftieth Gate of Understanding, a level beyond intellect and structure. By tapping into this level, he could reveal a light of 'not caring' about justice, in which nothing matters, and everything is equal.

Haman's desire was to hang his enemy, Mordechai, on a tree fifty cubits high. Fifty is the number that is above the realm of the seven, beyond good and evil, for the fullness of seven is seven times seven, i.e., forty-nine. One who ascends beyond the number forty-nine reaches fifty, which is the number beyond Creation itself. Earlier sources explain that the name Haman has the numerical value of 95, and with the Kolel, adding one for the entirety, it equals 96, which in turn is the numerical value of נ' אמה / fifty cubits" (*Rokeach*, Hilchos Purim). In other words, the essence of Haman is connected with the realm beyond 'good and evil'.

Furthermore, the Medrash relates that Haman took the fifty-cubit-high tree from the *Kodesh haKodashim* / Holy of Holies (*Pirkei d'Rebbe Eliezer*, 50. *Medrash Talpiyos*, Achashverosh). This means that Haman is aiming for the highest place of Transcendence, the Divine level of Keser (The *Yalkut* writes that he took this plank from the Ark of Noach: *Rokeach*, Hilchos Purim). Haman wanted to take the tree from the holiest place in the world, the Holy of Holies, the place where the Ark of the Covenant stood. The Ark of the Covenant "had no measurement," meaning it was beyond all opposites, the level of Keser, where everything belongs, even things that are in the category of the "impossible of impossibilities."

This transcendence is subtly hinted at in Haman's very name: *Ha-Mahn* / Is it the Manna?" (*Mahn Hu*: Shemos, 16:15). The Manna was described as white, colorless, and undefined, capable of taking on any taste the eater desired. It was the food of *Sovev*, a spiritual sustenance that adapted to consciousness itself. Just as the Manna had no fixed flavor, so too the energy Haman sought was beyond definition, capable of sustaining both good and evil alike.

In this sense, Haman's use of the lot was not incidental; it was essential. He intuited that only by accessing the Divine light that lies beyond all differentiation could he hope to succeed in his evil plan. Haman sensed that there is a superrational plane from where good and evil can draw equally. A sphere where no moral strings are attached, and good and evil are equally capable of receiving and being nourished. He wished to tap into a spiritual space that exists outside the context of Creation, where, "As for your many sins, can they harm Him?...and if you acted righteously, will it benefit Him?" (*Iyov*, 35:6-7). This is why, even if it was not known by his conscious mind, he cast a lot.

THE OHR OF *MAKIF* (*IGUL* / CIRCLE) IN *GALUS* / EXILE

To review, the number seven is associated with the natural order, the seven days of creation, rooted in the seven lower Sefiros. Each of these contains seven levels within itself, forming the structure of forty-nine, the full unfolding of the natural world. And the Fiftieth Gate reaches beyond to the *Makif* / Surrounding Light, the Ohr haSovev, that which transcends all comprehension and definition. And so his gallows, grotesque an image as it was, had the power to channel the ungraspable power of 'fifty' and harness it for destruction.

In truth, the entire concept of *Galus* / exile, whether it be physical, emotional, or spiritual, is rooted in Makif, also referred to as *Igul* / the Circle. In the words of the Alter Rebbe: "And behold, exile is a state of sleep, a withdrawal of intellect — the three intellectual faculties bound together and hidden. Thus, the soul draws its vitality from Above, from a realm called *Igulim* / Circles, in which there is no concept of higher or lower, but all is equal, integrated, and unified without separation or distinction.... Yet for this level to be revealed below, it can only come through the sleep and concealment of intellect that occurs in exile" (*Torah Ohr*, Vayeshev: והנה בגלות הוא

בבחי' שינה והסתלקות המוחין תלת כלילן כו' ואז נשמתו מושכת לו חיים מלמעלה כו' ושם הוא בבחי'
עגולים שאין בהם בחי' מעלה ומטה רק הכל בהשוואה אחת ובהתכללות והתאחדות כל העניינים בלי שום
(.פירוד והתחלקות ...אך להיות בחי' זו בגילוי למטה אינה כ"א ע"י בחי' שינה והסתלקות המוחין בגלות

Galus is alienation and separation from one's home or Source. In the state of Galus, we experience estrangement and misalignment, clarity fades, ambiguity reigns, and good and evil seem to coexist without distinction. Galus is like a dream, where contradictions flow together, where elation and despair can alternate within moments. One moment offers purpose and presence, the next, emptiness and confusion. One moment we feel high and connected, the next, low and estranged. This can be beyond disorientation; it can be a disintegration of moral and spiritual certainty.

In the unfolding Purim story, King Achashverosh emerges as a figure of striking impartiality. He does nothing on his own volition, acting only upon the advice of others. Ironically, he executes his wife on his advisor's word, and then executes that very advisor at his wife's behest. Achashverosh also represents the King of the World, of Whom it is said, *Achris v'Reishis Shelo* / "The end and the beginning are His". Indeed, Chazal teach that every time the word *haMelech* / 'the king' appears in the story (as opposed to simply *Melech* / king) this too refers to the King of the Universe (*Medrash Rabbah*, Esther, 3:10. This does not negate the historical narrative about the actual king Achashverosh, rather it teaches us that the earthly king was but a reflection of the (Divine) King: *Resisei Layla*, 19).

King Achashverosh thus represents the level of Makif, the *Keser* / crown above the head, above reason, beyond system and judgment. It is a realm of radical possibility, where existence simply is, undefined by inner structure, without subjective rational evaluation or interpretation.

Achashverosh represents the level of Makif, the circle, the deep space beyond the world of order of higher and lower. Achashverosh, the Megilah tells us, reigned "from Hodu to Kush." Chazal (*Megilah*, 11a) offer two opinions: these provinces were either at opposite ends of the earth or right next to each other. In this paradox lies the essence of the circle, where the most distant and the most adjacent become indistinguishable. It also suggests that his kingdom encircled the entire globe, from Hodu all the way around to Kush, the province adjacent to Hodu. In other words, he is the King of the Circle (also the circle from *Hodu* / 'praise' all the way around to *Kush* / 'darkness'). Even his feast, which lasts 180 days, reflects this. The number 180 is spelled ק״פ; Kuf (100), Pei (80), which is the etymological root of the word *Hekef* / הקף / surround, encircle. In a circle, there is no hierarchy, no bias, no differentiation, just pure potentiality (Thus the circumference of the earth is divided into 360 *Ma'alos* / degrees, as the Rambam writes in the laws of *Kiddush haChodesh*, and from one 'horizon' [meaning 'hemisphere'] across to the other there are 180 Ma'alos).

When Haman accuses the Jews, he says to the King, "There is a certain people scattered abroad and dispersed" (*Esther*, 3:8). The phrase *Yeshno* / "there is", can also be read as 'They are asleep.' Haman is alluding to the fact that exile is a state of sleep. Haman subtly invokes the idea that the Jewish People are spiritually dormant, and appeals to the King who, on this level of Makif and *Igul* / Circle, is also 'asleep' so to speak. He is the Transcendent King, 'dwelling in' the realm of Keser, beyond caring and judgment, where anything is possible, even consenting to a decree that would kill His true 'wife', Klal Yisrael.

BY BEING AYIN, YOU ALLOW THE
ULTIMATE YESH TO BE REVEALED

Yet this is where the story takes an unexpected turn. The very Makif that Haman tried to manipulate, the source of formlessness where law and order seem irrelevant, turned against him. The same power of Makif that Haman desired to imply to render insignificant order and 'law', to disregard a universe where results are in direct consequence to actions and where righteousness breeds blessings, was used to annul the decree. Makif is beyond form, but that also means it is beyond old forms and new forms. It cannot be controlled or predicted. Haman's decree was drawn from Makif, and it was through that same Makif that it was reversed. The new law did not evolve from the old; it replaced it entirely. In the realm of Makif, transformation is not gradual; it is absolute.

Makif is the realm of pure potentiality, and only over time does it become actualized through the immanent Light of Memaleh. In other words, first an idea exists in Makif and only afterward does it take form, becoming defined, individualized, and manifest. *Golem* / substance and *Tzurah* / form is another way to describe potentiality versus actuality, existence versus form, or emptiness versus fullness. To reshape a vessel, for example, one must first erase the old form. If you wish to turn a silver plate into a cup, you must first soften or melt it down by heating it, undoing its form, before shaping it anew. So too spiritually, to alter your reality, you must first elevate it to the level of Makif, to that pure, 'melted-down', undifferentiated state of Golem, and from there, recraft it, allowing new possibilities to emerge.

When Esther invites the king to her feast and explicitly includes Haman in the same breath, "the king and Haman," she is engaging in a profound spiritual act. By equating the two, the sovereign and his minister, she shakes them loose from their fixed identities, melting down their defined forms. In doing so, she perceives them not as distinct people locked in hierarchical roles, but as Golem, unshaped potential, prior to form. She calls forth their formless essence, and by invoking the Makif, the undifferentiated light beyond all structure, she dissolves the negative power of Haman at its root. Haman had reached into the realm of Makif in an attempt to destroy, but in Makif, 'everything' and 'nothing' are both possible. Esther connects to this level and uproots the existence of Haman at his source.

From another angle, Esther ascends inward and upward into the *Ayin* / nothingness that precedes all *Yesh* / manifestation. From this place she reshapes reality, for the positive. On the surface, we call ourselves *Ani* / 'I'. But this separate sense of self is an illusion, a mirage, a transient image that labors under the notion of separateness and fragmentation. The only true I is the ultimate I, the essential Yesh, the Divine I that pulses through all existence. This One I is manifest in all the individuated 'i's of the world. In order to access that ultimate I, one must first deconstruct the false ego-self, the illusory Ani, and return it to Ayin, to emptiness, to egolessness. From there, the Ani reemerges as a true vessel for Divine action: *Ani Hashem* / 'I am (one with) Hashem.'

When Esther beholds the desperate reality of her people, she sees that within the visible Yesh, the fixed form of reality, the way things are right now, all seems dark, hopeless, and doomed. Yet, she declares with radical surrender: "I will go to the king, though it is against the law... and if I perish, I perish" (*Esther*, 4:16). To appear before the king unbidden was to risk death, but she chooses to go nonetheless. In doing so, she substitutes her egoic Ani for the infinite Ayin, and in that ultimate act of self-negation, she unlocks a miracle. In her Ayin-state, having placed herself fully aside, the true Yesh of existence is revealed, Divine blessings and life begin to flow, and transformation is set in motion.

ESTHER IS *MALCHUS,* BOTH *AYIN* AND *ANI*

Esther embodies the quality of Malchus and thus is *Ayin* / nothingness, as Malchus has "nothing of its own." Regarding Esther, it says, כי אין לה אב ואם / *Ki Ein (Ayin) Lo Av v'Eim* / "for she had neither father nor mother" (*Esther*, 2:7). She has "no parents," as she comes from the quality of *Ayin* / nothingness. Yet, when she pleads for her people, she says, כי נמכרנו אני ועמי... כי אין הצר שוה בנזק המלך / "For we are sold, I (אני / *Ani*) and my people... Instead, the enemy has (אין / *Ein* or *Ayin*) 'not' sufficiently recompensed the king...." (7:4). By this, she declares that she is embodying both the *Ayin* / nothingness and the *Ani* / self rooted in the Ultimate Ani, the Yesh of Keser, the transcendent source beyond all duality, as will shortly be explained.

Indeed, a radical transformation unfolds. That which was meant for destruction becomes the very source of salvation. The Pur, the lot cast by Haman, becomes the wellspring of joy. From the place of Pur, from the realm of Ayin that Haman sought to misuse, comes Klal Yisrael's deliverance. As such, the Yom Tov is not called *Pur*, singular for lot, but *Purim*, 'lots' in the plural. There are, in fact, two 'lots': one of destruction and one of salvation. One was aimed at erasing the Jewish People, and one gave birth to a new form, a renewed and elevated existence of the Jewish People. We commemorate not only the lot of Haman, but also the miracle that came about through the place of 'lot', Ayin, which allowed for new life to emerge.

The old 'form' of the Jewish People, which was threatened with annihilation, crumbled, as connoted by the word *Pur*, from the root *Porer* / 'crumble'. There was a dissolution, melting-down, or crumbling of the negative decree, and a positive decree and a new reality was born. Hence, the word Purim is related to the word *P'ru*, as in *P'ru u'Revu* / "Be fruitful and multiply." Haman sought to wipe us out, to bring us to a final end, but instead, we multiplied, flourished, and became stronger and more fruitful than ever before. From the edge of inconceivable annihilation, an inconceivably great redemption was born. The Purim miracle set into motion the return of many from the Babylonian exile, and ultimately, this led to the rebuilding of the Second Beis haMikdash in Yerushalayim.

CONNECTING TO THE ESSENCE, BEYOND *MAKIF*, WHERE *YESH* AND *AYIN* ARE ONE

On a more subtle and profound level, Haman's fatal miscalculation lay in his failure to grasp the deepest truth of all reality: beyond all levels, beyond even the Infinite Light of Sovev Kol Almin, there is *Atzmus* / the Divine Essence. Atzmus is, so to speak, not a force or Light or even an aspect of the Divine, but the Essence of All Reality. It is not bound to any descriptions, not even 'Infinite', for even Infinity is a formless 'form', distinct from finitude. Atzmus is beyond both form and formless, beyond 'beyondness'. From this space of Essence, there emerges the possibility of true *Bechirah /* choice.

Authentic Bechirah can only emerge from a place not bound by reason, not compelled by logic, causes, or conditions. It must arise from a source that is itself unshaped by anything else, 'namely' from *Etzem /* Essence. Haman did not know that the Etzem of the Creator chose and chooses the Etzem of Klal Yisrael. This Divine choice is not for what the Jewish People do, nor how they appear, nor even how they serve, but who they are at their core, beyond all garments and definitions. And the Etzem-choice of Klal Yisrael is always for blessing, life, and eternity (See at length Ma'amar BaYom Ashtei Asar, *Sefer haMa'amarim Melukat*, 3, pp. 99-110).

The Bechirah of Atzmus is in "the souls of the righteous" (בנפשותן של צדיקים נמלך: *Medrash Rabbah*, 8:7). In other words, although Atzmus is 'beyond good and evil' as it were, there was yet a Divine choice in the Etzem of goodness, righteousness, life, and blessing. This means that even a lottery, and what seems to be 'random' or arbitrary, is designed and orchestrated from on High. There is a saying by the Geonim: "One who does not follow a lottery is like one who does not follow the Ten Commandments" (העובר על הגורל כעובר על עשרת הדברות: *Teshuvas haGeonim* (Yerushalayim), 60. *Shu'T Chavos Yair*, Siman 61. *Likutei Sichos*, 13, pp. 114-115. Regarding the lottery of Haman, see *Pri Tzadik*, Shemos). This is why the decree of annihilation could not succeed. Haman was playing with what he thought was randomness, so he cast a Pur, a gamble into the hands of fate. But he did not understand that even what appears arbitrary, even what appears beyond order, is concealed in the palm of the Divine, and the Etzem eternally chooses the Etzem of Klal Yisrael (It is noteworthy to point out that in the קרוב"ץ / poem for the last day of Pesach it states: ומאז בחלקו עלו מחלשים שבעים. וסגלם לו לחבל נחלה מקבעים / "And from then, by lot, they were apportioned from the seventy. And He treasured them as His inheritance, set apart for Him." The KolBo explains that this means the Holy One, blessed be He, cast lots together with the seventy ministering angels above, and to each angel fell one nation, while Klal Yisrael fell to the portion of the Holy One Himself. Thus, the original choosing of Klal Yisrael by Hashem to be His People came about by a lot).

Hence, the Pur leads to Purim, the celebration of that which is 'beyond the Beyond'. It is the day when we do not distinguish between "Blessed is Mordechai" and "Cursed is Haman," not because good and evil are the same (*Chalila* / G-d forbid), but because we touch a level where true choice itself originates — not in morality or merit, but in Essence. Even while the Divine is 'beyond good and evil', Atzmus made and continues to make a choice, for goodness, for righteousness, for life, and for blessing. That choice is eternal. That choice is Klal Yisrael.

One of the deepest paradoxes is that Hashem is not bound by human constructs or values, yet, from that very place of boundlessness, He chooses the 'construct' of goodness over evil. It is not because He has to, but because He wants to. And His choice in life, in blessing, and in Klal Yisrael is eternal, because it comes from Atzmus, which is unchanging.

When Haman, humiliated, leads Mordechai through the streets of Shushan, marking the first visible shift in the swelling tide of redemption, he proclaims, ככה / *Kachah* / "*Thus* shall it be done to the man...." On the surface, this is merely a phrase of royal formality, but the Maggid of Kozhnitz, in the name of the Holy Baal Shem Tov, reveals a deeper resonance: ככה / *Kachah* is an acronym for כתר כל הכתרים / *Keser Kol haKesarim* / the Crown of all Crowns, the Essence beyond reason and judgment. Meaning choosing is not the result of merit, pending Divine favor. The Essential choice of Klal Yisrael does not mean that Klal Yisrael's righteousness impinges on or colors the Essence's 'bias'. In fact, no quality of Klal Yisrael, whether desirable or undesirable, compels the Divine Essence to respond. Rather, Etzem chooses us unconditionally, from a place beyond cause and effect, from the innermost delight of the Divine Essence. This choice is not a reward or even a set of expectations and responsibilities; it is a Divinely 'innocent', simple desire rooted in ultimate, untouched freedom.

Why is there a choice at all? Why would a radically uninfluenced freedom, without needs or agendas, make a deliberate choice to love and redeem Klal Yisrael? ככה / *Kacha* / 'just because'. In Hebrew, when one is asked למה עשית את זה / 'Why did you do that?' the other replies ככה / *Kacha* / 'just because'. There is no justification, logic, or lack. This is a freedom so radical that it resists explanation, the freedom of Divine Will. Hashem's choice of Klal Yisrael is the most unconditioned form of choice: it is ככה / *Kacha*, just because the Essence is one with Our Essence. This utterly simple Will is called of כתר כל הכתרים / *Keser Kol haKesarim*, Essence to Essence (Keser Kol haKesarim is the 'space' where Divine *Yediah* / knowing and complete human Bechirah, Ayin and Yesh, are all paradoxically unified as one. Hence, the Name ככה is connected with the ultimate redemption and the complete elevation of all souls: *Kesem Ofir*, Megilas Esther, 6:9. *Toldos Yaakov Yoseph*, the end, Os 16).

Sovev is the Infinite Light, Memaleh the Finite Light; these are two 'manifestations' of the Creator, but they are not the Creator

Himself. These are forms of Light; they are revelations, expressions, not the Etzem. Just as a ray of sunlight is an emanation of the sun, but not the sun itself, so too, Memaleh and Sovev are but emanations of the Etzem. The true Etzem, Hashem's Own Being, is beyond both finite form and formless infinity. It is beyond all notions of causality, purpose, region, and reason. Even calling Etzem the 'Source' of Light, already describes a type of 'region' and 'function'. And yet, it is paradoxically Etzem that chooses, wills, and desires the souls of the righteous.

In truth, there is no 'why' this choice occurs — to ask 'why' is to assume a need, and something that will fulfill what is missing. When a person eats, it is because he is hungry and needs nourishment. When one studies, it is because he seeks knowledge he does not yet have. All "whys" are bound up with deficiency and striving to fill that deficiency. But Atzmus, the Divine Essence, is absolute Wholeness. It is complete, lacking nothing, and therefore needs nothing. There is, in fact, no 'outside' at all. Besides Etzem, there is nothing, for all that exists is but an expression of Essence 'within' Essence, like a ray within the sun.

Moreover, the question 'Why' implies that a cause precedes an effect. For example: 'Why do I act in a certain way? Because I want to be a good person.' This assumes that the concept of 'goodness' exists prior to, and independent of, my action. But with Hashem, the Creator and Essence of all Existence, such reasoning cannot apply. We cannot claim that Hashem created the world *because* Hashem needed something from it or had some other reason or purpose, such as 'Hashem was lonely,' Heaven forbid. That would imply that the reason preceded the Creation. The only way we can speak of Hashem's choosing is in the language of ככה / *Kacha* / "just because." It is not rooted in a prior cause, but in the pure overflow of Divine Essence, which is directed toward Klal Yisrael, yet being already eternally and intrinsically bonded with Klal Yisrael.

MESIRAS NEFESH / ATZMUS ALLOWS FOR THE OHR MAKIF TO ENTER INTO A PENIMI

Mesiras Nefesh, often translated as 'self-sacrifice', in its deepest sense means transcending the basic instinct for self-preservation, the ego's drive to survive and perpetuate itself. It is a surrender of the self-centered will, letting go of control and fear, in order to awaken and activate the Divine instinct within our *Neshamah* / soul, our *Etzem* / essence. Through this profound act of letting go, of transcending ego and instinct, we connect to our true Essence, and it is through this connection that we are able to draw down Makif, the transcendent, all-encompassing Divine light of Sovev, into Penimi, the inner world of Memaleh, form, structure, and personal experience.

And this, in truth, was the miracle of Purim: even from the perspective of the lower Makif, the level of reality that seems beyond distinctions of good and evil, destruction was never truly possible. Why? Because the Jewish People managed to draw down Makif into Penimi. The Divine light that is ordinarily removed from the world of distinctions, beyond measure and morality, was brought into detail, into life, into lived reality. Yet for this integration to occur, for Makif and Penimi, transcendence and immanence, to merge, the Jewish People had to awaken their deepest self, the self that includes and harmonizes all dimensions, a soul-root that holds within it both infinity and finitude, order and transcendence.

They needed to become conscious of their essence, which includes and reconciles all expressions, and finds no contradiction between them; their paradoxical 'inclusive transcendence'.

There are times in our spiritual, intellectual and emotional growth processes when we move in a steady, incremental fashion. We build upon yesterday's efforts, climbing a ladder one rung at a time. This measured movement is rooted in our finite, defined, individual self. There are other times when we move through leaps, breakthroughs that are not sequential, instantaneous, or seemingly unrelated to our previous steps. These quantum leaps arise from a deep place within us called Makif, a dimension beyond the intellect and its calculations, and also beyond our infinite, formless, unmanifest self. Makif allows for sudden radical transformation, because it is not bound by logic or progression.

The Jewish People of that generation, despite their earlier spiritual shortcomings (which can be seen as the original cause of their predicament) stood firm for an entire year in a state of Mesiras Nefesh (Alter Rebbe, *Torah Ohr*, Megilas Esther, 91b. 97a. 99b). This was not a fleeting moment of sacrifice but a sustained posture of inner surrender. They reached a level of Makif beyond measure, in which their past no longer dictated their present. Still, their true greatness was not just in reaching that high spiritual level; it was in their ability to translate that transcendence, that fire of Mesiras Nefesh, into the rhythms of their everyday life.

Unlike at Sinai, where we 'expired' from the overwhelming Light and ecstasy of the experience, and had to be revived repeatedly, during the year of Purim, we did not expire. We lived and endured. From the moment of the decree until its nullification a year later, we absorbed our spiritual awakening and integrated it into every detail of life.

The Hebrew word for year is *Shana*, from the same root as *Shinui* / change. A year represents the full cycle of time, its seasons, transitions, and transformations. That we sustained our Mesiras Nefesh for a full year shows that we did not merely touch Makif in a moment of inspiration; rather, we carried it through every phase of life. We lived it in heat and cold, joy and fear, light and shadow.

Klal Yisrael, in unison, made the Makif permeate the Penimi. And when the power of Makif is fully integrated into the world of form, harm cannot touch innocent lives. The very structure of reality changed: Makif infused the world of cause and effect, where righteousness gave birth to blessings, and the decrees of destruction lost their hold. Haman's plot dissolved, not only because it was overturned from the outside via the king, but because the very root of reality had shifted, the whole universe had changed, through the simultaneous inner work of Klal Yisrael.

Mirroring the King Above who awakens from a state of slumber (as will be explored), the mighty king below, Achashverosh, too, finds sleep fleeing. In his inability to sleep, he summons his servants to read to him from the *Sefer haZichronos Divrei haYamim* / "The Book of Remembrances and Chronicles." This scroll recounts the history of his reign, his deeds, and the unfolding of events in his kingdom.

Sleep is a Makif (Igul) reality, circular and undefined. When the king wakes up from this enveloping Makif, he seeks to understand why; he seeks clarity on his narrative. He asks to be read from the book of written accounts, the words that anchor time, the stories of the past that have shaped the present. The king desires that these accounts and forgotten memories be read aloud, symbolically bridging the 'transcendent' dream world with the 'immanent' waking clarity of detailed narratives. He is driven to relate the Makif of his 'not-knowing' to the conscious Penimi recognition of the details of his day-to-day life and reign. As if subconsciously following the lead of the Jewish People, he, too, is drawing the Light of Makif into Penimi.

It is in this context that the name *Purim*, on the surface, a Persian word expressing empty randomness, begins to reveal its deeper positive resonance. It is, in fact, a profound name for this Yom Tov. Purim celebrates the highest form of transformation: redemption, and not despite the negative decree, but by means of the negative decree. By touching the very root of 'randomness' within the Makif, it is transformed and drawn down into a new Penimi. This transformation is made possible through our Mesiras Nefesh, by which our soul connects with its Etzem, beyond both Makif and Penimi, with the Etzem of Elokus, the Divine Essence itself. Only by connecting to a reality that is beyond opposites can these opposites come together and manifest redemption.

The idea of the Makif becoming fully integrated within the Penimi, the internal vessel, is beautifully reflected in a profound aspect of the Purim story. As explored earlier, Chazal say (*Shabbos*, 88a), "'And they stood under the mount…' This teaches that the Holy One, blessed be He, overturned the mountain upon them like an (inverted) cask, and said to them, 'If you accept the Torah, good. If not, there shall be your burial'… This furnishes a strong protest against the Torah." This moment, though filled with awe and revelation, introduced an element of coercion, casting a shadow of protest over the original acceptance of the Torah.

Yet centuries later, during the era of Achashverosh, a remarkable shift occurred: Klal Yisrael reaccepted the Torah, this time not from fear or compulsion, but out of love and inner resolve. The process that had begun at Sinai found its completion in Shushan and in the kingdom of Achashverosh. The external became internal. That which had once been imposed from Above, from the realm of Makif, now entered their inner world, their Penimi. So deep was this internalization that they embraced the very Megilah as part of Torah itself, and sanctified the celebration of Purim as an eternal Yom Tov to be celebrated every year. What was given from Above was now internalized Below, in their Penimi, their internal, practical experience.

Purim thus marks a turning point in the sacred relationship between Heaven and earth, a moment when humanity Below became not merely a recipient of Divine wisdom, but an active partner, even a co-creator, in its unfolding. It was then that man truly became a companion and co-conspirator in the ongoing revelation and articulation of Torah. This acceptance was not merely of the fixed and immutable written word, the Torah she-b'Kesav, sealed and absolute, resistant to alteration or human refinement. Rather, it was the dynamic, evolving dimension of Torah, the Torah She-b'Al Peh, the oral tradition, that was fully embraced. Unlike the written Torah, which is eternal in its words and form, a canonized absolute text, the oral Torah lives through interpretation, application, and the ever-deepening inquiry of the human mind.

In this, Purim stands apart. It was the moment when the Jewish People willingly, joyfully, and with full consent, embraced the task of becoming *Mechadshim* / innovators and unveilers of the Torah's infinite depths. They accepted not only the legacy of Torah she-b'Kesav, but the responsibility to expand its light through the prism of their intellect and soul, drawing forth new sparks all the while, of course, remaining completely rooted in the sacred framework of the received and revealed Written Torah. We can become Mechadshim, so long as the extrapolations are in accordance with the principles of Torah and its pedagogy.

Only during the story of Purim was Torah truly accepted *from within*, with desire, with devotion, with love and unfettered joy, and with the full flowering of human will in harmony with the Divine Will.

FROM BACK TO BACK TO FACE TO FACE

This process of revelation and the ultimate receiving of the Torah is referred to by the holy Arizal as *Panim el Panim* / face-to-face. At Matan Torah, the Divine turned toward us in full revelation, and we, in turn, faced Hashem, as the Pasuk says, פנים בפנים דבר ה' עמכם בהר / "Face-to-face Hashem spoke to you at the mountain" (*Devarim*, 5:4). Yet, on Purim, a new and deeper level of Panim el Panim emerged, an intimate encounter not through thunder and flames and intimidating power from Above, but through the filter of hiddenness and human initiative. A new dialogue between Above and Below began.

The Era of Prophecy began with the Giving of the Torah and continued through the time of the First Beis haMikdash. It was a period marked by open miracles, prophetic vision, and Divine clarity. With the destruction of the Beis haMikdash and the exile that followed, although the actual exile began already a few years before, the Heavens seemed to close. This ushered in a time of *Hester Panim* / concealment of Hashem's Face, in which Divine revelation no longer shone openly. This was actually a spiritual 'weaning', as a parent gently encourages a toddler to stand on its own, to begin the journey of gaining strength and maturity.

The story of Purim, as recorded in the Megilah, is paradoxical. On one hand, it is part of Tanach, the canon of Divine revelations and *Kisvei haKodesh* / sacred texts. Yet, unlike the Torah or books of prophecy, Megilas Esther was written by human hands, and maybe even adapted from the original writings of Persian chroniclers (שלחו

:לה קנאה את מעוררת עלינו לבין האומות. שלחה להם: כבר כתובה אני על דברי הימים למלכי מדי ופרס

Megilah, 7a).

The Megilah narrates human history and events, yet strikingly, the Name of Hashem does not appear even once (The Even Ezra explains on *Esther*, 1:1 that this omission is deliberate, for once the Scroll would be included in the royal chronicles of Persia, and translated, the sacred Name could have been rendered into idolatrous terms... והנכון בעיני מזאת המגילה חברה מרדכי, וזה

טעם וישלח ספרים וכולם משנה ספר אחד שהוא המגילה כטעם פתשגן והעתיקוה הפרסיים ונכתבה בדברי

הימים של מלכיהם והם היו עובדי עבודה זרה והיו כותבין תחת השם הנכבד והנורא שם תועבתם, כאשר

עשו הכותים שכתבו תחת בראשי' ברא אלהים ברא אשימא, והנה כבוד השם שלא יזכרנו מרדכי במגילה:

Mordechai, Megilah, 396. Alter Rebbe, *Shulchan Aruch*, Orach Chayim, 334:13).

The story of Purim unfolded in a crossroads of history, the end of one era and the beginning of another, and therefore, it is both from Above *and* from Below. It is a rabbinically initiated Yom Tov, prompted by Esther's request, yet it is canonized within Tanach, Hashem's word. The Megilah is a story that embodies the fusion of Divine revelation and human participation, the Above and the Below.

ACHOR B'ACHOR / BACK TO BACK

Relationships that operate in a top-down fashion can also be called *Achor b'Achor* / back-to-back. This is in contrast to the higher, more intimate level of *Panim el Panim* / face-to-face. A back-to-back dynamic may still feel deeply connected, even loving and close, but it lacks the fullness and reciprocity of mature relationships. A classic example is the relationship between parents and their small children. It is loving, devoted, and constant, seemingly face-to-face. Yet in truth, it remains Achor b'Achor most of the time, because it generally flows in one direction: the parent gives, and the child receives. The child clings, follows, and absorbs, but without full autonomy or dialogue. It is not yet a relationship of equals or of mutual revelation. It is a relationship of dependence, not encounter. In other words, in comparison to a mature relationship, this relationship is still considered Achor b'Achor.

Such was the nature of the relationship between Hashem and *B'nei Yisrael* / the 'Children' of Israel, during the prophetic era. Hashem revealed wisdom through prophets, and we listened and dutifully obeyed, like eager, young students. The Divine Presence was manifestly guiding us, especially when the First Beis haMikdash stood, when miracles abounded and Hashem's Panim shone openly. All those who lived during those periods of time intimately felt the Divine Presence. Yet, it was nonetheless a top-down relationship; it was about the Above, not the Below. Yet, Hashem desired a true relationship with us. And so, with the destruction of the Beis haMikdash and the onset of exile, the dynamic shifted. The *Hester Panim* / concealment of the Divine Face began (The Ohr of Ze'ir Anpin, the Divine Masculine and revelatory aspect left Malchus, our lived reality). This was not essentially a punishment, but part of a larger process of spiritual maturation. Just as a parent eventually withdraws to give the child space to grow, so too Hashem stepped back, creating the possibility for a new kind of relationship, one that is chosen, reciprocal, and rooted in freedom.

A DEEPER LEVEL OF *PANIM EL PANIM*: *TORAH SHE-B'AL PEH*

Within this framework, too, the story of Purim marks a turning point. It initiates a deeper level of Panim el Panim and a more mature, mutual relationship between the Below and the Above. Even the face-to-face revelations at Sinai and throughout the prophetic era, despite their brilliance, are Achor b'Achor in comparison to the inner, chosen intimacy that begins with Purim and that will one day culminate with the coming of Mashiach.

This process unfolds further with the rebuilding of the Second Beis haMikdash, a Temple not built through overt miracles from Above, but through human effort from Below. This shift mirrors the emergence of Torah she-b'Al Peh, the Oral Torah, which becomes the primary medium of connection. Unlike the Written Torah, which is received passively from Above, the Oral Torah requires human input, discussion, creativity, and partnership. It is the paradigm of Panim el Panim. In a true face-to-face relationship, one can 'step back' and even 'talk back', and one can freely choose. It is precisely this freedom and independence that makes the connection more real, more meaningful. No longer are we cornered with a mountain held over our heads. In the era that begins with Purim, we begin to choose the relationship anew, not out of fear or dependence, but from love and inner alignment. And that choice is what makes it enduring.

This higher, more mature face-to-face relationship is known as a *Bris* / covenant. A Bris is not a one-sided declaration, but a sacred bond that requires the willing consent of both parties. A *Bris haNesuin* / covenant of marriage cannot be declared בעל כורחו / *b'Al Korcho* / against one's will; there must be *Da'as* / awareness and consent for it to be valid and binding (*Kidushin*, 2b). This is the reason why לא כרת הקב"ה ברית עם ישראל אלא בשביל דברים שבעל פה / "The Holy One, Blessed be He, made a *Bris* / covenant with the Jewish People only for the sake of the matters that were transmitted *b'Al-Peh* / orally" (*Gittin*, 60b). That is, the *Ikar* / main element of our Bris with Hashem is revealed *Davka* / precisely with the revelation of Torah She-b'Al Peh, which is characterized by our active, freely-chosen participation. The essence of our covenant with Hashem is revealed most fully through Torah she-b'Al Peh, because it is here that our active, creative, and freely chosen partnership comes to light.

In the *Torah she-b'Kesav* / the written, revealed Torah, Hashem spoke *to* Moshe and the Prophets; in Torah She-b'Al Peh, Hashem speaks *through* the Sages. Similarly, in an Achor b'Achor relationship, Hashem reveals Himself to us from Above, and talks to us. In a Panim el Panim relationship, HaKadosh Baruch Hu no longer talks only 'to' us, but also through and with us. The encounter is no longer one-directional; it is a living partnership. Our voices are part of Hashem's revelation. Our questions, our insights, our very seeking, all become vessels through which Divine Wisdom and Presence are revealed.

The events of the Purim story occurred during the time of the *Anshei K'neses haGedolah* / Men of the Great Assembly. This was a 'supreme court' of 120 men, with about 85 rabbinic sages and 35 prophets, which would gather following the destruction of the First Beis haMikdash through the early period of the Second Beis haMikdash (Perhaps there were literally 120 sages at that time, or perhaps this number is symbolic, corresponding to the number of positions of authority in the kingdom, as it is written: "It pleased King Darius to appoint over the kingdom 120 satraps to be in charge of the whole realm": *Doniel*, 6:2. Or 120 could be a reference to deeper significance, for example, the 120 *Tzirufim* / letter combinations in the five letter Name 'Elokim', which represents judgment and judges, and because of this, Darius may have (unconsciously) chosen this number of ministers for the K'neses haGedolah).

The Men of the Great Assembly were the bridge across the chasm of this transitional age, shuttling Klal Yisrael from the age of the Prophets (Hashem talking *to* us) to the Sages (Hashem talking *through* us), and guiding us forward into the future toward a fullness of this new paradigm.

As mentioned earlier, Mishnah Avos (1:1) speaks of two transmissions of Torah: "Moshe received the Torah from Sinai and transmitted it to Yehoshua, Yehoshua to the Elders, the Elders to the Prophets, and the Prophets transmitted it to the Men of the Great Assembly." The first stage of 'transmission' thus begins with

Moshe, and it ushers in the Era of Prophecy. It continues through Yehoshua and the elders until it reaches the *Nevi'im* / Prophets. Up to this point, the word *u-Mesarah* / "and *he* transmitted it..." is used. Afterward, the same word comes in a plural form: *Mesaruha* / "and *they* transmitted it...." The plural "they" indicates a new kind of transmission occurring between the Prophets and the Men of the Great Assembly, shifting from the singular 'voice' of the Above to the multiple voices of the Below. What is more, Rashi comments that they, all the above-mentioned, transmitted the Torah *Zeh laZeh* / "from one to another," subtly implying multiple transmissions and human explanations and even discussions, branching out into the world of the many, the Below. The different endings of this verb indicate a nuanced shift from the predominantly Written Torah (although the Oral tradition was enfolded within it), to the Torah of the Sages.

The question is asked: why were they called the Men of the "Great" Assembly? The answer is given (*Yuma*, 69b): because they returned the crown of the Holy One, Blessed be He, to its former glory when they composed the Amidah, which says, *HaKeil haGadol, haGibor, ve-haNora* / "...the Great, the Mighty, and the Awesome Divinity." Originally, Moshe came and implored Hashem in prayer, saying, "The Great, the Mighty, and the Awesome" (*Devarim*, 10:17). Later, the Prophet Yirmeyahu / Jeremiah came and said, "The Gentiles, the minions of Nevuchadnetzar, are carousing in His sanctuary; where is His awesomeness?" Therefore, he did not say "the Awesome" in his (version of the) prayer (*Yirmiyahu*, 32:18). Doniel came and said, "Gentiles are enslaving His children; where is His might?" Therefore, he did not say "the Mighty" in his prayer (*Doniel*, 9:4). Finally, the members of the Great Assembly came and said, "On the contrary, the Might of Hashem, and the fullest expression of it, is that Hashem conquers His inclination and exercises patience toward the wicked."

This profound statement by the Great Assembly means that throughout Galus, HaKadosh Baruch Hu shows infinite 'Might' specifically by stepping aside, hiding, and by no longer imposing a top-down, Achor b'Achor relationship upon us. This way, Hashem allows the world to be, to run its course, so to speak, as an apparently detached and independent entity.

COLLECTIVE / PROVIDENCE VS. INDIVIDUAL / FREE CHOICE

In truth, the emergence of individuality and personal free will is directly proportional to the perceived distance from Mount Sinai. The closer we were to the revelation at Sinai, both historically and spiritually, the more we lived in a world shaped by collective experience, prophetic clarity, and overt Divine Providence. It was a time of archetypes, not individuals; of national destiny unfolding through miraculous intervention and direct communication from Above.

During the Era of Prophecy, the Divine Panim was more openly revealed. The supernatural was commonplace, and the Presence of Hashem was an undeniable force in the lives of the people. In such a reality, there is less room for ambiguity, and therefore, less space for personal autonomy and true *Bechirah* / free choice. The light was so overwhelming that the human being, the individual with his or her own choices, was, in a sense, eclipsed by it.

Yet, as history progressed, and especially with the shift into the era of the Sages, and the second Beis haMikdash, a new paradigm began to unfold. Divine Presence became more concealed; the miracles ceased to be open and obvious, and the voice of prophecy became dimmer. By means of this concealment, a space was opened for individuality to flourish. No longer living as archetypes in a grand, Divinely-scripted drama, human beings began to express themselves as unique souls with distinct inner worlds, questions, and choices. In this way, the concealment was not essentially a loss, but rather a transformation. Hester Panim is what allows the human 'face', the individual free choice, to emerge. In the absence of overwhelming revelation, we are given the dignity and the challenge of choosing, of seeking, of becoming. The Era of the Sages, of Torah she-b'Al Peh, is the age of dialogue, of interpretation, of dynamic engagement and sharing insights and Chidushim. Thus, the less obvious Hashem's Presence became, the more room there was for human Bechirah and conscious, personal relationship with the Divine (Paradoxically, the ultimate state of human consciousness, in the times of Mashiach, will be a full Panim el Panim relationship. In that era, both human Bechirah, genuine free will, and Divine Hashgachah will be revealed simultaneously, in perfect harmony. This profound convergence will be explored further later on).

At this juncture in history, Hashem ceased talking to us in a revealed, uni-directional manner, and now lovingly allows *us* to do the talking. We are thereby allowed to hear the echo of Sinai within our own consciousness and voice as we think and speak. In the language of the Ramban, "Even though the prophecy of the prophets, that which comes through vision and revelation, has been taken away, the prophecy of the Sages, which comes through the path of wisdom, has not been taken away; rather, they know the truth

through the *Ruach haKodesh* / Divine Spirit within them" (אַף עַל פִּי
שֶׁנִּיטְלָה נְבוּאַת הַנְּבִיאִים, שֶׁהוּא הַמַּרְאָה וְהֶחָזוֹן, נְבוּאַת הַחֲכָמִים שֶׁהִיא בְּדֶרֶךְ הַחָכְמָה לֹא נִיטְלָה, אֶלָּא
יוֹדְעִים הָאֱמֶת בְּרוּחַ הַקֹּדֶשׁ שֶׁבְּקִרְבָּם: Ramban, *Baba Basra*, 12a. See also Ra'avad, *Hilchos
Lulav*, Rambam, 8:5. Ra'avad, *Hilchos Beis haBechirah*, 6:14. See also, the Mabit,
Hakdamah, *Kiryas Sefer* וְהַתּוֹרָה שֶׁבַּע״פ אִי אַתָּה רַשַּׁאי לְאָמְרָהּ בִּכְתָב לִהְיוֹתָהּ גְּנוּזָה בְּנַפְשׁוֹתֵיהֶן
(שֶׁל צַדִּיקִים).

THE REVELATION OF CONCEALMENT

Hester Panim, paradoxically, is a revelation in itself, as it 'allows'
Hashem to speak through us, rather than merely to us. Our Sages
(*Chulin*, 139b) say, "Where is a hint of the name and events of אֶסְתֵּר
/ Esther in the Torah itself? From the Pasuk וְאָנֹכִי הַסְתֵּר אַסְתִּיר /
VeAnochi Haster Astir / "And I will certainly hide (from Klal Yis-
rael)…" (*Devarim*, 31:18). The name Esther is alluded to in the word
Astir / "I will hide."

At Matan Torah, we experienced the Aleph / Oneness of אָנֹכִי /
Anochi / the Divine 'I' openly through the revelation of the first of
the *Eser haDibbros* / the Ten Commandments, *Anochi Hashem* / "I
am (revealed as) Hashem…." With the story of Purim, however,
Hashem reveals the Divine 'I' through another Aleph: אַסְתִּיר / *Astir*
/ "I (Hashem) will hide." Now, the Anochi is 'revealed' *by means of*
deep concealment. We learn from the story of Esther and Purim
that the Oneness of HaKadosh Baruch Hu is deeply hidden within
the workings of nature and the flow of history. The revelation of the
light of Purim is that "Even in the concealment / darkness there is
light" (*Resisei Layla*, 53).

This is similar to the profound stillness shared between two deeply trusted friends, a comfortable silence that requires no words. In

such a bond, presence is felt without the need for constant affirmation. So too on Purim, though Hashem's name is absent from the Megilah, we celebrate that very silence. It is the quiet confidence of knowing that HaKadosh Baruch Hu is with us, even when not overtly speaking to us. Purim reveals the possibility of intimacy with Hashem not despite the darkness, obstruction, or duality of the world, but *within* it. It teaches us that even in the absence, even in the concealment, Hashem's presence is near. We trust that the silence is not empty, but full, that Hashem is still speaking, not to us, and not in a revealed way, but through us, and in an inner way, in the deepest recesses of our soul and consciousness.

THE SHECHINAH IS ALWAYS WITH US

Rebbe Shimon bar Yochai ("Rashbi") declares, שבכל מקום שגלו שכינה עמהן / "In every place they (Klal Yisrael) were exiled, the *Shechinah* / Divine Presence was with them." Rashbi gives examples: "In the Egyptian Exile the Shechinah was with them, in the Babylonian Exile the Shechinah was with them; the Divine Presence never abandons us (*Megilah*, 29a). The Medrash (*Eicha Rabbah*, 1:54) adds further, for example, גלו ליון שכינה עמהם / "They were exiled to Greece, and the Shechinah was with them." And, גלו לעילם שכינה עמהם / "They were exiled to Elam, and the Shechinah was with them," as the Pasuk says (*Yirmeyahu*, 49), ושמתי כסאי בעילם / "And I will set My Throne in Elam," implying that even there, the Shechinah dwells.

Where is Elam? In the book of Doniel (8:2) it says, "I was in Shushan *haBira* / the Capital, which is in the province of Elam." This tells us that "Elam" refers to Shushan (Alter Rebbe, *Torah Ohr*, Hosafos, Megilas Esther). The Hebrew word for darkness, *Choshech* / חשֶׁך, has a numerical value of 328. Double darkness (328+328) equals 656, which is the numerical value of שׁוּשַׁן / Shushan. As such, even in the double concealment and exile (*Hastir Astir*) of Shushan, "My Throne," the Shechinah is revealed.

Purim comes to teach us that the Divine Presence is found even within the unfolding of nature itself, even within what appears to be compounded darkness. Even in the deepest exile of estrangement and alienation, the living Presence of Hashem is there.

Though the story of Purim took place during the Persian exile, it also alludes to the final exile, our current extension of the Roman Exile, which is rooted in the double dark forces of Esav and Amalek.

The entire story of Purim is a battle against Amalek and the eradication of Amalek, the ancestor of Haman. The nearly two thousand years of the Roman Exile, at its core, is a struggle against Amalek. As such, the Purim story stands as a guidepost and a light for us, a message planted in history to prepare us for what was to come. The story from within the Persian Exile whispered to us across the centuries that there would come another, even deeper and much longer exile, when Amalek would rise again, cloaked in new forms. In this fourth and final exile of Klal Yisrael, darkness will be so compounded and thick that it conceals its own concealment. Its darkness is so deep that one no longer knows that it is dark; one is so confused that they do not realize they are confused, one is so misdirected that they stop even considering that they could be misdirected.

In this time, darkness masquerades as light. And yet, even there, in that place of doubled darkness, Purim reveals a profound truth: the light of Hashem, the light of the Shechinah, the light of holiness, of meaning, of clarity and purpose, may be hidden, but it is never absent.

THE REVELATION OF CONCEALMENT

Purim reveals that intimacy with Hashem is found not 'outside of' the darkness and concealment of the world, but within it. In silence and hiddenness, Hashem's Presence speaks through us, from the depths of our soul. This comes to teach us that there is Light even within our own darkness and apparent concealments. Yet, even when the concealment *remains* a concealment, there is light; the concealment itself shines. The hiding itself becomes a kind of revelation, the mask reveals the Face. If the concealment were to vanish the moment we sensed the Divine within it, it would be a paradigm of clarity, not of Purim. It would be more of a top-down revelation. But Purim teaches and reflects something deeper: even the *He'lem* of Galus contains within it Geulah (Hence, the root of the word *Megilah* / מגילה is גל / *Gal*, which is also the root of both *Galus* and *Geulah*).

A NEW REALITY IS BIRTHED IN THE WORLD

All of this represents a tremendous paradigm shift in our relationship with Hashem, and Hashem's relationship with the world. Regarding the Pasuk (*Tehilim*, 102:19), "May this be written down for the coming generations, that a people yet to be created may praise Hashem," Chazal say, "May this be written down for the coming generations...' This refers to the generation of Mordechai, which was leaning towards death, and 'A people yet created may praise

Hashem'... This means that Hashem created a ברייה חדשה / new Creation" (*Medrash Rabbah*, Vayikra, Emor, 30).

By means of the story of Purim, a new world has come into being. Through the lived experience of Klal Yisrael, a new dimension of reality was unveiled, one that had never been fully accessed before. A new kind of relationship with HaKadosh Baruch Hu began to emerge, one more intimate, more hidden, yet no less true. This new reality carried radical implications for all of humanity, as well, and for all forms of 'lower wisdom', including philosophy, the sciences, and all other areas of human inquiry and development.

Purim's quantum shift in the way the Creator reveals Himself to Creation sent ripples throughout the entire cosmos. What unfolded then within the realm of Torah and the awakening of Klal Yisrael, within the *Penimiyus* / the inner soul of the world, reverberated outward and reshaped the *Chitzoniyus* / the external face of reality. At that pivotal moment in history, similar paradigm shifts were taking place across the globe, and cultures everywhere began to undergo profound transformations. Some theorists refer to the period of Purim as the Axial Age, a time when long-held certainties began to dissolve (פר / crumble), and humanity turned sharply inward, asking deeper, more essential questions about meaning, the purpose of life, and the nature of existence. That seismic shift, sparked by Purim's Light, continues to shape the world today. We are still living in the Era of Purim, a Purim world.

FROM THE NAME 'HASHEM' TO THE NAME 'ADO-NOI'

All earlier Yamim Tovim, recorded and commanded in the Five Books of Moshe, celebrate miraculous and extraordinary events such as our going out of Egypt, receiving the Torah at Mount Sinai, and being embraced by the Clouds of Glory as we journeyed through the Desert. These events speak of an open revelation of Hashem's Infinite Light, as it were. They are supernatural meta-events that occurred outside the normal limits of time and space, causality, and nature. With the story of Purim, a paradigm shift occurred. Now Hashem speaks and reveals purpose and destiny through us, and in oneness with the limits and workings of time and space, causality and nature.

This shift in relationship is expressed in two principal Names of Hashem: the Name 'Hashem' (the Unspeakable Name: Yud-Hei-Vav-Hei), and the Name Ado-noi (the name of G-d that, out of great reverence, we pronounce in place of the Unspeakable Name). Previously, Divine revelation was predominantly in the mode of the Name 'Hashem.' Since Purim and onward, Divine revelation has been in the mode of 'Ado-noi'.

The Name of Hashem, Yud-Hei-Vav-Hei, when rearranged, can spell out the words *Hayah* (Hei-Yud-Hei) / 'It was,' or past tense, *Hoveh* (Hei-Vav-Hei) / 'It is,' or present tense, and — when you exchange the Vav for another Yud (because the Vav is, in a sense, an elongated Yud), you create the word *Yihiyeh* (Yud-Hei-Yud-Hei) / 'It will be,' or future tense (This deciphering of the Name of Hashem is first recorded by the Chasidei Ashkenaz. Rebbe Yehudah haChasid, *Sefer Gimatriyos*, 78. His son-in-law, Rebbe Eleazar Worms, *Siddur Rokeach*, p. 21. See also Pirush Rebbe Yehuda Bartzaloni on *Sefer Yetzirah*).

In this way, the Name 'Hashem' represents a totality of all past, present, and future, and simultaneously a complete transcendence of time. Hashem is thus 'the Timeless, Infinite Being-ness' or 'the Eternal One'. However, the way the Name Hashem is actually indicated and pronounced today, in our post Beis haMikdash era of exile, is "Ado-noi." The Name Ado-noi is the manner in which we can get a grasp, as it were, of the Infinite, Ineffable One within this finite world of limitations. In this way, 'Ado-noi' is the manifestation of the Infinity of 'Hashem' enclothed and concealed within finitude.

HaTeva / the (finite world of) nature, in numerical value, is 86. This is also the numerical value of the phrase *Kli Yud-Hei-Vav-Hei* / "the vessel of the Name Hashem" (*Kli* is spelled Chaf/20, Lamed/30, Yud/10 = 60; the Name 'Hashem' is spelled Yud/10, Hei/5, Vav/6, Hei/5 = 26). Thus, 'nature' is the vessel that now 'contains' the revelation of Hashem's Infinite Light. This world is the 'glove' in which the transcendent 'Hand of Hashem' is vested and operating, albeit in hidden and mysterious ways.

Maseches Megilah, which speaks about Purim, opens with the teaching, "The Megilah is read on the 11th, 12th, 13th, 14th, and 15th (of the month of Adar); לא פחות ולא יותר / no less and no more" (Mishnah, *Megilah*, 1:1). The words of the Mishnah, לא פחות ולא יותר / "...no less and no more" are a little peculiar. It seems the Mishnah should have said, "...not *before* and not *later*." (Although perhaps the Mishnah wishes to phrase this statement in a similar fashion to the other Mishnayos that use this phraseology, although in those it appears in the context of measurements: *Shabbos*, 137a. *Eiruvin*, 57b. *Yuma*, 26b). On closer inspection, however, the words "less" and "more" seem to hint at the idea of a number. What could be that number? The days on which the Megilah may be read, the 11th, 12th, 13th, 14th, and 15th, are a spiritual equation: 11+12+13+14+15, equaling 65, which is the numerical value of the Name Ado-noi. The days before and after the period when the Megilah may be read are the 10th and the 16th of the month, and 10+16 equals 26, the value of the Name Hashem. In this way, the Mishnah can be interpreted as follows: 'The Megilah is read in (the consciousness of) the imminent Name Ado-noi; no less and no more — not in (the direct consciousness of) the transcendent Name Hashem' (*Shaloh haKadosh*, Torah She-b'Kesav, 329, 1. 330, 2. The Name 'Esther' is numerically 661. 'Ado-noi' in its full filling is 671. Within 'Esther' the Yud / 10 is hidden).

Ado-noi stems from the word *Adon* / Master. The Name Ado-noi can shift in form; it adapts according to the human relationship it reflects, for example, *Ado-ni* / 'my Master' and *Ado-neinu* / 'our Master'. In contrast, the ineffable Name Hashem never changes. It is always the same, untouched, unaltered, transcendent. One does not say *Hashemi* / 'my' Hashem, because this Name exists beyond all relational context, beyond time, space, or personhood. Whereas 'Hashem' is beyond relationship, 'Ado-noi' expresses the Divine as encountered within a relationship, in the ways that G-d is known to us. It is the Name of immanence, of Divine closeness. The profound depth of the Purim story lies in this very closeness, in our ability to connect with the Divine not only by transcending our limitations, but also from within them. On Purim, and thereafter, Hashem (the Transcendent One) meets us within immanence, within our life story, within nature, within our lived experiences, within our minds and consciousness, within history, and within a hidden, intimate relationship.

Moreover, this is how the *Yetzer* / 'inner drive' for idol worship was nullified by the men of the Great Assembly soon after the events of the Purim story (*Yuma*, 69b). The impulse toward idolatry stems from a longing to experience the Divine within the immediacy of life. When the Divine is perceived as utterly transcendent, beyond all nearness and relatability, the soul yearns for and seeks a point of contact, a bridge, an intermediary through which it might encounter the Infinite within the finite. Yet, even if such a bridge would initially seem effective, it would soon become the seeker's main focus, and they would end up serving the intermediary rather than the Divine through it. Purim transformed this paradigm. Through the unfolding of its hidden miracles, it was revealed that the Divine is not distant, but already present within the immediacy of experience, within the seeming randomness of history, and within the garments of nature and human choice. This revelation prepared the world for the dissolution of idolatry, and any perceived need for false intermediaries naturally fell away (See *Ya'aros Devash*, 2:2).

TRANSITIONING FROM *'ACHOR B'ACHOR'* TO *'PANIM EL PANIM'*

As discussed, there are two primary paradigms of relationship between HaKadosh Baruch Hu and the world: Achor b'Achor and Panim el Panim. When moving from any state to another, there is a third, transitional stage that connects and transforms the first into the second. Our relationship with the Creator began with an Achor b'Achor connection. This stage is also referred to as *Zivug T'midi /* constant unity, like the bond between a nursing child and its mother, a closeness so complete that separation is unthinkable and not even possible. The child is ever near, yet still never fully aware of the other as Other. It is a connection defined more by dependency than mutuality. This was the kind of relationship Hashem had with us from when we were taken out of Egypt and brought to Matan Torah until the end of the First Beis haMikdash (Although within that period, during the times of the *Shoftim* / Judges, there was also a relative Divine withdrawal and concealment.) In the words of the *Navi* / Prophet Yirmeyahu, "Thus said Hashem, 'I counted in your favor the *Chesed* / devotion of your youth, your love as a bride, לכתך אחרי / *how you followed Me* in the wilderness, in a land not sown'" (*Yirmeyahu*, 2:2). This hints at the fact that we "followed" Hashem אחרי / *Acharei*, on the level of *Achar* (אחר) / the back, and yet it was counted as Chesed.* This was a stage of uni-directional relationship. Like children walking behind their parents, we followed Hashem through the wilderness. When we obeyed, we were protected. When we disobeyed, we were disciplined. It was a relationship of profound closeness, but not yet one of full maturity. We were near, but not yet independent, as individuals in a face-to-face relationship.

This was the Age of Prophecy, as discussed. It was an imposed relationship, as it were (Maharal, *Ohr Chadash*, Hakdamah), in which we could only "devotedly" receive from Above. If we needed to know, for example, whether to go out to battle or not, we would simply ask the Cohen Gadol, the High Priest, to request a prophetic insight via the Urim v'Tumim, the sacred Divine Name that was placed within, or was part of, the *Choshen* / breastplate. Similarly, during our travels through the Desert, we would move or stay put

---

* In truth, there are four stages: Panim and Achor are the two extremes, and between them lie *Yemin* / the 'right side', aligned with Chesed, and *S'mol* / the 'left side', aligned with Gevurah: Ramaz, *Zohar* 3, 93a. *Ma'amar Vayehi Omen Es Hadassah*, 5713, Chap. 2, p. 102. This means that a person may be operating on the level of Achor, the "back" rather than Panim, and yet still remain connected to the attribute of Chesed, as indicated in the above description.

depending on the Divine Pillars of Cloud and Fire; if they moved, we moved, if they stayed put, we stayed put. "Upon the word of Hashem we rested, and upon the word of Hashem we traveled" (*Bamidbar*, 9:23).

To enter into a more mature and conscious relationship with HaKadosh Baruch Hu, we needed to pass through an experience of Gevurah, of separation, distance, and concealment. The second stage, therefore, was marked by the destruction of the Beis haMikdash and the subsequent exile to Babylon and Persia. In order to evolve from a 'back to back' relationship to a 'face to face' relationship, there needed to first be a *Nesirah* / severing,* a process of sepa-

---

* In greater detail: On a cosmic level, prior to the Nesirah, there was *Mochin* / intelligence / vitality, but only flowing into ZA (the masculine, transcendent Sefiros, "Kudsha Brich Hu"). ZA, in turn, was *Mashpiah* / continuously transmitting Mochin to Malchus (the feminine, receiver, "K'neses Yisrael"), and all this was done in a way of Achor b'Achor (since Malchus has no vitality of its own, it needs to be fed Mochin from ZA or beyond.)

When ZA is aroused (with *Kishui* / arousal, *Kiviyachol* / so to speak), there is a live, animated Eiver, organ, and it can be and is unified with *Nukva* / Malchus.

The act of Nesirah alters this dynamic between ZA and Malchus, changing it from a one-dimensional active giver and passive receiver to a relationship that is more equal, dialogic, and mature.

At first, Malchus is dependent upon ZA for Mochin and vitality (in a Back to Back way), followed by the Nesirah, the separation between ZA and Malchus, which eventually leads to a higher level of unity between ZA and Malchus (face to face).

Experientially, the way people experience the *Yichud* / unity of ZA and Malchus is by sensing the *Mochin* / Divine Purpose and Intelligence hidden within *Teva* / nature. We see that Teva exists, but if we are spiritually mature, we can sense within Teva the hidden Hand of Hashem guiding everything, we experienced within our reality, our Malchus, the Divine Presence (of ZA), and felt the Hand of Hashem in all of life.

The time of the First Beis haMikdash was a time of *Nevuah* / prophecy and miracles; the Hand of Hashem was openly revealed in nature. Then came the *Nesirah* / separation, the destruction and exile. The purpose of the Nesirah was so there could be a Panim el Panim relationship, allowing for a revealing of Torah She-b'Al Peh. Yet, during the Nesirah, there is a movement away, a sense that Hashem has left us (Chas v'Shalom). We feel alone and rejected, like a divorced woman, or an abandoned child. And that is what Klal Yisrael tells the Prophet Yechezkel: 'Hashem has divorced us.' This is because now ZA and Malchus are no longer 'attached at the hip'. Of course, the purpose of the Nesirah is to eventually reach a deeper connection, but Malchus feels (meaning 'we' feel) abandoned, alone, and divorced.

In such a state, it seems as if *Elokim Yashen* / 'Hashem is sleeping.' Haman says, "The G-d of Klal Yisrael is asleep." Indeed, during the period of the Purim story, Klal Yisrael was in great danger and *Tzarah* / distress. At such times, experientially, we feel as if nature has its own rules, as if Hashem is not ruling it. There is an appearance of randomness, like the *Goral* / lottery of Haman. This is what many of Klal Yisrael originally thought when the decree of Haman became known: 'Hashem has left us, and now nature has taken over, and it is might over right.'

Yet, during the Nesirah, where ZA is turning away and separating from Malchus, Malchus is not left without Mochin altogether. Yes, ZA is separate from Malchus and is no longer moving Mochin into Malchus, however, Malchus receives Mochin from *Av'ah* (Chochmah and Binah and even higher). This Mochin is not the 'Mochin of Creation' (as the Mochin of ZA), since Av'ah is Higher than this world which is 'created by' ZA — the six Sefiros being the Six Days of Creation (like a six-sided cube of Creation with Shabbos / Malchus in the center) — rather it is a Mochin from beyond Creation. The separation then opens up the space for an even higher level of revelation to occur within the apparent concealment.

The Mochin within Malchus that is experienced (during the Nesirah) is experienced as a sense that even though nature seems to function on its own, we have *Emunah* / higher Mochin that everything is going to work out for the best (even if we do not yet intellectually know how). When we experience this form of higher Mochin in Malchus, as during the time when the Purim narrative was unfolding, true we do not have the revelation of ZA in our Malchus, meaning, we are 'asleep', dissociating from the practices of Torah (ונשי ומ תורצמה / "They are asleep from (not doing) Mitzvos": *Megilah*, 13b, and ZA is essentially Tiferes, and Tiferes is Torah... הרות ותמ ז ותמ ותראפתהו: *Berachos*, 58b). Yet, despite the lack of Torah, there is awakened within us (Malchus) a *Tenuah* / movement of total *Mesiras Nefesh* / self-sacrifice (and Mesiras Nefesh is connected with the level of Chochmah within Klal Yisrael: *Tanya*, 18). In this state of Nesirah, there is a tremendous sense of longing and yearning to connect, until the point of Mesiras Nefesh, as the revelation of Chochmah comes down and is revealed even in the Guf, the body of Klal Yisrael.

What is more, even after the Nesirah and the *Yichud* / reunification of ZA and Malchus in a mode of Panim el Panim, where Malchus is enlivened directly from ZA, the Mochin from Av'ah still remains enclothed within the Malchus. This is the *Chidush* / novelty of ration. Imagine two people who are literally attached to each other back to back; what happens when they wish to encounter each other face to face? To do so, they need to first detach and move away from each other so that they can then turn around to face each other. This temporary disconnection allows for a re-connection on an entirely new level, not one of dependence, but of mutual recognition and love. It is through this purposeful distancing that the path is cleared for a higher and more conscious bond.

Continuing with the developmental paradigm we have been exploring to understand these relational dynamics, the stage of Nesirah can be likened to the difficult but necessary years of adolescence. Adolescence is a time when both parent and child begin to detach, to move 'away' from one another, not in rejection, but in order to create the space needed for individuation. The child is no longer entirely dependent on the parent and begins to carve out an identity of their own. Though the parent desires this growth and autonomy, it is often a painful process, marked by misunderstandings, distance, and a disruption of the easy intimacy that once was. The patterns of communication and connection that served in earlier stages begin to fall away. The natural impulse of the parent to give freely and unconditionally may now need to be tempered. Unrestrained giving, once nurturing, could now hinder the child's emer-

---

Purim, which, in this way, is beyond the level of Shabbos and Yom Tov. The mature reunification of Malchus and ZA is thus on a higher level than the initial relationship of open revelation and childlike dependence, when Malchus has all its Light from ZA, because now, Malchus (in addition to the Mochin from ZA), still has the Mochin from Av'ah (as the level ZA, who also has their Mochin from Av'ha), and the relationship between ZA and Malchus are more mutually independent and thus more Panim el Panim, although the deepest level will be in the times of Mashiach, as will be explored.

gence as an independent self. It takes Gevurah, strength to withhold, to allow the child to struggle, and to discover themselves. Yet
this stage is not a breaking of the relationship, but a transformation
of it. Because only through this process of temporary disconnection can a deeper, more honest, and mature person-to-person relationship emerge, a healthy relationship not rooted in dependency,
but in mutuality, respect, and conscious choice.

THE PURIM STORY BEGINS WHEN THE KING IS SLEEPING & THE SALVATION BEGINS WHEN THE KING IS AWAKENING

In this cosmic, and thus microcosmic, state of slumber, the Sages
and leaders of Klal Yisrael perceived the great peril their people
faced. It was a time of deep spiritual sleep. The Jewish People no
longer experienced a conscious, living relationship with HaKadosh
Baruch Hu, and, as it were, even Hashem Himself was in a state of
Divine slumber. It was a time when a double measure of concealment had descended upon the world.

Below, the people were spiritually asleep. Above, the light of the
Divine was veiled. There was no awakening from Below, nor was
there any longer an arousal from Above. The flow of connection
had stalled on both ends. The danger was not merely political and
physical; rather, these symptoms were the effects of the spiritual
and existential danger that was occurring cosmically. Being that
this narrative of Purim unfolds within this in-between time, between awakening from Above, as in prophecy, which is coming to
a close, and the awakening from Below, which has not yet come,
they stood on the brink.

Haman, whom the Arizal identifies as a master astrologer, intuited this truth (ונודע כי המן הרשע היה אוסטרולוגוס גדול :Sha'ar haKavanos, Purim, Derush 1. In Pri Eitz Chayim, the terminology is והנה המן הרשע היה מכשף גדול / "And behold, Haman the Wicked was a great magician": Pri Eitz Chayim, Sha'ar Chanukah, Purim, 5). Haman recognized the moment, the alignment of this dual concealment, and devised his wicked plot. Precisely because the bond between Klal Yisrael and Hashem seemed dormant, he believed that he could sever it entirely, Heaven forbid. His aim was not just persecution, but total annihilation, to destroy a people who, in his eyes, had fallen asleep and whose G-d, so to speak, had turned away and was asleep, as well.

But the Sages of the generation, and Mordechai and Esther, understood the depths of the moment. In response, they called for a three-day fast, day and night, to awaken the people from their spiritual stupor. Through fasting, prayer, and introspection, the nation began to stir. From within their double concealment, a cry rose, and this cry from Below aroused Heaven Above. Their tears tore through the veil, and the great reversal began. The first flicker of the miracle is recorded in the Pasuk, "On that night, the king's sleep was disturbed" (Esther, 6:1). On the surface, this refers to Achashverosh, king of Persia. Yet, the Sages reveal its deeper resonance; it alludes to the King of All Kings, the Holy One, blessed be He. As the Medrash teaches (Esther Rabbah, 10:1), "The heavens and the throne of the King of Kings trembled, as He saw His children in distress."

Halachic authorities (Darkei Moshe, Orach Chaim 690. Magen Avraham ad loc., 17) instruct that when reading these words in the Megilah, one should raise their voice, for these words mark the very heart of the miracle (*Megilah*, 19a). This Divine awakening from slumber is the turning point. Indeed, throughout the Megilah, the phrase "the king" often hints at the King Above. And here too, the Sages say (*Megilah*, 15a): "On that night, the sleep of the King of the world was disturbed." In the words of Dovid haMelech (*Tehilim*, 78:65), "Then Hashem awoke as one who had slept, like a warrior shaking off wine." All this was awakened by our cries, our longing, and our return, the return of His beloved children. We stirred the Heavenly compassion.

Hashem beheld His children's need, just as in Egypt, centuries prior. Yet, this time, it was not the cry of a child waking up and reaching instinctively for its mother. This awakening of Klal Yisrael was the awakening of a mature soul, a nation no longer seeking miracles alone, but a deeper, reciprocal relationship with the Infinite. This was a new stage in our connection, a turning from back-to-back to face-to-face, on a deeper level.

Indeed, everything in the story begins to shift on that fateful night when "the King" cannot sleep. It is not just personal insomnia; it symbolizes a cosmic awakening from Divine slumber. And so, as we read the words "On that night, the King's sleep was disturbed," we raise our voices, for this moment stirs us, stirring the Divine Presence, and the hidden hand of Providence begins to move history forward once more.

The awakening of the King is the beginning of the third stage, the return from Divine slumber to the deeper state of Panim el Panim relationship between Hashem and His people. This night is the hinge of history. It marks the turning point within the darkness of the Persian exile, setting into motion not only the salvation of the Jewish People, but also the eventual (continuation of the) rebuilding of the Second Beis haMikdash. It paves the way for the spiritual renaissance of Torah She-b'Al Peh, the flowering of the era of Chazal, the Sages of the Mishnah and Talmud, who would illuminate exile with the inner light of Torah.

SPIRAL STEPS

The terminology we have been using, Achor b'Achor, Nesirah, and Panim el Panim, originates in the teachings of the holy Arizal. The Alter Rebbe teaches (*Sefer haMa'amarim*, 5565) that whatever the Arizal taught in esoteric language and Kabbalistic abstractions, the Baal Shem Tov was able to bring it into the world of experience, by expressing it through a *Mashal* / parable or metaphors that touch the heart and imagination. One such metaphor by the Baal Shem Tov (*Ohr haTorah* [The Magid], Eikev) to explain the process we have been discussing is that of a spiral staircase. In Yiddish (and German), a spiral staircase is called *Shvindal-Trep* / spiral step (Rashi, in *Melachim* 1, 6:8 writes, "A *winding staircase*, and that is called in our language... the commonly used term, *Shvindel Steig*": ל"ד שטיי"ן ושם המורגל שווינד"ל אשכנז ווינ"ל ובלשון (שט"י. This image captures the essence of ascent, unity, through seeming descent, separation, of drawing closer even while appearing to move away, a perfect parallel to the journey from Achor b'Achor, through Nesirah, to Panim el Panim. Just as a spiral staircase turns away in order to rise, so too, we at times must turn, detach, and reorient to ultimately encounter the Divine face to face.

In the unfolding of history, Hashem, as it were, needed to "separate" from us, to create a sense of distance, so that we could begin to experience true independence and develop the sense of responsibility necessary for a mature relationship. This Divine withdrawal was not abandonment (Chas v'Shalom) but empowerment. It opened the space for us to rise into our own spiritual adulthood, to begin shaping, developing, and revealing Torah She-b'Al Peh with our own insight and effort, and to establish lives of holiness and elevation, even without the presence of the Beis haMikdash and revealed miracles.

In the early, pre-personal stage of life, an infant perceives no clear boundary between self and mother, nor between self and world. The lines between inner and outer are blurred; the external world is experienced as an extension of the self. As the child matures, they gradually become aware of their own physical limits, where their body ends, and the outside begins. Still, at this stage, parents and siblings are often felt as parts of the self, familiar, responsive extensions of the child's will. When the infant cries, he is fed. When he dirties himself, he is cleaned. When tired, he is soothed to sleep. Life is seamless and immediate. Only when the parent begins to withhold, delaying the response, resisting the impulse to immediately satisfy every need, does the child begin the slow, painful, but essential process of individuation. Through many gradual and layered stages, the child develops inner strength, resilience, and autonomy. Eventually, a healthy adult no longer needs to live under the constant care of the parent. Indeed, at some point, the parent may even 'exile' the child, lovingly, for their own good, urging them to step into the world on their own.

So too with us and HaKadosh Baruch Hu. Although the Divine Presence is no longer as palpably felt as it was in the days of prophecy and open miracles, a new and deeper form of relationship has become possible. This is the paradox of *Galus* / exile. On one hand, the severance from our earlier, dependent state can leave us feeling alone, adrift, even abandoned. Yet it is precisely within this ache of separation that a truer yearning arises, one not born of need alone, but of love. It is this yearning that allows us, perhaps for the first time, to consciously and freely choose to accept the Torah. The relationship is no longer passive, rather, requires our presence, our commitment, our voice. We become deeply present in a way we had not been before, for now the relationship relies on our own active participation.

To fully grasp the nature of this transformation, we must delve deeper into the meaning of Galus, not merely as exile, but as the fertile ground from which the deepest connection can grow.

DIVINE SLUMBER

Galus, or exile, is not merely a geographical displacement; it is an existential disorientation. It is the aching sense of estrangement, of being disconnected and alien within one's own self. In our relationship with the Divine, *Galus* is the feeling of separation, a painful sense that Hashem is absent, asleep, so to speak; that the Creator has withdrawn, leaving the world to drift as if unguided and left to its own devices. This is indeed very painful, but, like all movements and stages of human development, it is required. It is a temporary concealment that fosters independence and deepens capacity. Like the spiral staircase that winds away before it rises, this momentary distance is the only path to a higher, truer reunion, a more mature and authentic encounter with the Infinite.

The events of Purim beautifully illustrate this dynamic of hiddenness and emergence. During the Persian exile, a time devoid of open miracles, prophecy, or direct revelation from Above, an orphaned, displaced Jewess named Esther rose unexpectedly to become queen of the vast Persian Empire. Through her hidden courage and providential ascent, the Jewish People were saved from Haman's diabolical plot, and eventually, the Jewish People were granted permission to complete the rebuilding of the Second Beis haMikdash (*Ezra*, 4). This restoration ushered in a new spiritual era, the flourishing of the Torah she-b'Al Peh, the Oral Tradition, and the golden age of the Sages that began during the Second Beis haMikdash period.

Yet, all of this unfolded within a time of cosmic slumber, a period steeped in prejudice, vulnerability, and apparent Divine silence. When Haman, the wicked antagonist, lobbied the king against the Jews, he said: ישנו עם-אחד / "There is a certain people scattered and dispersed..." (*Esther*, 3:8). The phrase "there is" in Hebrew is ישנו / *Yeshno*, which can also be read as 'They are sleep,' as in ישן / *Yashen* / sleeps (ישנו literally means 'there stands out', since the correct term for 'there is' is simply יש / *Yesh*: Maharsha, *Megilah*, 13b). Haman was subtly referencing not only the Jewish People's dormancy but also, as the Medrash teaches (*Esther Rabbah*, 10:1), the slumber of their G-d: אלקיהם של אלו ישן הוא / "The G-d of these people is *Yashen* / asleep." Exile, in this view, is not just displacement, it is sleep, Divine sleep.

As mentioned earlier, all transformations from a back-to-back to a face-to-face relationship begins with a painful separation. In our relationship with HaKadosh Baruch Hu this is also true. The stage following 'back-to-back' is 'Hester Panim', a withdrawal, a concealment of Presence. There is a sense of absence, of being ripped away from everything good and holy in life. But deeper still is *Hastara b'Toch Hastara* / concealment within concealment, a kind of Divine anesthesia, and a darkness so dark that we begin to think it is light, a concealment so concealed that we start thinking that there is no concealment at all. This double hiddenness of *Haster Astir Panai* / "Hide, I will surely hide, My Face" (*Devarim*, 31:18), is specifically connected with the Purim story and the main protagonist, Esther, whose name is connected with the above Pasuk (*Chulin*, 139b). She is hiddenness within hiddenness.

Therefore, precisely because the separation and concealment of exile was so devastating, dark, and agonizing for both the Jewish People and for HaKadosh Baruch Hu, an anesthetic was needed to begin an arousal and reawakening. When a young adult leaves the protective shelter of the 'nest' but has not yet developed the tools for healthy self-soothing and resilience, they may tragically turn to harmful substitutes, such as substance abuse, addictions, or self-mutilation (may the Compassionate One spare us) in order to numb their pain and anger of loss and transition. Rest and sleep are necessary for our bodies and minds to survive significant changes and traumas.

Just as a patient needs to be put to sleep in certain surgeries, both humanity and Divinity needed a numbing of the pain of the first exile from the Beis haMikdash, an anesthetic of sorts that would allow for renewal and reconfiguration. Sleep, in this sense, becomes mercy: a state of anesthesia to soften the agony of disconnection, to allow for the inner reconfiguration, healing, and eventual rebirth.

The days of exile and Divine separation awaken profound sorrow and deep anguish, both for the Jewish People, who suffer the pain of distance from their Creator, and for the Holy One, blessed be He, who suffers along with His children. As the Sages teach (*Chagigah*, 15b): "My head hurts, my arm hurts," a Divine expression of shared pain and empathy. This is compared to a young child or adolescent breaking away from their parents. The transition into adulthood carries great risk. If the child lacks the inner strength and tools to navigate the alienation of this separation, they may fall into deep despair. In such a vulnerable state, they may turn to self-numbing, as mentioned. Yet this is the very time when one must do the opposite: to strengthen the body, nourish it with wholesome food, and abstain from harmful influences. It is through this strengthening that one overcomes the loneliness and pain of separation. So too, during this time of spiritual transition, the Jewish People were called to fortify themselves, to cultivate inner strength in the face of divine concealment. And just as a patient undergoing a difficult surgery must be put to sleep so they do not feel the pain of the procedure, so too a deep slumber descended upon both Klal Yisrael and the Divine Presence. This sleep, a kind of spiritual anesthesia, was necessary in order to survive the trauma of this painful transformation.

This story takes place in the double darkness of the final phases of the Persian exile. Yet, as with all exiles and nights, the darkest hour comes right before dawn. This was the time of Divine Slumber and of Nesirah, when the relationship between us and Hashem transitions from Achor b'Achor to Panim el Panim.

At this sacred turning point, the pain is greatest. For in the Ne-sirah, the former connection is severed and the new closeness has not yet come into being. One feels not only distant, but as if drift-ing further apart. Imagine two figures once standing back to back. One begins to turn, and in that turning, for a moment, the dis-tance is greatest. Yet this very movement, this painful pivot, is not a retreat but a preparation, the sacred choreography that will allow them to meet face to face. So too was Purim: a moment of veiled distance that concealed within it the seeds of the deepest closeness yet to come.

This meta-historical process described in the Purim story is parallel to the *Nesirah* / surgical separation and re-configuration of Adam and Chavah / Eve. Originally, Adam and Chavah were created as a single body: "And G-d created Adam in His image… male and female He created them" (*Bereishis*, 1:27). That is, Adam and Chava were initially created as a single being, with two faces gaz-ing in opposite directions, connected back-to-back (*Medrash Rabbah*, Bereishis, 8:1. *Eiruvin*, 18a); they were conjoined, but also paradoxically alone, without a real relationship with the *other*. Although they were merged as one, the Torah says, "It is not good for the man to be alone (back-to-back); I will make a helper *against* him (face-to-face)" (*Bereishis*, 2:18). Therefore, "Hashem caused a deep sleep to fall upon Adam… and He took one of his sides…" (*Bereishis*, 2:23), in order to separate them. It was only in this state of *Durmita* / sleep that a *Nesirah* / severing could occur without completely over-whelming Adam and Chavah. Only through this surgical opera-tion could they begin to "know" each other, challenge each other, be "helpmates against" each other, and thus really help each other to grow.

HELPER / AGAINST:
TORAH RISING FROM THE BELOW

We can only truly receive the gift of a helper, an Ezer, when that person also stands *Kenegdo* / opposite us, not in opposition, but in presence, face-to-face, seeing us fully, reflecting us back honestly. Only when two individuals stand across from one another by their own volition, by choice, not compulsion, can they authentically give and receive love, feedback, and growth. And because they stand freely, they also hold the power to walk away.

It is precisely this risk, the possibility of disconnection, that renders true connection so precious. For when a relationship endures not by force, but through choice, it awakens a deeper sensitivity, a more conscious presence, within both partners.

One cannot truly help another or be helped by them unless they are standing face to face, able to see one another, to reveal their countenance to each other. When two people willingly choose to stand opposite one another, with open hearts, they can give to each other, receive from each other, and come to truly love one another. On the other hand, if things are not going well between them, they still have the option to walk away. Precisely, it is this possibility that deepens the bond between them, because the relationship is rooted in free will. As long as they remain together, it is clear that they have chosen to stay, not because they were forced to, but because they desire it. When each one knows that the other is present by choice, not compulsion, it awakens a deeper sense of closeness, a more powerful connection.

So it is with our relationship to HaKadosh Baruch Hu. In exile, when the Divine Countenance is concealed, and the bond is no longer automatic, the relationship becomes more intimate, not less. It is no longer sustained by proximity alone, but by pursuit. No longer guaranteed, it must be chosen. Indeed, that choice, amid distance and silence, is what renders it so powerful, for we are no longer tethered to the 'back' of the Divine, carried along unconsciously. Now, every step toward connection must come from within us, and that, paradoxically, is what makes it truly ours and meaningful.

When we stand in exile, we are granted the unique opportunity to feel a closeness to HaKadosh Baruch Hu that may surpass what we experienced while dwelling in our land. This bond is entirely rooted in our own will; it is not imposed upon us by geography, circumstance, or national structure, but rather a connection that flows from the deep desire of the Jewish soul to draw near to its Creator. Yet this gift carries a paradox, a blessing with a thorn. Precisely because the relationship is built on choice, we also have the painful possibility to walk away, and tragically, there have been those who did. But therein lies our great power: on one side, the freedom to turn away entirely, G-d forbid, and on the other, the power to forge a deeper, more elevated bond, precisely because it emerges from our own choosing.

When we choose to connect with the Source of Life, our lives become fuller, more textured, resonant, and alive. This is the beauty and sweetness of the Torah She-b'Al Peh, the Oral Torah, which in many ways surpasses the written Torah She-b'Kesav. For the Written Torah is fixed, etched in sacred ink, gifted from Above. But the Oral Torah is alive, breathing through our choice, our yearning, our effort to become partners in Divine revelation.

At the culmination of the Megilah, when all was transformed, and everything was turned around, the Megilah says, ליהודים היתה אורה / "And for the Jews there was *Orah* / אורה / Light." Our Sages say this *Orah* refers to Torah (*Megilah*, 16b), while the Pasuk (*Mishlei*, 6:23) says כי נר מצוה ותורה אור / "For Mitzvah is a lamp and Torah is *Ohr*.'" Interestingly, the Book of Mishlei uses the word *Ohr* / אור, in the masculine form, while the Megilah uses *Orah* / אורה, in the feminine form. Why the difference? The light revealed on Purim is the light of the Torah she-b'Al Peh, the Oral Torah, and the feminine term *Orah* refers to this feminine dimension of Torah, the aspect that rises from Below. It is not the fixed revelation from Above, but the flowing light that emerges from within. On Purim, we merited to receive the Torah fully, willingly, lovingly, not imposed from Heaven, but awakened from within us, and this is reflected in the beginning of the flowering of Torah she-b'Al Peh.

This is also the deeper reason why the Yom Tov of Purim was initiated by Esther, a woman, and her scroll recounting the story of Purim is called *Megilas Esther*.

Torah is the bridge through which the Creator creates reality and through which we connect to our Creator, the holy medium of relationship. Yet, like any bond, the relationship must be mutual. A healthy relationship breathes with reciprocity and rhythms in a sacred dance of giving and receiving. At the time of Purim, a profound shift occurred; we accepted the Torah anew, not merely as a command from Above, but as an internalized commitment, a love born from within. The Makif began to become Penimi, no longer only surrounding from beyond, but entering inwardly, becoming personalized, internalized.

During the prophetic age, man received the Divine influx passively. But from Purim onward, a new symbiosis formed; we began to rise, to engage, to partner actively in the unfolding of Torah. No longer were we merely vessels receiving; we became co-creators, interpreters, builders of the Oral Tradition. Purim thus stands at the crossroads of spiritual history, marking the end of the 'open miracle' period. "Why is Esther compared to dawn? To teach us: Just as the dawn is the end of the night, so too Esther is the end of all miracles" (*Yuma*, 29a). Purim comes at the conclusion of the canonized revelation, and also with the dawning of a new light, the flourishing of Torah She-b'Al Peh.

This liminal nature of Purim is reflected in the scroll of Esther itself. When Esther requested that Purim be established as a national Yom Tov, the Sages argued. When she responded, they readily agreed. However, when Esther asked that Megilas Esther be enshrined as part of the written canon, the matter sparked a greater debate (*Megilah*, 7a: שלחה להם אסתר לחכמים קבעוני לדורות, שלחו לה קנאה את מעוררת עלינו לבין האומות. שלחה להם, כבר כתובה אני על דברי הימים למלכי מדי ופרס..... שלחה להם אסתר לחכמים כתבוני לדורות. שלחו לה, הלא כתבתי לך שלישים שלישים ולא רבעים, עד שמצאו לו מקרא כתוב בתורה).

Even generations later, the Sages questioned whether the Megilah is truly part of the written Torah in all aspects, or if it belongs more to the oral realm (אמר רב יהודה אמר שמואל אסתר אינה מטמאה את הידים. למימרא דסבר שמואל אסתר לאו ברוח הקודש נאמרה והאמר שמואל אסתר ברוח הקודש נאמרה נאמרה לקרות, ולא נאמרה ליכתוב). This very ambiguity reveals the essence of Purim, it is the hinge between the Written and the Oral, between Divine descent and human ascent. The Megilah is both text and subtext, hidden and revealed, written and spoken. It embodies the mystery of Torah becoming truly ours.

Either way, Purim and the Megilah represent the beginning of the rising of the feminine principle, and thus it was Esther herself who proposed to establish the Yom Tov and Megilas Esther.*

---

* The Giving of the Torah, *Matan Torah*, is described by the Sages as a wedding between HaKadosh Baruch Hu, the Groom, the 'masculine principle' and Klal Yisrael, the Bride, the 'feminine principle' (see *Ta'anis*, 26b: ביום חתנתו זה מתן תורה). At that moment, a covenantal relationship was forged, but one that reflects a top-down dynamic. This is symbolized by the image of the Mountain suspended above the people's heads, indicating a certain coercive transcendence, an overwhelming Divine Presence that leaves little room for human initiative. This cosmic marriage is reflected in the microcosmic marriage as well. While marriage needs to be consensual on both ends, on the part of the 'receiver', it is more passive (There needs to be דעת / conscious choice and awareness on the part of the groom and bride: *Kidushin* 2b.) The simple reason for the bride's Da'as is as Rashi explains: any time there is a *Kinyan* / acquisition, in addition to the Da'as of the קונה *Koneh*, the one who acquires it, דבעינן דעת המקנה / "There needs to be Da'as of the *Makneh* / the giver of what is being acquired": Rashi, *Kidushin*, 44a. (Note that Rashi, in *Yevamos* 19b, writes that it is a teaching from a Pasuk that we know that Kidushin requires the Da'as of the Makneh: והלכה והיתה לאיש אחר מדעתה משמע. See *Chidushei Chasam Sofer*, Baba Basra, 47a.) Yet, a bride's consent is more essential. In the words of the Ran, *Nedarim*, 30a: אלא מכיון שהיא מסכמת לקדושי האיש היא מבטלת דעתה ורצונה ומשוי נפשה אצל הבעל כדבר של הפקר.

This model reveals the original cosmic structure: a relationship initiated from Above, with the feminine receiving from the Above. Klal Yisrael 'accepted' the Torah מדעתה / with her consent, yet it was more about the Above than the Below.

As history unfolds, the feminine, also referred to as Malchus, K'neses Yisrael, or the Shechinah, begins to rise more and more. The original relationship was more top-down. But the ultimate goal is of a fully reciprocal, face-to-face connection, Panim el Panim, in which the feminine becomes an active, equal participant. Chazal tell us, מפני מה אמרה תורה כי יקח איש אשה, ולא כתב כי תלקח אשה לאיש מפני שדרכו של איש לחזר על אשה ואין דרכה של אשה לחזר על איש. משל לאדם שאבדה לו אבידה מי אבידה מי חזר על מי, בעל אבידה מחזר על אבידתו / "For what reason did the Torah say, 'When a man takes a woman…?' Because it is the way of a man to pursue a woman, and it is not the way of a woman to pursue a man. The Gemara cites a parable of a man who lost an item. Who searches for what? Certainly, the owner of the lost item searches for his lost item": *Kidushin*, 2b. Yet (in one version) the Ritva (ibid.), adds that this pattern is actually a result of the curse from the Garden of Eden. One of the 'curses' Chava bore was the paradigm of "And he shall rule" (*Bereishis*, 3:16). According to this view, the male-dominant *Kidushin* / wedding structure is part of a fallen order, a distortion

SWEETER THAN WINE

"*Kneses Yisrael* / the congregation of Israel said before the Holy One, Blessed be He: 'Master of the Universe, the statements of Your beloved ones (the Sages) are more pleasant to me than the wine of the written Torah itself'" (*Avodah Zarah*, 35a). This sweetness comes from our wanting the relationship, wanting closeness and communication with Hashem. Torah She-b'Al Peh is not a forced connection, as the image of a mountain suspended over our heads when we originally received the Torah. Torah She-b'Al Peh is Divine communication that comes from within, expressing our yearning to be together, and our active commitments to each other. This is the essence of Purim and, by extension, Adar.

The "pleasantness" and pleasures of such a mature relationship are experienced precisely because we are no longer engaged in an Achor b'Achor dynamic; it is not a *Zivug Temidi* / constant unity. If it were constant, it would not be sweet. תענוג תמידי אינו תענוג / "Continuous pleasure is not (considered) pleasurable" (*Likutei Amarim* [the Maggid] 168, in the name of the Baal Shem Tov). The desire of separate entities to reunite, and the electrifying experience of real face-to-face connection, is what gives rise to such great pleasure in both the receiver and giver.

---

destined to be undone in the Messianic future. In that time, the feminine will have risen fully. As the prophet says, נקבה תסובב גבר / "The woman will surround/transcend the man" (*Yirmeyahu*, 31:22). In other words, we, Klal Yisrael, will no longer merely be receptive, but active, in a complete Panim el Panim relationship. Then, Kiviyachol, both partners will be fully present, and contributing, to each other.

Repetition dulls joy. Hearing people talking about nonsense is not pleasurable, yet hearing a parrot mimic a few nonsensical words evokes pleasure (*Keser Shem Tov*, 407). Pleasure comes from a novel or unusual experience or perception. When we, in a state of separation, reach out to HaKadosh Baruch Hu to fully receive the Torah and are able to *Mechadesh Chidushim* / create novel insights in Torah, it causes pleasure, both for us and On High, a pleasure that is "more pleasant than wine." Precisely because of the absence of clear revelation from Above, a new, deeper level of revelation and relationship is able to emerge and flourish.

At Matan Torah, we were swept up in an overwhelming, so awe-inspiring Divine revelation. Our acceptance of the Torah was, in a sense, compelled by infatuation and squeezed under the weight of the Presence of the Infinite. The events of Purim, on the other hand, occurred in private moments and in the quiet shadows of exile, without miracles or open revelations. Nevertheless, then we embraced the Torah with passion and with choice. No longer were we under spiritual duress; we were motivated by mature love, freely-chosen commitment. We were seeing our Divine Beloved eye-to-eye.

Purim, says the holy Arizal, is the revelation of the *Ohr d'Yesod d'Abba* / the illumination of the quality of "intimacy" within the Divine Father. The Baal Shem Tov teaches that Yesod corresponds to the world of *Ta'anug* / pleasure (שמעתי ממורי שאדם נקרא צדיק בסוד צדיק יסוד עולם כשיש לו תענוג גדול בעבודת ה': *Toldos Yaakov Yoseph,* Va'eschanan, p. 179b) Indeed, when giving a gift, the deeper the pleasure in the act of giving, the more the giver wishes for the receiver to receive it (ובחינת יסוד היא, על דרך משל, ההתקשרות שמקשר האב שכלו בשכל בנו ... ומדבר עמו פנים אל פנים באהבה

וחשק... כי על־ידי החשק והתענוג, מתרבה ומתגדל שכלו בהרחבת הדעת להשפיע וללמד לבנו וכמו

על דרך משל בגשמיות ממש, רבוי הזרע הוא מרוב החשק והתענוג, ועל־ידי זה ממשיך הרבה מהמוח:

Tanya, Iggeres haKodesh, 15).

Abba is a term for the Sephirah of *Chochmah* / wisdom, which is experienced as *Bitul* / self-transcendence, transparency, openness, and utter receptivity. Yesod of Abba, then, is the pleasure that arises from encountering or enacting such selfless wisdom. It is the delight of dissolving the ego in the presence of truth.

This is the unique Ta'anug, the pleasure and sweetness of *Kabbalas haTorah* / acceptance of Torah that we taste on Purim. It is not the awe-struck surrender at Mount Sinai, when our souls left our bodies from sheer overwhelm, when the mountain loomed over us. There, too, we reached Bitul — but not Ta'anug. On Purim, *we* initiate the experience; it is not imposed, it is what we want with all our heart. In the absence of open revelation, in a world where Divine Presence is hidden, we find our resources within, and in doing so, we taste the joy of Bitul, the sweetness of selfless union with Divine Wisdom. In Yiddish, this taste is called the "*Gishmak In Kabbalas haTorah* / the relish, the delicious satisfaction in receiving the Torah." Even deeper, since Chochmah is connected with *Mesiras Nefesh* / total surrender of the ego, the Yesod of Chochmah is the Gishmak of Mesiras Nefesh, the ineffable *Taanug* of Bitul.

At Matan Torah, the dominant emotion was Yirah, awe, reverence, even trembling. The encounter was so overwhelming, so saturated with Divine revelation, that all we could do was stand back in sacred fear. As the Pasuk describes: "And all the people saw the voices and the torches, the sound of the shofar, and the smoking mountain, and the people saw and trembled, and they stood from afar" (*Shemos*, 20:15). Our souls expired from the indescribable grandeur and intensity. By contrast, the Purim experience is one of *Ahavah* / love. Hiddenness replaced spectacle, but it was precisely in that concealment that something deeper emerged: a conscious, intimate closeness to Hashem. Without thunder or flames, the Jewish People chose again, this time from within and with love. As our Sages teach, "They re-accepted it in the days of Achashverosh," not out of fear, but out of love and commitment. This re-acceptance was not coerced by a booming voice from the Heavens; it was animated by an authentic impulse within us, bolstered by our certainty of heart.

At Sinai, we stood back in awe. On Purim, we stepped forward in love.

An allusion to this idea is hidden in the words *Har Sinai* / Mount Sinai, which is numerically 335 (*Har* is Hei/5 plus Reish/200; *Sinai* is Samach/60, Yud/10, Nun/50, Yud/10 = 335). The word *Purim* is numerically 336 (Pei/80, Vav/6, Reish/200, Yud/10, Mem/40 = 336). Hence, *Purim* equals *Har Sinai* plus 1. What is the extra '1' in Purim? It is the *Echad* / one. *Echad* means one, but in numerical value, *Echad* is 13, which is also the value of the word *Ahavah* / love. As such, Purim is 'Har Sinai plus love'. There was one element missing at Sinai, and that was *ourselves*; our love, our choice, our desire.[*]

---

[*] On Purim we are asked to send מנות איש לרעהו / "gifts one to another." The Mitzvos of Purim are meant to foster love and unity. The above words have the same numerical value as שמע ישראל ה׳ אלקינו ה׳ אחד / *Shema Yisrael, Hashem Elokeinu, Hashem Echad* (Komarna, *Kesem Ofir*, 10:19). To give to another with love is to truly express the reality of Hashem Echad.

From the time of Purim onward, we stepped into a more active role in our relationship with the Divine. No longer merely *recipients* of revelation, we became *co-creators* in the unfolding revelation of Torah. As partners in the covenant, empowered by the principles given at Sinai, we were able to initiate something unprecedented, a new Yom Tov, born not from an explicit command but from a hidden collective revelation.

PURIM AS AN ALLUSION TO ALL THE YAMIM TOVIM

Purim represents the loving acceptance and re-affirmation of all Torah with all its commandments and mandated Yamim Tovim. This is illustrated by the fact that the five letters in the word *Purim* (Pei, Vav, Reish, Yud, Mem) are an acronym for all the Torah's *Yamim Tovim* / holy days of the year. Pei stands for *Pesach*, Vav for *v'Sukkos* / 'and Sukkos' (Sukkos also celebrates the journey in the Desert following the Exodus from Egypt, and so it is appropriately connected to Pesach with 'and'). Reish stands for *Rosh Hashanah*, Yud for *Yom Kippur*, and Mem for *Matan Torah* / 'Giving of Torah', referring to the Yom Tov of Shavuos.

When Klal Yisrael re-accepted the Torah with wholehearted desire, they reaffirmed and reabsorbed the essence of all the other Yamim Tovim. Thus, Purim does not merely *allude* to the Yamim Tovim (as do the letters of the word *Purim*) but Purim itself embodies qualities and elements of all the Yamim Tovim of the year.

Purim is similar to Pesach in that it is a day of redemption, a celebration of national salvation and liberation (Although this is to a lesser degree than Pesach, as after the events of Purim, we still remained 'servants' to the powers of the world: *Megilah*, 14a). This day echoes the spiritual ascent of Shavuos, for on Purim we renewed and deepened our acceptance of Torah. It mirrors Rosh Hashanah, as the fate of the Jewish People 'hung in the balance', and as the *Sefer Zichronos / Book of Remembrances* was opened in the court of the king below and the King Above.

Purim aligns with Yom Kippur, a day of profound Teshuvah and spiritual realignment. In fact, Yom Kippur is called *Yom haKi-Purim*, which can be interpreted as the phrase 'a day that is like Purim', suggesting that the qualities of Purim surpass even the sanctity of Yom Kippur. And just like Sukkos, which celebrates the Clouds of Glory and Divine sheltering, Purim is a testament to Hashem's hidden protection amid our exile. Moreover, both are celebrations of unbounded joy. Sukkos is the time of our joy, and Purim too is a day of great joy: ליהודים היתה אורה ושמחה וששן / *LaYehudim Haysa Orah v'Simchah v'Sason* / "For the Jews there was light and joy and happiness..." (*Esther*, 8:16).

SUMMER VS. WINTER MONTHS

Our re-acceptance of Torah on Purim aligns with the time of year in which it occurs. A year unfolds into two spiritual stages. The first six months, from Nisan to Tishrei, are marked by a paradigm of *Isarusa d'leEila* / arousal initiated from Above. The second six months, from Tishrei to Adar, are governed by *Is'arusa d'leTata* / arousal initiated from Below, by us.

These stages are reflected in the seasonal cycle. Summer is luminous and revealed, radiant with sunshine and flourishing growth. It is revealed Light shining downward. Winter is concealed, quiet, and inward, a time of hibernation, rest, concealing hidden potential. Winter is the level of humanity, which, through action and friction Below, kindles warmth that rises upward. It is inner Light.

In the winter, the sunlight from Above decreases, mirroring the slumber of the King, the Source of Life. The days shorten and the cold increases, driving us inward, both physically and spiritually. Nature recoils: leaves fall, colors fade, animals hibernate, and the earth becomes still. Life appears dormant. The cold suppresses growth; vegetation within the ground becomes too weak to sprout and break through the surface. Creation as a whole seems to hibernate, and even humans may sleep more in the winter, all mirroring the 'slumber' of Klal Yisrael, Below, vulnerable in exile.

When the seasons turn, the transformation is felt viscerally. We shed the weight of our heavy clothing and awaken, like buds turning toward the sun to 're-accept' its life force. Summer unfolds with ever-lengthening days, light expanding both outward and inward. It is a time of freedom and increased self-revelation. The revelation from Above inspires revelations from Below.

The four seasons are related to the four letters in the Name of Hashem, Yud-Hei-Vav and Hei (*Pardes Rimonim*, 21:16). Yud (י), which looks like a small seed or sprout, corresponds to the spring. The more expansive and filled-out letter, the upper Hei (ה), refers to summer, when life and the world feels full of life. Vav (ו), a connecting letter (meaning 'and') corresponds to the fall, a season in which we connect to others and to the Divine. The final Hei, being a silent letter, represents the barren winter months.

י / Spring

ה / Summer

ו / Fall

ה / Winter

In the two-season model of the year, the six summer months (spring-summer), from Nisan to Tishrei, correspond to Yud-Hei, the 'upper' part of the Divine name. 'Yud-Hei' represents the higher reality, the realm of 'Giving', the flow of Divine light from Above. The six winter months, from Tishrei to Adar, correspond to Vav-Hei, which represents the lower reality, Creation, human participation and receptivity, Below.

Summer months / Yud-Hei / the Giver / the Light Above

Winter months / Vav-Hei / the Receiver / the Vessel Below

Within the dynamic of the Divine itself, the six summer months represent the masculine aspect of the Creator, so to speak, which bestows a flow of Light; whereas the six winter months represent the feminine absorption of that Light (*Koheles Yaakov*, Yud Beis Chodesh).

Similar to the masculine-feminine metaphor, the six warm summer months are an expression of *Ohr Yashar* / direct descending light, and the six colder months are an expression of *Ohr Chozer* / returning, reflected light that rises from Below (*Arizal, Likutei Torah, Vayeitzei*). In the summer, the Divine Light moves from Above to Below, in the mode of 'direct light.' Thus, the world appears more alive in this half of the year, as there is a more revealed flow of Divine light down into the world. This is the same as our original position, with the summer in a masculine, giving posture, and the winter in a feminine, receiving and reflective posture.

Ohr Yashar corresponds with the idea of *Is'arusa d'leEila* / awakening from above. For example, the light of *Geulah* / redemption that flows down to us from Above in the month of Nisan is an Is'arusa d'leEila. In Nisan, we were redeemed from Egypt not through our own merit, but through miraculous intervention, a Divine arousal from Above. Similarly, Shavuos commemorates the giving of the Torah, a top-down revelation of infinite wisdom, so much so that we felt as if a mountain was suspended above our heads, as explored earlier.

The winter-fall months are a time of Ohr Chozer and *Is'arusa d'leTata* / awakening from Below. We begin the fall with the month of Tishrei, the seventh month, seven representing the natural world Below, created in seven days. Rosh Hashanah is a time of judgment and celebration of our existence and purpose in this world. Yom Kippur is a time of atonement and the inner work of *Teshuvah* / recalibrating our internal system and elevating our humanity. These are expressions of Is'arusa d'leTata, human arousal from Below. The light is not granted freely; we must generate warmth from within.

On Sukkos, the Sukkah recalls both physical booths and the Clouds of Glory that protected us. Though those clouds began in Nisan, the Sukkos festival is celebrated in Tishrei. According to one view, we earned those clouds through our Teshuvah on Yom Kippur, a light we initiated from Below (*Pirush haGra,* Shir Hashirim, 1:4. See also *Targum, Shir Hashirim,* 2:17).

This distinction clarifies why the winter Yamim Tovim do not revolve around open miracles. Rather, they mark moments of human effort, inner transformation, and the cultivation of our own spiritual nature. They focus on our relationship to the natural world and the assiduous cultivation of our human nature. This approach to our lives and relationships activates the returning-light through an awakening from below, and the feminine receiver, in turn, becomes a giver in her own right.

Summer / *Ohr Yashar* / direct light flowing from Above to Below

Winter / *Ohr Chozer* / returning light flowing from Below to Above

Now we return to Purim, which falls in Adar, on the cusp of the full moon of the final month of the lunar year. At the culmination of this entire lower cycle, the receiver is at peak of its power and potential. While the solar year began back in Tishrei, on Rosh Hashanah, the lunar year begins on the First of Nisan.

The sun, steady and self-luminous, represents the masculine, the Mashpia, the Giver.

The moon, reflective and changing, represents the feminine, the Mekabel, the Receiver.

Purim is an expression of the fullness of the moon at the fullness of the lunar year. It is the celebration of the feminine, of hidden light, of Esther, of Knesses Yisrael, which are all symbolized by the moon.

At Sinai, we received Torah from Above, amid blinding, sun-like spiritual brilliance. At Purim, we received it again, from Below, amid the glow of the moon within the dark spiritual 'night' of exile. There began the era of Torah she-b'Al Peh, which, too, is likened to the moon, as it illuminates the darkness of exile. (In the language of *Rabbeinu Bachya*, את המאור הגדול לממשלת היום זו תורה שבכתב ואת המאור הקטן לממשלת הלילה זו תורה שבעל פה. Bereishis, 2:3. Note, that there are 53 Torah portions, the word Chamah/sun is numerically 53. Torah she-b'Al Peh is connected to the moon and the feminine, hence, Esther is the essence of the Purim story. וידוע דתורה שבכתב נמשל לזכר המשפיע. ושבע״פ לנקבה המקבלת. *Haamek Davar*, Shemos, 29: 41).

Thus, Purim, hidden, disguised, seemingly a 'mundane' day, is actually the day of deepest revelation. It is the beginning of the full embrace and partnership between the light of the 'sun' Above, and its reflection in the 'moon' Below, between Giver and Receiver.

FULL FACE-TO-FACE: INITIATING THE YAMIM TOVIM OF THE FUTURE

Although Purim represents a momentous face-to-face encounter between the Infinite and humanity, it is still not yet the fullest, deepest manifestation of face-to-face communion. On our side, the human side, our face was revealed. We were no longer hiding, no longer only clinging to the Creator as a child to a Parent. We had matured into mental, emotional, and spiritual adulthood, standing upright, choosing our relationship with the Divine, rather than passively receiving it. We did step into our strength. Yet, from our perspective, the 'Face of Hashem' is still hidden.

Even after the ecstatic miracle and tremendous salvation of Purim, the exile was and is not over. In the words of Chazal, אכתי עבדי אחשורוש אנן / "We are still servants of Achashverosh" (*Megilah*, 14a). The miracle was great beyond conception (*Ad d'Lo Yada*), but the redemption was paradoxically incomplete. The face of Hashem remained in concealment, Hester Panim. Even when we returned to

Eretz Yisrael to rebuild the Second Beis haMikdash, it lacked the open revelation of Divinity that filled the First Beis haMikdash. No fire was descending from Heaven, no Ark was resting in the Holy of Holies, no Divine Voice was speaking from between the Cherubs, and the *Shechinah* / Divine Presence was no longer fully manifesting for all to see. Thus, it was destined to be destroyed once more, and so it was.

Hashem's face was still in hiding. The Divine *Anochi* / "I Am" was still in *Astir* / "I will hide," in exile.

To review, there are three stages to our historical spiritual journey:

In the first stage, the prophetic period and time of the Written Torah, there were constant open miracles, clear Divine communications, and overwhelming spiritual light. Yet, we, the human recipients, were in an immature state, like infants held tightly by a parent, unable to properly receive this light, unable to turn and face the Infinite on our own.

In the second stage, the *Nesirah* / severing cut us loose from that spiritual attachment and dependency and forced us to stand on our own feet. We were forced to mature until we had the power to turn around and become an *Ezer Kenegdo* / "helper opposite Him," facing Hashem, not clinging blindly but choosing intentionally. This new stance, revealed in the Purim miracle, began our face-to-Face relationship, but it was, and is, only partial. Even while our face is turned toward Heaven, the Divine Face remains partially veiled. The Shechinah is still hidden in exile. The Anochi, the I of the One, remains to this day in a state of *Hastarah* / concealment.

Only with the coming of Mashiach will our relationship be truly and fully Panim-el-Panim, with nothing held back on either side. Then both faces, ours and Hashem's, will be fully open, fully revealed, fully aligned. The Alter Rebbe remarked that Purim is a foretaste of the future, a glimmer of the days of Mashiach, of the World to Come (*Reshimos*, 6. Purim).

"In the beginning, all beginnings were from Pesach, and thus all commandments are in remembrance of the Going out of Egypt. But now..." (*Likutei Moharan*, Tinyana, 74). In the Torah, Pesach was and is the foundational Yom Tov, the first of the Torah's three pilgrimage Yamim Tovim/Holidays, Pesach, Shavuos, and Sukkos, and many Mitzvos are in fact done "in remembrance of the Exodus from Egypt." Yet something profound occurred in the year of the Purim story. The three-day fast that Esther and Mordechai enacted was during Pesach, and in that year, it took precedence over the celebration of Pesach itself. As one, the Jewish People fasted and did not eat the Matzah or drink the wine on Pesach night. The Mitzvos of Pesach were temporarily set aside during these urgent moments (*Megilah*, 15a, Rashi. See also Rambam, *Hilchos Mamrim*, 2:4. Although, according to another perspective, perhaps they did eat Matzah: *Aruch l'Ner*, Yevamos, 121b. *Shu'T Arugas haBosem*, Orach Chayim, 180).

This symbolic pushing aside of the observances of Pesach hints at the power of Purim. In fact, in the future times of Mashiach, all Yamim Tovim will draw their light from Purim, rather than from Pesach. While Pesach, the first of Yamim Tovim, focuses on the past, Purim is rooted in the future; it is the 'end' of the past Yamim Tovim and the 'first' Yom Tov of the future.

The root of the word *Purim* / פורים can also be linked to the word פירור / *Pirur* / crumb or fragment, as in breaking something down into small pieces. So do we learn in the laws of Chametz that in preparation for Pesach, one may מפרר / "crumble and scatter (Chametz) to the wind," in order to nullify it (*Pesachim*, 21a). This correspondence between Purim and crumbling and nullifying is fitting since Purim stands at the culmination of all the Yamim Tovim and the end of all miracles ("Esther is the end of all miracles": *Yuma*, 29a), and Purim is also, in a sense the 'preparation' for Pesach and the beginning of all redemptions, including the future redemption.

As such, the word פורים contains the word *Peru* / פרו / to be fruitful, suggesting increase, flourishing, and the bringing forth of a new Creation. Hence, Purim is not only the ending point of the cycle of sacred days, but also the beginning of something new: it is the first Yom Tov of the future, a new world, the World to Come. Even in the present, Purim itself multiplies and expands, impregnating the future, removing all negativity from the fabric of time, and giving birth to the unimaginable eternal joy and peace of the future.

ESTHER THE ORPHAN & OUR OWN BREAK FROM THE PAST

Upon introducing Queen Esther, the Megilah emphasizes that אין לה אב ואם / "...she had neither father nor mother." She was a complete orphan, bereft of both parents. This detail is not incidental, nor mere circumstance or happenstance. In truth, nothing in the Megilah is happenstance, and this very point is what the story of Purim comes to teach us: that nothing is random in the universe.

Every event, every detail, is purposeful and Divinely orchestrated. Esther's orphanhood is profoundly connected with the essence of Purim itself, which marks not continuity with the past but the birth of an entirely new paradigm.

For the most part, children define themselves in relation to their parents, either by following in their ways or by rebelling against them. Yet in both following and rebelling, there remains a continuity. Their path is shaped, whether in harmony or in contrast, by the imprint of their upbringing. In this sense, the past always carries forward into the future.

Purim, however, represents a wholly new model of Divine relationship with Creation based on the revelation of Torah she-b'Al Peh, and thus a new type of miracle. Purim was not an open miracle descending from Above and disrupting nature; rather, it is a miracle that emerges from within nature itself, the hidden thread of Divine Grace that HaKadosh Baruch Hu has woven seamlessly into the ordinary unfolding of history.

To awaken and usher in such a shift in the nature of miracles, there needed to be an influencer who could spark radical newness, unbound from inherited patterns and previous paradigms. Thus, the heroine of the Megilah is an orphan, not programmed by parental influence, able to envision and channel a salvation that was unlike anything that had come before. This is similar to the holy Baal Shem Tov, the awakener of Klal Yisrael and revealer of *Toras Chasidus* / the redemptive teachings of Chasidism. Orphaned from both parents at a tender age, he too became a vessel through which an entirely new light entered the world, a revolutionary path in Avodas Hashem, opening the wellsprings of joyful salvation and renewing the soul of Klal Yisrael.

It is important to realize that the themes of Purim are not only about Esther, nor her story as a historical moment, but rather they are a call to us to awaken now, in our own lives. So often, we carry the weight of our past, the stories of our mistakes, wounds, and early achievements, unconsciously dragging and dropping them into our future. Like children bound to the limitations of their parents, we live in reaction to our own past, whether we are repeating our patterns or rebelling against them. In both cases, the past still governs the present. Yet, Purim teaches us the secret of Esther: to become, in a sense, an 'orphan' in a positive metaphorical sense, meaning to release our hold on 'where we came from', and allow ourselves to come into the present moment without baggage. When we can cancel our automatic 'subscriptions' to 'yesterday' and 'last year', and 'when I was young', we can stand firmly in the now, joyfully open to new perspectives and a new world.

Miracles are born in this space. If we cling only to what has been, our future can be nothing more than an echo of our past. But if we let go, if we become open and unbound, we allow completely new light to flow into our lives, with unprecedented salvations, transformations, and abilities. Just as Esther, by letting go of her identity and fears, received the ability to receive a redemption unconnected to the past, so too must we, on whatever level is appropriate for us. In our own way, each of us can step into a state of deep openness where the Infinite can act through us in ways we could never have imagined, drawing down blessings and miracles beyond what our inherited worldview might have dictated.

PURIM & THE TIMES OF MASHIACH
AND ULTIMATE UNITY

Part of the cosmic breakthrough of Purim is not only that it inaugurates a new revelation of Torah, and a new category of miracles, within *Galus* / exile, but it also signals the beginning of Galus being מפרר / 'crumbled and scattered to the wind' for all time. From Purim onward, new currents in history have begun to flow, which will finally פרו / 'come to fruition' with the coming and revelation of Mashiach (Hence, although אסור לאדם שימלא פיו שחוק בעולם הזה / "It is forbidden for a person to fill his mouth with laughter in this world": *Shulchan Aruch, Orach Chayim*, 560:5. Yet, regarding Purim (or Simchah for a Mitzvah), there is leniency: *Taz*, ad loc. On a deeper level, this is because Purim is connected with Olam haBa, beyond *Olam haZeh* / this world).

In the story of Purim, we witness the first flowering of the ultimate face-to-face relationship, one that will in time reveal both the fullness of Hashem and the fullness of humanity in יחוד שלם / complete unity. The purpose of Creation, the mutual unveiling of Creator and Creation, begins to unfold like soft rose petals within the quiet, hidden miracle of Purim.

That is why Purim (and Yom Kippur) will never be nullified even in the Messianic era, even though other Yamim Tovim may no longer apply or will perhaps be superfluous.*

Medrash Rabbah, Mishlei, 9:2. *Yalkut Shimoni*, Mishlei, 1,304. *Sefer Chasidim*, 369. *Torah Ohr*, Megilas Esther, p. 90d. See also Rambam, *Hilchos Chanukah, Megilah*, 2:18. The language is כל ספרי הנביאים וכל הכתובים עתידין לבטל לימות המשיח חוץ ממגלת אסתר, which means the 'books' will be superfluous, besides *Megilas Esther*. Yet, the language of the Arizal is כל המועדים עתידים לבטל, חוץ מן הפורים / "All the Yamim Tovim will be nullified (superfluous), besides Purim: *Pri Eitz Chayim*, Sha'ar haPurim, 5 (The Me'iri writes that the does not mean

In the beginning of human history, the dominant revelation was the *Anochi* / "I" of Hashem. The universe was flooded with Hashem's light. The collective soul of Israel dwelled in this radiant Oneness, from the Exodus through the First Beis haMikdash, but we were like infants in a cradle, nurtured, protected, and not yet individuated. We had not yet found our own Anochi.

We lived in a 'unity' of dependency, far from a mature, mutual relationship. There was an overpowering revelation of *Yediah* / Divine foreknowledge and *Hashgachah* / overseeing of our lives, with a minimal degree of *Bechirah* / free choice.

Only when we were cast into exile, scattered among the nations, and largely deprived of our spiritual homeland, did the possibility emerge for our own identity to arise. We were no longer bound by the compelling sense of Divine proximity and overt miracles of the Beis haMikdash. We now needed to begin making choices freely. In order to connect ourselves consciously with HaKadosh Baruch Hu, we needed to make efforts to clarify our Bechirah within this new atmosphere of separateness and distance.

דרך צחות אמרו כל הכתובים יבטלו ומקרא מגלה לא תבטל ולא שיבטל ספר מן הספרים הנאמרים literally. בנבואה או ברוח הקדש אלא כך הוא אומר שאפילו תבטל קריאתם בצבור קריאת מגלה זו לא תבטל שעקר תקנתה היתה לקריאת צבור: *Makos*, 23b). Yet, it seems from the writings of the Rambam, that he is only referring to the Yamim Tovim that are recorded in *Megilas Ta'anis*, and not the Yamim Tovim of the Torah. The forgetfulness will be upon all the troubles we have endured and the Yamim Tovim that were instituted because of those troubles, but not upon the Yamim Tovim of the Torah. As the Rambam writes, "All the books of the Prophets and all the Holy Writings will be nullified in the Messianic era, with the exception of the Book of Esther. It will continue to exist, as will the five books of the Torah and the laws of the Oral Law, which will never be nullified. Although all memories of the difficulties endured by our people will be nullified, "For the former difficulties will be forgotten and they will be hidden from My eye," the celebration of the days of Purim will not be nullified, as it says: 'And these days of Purim will not pass from among the Jews, nor will their remembrance cease from their seed'": *Reshimas haTalmidim*, Griz, Megilas Esther, 9:28.

In order to move into this new paradigm of relationship, there first needed to be a slumber, a period of dormancy for both parties, Divine and human. Only in that slumber could the Nesirah, the severance, occur. And only through that severance could the 'two' turn to face one another in mutual acknowledgment, allowing an 'individuated union' to arise for the first time in Creation.

Suddenly awakened from our slumber by the threat of annihilation, we leapt to our feet as a people and realized that we could only be connected to our Source and Protector through our own choosing. No longer would we be connected by overwhelming supernatural miracles or coercions, but we would ourselves connect through quiet acts of free will. In this moment, we revealed our Anochi, and our eye-to-eye, 'I to I' relationship with Hashem.

Indeed, the entire construct of Bechirah is rooted in the Nesirah (Ramchal, *Kelalim haRishonim*, Klal 28), as the severing allows for the emergence of individuality and participation in our destiny.

During the events of Purim, this mutual relationship was, of course, still in its infancy. But it had begun. In the end, this mutuality will mature into the Complete Redemption. Then, the Divine 'I' and our 'I' will shine in full harmony. This will not come to be through an erasure of oneself, but through the full emergence of our humanity, held in union with the Divine Essence. It is not dissolution into Oneness, but a 'unified duality', like two friends face-to-face in honesty and deep communion. Such is the true revelation of *Atzmus* / Essence — both the Creator's and our own, as One.

We are, in Essence

Not servants to a King

Not children to a Parent

But a beloved to our Beloved

And this is the reason the world was created

MIRACLES VS. NATURE, REVELATION VS. INNOVATION, DIVINE PROVIDENCE VS. FREE CHOICE

In the earlier epochs of Creation and humankind, the world still pulsed with the fresh vitality of its origins. As we were so close to our Source, we could feel the warmth of the Divine Breath animating the world around us. Even when humanity veered, whether by eating a prohibited fruit like a rebellious toddler, or falling into idolatry and distorted worship like a confused adolescent, it was merely misguided, unconsciously reaching out for spirituality and transcendence. We apologized for our mistakes and went back to living in wonder, awe, and a certain innocence.

In the ancient world, where the workings of nature could not yet be postulated by laws of physics and reason, human beings lived in a far more immediate and revealed relationship with Spirit. There was simply nothing else to lean on, no alternative framework to explain existence and give one a sense of security. Some skeptics might argue this was due to primitive thinking and a lack of intellectual development, but one could just as easily suggest the opposite: people were closer to their origin, to the Creator, and lived in intimate dialogue with Divine Mystery. If they dwelled in wonder and reverence, it was not because they were ignorant, but because they were more sensitive and attuned spiritually. Hence, rather than seeking to dissect reality or holding the world at arm's length, they surrendered to its sacredness. Whether for better or worse, they were much more 'spiritual' than 'empirical', living more in awe than in analysis.

In this world of dialogue and wonder, ancient humans had a greater sense of the collective than the individual, and this cultural phenomenon was part of their connection to transcendence. For this reason, even the figures in the Torah, although they were certainly individuals with personal lives, also embodied universal patterns and truths; they are spiritual archetypes of all human dynamics and teaching symbols that guide humanity for all time.

For the most part, the Torah's narratives of these figures are dramas of revealed Hashgachah, of Hashem's direct orchestration, and not journeys of autonomous beings with full choice. The history of the world and of Klal Yisrael as a people reads as a tapestry of Divine Presence, of Providence, and the manifestation of the timeless Panim of HaKadosh Baruch Hu.

Yet, as we moved further from Sinai and drew closer to the Final Redemption, the light of prophecy waned, and the Panim of Hashem became more hidden, until we entered the era of Torah She-b'Al Peh, the creativity and individuality of the Sages. Here, our consciousness became less related to timeless 'Presence', and more related to the world of *Z'man* / time and thus 'process'. We participated in a gradual unfolding of history and ideas, as opposed to witnessing miraculous events that instantaneously shifted reality. In an era of individualism and creativity, life is less about the collective. The collective of Klal Yisrael no longer lived exclusively in one place (Makom), in Eretz Yisrael. Instead, the gaze of Torah, Halacha, and *Ruchniyus* / spirituality turned inward, toward the individual and to his or her unique relationship with the Divine.

Purim stands at this turning point between the collective and the individual, between the overt revelation of the Divine 'Anochi' and the world of concealment and Hester Panim, where humanity's face is finally revealed, and human individuality emerges in its full glory. Yet the revelation of human individuality is not the end of this process. Individuality will blend more and more into a paradoxical synthesis of the Divine 'I' and the human 'I', and the supernatural and the natural. In the future, there will be openly revealed miracles that are paradoxically integrated with the functioning of the natural world. There will also be a synthesis of the collective and the individual, and *Makom* / space and *Z'man* / time.

In fact, today, as we are living at the edge of redemption, this future is beginning to take shape in front of us. No matter how this phenomenon may be interpreted, it is fascinating to note that a very significant percentage of Klal Yisrael is once again living in one *Makom* / place, in the Holy Land of Eretz Israel, and once again we are witnessing revealed miracles from Above to all of Klal Yisrael and for the entire world to see.

Even more amazingly, the miracles now being displayed to Klal Yisrael, and to the entire world, are revelations of the Above, in total harmony with human beings, Below. In this cosmic joint revelation, the Divine Panim is bringing miraculous help and revealed miracles that are inseparable from the human Panim, tremendous human ingenuity, and *Mesiras Nefesh* / devotional self-sacrifice.

Through the openly publicized teachings and presence of great Sages and Rebbes, the Oneness of Hashem, and our understanding of it, has been revealed more and more. At the same time, our ability to freely choose, and our understanding of this ability, has become more and more refined. Astonishingly, these paradoxical realities, Hashgachah and Bechirah, are right now being revealed in synthesis and simultaneity. This is perhaps possible today due to the flexibility of the contemporary mind. Only a deeply curious mind, without substantial prejudices and assumptions about the nature of reality, can truly behold this paradox as truth.

The teachings of the Baal Shem Tov declare and reveal, and draw down into this world, the highest, deepest levels of Achdus Hashem. The Divine Presence shines within every detail of existence, and there is total Hashgachah Pratis in every blade of grass. Divine Presence fills all things; not a thought, moment, or movement in Creation is outside of Hashem's providence. Every detail of our lives, and every momentary sparkle of sunlight upon a rippling river, is a manifestation of the Infinite. A leaf sways in the wind only when it is willed from Above. This Divine Providence is utterly intimate: every inner experience, and every event in the universe, is part of an intentional and loving orchestration (See *Yahel Ohr*, Tehilim 132, regarding the proof text in Chazal from *Chulin*, 63a. Yerushalmi, *Shevi'is*, 9:1. Perhaps, this idea of Hashgachah Pratis is also related to what the Gra, who lived in the times of the beginning of the revelation of Chasidus, means when he explains that every element of existence is encoded in Torah and that all of life is part of a greater script, a cosmic unfolding of the original script. These are his words: "The general principle is that everything that was, is, and will be until the end of time is included in the Torah — from *Bereishis* to *l'Einei Kol Yisrael* (the final words of the Torah). And not only the generalities, but even the details of every species and of every individual person in particular — everything that will happen to them from the day of their birth until their end, and all their reincarnations, and all the particulars and the particulars of those particulars. And likewise, everything about each species of animal and beast, and every living creature in the world, and every plant and shrub and inanimate object, all their particulars and the particulars of their particulars within each and every species and individual member, until the end of time, and everything that will happen to them, and their spiritual roots." In the actual words of the Gra, Pirush, *Safra DeTzniusa*, 5: והכלל כי כל מה שהיה והוה ויהיה עד עולם הכל כלול בתורה מבראשית עד לעיני כל ישראל. ולא הכללים בלבד אלא אפילו פרטיו של כל מין ומין ושל כל אדם בפרט וכל מה שאירע לו מיום הולדו עד סופו וכל גלגוליו וכל פרטיו ופרטי פרטיו. וכן של כל מין בהמה וחיה וכל בעל חי שבעולם וכל עשב וצומח ודומם וכל פרטיהם ופרטי פרטיהם בכל מין ומין ואישי המינים עד לעולם ומה שיארע להם ושרשם. Note also, Ramban, *Devarim*, 32:40: היא כוללת כל העתידות למו / "The Song contains everything that is to come upon them, to Klal Yisrael").

Yet, simultaneously, with the tremendous revealing of Hashgachah Pratis, we are also witnessing the unfolding of a deeper awareness of the individual and his Bechirah. This is happening in a world culture that more than ever before celebrates the dignity of the individual human being, the sanctity of personal choice, and the flourishing of individual creativity.

The synthesis between has been steadily rising in the course of human history until a breakthrough in alignment with the Zohar's prediction that in the Sixth Century of the Sixth Millennium (corresponding to 1740-1840 in the secular calendar), there would be "an outpouring of both the higher and lower wisdoms."

During this period, there was an emergence of modernity, the cry for liberty, and the rise of representative democracies, championing the choice to choose one's government. The stage was being set for our contemporary sense of sanctity in individual needs, personal uniqueness, and rights to Bechirah and self-determination. This was not merely a political or cultural shift but a nascent spiritual revelation from on High and part of the eventual revelation of our ultimate oneness with the all-inclusive 'Individual', *Atzmuso Yisbareich* / His blessed Essence.

As a result, we are beginning to witness the revelation, in our own consciousness, of the absolute Oneness of the Creator, simultaneous with the autonomy of man, Hashgachah Pratis, *and* Bechirah Chofshis as a paradoxical unity. In fact, more and more people can now understand and feel how both Hashgachah and Bechirah are reflections of the same ultimate Atzmuso Yisbareich.

True, on the surface, the idea that Divine Yediah and Bechirah Chofshis coexist can seem incoherent. That these could both be true simultaneously defies conventional logic and all previous modalities of thinking. But in a deep, intuitive level of knowing, we can perceive that predetermination and choice do not contradict each other; rather, they complement each other. They overlap in a mystery that transcends their apparent duality. There is a higher synthesis in the revelation of Atzmus, the Essence of the Creator, which contains both Infinite and finite, revelation and concealment, *Da'as* / knowing and *Lo Yada* / not-knowing.

There was a time when time and space were seen as fixed, absolute dimensions. With the advent of quantum theory, and the relativity of 'waves or particles', portions of humanity have begun to perceive reality as layered, dynamic, and often filled with seemingly contradictory truths. This shift is not incidental; it is a preparation for a global awakening to our ultimate spiritual reality. It is a sign of Atzmus becoming more manifest in collective consciousness. As people are learning to think in terms of paradox, the Essence of the Infinite, which holds within it all opposites in perfect unity, can be revealed with greater accessibility, and be assimilated with greater ease into more and more people's thought, speech, and action.

What unfolds in the realm of the "lower wisdom," in science and philosophy, is not separate from the higher truths, the 'higher wisdom' of the Oneness of Hashem that is being revealed. The lower wisdom is part of the revelation. And at the same time, it becomes the vessel through which those higher, paradoxical truths can be integrated into the collective human mind.

The Alter Rebbe once said that Kabbalah speaks of the Names of the Holy One, blessed be He, and His revelations, whereas the teachings of Chasidus correspond to the realm of נגילה ונשמחה בך / "Let us be glad and enjoy You," rejoicing in the Infinite Light of the Atzmus of Hashem" (Rebbe Rashab, *Toras Shalom*, 19 Kislev, 5669: דהקבלה מדברת על שמותיו של הקב"ה וגילוייו, ואילו תורת החסידות היא בבחינת נגילה ונשמחה בך, בא"ס עצומ"ה. See also *Toras Shmuel*, 5638).

The teachings of the Baal Shem Tov and Chasidus are not merely explanations of Divinity, of Hashem's Infinite Light, but rather revelations of Essence itself, so to speak. And the more Atzmus is 'revealed', so too is the nature of human potential and free choice.

In the time of Mashiach's arrival, this unity will be fully manifest. The Face of Hashem and the face of man will meet. Absolute Divine foreknowledge and human agency will kiss. Providence and invention will be instinctually recognized as one truth.

THE DATE OF PURIM

Now it is understood why this Yom Tov is called *Purim*, and why, 'coincidentally', the Yom Tov is positioned in the month of Adar. Let us explore the date in greater detail, in order to appreciate the interconnectedness of all the expressions of this Yom Tov.

Torah She-b'Kesav, the Written Torah, as mentioned, is deeply rooted in *Makom* / space. The structure and words in Torah She-b'Kesav are all precise and exact, each letter measured, as if with geometric precision. Even the times within the Torah are fixed. For example, Rosh Hashanah always falls on the First of the Seventh Month. Yom Kippur on the Tenth, and Pesach begins on the Fourteenth of Nissan. These points in 'Torah She-b'Kesav time' are Divinely defined and absolute, the dates immovable, as if they are affixed to precise coordinates in space. In Torah She-b'Al Peh, by contrast, there is relative flexibility and dynamism, less like Makom and more like humanly defined *Zeman* / time. For example, since Written Torah does not explicitly state that Matan Torah occurred on the day of Shavuos, it 'allows' human wisdom to confirm the date. The Oral Torah, hence, develops a debate: 'Did Matan Torah fall on the day of Shavuos, the Sixth of Sivan, or did it actually fall on the Seventh of Sivan?' In Torah She-b'Al Peh's reading of time, time is not fixed or static; it is alive, dynamic, and in constant dialogue. The dates of its Yamim Tovim are discovered through creative exploration.

This creative exploration of time reaches its fullest expression in Purim. Here, we encounter a Yom Tov whose date can differ from Makom to Makom: it is the Fourteenth of Adar in most locations, and the Fifteenth in walled cities. This is a Yom Tov that shifts with context, geography, and memory. And so, although Megilas Esther is part of the *Kisvei haKokdesh* / sacred and canonical writings of Torah She-b'Kesav, it still bears the imprint of Torah She-b'Al Peh. It introduces a Torah teaching that is not etched in stone or Makom, but rather inscribed upon the watery flow of living moments, in the evolving, historical story of Klal Yisrael, wherever they happen to be.

To gain a deeper understanding of the 'time' of Purim, let us begin with a number of questions, and then as the answers unfold, deeper interpretations will surface.

QUESTION ONE:

On a simple level, the fourteenth and fifteenth days of Adar were chosen for Purim, being that these were the days that Klal Yisrael rested. On the thirteenth of Adar, the Jews throughout the empire fought for their lives. On the fourteenth, they rested and celebrated their survival, except in Shushan, where the battle raged on for an additional day. In Shushan, the Jews rested and celebrated on the fifteenth day of the month. In order to give special honor to the Holy Land, our Sages established that all cities that were surrounded by walls in the time of Yehoshua would also celebrate Purim on the Fifteenth of Adar, just as in the walled Persian capital of Shushan.

This begs the question: why is there a division between the day of the miracle and the two days of 'rest'? In contrast, for example, on Pesach, the celebration of the miracle of *Yetzias Mitzrayim* / Exodus from Egypt occurs on the same day as the liberation. During the Purim story, the actual miracles of salvation occurred on the Thirteenth of Adar outside of Shushan and on the Four-teenth within Shushan, but the actual days implemented as cele-brations are on the days *after* the miracles. Why is Purim different from Pesach in this respect?

QUESTION TWO:

Another striking difference between Purim and other Yamim Tovim is that Purim is celebrated for only one day, whereas others can span multiple days, such as seven days of Pesach and seven days of Sukkos. Of course, this duration reflects the nature of the histor-ical event that is celebrated. Chanukah, for example, is eight days because it commemorates an eight-day miracle. What is it about Purim's essence that lends itself to just a single day of celebration, like Yom Kippur?

QUESTION THREE:

Why is Purim, a one-day celebration, paradoxically observed on different days by different communities? At first glance, this raises a Halachic question: how can one Mitzvah be performed on dif-ferent days in different places? Doesn't this violate the principle of לא תתגודדו / "Do not form separate factions," as the Torah warns against dividing the nation into groups? (*Devarim* 14:1. Chazal interpret this Pasuk to mean, לא תעשו אגודות אגודות: *Yevamos*, 13b. Indeed, the Gemara asks this question and answers, תנן התם: מגילה נקראת באחד עשר, ובשנים עשר, ובשלשה עשר, ובארבעה עשר, ובחמשה עשר, לא פחות ולא יותר אמר ליה ריש לקיש לרבי יוחנן איקרי כאן לא תתגודדו, לא תעשו אגודות אגודות אמר אביי כי אמרינן לא תתגודדו כגון שתי בתי דינים בעיר אחת...אלא אמר רבא כי אמרינן לא תתגודדו כגון בית דין בעיר אחת, פלג מורין כדברי בית שמאי, ופלג מורין כדברי בית הלל. אבל שתי בתי דינין בעיר אחת לית לן בה. In other words, the question here is not so much a technical Halachic question, rather, a more philosophical, Penimiyus question).

Many Rishonim raise this issue at the beginning of Maseches Megilah. The Ritva explains that the prohibition of לא תתגודדו / "Do not make factions," only applies when groups argue and disagree, each believing the other to be mistaken, thus creating an illusion that there is more than one Torah. "But in the case of Purim, from the outset, the Sages established two distinct days of observance, with full agreement among the communities. Each group acknowledges the other's practice as valid and everyone agrees that each one is doing as he should" (אבל בענין מגלה ליכא אגודות אלא בשהאגו' חולקים אלו עם אלו וכסבורים שהכל היה להם לעשות שטה א' ואלו מורים על דבריהם ונעשה תורה כב' תורות אבל הכא כך היתה התקנה מתחלה שיהיו חולקים בזמניהם וכלם מודים זה לזה שעשויה כראוי לו ובהא ליכא אגודות כלל).

Nevertheless, the deeper question remains: why from the outset, did the Sages choose to establish the Mitzvah of Purim in this unusual way, dividing the celebration between two days? The Ramban voices this question with striking candor: "I am very astonished; what prompted them to do this? What compelled them to split the Jewish People into separate groups for this Mitzvah? Even though there is no violation of לא תתגודדו / "Do not make factions," since it is similar to two separate courts in different cities still, why was it *initially* established this way? Moreover, where else do we find such a division in Torah Law? For the Torah says, 'One Torah and one law shall be for you,' and any enactment of the Sages should mirror the 'enactments' of the Torah itself" (אני תמה מאד, מה ראו על ככה ומה הגיע אליהם לעשות ישראל אגדות במצוה הזו ואע"ג דליכא הכא משום לא תתגודדו דהו"ל שני בתי דינים בשתי עיירות כדאיתא בפ"ק דיומא מ"מ לכתחלה למה חלקום לשתי כתות. ועוד היכן מצינו בתורה מצות חלוקה בכך והתורה אמרה :תורה אחת ומשפט אחד יהיה לכם וכל דתקון רבנן כעין דאורייתא תקון

Ramban, *Megilah*, 2a).

This is truly something unique about the Yom Tov of Purim over all other Yamim Tovim, in that originally at its inception, there were multiple days for celebration established.

QUESTION FOUR:

Many hundreds of years ago, a day of Rosh Chodesh, beginning a new month, would be established when two witnesses appeared before the *Sanhedrin* / High Court in Yerushalayim and testified that they had seen the new moon. Once their testimony was accepted and the court declared the new month, messengers were dispatched to Jewish communities throughout the Land to inform them that, for example, Sunday would be Rosh Chodesh. This was especially important in months that contained Yamim Tovim, as people needed that information to determine the date on which they would observe the Yom Tov. Certain locations were more than a fifteen-day journey from Yerushalayim, and messengers would not be able to get there before the Yom Tov (the Fifteenth of Nissan is Pesach and the Fifteenth of Tishrei is Sukkos), so those communities observed the Yom Tov of Pesach, for example, with an extra day of observance just in case. If Rosh Chodesh Nisan had been declared on the expected day, then in retrospect, the first day of Pesach would have been properly observed on the Fifteenth. But if the moon had not been visible on the presumed night of Rosh Chodesh, and so Rosh Chodesh had thereby been delayed, then the first day they observed would have retrospectively been on the Fourteenth of Nisan, and their second day of observance would have been on the correct date. This law is referred to as ספיקא דיומא / *Sefeika d'Yoma* / uncertainty of the day.

After a fixed, mathematical Jewish calendar was established, those distant communities, and today, all communities in the Diaspora, continue to uphold the tradition of observing two days of Yom Tov, for various Halachic reasons. This leads to an important question regarding Purim. Why was Sefeika d'Yoma not observed for Purim in places that were more than a fifteen-day journey from Yerushalayim?*

QUESTION SIX:

Another intriguing aspect of Purim is that most of the world celebrates it on the Fourteenth of Adar. Why is Purim, unlike the major Yamim Tovim that fall on the fifteenth day of their respective month, primarily celebrated on the fourteenth day? What is the deeper significance of the number 14 in the context of Purim? We should then also ask, what is the deeper connection between

---

* The simple answer why we do not enact the principle of ספיקא דיומא / Sefeika d'Yoma is because Purim like Chanukah is *mi-d'Rabbanan* / from our Sages, and thus ספיקא דרבנן לקולא / Any place there is ספיקא / doubt in matters of Rabbinic law we rule leniently. Hence, both on Chanukah and Purim there is no ספיקא דיומא / Sefeika d'Yoma. See *Avudraham*, Chanukah. *KolBo*, 44, והטעם לפי שחנוכה ופורים מדבריהם ולא החמירו בה כל כך. Although see *Minchas Chinuch*, Mitzvah 301:6. *Turei Even*, Rosh Hashanah, 18b. *Arvei Nachal*, Chanukah 1. There are other reasons offered, for example, since the Pasuk in *Megilas Esther* (9:28) says, לא יעביר / which can also mean, 'Do not pass over,' i.e., only on the days mentioned, the Fourteenth or Fifteenth, should Purim be observed, but not a day later (והא דלא עבדינן ספיקא דיומא כמו ביו"ט של גליות משום מרדכי ואסתר לא תיקנו לעשות ספיקא דיומא אח"כ להוסיף על דבריהם. ועוד דלא יעביר כתיב ועוד דכל החדש נהפך לשמחה: *Kaf haChayim*, Orach Chayim, 688:15. Note, *Sichos Kodesh*, Purim, 5719). Yet, it seems that Rebbe Chayim Vital would practice the Fifteenth of Adar as a semi-Yom Tov (without reading the Megilah or saying *Al haNisim*) because of Sefeika d'Yoma: *Sha'ar haKavanos*, Purim, Derush 1. There are opinions that all should recite the *Al haNisim* prayer addition on the Fifteenth of Adar as well: Maharil, *Hilchos Purim*, 7. The custom of some Tzadikim is in fact to recite *Al haNisim* in their silent prayer: *Nimukei Orach Chayim*, Siman 693:1. Yet, this is not the common practice, as can be seen from *Mordechai*, Megilah, 9.

Shushan Purim, celebrated on the Fifteenth of Adar, and the idea of 15?

QUESTION SEVEN:

Another dimension worth exploring is the unique way Purim is celebrated. Unlike most other Yamim Tovim, Purim remains a 'weekday' in its Halachic status, meaning it is not consecrated as a holy day in the formal sense, and no category of work is inherently forbidden. Most Yamim Tovim are marked by *Kedushas haYom* / a sanctity of the day, which places upon it a set of restrictions and prohibitions that express the day's holiness. In fact, the Torah's definition of a Yom Tov is the prohibition of doing work (ששת ימים האלו שאסרן הכתוב בעשיית מלאכה... הן הנקראין ימים טובים: Rambam, *Hilchos Shevisas Yom Tov*, 1:1. Rashi, *Megilah*, 5b). Purim has no such Halachic limitations. Interestingly, the Megilah recounts that Mordechai desired Purim to be established as a full Yom Tov, with restrictions on work just like other Yamim Tovim, but his request was not accepted (*Megilah*, 5b: הספד ותענית קבילו עלייהו, מלאכה לא קבילו עלייהו. דמעיקרא כתיב שמחה ומשתה ויום טוב. ולבסוף כתיב לעשות אותם ימי משתה ושמחה, ואילו יום טוב לא כתיב). Instead, in many communities, refraining from financial or mundane work on Purim is observed only as a *Minhag* / custom, not as binding law.

THE ANSWERS:

The first question raised concerns the division between the day of redemption and the day of rest and celebration. On a basic level, this separation into two distinct days is rooted in the nature of the miracle itself. Unlike other Yamim Tovim, which commemorate open and revealed miracles, the miracle of Purim was *Nistar* / hidden and clothed in the natural order and unfolding of time. It unfolded subtly, without overt suspension of nature, hence, aligning with the zodiac sign of the month of Adar, *Dagim* / Pisces, symbolized by fish submerged in water, hidden from view. Therefore, the celebration of Purim is not focused on *how* the Jews were saved, since that process lacked obvious supernatural elements, but rather on the simple and powerful fact *that* they were saved. This differs from Pesach, for example, where the *how*, the dramatic and visible plagues and miracles, is an essential part of what is remembered and celebrated. Because the salvation of Purim emerged through a natural progression of events, the miraculous elements of those events were not immediately recognizable. The full clarity of the miracles and the joy came only afterward, on the day after the danger had passed. Hence, the Yom Tov was designated for the day after the actual battle: the Fourteenth for most of the world, and the Fifteenth in Shushan, where the fighting continued an extra day (Although, Rashi writes that the main miracle was on the Thirteenth (דעיקר הנס בו היה: Rashi, *Megilah*, 2a), still, the full revelation of what happened on the Thirteenth — the decree of Achashverosh that the Jews were allowed to defend themselves — occurred on the next day. See also Rosh, *ad loc.*).

This is the simple reason, as we do not celebrate the miracle itself since it was a miracle that was deeply hidden, but rather celebrate that we were saved. But if we look a bit deeper and approach these events from a more subtle and nuanced perspective, a new layer of understanding begins to emerge.

The entire Purim story is about unity. Esther says, "Go and gather the Jewish People," to counter Haman's declaration that "There is a people, who are scattered and dispersed." Understanding this principle will also help us understand why the celebration of Purim is celebrated on two different days.

As previously explored, there are two fundamental modes in which Divine Light is revealed: Ohr Makif, the surrounding, transcendent Light that hovers beyond the cosmos and beyond human consciousness, and Ohr Penimi, the internal, immanent Light that is drawn inward and integrated within the cosmos and consciousness. In the world of Makif, also called *Sovev*, multiple realities can coexist simultaneously. Contrastingly, in the realm of Penimi, everything unfolds in sequence, with precision, measure, and discernible distinction.

Take, for example, the miraculous events of Pesach and the Exodus from Egypt. These were awakened through a revelation of Ohr Sovev, a light so transcendent that it shattered boundaries, and in doing so, it simultaneously brought salvation to one nation and destruction to another, as the Zohar teaches: "At that very moment when judgment was present for the Egyptians, *at that very moment* mercy was present for Klal Yisrael…, as it is written, 'And Hashem struck Egypt, striking and healing'; striking for Egypt, and healing for Klal Yisrael" (בההוא ממש דאתשכח דינא למצראי, בההוא ממש אתשכח רחמי לישראל. הדא הוא דכתיב: וראיתי את הדם ופסחתי עליכם... תני רבי חזקיה: כתיב ונגף ה' את מצרים נגוף ורפא נגוף למצרים ורפא לישראל: *Zohar*, 2, 36a). Purim, too, draws down a revelation of Makif, but a deeper, more penetrating one. This is a Makif that penetrates and becomes Penimi, entering and transforming the inner being. As explained, Purim is rooted in *Keser she–b'Kesarim /* the supernal crown of crowns, the ultimate peak of transcendence, the Essence in which the Infinite and finite are fused as one. Here, the loftiest revelations do not remain aloof but descend into the particulars of consciousness, into the very fabric of our lived experience. In contrast to the all-at-once redemption of Pesach, Purim unfolded in stages, as processes are gradual and layered in the realm of Penimi. First, there needed to be an elimination of negativity, a dissolution of external and internal enemies, which occurred on the day before Purim, when Klal Yisrael stood up to their enemies. Then came the revelation of light, the joy of redemption and transformation, the revelation of *Orah v'Simchah v'Sason* / "Light and Joy and Celebration."

When that which is beyond time and space is drawn into the confines of time, it manifests suddenly, all at once. Purim emerges from a plane that transcends time and space, multiplicity and materiality, and it is thus fittingly established as a one-day Yom Tov, 'all at once'. Yet Purim also exemplifies the interplay between Makif and Penimi, between timelessness and time. As such, while Purim remains a one-day Yom Tov, not all celebrate it on the same day. It is both 'one' and 'two'.

This duality-within-oneness reflects a deeper truth: Divine Oneness does not erase individuality, but rather illuminates it from within. The same transcendent light is absorbed uniquely by each person, in each place and each moment, differently. The Makif beyond distinctions becomes Penimi, and in the world of Penimi, distinctions do matter. Deeper unity does not require uniformity, but it can shine in the harmonious integration of differences.*

---

* A city that has a *Safek* / ספק, a doubt, as to whether it was surrounded by a wall in the times of Yehoshua bin Nun or not: when does one read the Megilah? The Rambam writes, עיר שהיא ספק ואין ידוע אם היתה מקפת חומה בימות יהושע בן נון או אחר כן הקפה קוראין בשני הימים שהן י"ד וט"ו ובליליהם / "A city that is in doubt, and it is not known whether it was surrounded by a wall in the days of Yehoshua bin Nun or only later, one reads on both days, on the Fourteenth and on the Fifteenth, and on their nights": *Hilchos Megilah*, 1:11. This is also the ruling of the Shulchan Aruch, which states that one should read both days due to the doubt, though on the Fifteenth without a blessing... כרך שהוא ספק אם הוקף בימי יהושע אם לאו קורין

באַרבעה עשר ובחמשה עשר ובליליהון ולא יברך כי אם באַרבעה עשר שהוא זמן קריאה לרוב העולם / "A walled city that is in doubt whether it was surrounded in the days of Yehoshua or not, one reads on the Fourteenth and on the Fifteenth and on their nights, but recites the blessing only on the Fourteenth, since that is the reading time for most of the world": *Orach Chayim,* 688:4. This ruling is based on the Gemara, *Megilah,* 5b: חזקיה קרי בטבריא בארביסר ובחמיסר מספקא ליה אי מוקפת חומה מימות יהושע בן נון היא אי לא. רב אסי קרי מגילה בהוצל בארביסר ובחמיסר. מספקא ליה אי מוקפת חומה מימות יהושע בן נון היא, אי לא / "Chizkiyah read the Megilah in Teveria on both the Fourteenth and the Fifteenth because he was uncertain whether it had been walled from the days of Yehoshua bin Nun or not. Rav Asi read the Megilah in Hutzal on both the Fourteenth and the Fifteenth, because he too was uncertain whether it had been walled from the days of Yehoshua or not."

Yet, the Ran's perspective is that one needs only to read on the Fourteenth of Adar: ולענין עיירות המסופקות אם הן מוקפין חומה מימות יהושע בן נון או אי לא הורו הגאונים ז"ל שהולכין בהן אחר רוב עיירות שרובן אינן מוקפות חומה מימות יהושע וקורין בהן בי"ד ועוד שאפילו תאמר שהוא ספק שקול ה"ל ספק של דבריהם ולקולא ונמצא פטורות בשניהם ומבטל ממנו בודאי מקרא מגילה לפיכך קורא בראשון ופטור בשני ודאמרינן בגמרא / אטבריא והוצל שהיו קורין בהן באַרבעה עשר ובחמשה עשר במדת חסידות היו נוהגין כן / "As for towns in doubt whether they were walled from the days of Yehoshua bin Nun or not, the Geonim ruled that we follow the majority of cities, which were not walled, and therefore they read on the Fourteenth. Moreover, even if it were a balanced doubt, it would be considered a Rabbinic doubt, in which case we are lenient. Thus (technically) they are exempt on both days, but if so, the Mitzvah of reading the Megilah would effectively be nullified. Therefore, one reads on the first day and is exempt on the second. And what we find in the Gemara about the communities of Teveria and Hutzal reading on both days that it is merely a *Midas Chasidus* / a pious custom": Ran on *Megilah,* 2a. At first glance, this Ran seems to contradict another Ran in Pesachim.

In *Pesachim* 108a, the Gemara discusses which of the four cups of wine at the Seder require reclining. One opinion holds that it is the first two cups: דהשתא הוא דקא מתחלא לה חירות / "Because now freedom begins." Another holds it is the last two: ההיא שעתא דקא הויא חירות / "Because it is at this time (the end of the Seder) that freedom truly is." The conclusion is: אידי ואידי בעו הסיבה / "In the end, both opinions are accepted, and all four require reclining."

The Ran asks: since the four cups are a Rabbinic Mitzvah, and the rule is ספק דרבנן לקולא / *Safek d'Rabbanan LeKula* / in cases of Rabbinic law, when in doubt, we are lenient, why not suffice with only two cups? He answers, 1) Reclining for all four is not burdensome, so there's no reason not to recline by all four. 2) If we are lenient, we risk that no reclining will be done at all, and thus נמצאת תקנת חכמים נעקרת / "The enactment of the Sages would be totally uprooted": Ran on the Rif, *Pesachim* 23.

This seems to contradict the Ran in Megilah, where in the place of doubt, we only need to read on the Fourteenth, why not both days, as we recline by all four cups? As the Rambam and the *Shulchan Aruch* rule: *ibid.* See *Mishneh laMelech,* ad loc. *Shu'T Eretz haTzvi,* 1:54.

A possible resolution is as follows: In the case of the four cups, if one reclines only for the first two cups, one is in effect ruling against the opinion that requires reclining for the last two cups, and vice versa (A similar ruling is found in *Shulchan Aruch*, Yoreh De'ah, 111:5: היו כאן שתי קדרות של היתר ולפניהם שתי חתיכות אחת של היתר ואחת של איסור ונפלה אחת לתוך זו ואחת לתוך דרבנן באיסור אפילו שתיהן אסורות זו. This is because, as the Shach, *ad loc.*, writes, ששתיהן כאן אבל של היתר אם אתה תולה האיסור בא' ומתיר השני הרי אתה אוסר א' מהן מהיתירו וא"כ כיון שאתה אוסר עכ"פ אחד מהן מאי חזית דאסרת להאי דלמא איפכא ועכ"כ שתיהן אסורות).

Whereas with regard to reading the Megilah, even if we read the Megilah only on the Fourteenth, this in itself does not negate the Fifteenth, because the Fourteenth is the established day for reading the Megilah for unwalled cities. Reading on the Fourteenth does not exclude the Fifteenth. Rather, it is a matter of location; those who read on the Fourteenth do so because in their place the Mitzvah is on that day, not to the exclusion of the Fifteenth. Hence, if one has read on the Fourteenth and then relocates on the Fifteenth to a place where the Megilah is read on the Fifteenth, he too must read the Megilah again on the Fifteenth, despite having already fulfilled the Mitzvah on the Fourteenth, as he is in a new location. This shows that the two days are not in contradiction but apply differently depending on location. See *Bi'ur haGra*, Orach Chayim, 688:5. See also *Bi'ur Halachah*, ad loc.: שבן עיר שעקר דירתו בליל ט"ו והלך לו לכרך נתחייב כאן וכאן.

In other words, in the case of the four cups, there is a *Safek b'Din* / a doubt in the law itself, whether one must recline for the first two cups or the last two. Since the Halacha itself is unresolved, there is no *Vadai* / certainty at all. By contrast, with respect to the doubt regarding whether a city was walled in the days of Yehoshua or not, there is no doubt about the law; unwalled cities read on the Fourteenth, and walled cities on the Fifteenth, the only doubt is the *Safek b'Metziyus* / a factual uncertainty. Therefore, such a doubtful city is treated as a Vadai with regard to the Din, the law. Accordingly, such a city reads on the Fourteenth as a Vadai, for that is the universal obligation of the majority of places, and once the Megilah is read then, there is no requirement to repeat the reading on the Fifteenth.

On a deeper, *Penimiyus* / inner level, the *Ohr* / Light of Purim shines from such a transcendent source that it is beyond all categories and distinctions. It is rooted beyond the *Sha'ar haNun* / the Fiftieth Gate, beyond even the realm of Sovev Kol Almin, the encompassing light, rooted in Etzem. Because it is so exalted, it does not exclude the particulars, the Peratim, but rather embraces and permeates them. It is a Makif, a Surrounding Light that paradoxically enters the Penimi, the inner vessels. Hence, as explored in great detail, Purim is the only Yom Tov celebrated on different days in different locations. The very structure of Purim allows for multiplicity within unity, difference without contradiction. Thus, even in a place of doubt, a city whose status is uncertain, the Ran rules, one reads on the first day and is exempt on the second. For the light of Purim does not demand uniformity; it manifests uniquely in each setting. Each day, the Fourteenth and the Fifteenth, has its own integrity, its own channel of revelation.

The revelation of Purim emerges from a "place" that is beyond the finite, but also beyond the Infinite, and even beyond the very category of 'beyond'. Purim is rooted in *Atzmus haNe'elam* / the Hidden Essence (so to speak), that which is simultaneously most concealed and most present.

True Infinity is not defined by limitlessness; it is freedom from *any* definition. It is not bound by the finite, nor by the infinite. Even the Endless Light, the expansive Ohr haMakif, is not the Source itself, but a mere emanation. The Emanator, the Essence of Hashem, transcends all dualities, even the duality of finite and Infinite, and even the designation as the 'Source' of either.

Precisely because we are speaking of absolute, inclusive Transcedence, definitions and limitations fall away. Individuality and particularity are not contradictions to the Essence, they are expressions of it. The Essence is present both as context and content, being and non-being, form and formlessness. The universe of multiplicity is not outside Divine Oneness, it is contained within it. Thus, when Atzmus is revealed (although this statement itself is contradictory), it does not erase distinctions; it illuminates them. Individuality is not nullified in the face of the One — it is embraced by it. The One manifests Itself through the many. Purim is one day, which

---

But even more profoundly: Purim itself is the Yom Tov that dispels doubt. In the end, there is no uncertainty (only holy doubt). Therefore, reading on the Fourteenth in a place where there is a *Safek b'Metziyus* / factual doubt is a revelation of Vadai, certainty in the very place of Safek, showing that even what appears as doubt is itself part of Divine certainty.

reflects Oneness, but that Oneness is not a uniformity. It is celebrated in distinction, on different days, in different ways, according to each place and person. Unlike other Yamim Tovim which are anchored to a single fixed date, Purim was *originally* fluid, originally instituted on different days, so much so that centuries ago, the Megilah reading could have been observed on the 11th, 12th, 13th, 14th, or 15th of Adar. As the Ultimate Oneness and Unity is not threatened by multiplicity, but expressed through it. Precisely in the celebration of individuality, the unity of the Essence becomes truly known.

NO SEFEIKA D'YOMA REGARDING PURIM

Grasping this truth allows us to uncover a deeper reason why Purim stands apart from other Yamim Tovim in two significant ways: Purim does not observe the usual Halachic uncertainty of dates of Sefeika d'Yoma. And Purim, Halachically speaking, remains a weekday, with no prohibition on performing specific forms of work.

In addition to the reasons offered previously, from a purely historical perspective, the absence of Sefeika d'Yoma, and why such doubt was not originally taken into account, makes perfect sense. Sefeika d'Yoma arose in cities and regions distant from Yerushalayim, where it was uncertain on which day Rosh Chodesh had been declared. However, during the time of the Purim story, which occurred after the destruction of the First Beis haMikdash, most Jews lived in Persia and Babylonia, regions within fifteen days' travel from Yerushalayim. This proximity meant they would have received timely notice of Rosh Chodesh, and so no uncertainty arose regarding the proper day of celebration. Additionally, for this reason, when Mordechai and Esther established Purim, they too did not take the idea of Sefeika d'Yoma into consideration.

Yet beyond the historical and Halachic logic (*Mordechai*, Megilah, 775. *Birkei Yoseph*, Orach Chayim, Siman 688:11), lies a deeper, more spiritual explanation, one that aligns with the very paradigm we have been exploring: that which is sourced above time manifests in the least time possible. Purim, like Yom Kippur, the other single-day Yom Tov in the Diaspora, is a day that draws from a level beyond process, beyond structure, beyond time itself. Purim, like *Yom haKi-Purim*, is a revelation of Essence, not just an expression of the Infinite Light or a Divine Attribute. It is higher than 'high', deeper than 'deep', and even beyond the concept of high and deep altogether. Essence transcends all categories, and so its manifestation requires no unfolding. Essence is immediate, whole, and indivisible. Thus, like Yom Kippur, Purim is one day (Although, the technical reason why Yom Kippur is always only one day is because of the danger of fasting for two days... משום דיש לחוש שיבא לידי סכנה: Rama, *Orach Chayim*, 624:5).

WORK ON PURIM

This helps us understand the other unique puzzling feature of Purim: despite its unparalleled spiritual heights, it is not treated as a sacred day of rest. It remains a weekday, with no prohibition on any type of *Melachah* / labor. If Purim reveals such an exalted light, deeper even than other Yamim Tovim, should it not, all the more so, be treated with the sanctity of rest and cessation?

Let us take a closer look at why *Melachah* / creative labor is prohibited on Shabbos, and (with a couple of exceptions) on Yom Tov, and how this sets the stage for an understanding of the unique nature of Purim.

In the grand unfolding of Creation from the *Ohr Ein Sof* / Infinite Light to a universe of defined and finite matter, there is a defined linear descent, a hierarchical progression. The Light emanates from its Source, contracts in Tzimtzum, expands, and continues to descend, ultimately crystallizing into the tangible world and bodies we inhabit. The higher, inner, more spiritual realms remain Above (so to speak), while the physical world is situated below, a reality structured by clear hierarchy: the upper worlds are refined, subtler, the lower worlds coarser and more physical. This great unfolding begins as pure Spirit and eventually degrades and evolves into dense, tangible matter.

During the normal course of development, the upper remains upper, the lower, lower. On Shabbos or Yom Tov, there is a melding of the two. On Shabbos, the lower realms ascend toward the higher realms. The Torah uses the word ויכולו / *VaYechulu* to describe the completion of Creation, a word related to כליון / *Kilayon*, which implies expiration or a yearning of a finite being to dissolve into the Infinite. These words speak of the ascension of the week Upward. When Creation rises to this elevated state, physical labor, actions aimed at transforming or mending the material world, are not only unnecessary but prohibited. On Yom Tov, this dynamic is reversed. A Light from Above, the spiritual root of the miracle associated with that Yom Tov, Pesach with the Light of Chesed, Divine Giving, for example, descends into the lower worlds. In this case, it is not that the lower world ascends, but that the higher world descends to us. Yet, because this light is so lofty, it overwhelms the vessels of the mundane world, and therefore work is restricted; the lower world cannot hold this higher Light without it becoming nullified in its presence. Not doing work is the way this nullification is manifested. In summary, the 'lower' is either elevated as on Shabbos, or it is permeated and consumed with the revelation of a higher Light, as on Yom Tov.

These movements, elevation on Shabbos and revelation on Yom Tov, make sense within a model of spiritual hierarchy, where holiness is either drawn down or ascended toward. Purim, however, does not fit this vertical paradigm. It stands outside the maps of 'higher and lower', because it is not a day of accessing Light but of Essence.

Whereas other Yamim Tovim are celebrations of emanations, of Lights that emerge from the Infinite, Purim is a revelation of the Source Itself, the Emanator, Atzmus, that which is beyond high and low, beyond all relational dualities. As such, on Purim, there is no need to elevate the mundane, nor to avoid it. There is no conflict between sacred and secular, body and soul. For the essence pervades all, without canceling and without separating.

This is why Purim is a *Yom Chol* / 'weekday'; it is not because it lacks holiness, but because Purim itself sanctifies the weekday, without a need to ascend to Light Above or receive and reveal Light below. The *Kedushah* / tremendous holiness of Purim does not 'lift us up', it is already essentially within us, illuminating the ordinary from the inside out.

PURIM & THE BODY

This is also why we celebrate with our bodies on Purim. We eat, we drink and rejoice, not in spite of our physicality, but through it. The joy of Purim must be felt in the flesh, because in the realm of Atzmus, there is no division between spirituality and flesh; all is included within the One.

This is the deeper meaning, as the Maharal explains (Hakdamah, *Ohr Chadash*), behind the Mitzvah to drink on Purim "until one no longer knows the difference between 'Blessed is Mordechai' and 'Cursed is Haman.'" Normally, the body and mind are in tension. The intellect desires clarity, while the body craves indulgence. But on Purim, that split is healed, and there is no longer any inner dichotomy. As such, we are invited to release the grip of binary thinking, to let go of the mind for a moment, and to allow the Essence of our deepest self, the spark of the Divine within, to flow through the body and the experience of distinctions, revealing that there is no actual contradiction.

Purim is the sanctification of the body, the weekday, the finite, the individual, the story of our life, the Penimi. We do not sanctify this level of reality because it is lesser or 'unspiritual', rather because in truth, it too is contained within the All. Actually, it is already essentially sacred; we just need to open our eyes to that most profound truth.

Everything is within Essence. As such, 'Essential' holiness does not require ascension from the world, nor a revelation of the Infinite. On the contrary, the weekday remains a weekday, and yet it is saturated with Hashem's Presence. This is the secret of Purim:

on this day, we do not realize holiness through withdrawal from the world, but by simply existing as we are, without a need to cease from work. Our work and body shine with the reality of Hashem's Essence.

A telling Medrashic teaching states that the Yom Tov of Purim, unlike all other Yamim Tovim, will never be nullified or rendered obsolete, even in the time of the ultimate redemption (as cited earlier). On a simple level, this suggests that while other minor Yamim Tovim established during exile will no longer be relevant in the era of complete Geulah, Purim remains the exception, for its salvation is of such magnitude that it will continue to resonate even in the Messianic future.

Yet, more profoundly, this Medrash is to be taken literally: even the major Yamim Tovim will become, in some sense, superfluous, 'like a candle in sunlight'. In the radiant light of redemption, the unique illuminations of each Yom Tov will be overshadowed by the all-encompassing brilliance of Geulah. They will still exist, but like lamps in daylight, their distinctiveness will fade.

Nevertheless, Purim will still shine. It will still be seen, still be felt, still be necessary, because Purim is not merely a celebration of a past event, but a revelation of the Truth of Truths, rooted not in *Seder haHishtalshelus* / the chain of emanation, but in the Infinite Essence Itself — *Atzmus Ein Sof.* That which is of Essence can never be diminished or eclipsed, not even by the most exalted revelations of the future. And so, Purim stands alone, eternal and luminous, even in a world ablaze with revealed Divine Light.

It is important to recognize that, on a revealed level, within the paradigm of *Giluyim* / Divine revelations, the other Yamim Tovim hold a more visibly elevated status. This is reflected in the Halachic restrictions on certain Melachos, as these Yamim Tovim commemorate open and manifest miracles. The Divine light that animated those events is tangibly felt and clearly discernible. Purim, by contrast, draws from the Etzem, the Essence itself, a level beyond all *Giluyim* / revelations.*

THE SIXTH & SEVENTH MILLENNIUM

There are Six Millennia that correspond to the six weekdays of *Avodah*, spiritual and actual work. We are still in the Sixth Millennium, near the end of the era of the 'weekday', of work, effort, struggle, and preparation.

The Seventh Millennium will be an era of *Sechar* / reward, a time of rest, when every day will be like Shabbos, full of peace and spiritual delight.

Beyond that lies an even higher dimension: the Eighth Millennium, which will transcend both 'work' and 'reward'. It can be said

---

* Herein also lies the distinction between Yom Kippur and Purim. Yom Kippur is connected with Etzem, yet in a way that is also 'revealed' in Giluyim. It is a day of Essence *as expressed*, and thus it carries the full weight of Divine revelation, including the absolute cessation of all work. As recorded in the Megilah, Mordechai wished that Purim too should become a day on which work is forbidden, that Essence should embody and fully penetrate the realm of revelation, yet that request was denied. Only Yom Kippur holds such potency, for it is a Divinely initiated Yom Tov, originating from Above. Purim, though drawing from a deep source, arises through human initiative, and man, even the greatest of men, cannot compel Essence to manifest within the parameters of revelation. Yet, there is an element within Purim that, in a way, is even higher, or deeper, than Yom Kippur, as will be explored.

that this time will be connected with Purim. And beyond even these time periods, there are the Ninth and Tenth Millennia (and beyond), each representing ever-deeper states of Divine revelation. While these too will be explored, let us begin with the foundational paradigm of six, seven, and eight.

Again, in contrast to other important Yamim Tovim, on Purim we are allowed to perform *Melachah* / work and mundane actions. The outer reason given for our Sages not accepting the prohibition of Melachah is that Purim is a Rabbinic Yom Tov, and so its laws are less strict than the Written Torah's Yamim Tovim. On an inner level, however, the 'collective prophetic consciousness of K'neses Yisrael' was tapping into a deeper reason when it did not accept a prohibition of Melachah. Purim, they intuited, is so holy that it transcends the paradigm of 'holy versus mundane', and strict versus lenient. Thus, Purim has the ability to 'include' the mundane and work within its holiness, without disturbing its status as a Yom Tov. This is a most profound insight to contemplate.

Similarly, Megilas Esther is so holy that the Name of Hashem, meaning the 'revelation and manifestation' of Hashem, does not appear in it at all. But this is not because it lacks holiness or perhaps does not rightfully belong to *Kisvei haKodesh* / the canon of Tanach (Heaven forbid). On the contrary, the entire Megilas Esther is 'Hashem', hence there is no need for a *specific* revelation of Hashem's Name to appear in it. In truth, the entire Megilah is composed of Names of Hashem, and therefore, there is no need for the explicit mention of a particular Name. Thus, *every* word in the Megilah is a revelation of Hashem's Name. This, too, is the nature of Torah itself; it is nothing but Names of Hashem. Even more deeply, the Torah is one extremely long Name of Hashem (See Ramban, *Hakdamah Al haTorah*. *Zohar* 3, 73a, regarding the Chumash).

In the year of the original Purim, the three-day fast instituted by Esther in the month of Nisan 'pushed aside' the celebration of the first and most important Yom Tov in the Torah, Pesach. As such, Purim is rooted in a paradigm of temporarily 'pushing aside' normative fixed levels and observances of holiness for the sake of attaining something even higher. Similarly, certain actions are permitted by a prophet temporarily, in order to achieve a greater purpose. And on a deeper level, Purim is connected with the future, to the most radical realms of holiness, of which it is said: "In the future, Mitzvos will be nullified" (*Niddah*, 61b). This is because, in that time, the *Ner Mitzvah* / the Light of the Mitzvos will be like a candle in broad daylight: the entire world will be filled with the Glory of Hashem *Himself*, outshining 'His Light'. The essence of Purim reflects this future 'daylight', this great Glory of the Future.

This is why Purim, the culmination of all the Yamim Tovim and the beginning, the first of the Yamim Tovim of the future, is one of the Yamim Tovim most intimately tied to the Messianic era.

It is possible to say that we are allowed to do 'unholy' or mundane work on Purim because it is an 'Essence Yom Tov', one that transcends and includes the opposites of mundane work and rest, 'holy' and 'unholy', just as it transcends the opposites of 'blessed is Mordechai' and 'cursed is Haman.' On Purim, we realize that even the 'unholy' Haman brought us untold blessings. Purim is a Yom Tov that brings us to the most radical 'holiness' even within our so-called 'mundane lives'.

This is also the inner reason why we do not recite the blessing of *Havdalah* / separation at the end of Purim. The technical reason is that Purim is merely a Rabbinic Yom Tov, and we were allowed to do *Melachah* / work throughout the day. However, the inner reason is that the holiness of Purim extends seamlessly into the future, into the rest of the year and the rest of history. The sacredness of Purim includes everything, and so there is no Havdalah from anything. Such will be *Yemos haMashiach* / the Days of the Messiah, when we will have "a day that is all Shabbos," every day will be Shabbos, as there will be no 'Havdalah', no existential separation, between the weekdays and Shabbos, between the holy and mundane, every day will be revealed as holy and good.

EVERY DAY & EVERY YOM TOV
ANOTHER DIVINE ATTRIBUTE IS REVEALED

The Torah's structure of time is shaped by a profound inner pattern: the rhythm of six and seven. Six days of labor are followed by the seventh day of Shabbos. Six years of working the land culminate in the seventh year, Shemita, when the earth itself is granted repose. This cycle reflects a deeper spiritual cadence embedded within time.

This division of six and seven mirrors the seven emotive *Sefiros* / Divine attributes through which the Infinite Light is refracted into the world. These Sefiros serve as spiritual prisms, shaping how the Divine Oneness is perceived and experienced within the multiplicity of Creation.

The first day of the week (Sunday), as well as the first of the Six Millennia (see Ramban, *Bereishis*, 2:3), have the potential to reveal

Hashem's *Chesed* / kindness. Monday, and the second of the Six Millennia, have a potential to reveal *Gevurah* / strength and judgment, and Tuesday, and the third millennium, have the potential for *Tiferes* / harmony and integration. Likewise, Wednesday and the fourth millennium are of *Netzach* / Divine victory and perseverance, Thursday and the fifth millennium are of *Hod* / humility and gratitude, and Friday and the sixth millennium are of *Yesod* / connection and intimacy. Finally, Shabbos, and the seventh millennium, are of *Malchus* / Divine majesty and presence.

The days of the week with their emotive Sefiros parallel the Yamim Tovim of the year. Pesach is the revelation of the Chesed of Hashem, as Hashem reveals to us on this Yom Tov great 'kindnesses' beyond what we deserve (*Zohar*, 2, 170a). Rosh Hashanah, the time of Divine 'judgement', is connected with the Sefirah of Gevurah. Shavuos is connected with the attribute of Tiferes (והתפארת זו מתן תורה: *Berachos*, 58a), as the Giving of the Torah 'harmonizes' Heaven and earth. Rosh Chodesh is connected with Netzach, celebrating the perseverance of the Jewish People, who, like the moon, always renew and begin again. Sukkos is connected with the attribute of Hod, as on it we humbly express our gratitude (*Hodu*) for the atonement, which we received just days before on Yom Kippur. Shemini Atzeres is Yesod, as it is a day when we experience deep 'intimacy' with our Creator, and Shabbos is Malchus, as it is the day when we let go of 'doing', enter a state of 'presence', and bask in the 'majesty' of the Creator.

IF EVERY SUNDAY IS CHESED — THE LIGHT OF PESACH — WHY DO WE NEED PESACH?

If each day of the week corresponds to one of the Sefiros, one of the Divine attributes, then why are Yamim Tovim necessary at all? Why do we need designated Yamim Tovim, upon which to acknowledge the revelation of these emotive qualities? Shouldn't it suffice to acknowledge them on each of the weekdays? More pointedly, if Sunday is aligned with the Creator's attribute of Chesed, why do we not necessarily feel, every Sunday, the overwhelming Chesed of Hashem?

The question, then, is not merely structural but also experiential: why do we not sense the Divine *Shefa* / flow, as it passes through the Sefiros of the days of the week, with the same clarity and intensity as we do on the Yamim Tovim?

The Arizal reveals a profound truth. Indeed, even today, every Sunday embodies the Shefa of Chesed, just as Pesach does. However, the Chesed of Sunday, while rooted in the sublime Chesed of Atzilus, descends through the spiritual realms in a way that diminishes its power. First, it is filtered through Beriah, then through Yetzirah and Asiyah, where it is finally revealed in our physical world. By the time it is filtered enough to reach us on a 'mundane day', it is but a faint glimmer of the original, luminous Chesed of Atzilus. What transpires on the Yamim Tovim is that, on those days, the pure Shefa from Atzilus is revealed in its full intensity. On Pesach, the Divine Chesed in Atzilus *breaks through* the veils or 'filters' of Beriah, Yetzirah, and Asiyah, shining more directly into our world. On Pesach, we can experience the Divine Kindness, unfiltered and fully radiant. The same is true with all the Yamim Tovim of the year (*Machberes haKodesh*, Sha'ar Yetzias Mitzrayim. *Eitz Chayim*, Sha'ar Kisvei Mori, Inyanei haTefilah).

EVERY YOM TOV REVEALS ANOTHER DIVINE ATTRIBUTE

Each month is intrinsically linked to the spiritual quality of the Yom Tov that it carries. For instance, the entire month of Nisan is aligned with Chesed, which is the setting for Pesach. From a deep perspective, the Chesed of Nisan *gave rise to* Pesach, rather than Pesach giving rise to the revealed Chesed of Nisan. In other words, we do not commemorate the redemption of Pesach in Nisan just because we left Egypt in that month; rather, we left Egypt in Nisan because Nisan was already inherently a month of *Geulah* / redemption and expansive Divine Kindness. Indeed, long before the Exodus from Egypt, קבע בו ראש חודש של גאולה / "Hashem designated for them a Rosh Chodesh for Geulah" (*Medrash Rabbah,* Shemos, 15:11).

Before the year of the Exodus, Nisan already held a potential for the revelation of the Ohr of Chesed, but since that Light remained obscured from the world of Asiya, it was experienced as it would on an ordinary Sunday. Sivan's capacity to reveal the Ohr of Tiferes was dormant and hidden, and this Light was experienced as if on a regular Tuesday.

When the Exodus from Egypt and the Giving of the Torah occurred, these events refined the world and elevated human consciousness to become receptive to the higher Lights latent within their respective months. At the Exodus, the Ohr of Chesed from Atzilus was able to break through the veils of Beriah, Yetzirah, and Asiyah due to *Aseres haMakos* / the Ten Plagues softening the spiritual atmosphere, as it were. These miraculous plagues broke the illusion of separateness, 'cracked open' Pharaoh's heart, and awakened Klal Yisrael to the presence of the Divine, allowing the

Ohr of Chesed to be directly revealed in the world, outwardly and inwardly.

Similarly, the event of Matan Torah bridged Heaven and earth ("And Hashem ['Heaven'] descended upon Mount Sinai, on the top of the mountain, and Hashem called Moshe ['earth'] up to the top of the mount; and Moshe went up": *Shemos*, 19:20) creating a cosmic opening that allowed the Ohr of Tiferes to shine into this world, undiminished and unblemished. Yet, these events did not themselves draw down or create the Ohr of Chesed or Tiferes; they only cleared obstructions in front of the Light that was already there.

This reframes our entire perspective on the Yamim Tovim: we do not observe the Yamim Tovim primarily to memorialize events that occurred thousands of years ago. Rather, we observe the Yamim Tovim primarily to internalize the Divine Light revealed within those moments in the cycle of time. The ancient historical stories were simply cracking open resistance and dissolving the spiritual filters of Beriah, Yetzirah, and Asiyah, so that the Ohr of Atzilus can shine, with power and clarity, into our consciousness. The story is not the source of the Light; it is the moment the veil was lifted, the blockage broken, and the Light to flash forth. Each Yom Tov is an expression of a deeper, timeless reality. The story is just the key that opens the door.

This also sheds light on the teaching that our *Avos* / forefathers observed all of the Mitzvos (*Yuma*, 28b), and even celebrated the Yamim Tovim long before the historical events associated with them ever occurred (Rashi, *Bereishis*, 19:3).

How could the Avos celebrate Pesach, for example, before the Exodus had taken place? They were deeply attuned to the spiritual rhythms embedded within time, and they did not require the outer narrative to break through resistance. Their souls were already sensitive to the presence of Divine Light hiding throughout the sacred cycle of the year. For them, the Light of Chesed in Nisan and the Light of Tiferes in Sivan were accessible without the need for historical events to unlock the potential within these days. They lived in harmony with the inner pulse of Creation and were completely open to perceive and receive the treasures of Light stored away within the months of the spiral of time.

ALL THE DAYS OF THE WEEK WILL BE REVEALED AS YAMIM TOVIM

This structure allows us to understand a profound teaching on a deeper level. The Leshem writes (*Shevo v'Achlama*, De'ah, 2, p. 116) that in the future, every day of the week will become a Yom Tov. This means that every Sunday, the weekly day of Chesed, will be a revelation of Chesed equal to Pesach. In fact, the Chesed that lay dormant in all the Sundays of history will, in the eyes of all, shine forth without obstruction. In the language of the Arizal, the Chesed of Atzilus will be openly manifest in Asiyah, in our lived reality.

In the times of Mashiach, the Medrash tells us, there will be no Yamim Tovim except for Purim and Chanukah. The Leshem explains this: all days and all moments will be filled with the holiness that the Yamim Tovim once uniquely held. In other words, there will be 'no more' Yamim Tovim because there will be no more weekdays forming a contrast. There will be no more mundane context for the Yamim Tovim, for every day will be infused with Divine Light and every moment will be 'sacred time'. On the other hand, since each day of the week will still be different from the other days of the week, the attribute of each Yom Tov will shine through the attribute of the corresponding weekday.

Every Sunday, Chesed, will be Pesach, the Yom Tov of Divine kindness and redemption.

Every Monday, Gevurah, will be Rosh Hashanah, the Day of Judgment and awe.

Every Tuesday, Tiferes, will be Shavuos, the revelation of Torah, harmony, and truth.

Every Wednesday, Netzach, will be Rosh Chodesh, the eternal renewal of time and light.

Every Thursday, Hod, will be Sukkos, the joy of sheltering in Divine embrace.

Every Friday, Yesod, will be Shemini Atzeres / Simchas Torah, the culminating joy, the intimate union with Torah and Source.

Every Shabbos, Malchus, will always remain Shabbos, the crown of time, the embodiment of stillness and sovereignty.

We are also taught that while all the Yamim Tovim will be "nul-lified," Purim will endure. Even in the Seventh Millennium, when every day will radiate the sanctity of a Yom Tov, Purim will remain distinct because Purim transcends the paradigm of the Seven Days of Creation, and even the elevated consciousness of the Seventh

Millennium. Purim belongs to a deeper reality, 'the Eighth Millennium'.

Like the number 50 — which, as we will explore, is deeply connected with Purim — the paradigm of eight represents a step beyond seven, while still encompassing it. Eight transcends the natural cycle, yet it includes the completeness of seven within its embrace. In the future, though every day will become a Yom Tov, Purim will endure as an additional, distinct, transcendent light, an "eighth day" of sorts. And yet, this eighth will not stand apart from the week; rather, it will be infused *within* the seven days; there will not be a day added to the week. The light of Purim, in all its depth, will be revealed within each of the seven days of the week, which will all be days of Yom Tov, as explained. This means that Purim will take on a new character. Today, Purim is expressed within a world where Melachah, creative labor, is permitted. But in the Seventh Millennium, when Purim is absorbed into the full sanctity of the weekly cycle of Yamim Tovim, it will be expressed in the mode of complete cessation from labor, just like all the major Yamim Tovim. This multidimensionality of Purim is because Purim is rooted in *Etzem* / pure Essence, and an essence by definition both transcends and contains opposites. Etzem thus includes and surpasses the dichotomy of work and rest.

Today, Purim's transcendence is enclothed within the garment of a mundane day, but in the future, when Purim becomes fully revealed within the sevenfold structure of time, it will be enclothed in the radiant garments of Yom Tov, and labor will cease, not because it must, but because its all-inclusive essence will be fully felt, even in sacred rest.

The Seventh Millennium still operates within a world of distinctions, as it is a framework of six days followed by the seventh, Shabbos. The seventh day is the culmination of a linear progression, yet it remains within the structure of time. The paradigm of 'eight', however, belongs to an entirely different order. It unifies temporality and all distinctions into a greater, transcendent whole. It does not replace the 'seven' or the 'six'; rather, it includes, encompasses, and elevates them. As the Rashba describes it, the number eight is the *Shomer haHekef* / the encompassing circumference that surrounds seven. It contains the temporal cycle of seven within itself, and at the same time transcends it, revealing the harmony and oneness that underlies all divisions (*Teshuvas haRashba*, 1:9. See also *Ohr haTorah*, Vayeshev, 278:1).

Still rooted in a world of distinctions and opposites, the Seventh Millennium sanctifies time by 'nullifying' the labor of the six weekdays through the holiness of Shabbos. In the Seventh Millennium, every day will be Shabbos (and Yom Tov), and thus every day then will be a *Menuchah* / rest from *Melachah* / work. Yet the paradigm of 'seven' remains within the duality of work and rest. It is only in the paradigm of 'eight', which enfolds both six and seven within a unified wholeness, that the true essence of Purim will be fully revealed as a complete Yom Tov. As the 'day' of Essence, Purim is expressed both in the paradigm of Melachah ('six') and in the paradigm of Menuchah ('seven') simultaneously. From our current time-bound perspective, this is not simultaneous; rather, Purim is now expressed in the world of Melachah, while in the future, it will be expressed in the world of Menuchah.

Purim transcends binary patterns: holy and mundane, effort and surrender, action and stillness — all in one breath.

Currently, we still perceive the binary realities embraced in Purim. On this day, we need to ensure that we perform specific Melachos and Mitzvos, and yet also to experience *Lo Yada*, a letting go of self-consciousness and personal agency. We are called upon to have Da'as and *Kavanna* / intention in our accurate performance of the Mitzvos of Purim; without *Da'as* / conscious awareness, there is no real *Avodah* / spiritual work. Yet, we also have to let go, floating beyond knowing, focussing and striving, and even beyond *Avodah* itself.

On one level, the Melachos and Mitzvos of Purim are amplifications of daily obligations: we are always meant to love our fellow, but on Purim, we express that love through something we might not always do: Mishloach Manos, sending them gifts of food. We are always obligated to give Tzedakah, but on Purim, we must actively seek out those in need, and give without restraint.

On this day of total expansiveness, everything is done with all of our generosity, joy, and expansiveness. In this way, it is a paradigm of 'exaggerated doing'. Yet, on a deeper level, as Purim marks the culmination of the lunar year, it is the final miracle recorded in Tanach, an echo of the 'end of time'. Thus, it belongs not to the world of doing, but to a world beyond doing. It hints at the future, a time of ultimate reward and revelation. Thus, throughout Purim, but certainly toward the end of the day, after 'drinking' for a while and deeply celebrating the festive meal, we step into a world that is beyond action, beyond comprehension, into a place of pure presence. We reach a point of *Lo Yada*, beyond knowing, beyond conscious doing, an expanse of pure being.

EIGHTH, NINTH, AND TENTH MILLENNIA

In greater detail: the Seventh Millennium will be a time of *Yom sheKulo Shabbos* / a day which is entirely Shabbos (Mishnah, *Tamid*, 7:4. See also *Sanhedrin*, 97a. *Avodah Zarah*, 9a. There will also be an Eighth Millennium, an eighth existential dimension: see *Erchin*, 13b. Ramban, *Bereishis*, 2:3. Rabbeinu Bachya, *ibid*. Ramban, *Sha'ar haGemul*, 58. *Pirush* haGra, *Safra DeTzniusa*, 5). In this context, Shabbos means general rest. In the Seventh Millennium, every day of the week will be a refraction of the general Light of Shabbos into the different qualities currently manifesting as the Yamim Tovim. Indeed, Yom Tov is also called Shabbos, a day of rest (Shabbos simply means 'a day of rest', and sometimes the Torah calls a Yom Tov "Shabbos" (*Vayikra*, 23:15). Yom Kippur is called *Shabbos Shabbaton* / the Shabbos of Shabbos).

As already discussed, the seven days of the week correspond to the seven Sefiros of revealed Divine emotion and emanation. Yet, there are also three higher Sefiros: Chochmah, Binah, and Da'as (or Keser). These three are connected with the Eighth, Ninth, and Tenth Millennia (See Hakdamah, *Bris Menuchah*).

If the Eighth Millennium is understood as a *Yom she-Kulo Yom Kippur*, the Ninth Millennium will be a *Yom she-Kulo* Purim. Then, the Tenth Millennium will be simply *HaKol* / 'Everything', all millennia merged into a oneness in which each millennium, and each moment and phenomenon, is nonetheless 'distinct'.

If the Seventh Millennium is the Shabbos of history, a world beyond toil, beyond Avodah, a time of reward and serenity, then the Eighth is a realm that transcends even the distinction between serenity and toil. The Eighth Millennium encompasses both the six days and the Seventh Day, striving and stillness, longing and satisfaction, work and rest, doing and non-doing. From this perspective, the Eighth Millennium could be called *Yom Shekulo Purim* / a day (era) when every day is Purim. However, from an even deeper perspective, the Eighth Millennium can be referred to as *Yom sheKulo Yom Kippur*, a time when every day is Yom Kippur, and then the Ninth Millennium can be called *Yom sheKulo Purim*.

Purim, in a way, is higher than Yom Kippur, as we can tap into the essence of the day of Purim by feasting and even merely existing. On Yom Kippur, even though עיצומו של יום / "The essence of the day brings atonement" (*Shevuos*, 13a), one needs to do Teshuvah for the atonement to be effective. On Yom Kippur, one must return, reflect, and refine oneself. Purim reveals an even deeper intimacy with Divine Essence, reached not through striving, but through 'just being' (The Halacha follows the Sages, not Rebbe Yehudah, and one needs to do Teshuvah for atonement to be effective on Yom Kippur (וכפרתם לשבים: Ramban, *Vayikra*, 23:10). Yet, when one does Teshuvah, it is still the "essence" of the day that brings atonement. In the words of the Rambam, ועצמו של יום הכפורים מכפר לשבים / "The essence of the day of Yom Kippur brings atonement *for those who return*": *Hilchos Teshuvah*, 1:3. In other words, both Rebbe and the Sages agree that עיצומו של יום means there is an atoning 'essence' of the day. Their debate, rather, is whether one needs Teshuvah to activate or allow the power of this essence to take effect: *Likutei Sichos*, 4, p. 1150).

Yom Kippur, as a day of Essence, also includes transcendence and immanence. On the one hand, we fast, shedding the layers of ego, rising to a near-angelic state. Yet we remain alive, embodied, grounded in our humanity. The Mishnah teaches, "Seven days before Yom Kippur, the Cohen Gadol is separated from his home." The Sages interpret the term 'his home' as 'his wife'. Rebbe Yehudah says, "The Sages designate another wife for him lest his wife dies, as it is stated in the Torah, 'And it will atone for him and for his house.' In other words, it is imperative that the Cohen Gadol be a married man, and at no point on Yom Kippur may he be unmarried. One's spouse represents one's home, one's groundedness, the fullness and structure of one's human-ness. On the one hand, the Cohen Gadol is separated from his wife and is 'not at home', and on the other hand, he must be married, and therefore connected with his 'home'. He needs to fast and refrain from food, drink, and spousal relations, and yet, he must also be married and pray even about the weather. This is the Essence as expressed in Yom Kippur: a paradoxical harmony, in which opposites are not in conflict but in fusion, transcendence and immanence, angelic detachment and human presence.

Yet, Purim is even deeper than Yom Kippur: the purity that can be reached through a long day of fasting on Yom Kippur can be spontaneously attained through joyful feasting and drinking on Purim. Purim reveals the highest truth, a holiness beyond form, beyond division, beyond all sin and the need for Teshuvah, and beyond even what we normally call 'holy'. This is a glimmer of a paradoxical reality that will be attained in what is beyond the Eighth Millennium, a time that can be called *Yom sheKulo Purim*, a realm of time-space-consciousness in which every day and every moment is Purim.

Seventh/Shabbos, Eighth/Yom Tov, Ninth/Yom Kippur, Tenth/Purim

Another, even deeper, way of contextualizing the Seventh, Eighth, Ninth, and Tenth Millennia can be offered.

The Seventh Millennium is Yom SheKulo Shabbos, a time when all existence is suffused with the holiness of Shabbos and every day is Shabbos. The Eighth Millennium, associated with the world of Binah (Ramban, *Sha'ar haGemul*, p. 303), is Yom SheKulo Yom Tov. In this era, each day of the week shines in its proper place, as the Mochin of Binah permeate the seven lower Sefiros, thus every day is revealed as a festival, a radiant Yom Tov with a revealing of another of the seven Sefiros; Sunday Chesed, Pesach, and Monday Gevurah, Rosh Hashanah.

The Ninth Millennium, aligned with the world of Chochmah, transcendence, emptiness, Ayin, is Yom SheKulo Yom Kippur. As Yom Kippur, every moment in this millennium is elevated, steeped in a constant immersion in the world of transcendence.

The Tenth Millennium, corresponding to Keser, is beyond both *Yesh* / form and *Ayin* / formlessness, a dimension that dissolves the very distinction between fullness and emptiness, where the highest and lowest are utterly one, the secret of Radla, beyond knowing and distinctions, yet, paradoxically, including that as well. This is Yom SheKulo Purim, in which every day and every experience is a revelation of Purim and Radla.

The introduction to the mysterious and ancient *Sefer* / book called *Bris Menuchah* speaks of the Tenth Millennium and declares, על כן לא יוכל האדם לדעת מה יהיה באלף העשירי / "…Therefore, no human being can have Da'as, no definitive knowledge of what will transpire in the Tenth Millennium." The deeper meaning of this straightforward statement is that since the Tenth Millennium is bound up with Keser and Radla, it cannot be accessed through Da'as and awareness. Only through *Lo Yada* / "not knowing," transcending Da'as, can one touch upon this Reality. This is like Purim itself. The deepest flow of Divine Shefa and the loftiest spiritual light of Purim are not accessed through knowledge, but through Lo Yada, a holy 'unknowing' that opens us to a reality beyond all knowing and known, the hidden mystery of the Ein Sof Itself.

PURIM, YOM KIPPUR, AND THE DAYS OF THE WEEK

Interestingly, the contrasts between Purim and Yom Kippur are mirrored in the days of the week on which these Yamim Tovim may occur. Purim can only fall on Sunday, Tuesday, Thursday, or Friday, while Yom Kippur may only fall on Monday, Wednesday, Thursday, or Shabbos. Even in the flow of the weekly cycle, the divergent qualities of these two sacred days are subtly expressed.

The Mishnah (*Kelim*, 17:14) says, ויש במה שנברא ביום הראשון טמאה, בשני אין בו טמאה בשלישי יש בו טמאה, ברביעי ובחמישי אין בהם טמאה...וכל שנברא ביום הששי, טמא / "The laws of uncleanness can apply to what was created on the first day. There can be no uncleanness in what was created on the second day. The laws of uncleanness can apply to what was created on the third day. There can be no uncleanness in what was created on the fourth day and on the fifth day, except…

The laws of uncleanness can apply to all that was created on the sixth day."

There are things that were created on the first day of creation that are susceptible to ritual defilement when one makes vessels from them. For example, 'the land' was created on the first day, and earthenware vessels that are made from it are ritually defiled. On the second day, Monday, the firmament was created, and it bears no susceptibility to Tumah. On the third day, Tuesday, trees were created, and vessels made of wood are susceptible to impurity. On the fourth day, Wednesday, the celestial spheres were created, which are beyond the realm of impurity. On the fifth day, Thursday, birds and fish were created, and vessels made from them are not susceptible to Tumah (however, they can be Rabbinically susceptible to Tumah, therefore Thursday is in both categories). On the sixth day, Friday, beasts and animals and reptiles and mankind were created; if one made vessels from their bones or from their skins, they are susceptible to receiving ritual defilement. On Shabbos, nothing was created; hence, no potential for impurity was introduced.

Rebbe Bunim of Peshischa draws a profound insight from this: Purim can only fall on Sunday, Tuesday, Thursday, or Friday, days on which creation included elements that can become Tamei, ritually impure. Yom Kippur, by contrast, can only fall on Monday, Wednesday, Thursday, or Shabbos, days that are inherently beyond Tumah.

The deeper meaning of this phenomenon is striking. The Kedushah and Light of Purim descends into realms that can become impure, and transforms them from within, and thus includes them within its embrace. The Light of Purim enters the world as it is, with all its messiness, and uplifts it. Yom Kippur, on the other hand, exists in a realm beyond impurity. It is a day when the Yetzer haRa, the negative, ego inclination, is transcended (*Yuma*, 20a. *Zohar* Pinchas, Raya Mehemna, p. 255a), a day not of transformation within the world, but of transcendence above it. Fasting is the language of transcendence, of rising beyond the self and the physical. Feasting, however, when done in holiness, is the transformation of the self, the elevation of the body, the refinement of the ego.

Yom Kippur is fasting, while Purim is feasting. One ascends while the other draws down. One is exclusive transcendence, the other is inclusive.

Purim reveals a higher Light and deeper possibility. It is not just pure transcendence, pure detachment, and *Ayin* / no-thing-ness; rather, it is the transformation of this *Yesh* / existence, this manifest, observable world, *into* light and holiness. Purim reveals the absolute Oneness of Hashem in all and in everything. This experience of Purim is but a glimpse of the Divine Transcendent One Itself, which is beyond 'Transcendence'. This is an experience of a joy-soaked, radiant 'today', one with a future era, namely, *Olam haBa /* the World to Come.

As such, Purim is not about escaping the body, but about drawing Divine Light down into the body — and even deeper, revealing Light already within the body. On Purim, we reaccepted the Torah not in a posture of flight from ourselves and our bodies, but *with* our bodies, and our whole being, fully present and intact. At the time of Matan Torah, it is stated that with every Divine Utterance that came forth from the mouth of the Holy One, blessed be He, the souls of Klal Yisrael left their bodies (*Shabbos*, 88b). In other words, the experience of Sinai was so overwhelming that they could not integrate it within their physical existence, and their souls fled. Their spirits could not remain contained; they soared upward, unable to integrate the Infinite within the finite vessel of flesh. Indeed, knowing intuitively their inability to fully experience spirituality within the body, on the night before Matan Torah they went to sleep, and their sleep was sweet to them (*Medrash Rabbah*, Shir haShirim 1, 12:20). They reasoned that the best state in which to receive the Torah was not in the body, awake, but in the body surrendered, in a dreamlike state, detached from physicality, half there and half elsewhere (*Likkutei Sichos*, Vol. 4, pp. 964-965).

By contrast, in the days of Mordechai and Esther, we accepted Torah anew, not in sleep and dream, but from awake and fully present. The miracle began when נדדה שנת המלך / "The king's sleep was disturbed." Both the King Above and the king below could not sleep. In that moment, all were awake and embodied. The cosmos itself shook off its slumber and stood at attention, for we were opening to receiving the Torah with willingness and desire, into our very bodies, without separation from them or dissociation (*Torah Ohr*, Hosafos, Megilas Esther, 118b).

This is why Purim is connected with the word גוּף / *Guf* / body. For the word פור / *Pur*, in the system of At-Bash (in which the first letter Aleph is interchanged with the last letter Tav, the second letter Beis with the second-to-last letter Shin, and so on), translates to גוּף. Purim teaches us to embrace the body within the joy of Torah and spirituality; the body is not an obstacle, but a full partner and active participant in every detail of our spiritual practice and our holy joy. Moreover, Purim reveals that HaKadosh Baruch Hu chooses the bodies of Klal Yis-rael, revealing the *Kedushas haGuf* / the holiness of the body (גופא דילהון קדישא / "The body of a Tzadik is holy: *Zohar* 3, 70b).

THROUGH *AYIN*, WE GET TO HIGHER *YESH*

On Purim, we celebrate with eating and drinking, fully includ-ing the basic functions of the body in the boundless holiness of the day. On one level, this serves as a *Tikkun* / rectification for the way we afflicted our body and deprived it of food and drink on Yom Kippur. Yet at the same time, it is precisely through the fasting on Yom Kippur that we are now able to feast and include the body.

Fasting before feasting, denying the body before celebrating with the body, ensures that the inclusion of the body on Purim is done with holiness and not indulgence, with delicacy and transcen-dence and not with coarseness and *Grabkeit* / unrefined behavior. This is similar to the Ayin state that must come before the higher Yesh. One must pass through a state of *Hishtavus* / equanimity and detachment, before reaching a state of *b'Chol Derachecha Da'eihu* / "In all your ways know Him."

Only after stepping back from the world of *Yesh* / existence and physicality and immersing in *Ayin* / 'non-existence' or healthy emptiness can one re-enter this world and this body without being consumed by it. Temporarily unhooking from our constant con-sumption of food and drink ensures that our attachment to this world is not unhealthy clinging but 'holy re-attachment', egoless engagement with the world aligned with the Divine will. Before we can fully rejoice, we need to put aside our 'me', our egoic 'I', and view the world as Ayin, nothing in itself, empty, trivial, and transparent. And then we need to re-engage with the world, and even to desire it, but only because this Creation is the *Ratzon* / Will of the Creator. Such Divine desire is a radical and holy re-attachment to the world, born of radical detachment.

Emptiness precedes fullness. Fasting comes before feasting. For this reason, we 'empty' ourselves on *Ta'anis Esther*, the Fast of Esther, on the day before Purim. And this is also why Purim, in the twelfth month, is understood as the *culmination* of the fast of Yom Kippur, in the seventh month. Even in the historical Purim narrative, the pattern is clear: there was a three-day fast in Nisan, and only a year later, in Adar, did the miracle of Purim unfold.

Release of Yesh and immersion in Ayin must come before a higher Yesh can be born. Refraining precedes conscious reengagement, and avoidance of materialism precedes inclusion of the material world.

Furthermore, after the Purim story and the miracle already occurred, Klal Yisrael accepted upon themselves the cycle of all fast days throughout the entire year, what are called "the four fasts" which are mentioned in the Book of Zecharya (8:19). When it says in the Megilah (9:31) that Klal Yisrael accepted upon themselves דברי הצומות וזעקתם / "The obligation of the fasts (plural) with their lamentations," it refers not only to Ta'anis Esther (as explained by the Rambam, *Hilchos Ta'anis*, 5:5), but according to the Chasam Sofer (*Derashos*, Purim, based on the *Tashbeitz*, 2:227) also to the four fasts on which Klal Yisrael mourns the events around the destruction of the Beis haMikdash (Tzom Gedalya, the Tenth of Teves, the Seventeenth of Tamuz and the Ninth of Av). Before Purim, these fasts were not observed, as the people assumed the *Churban* / destruction and exile would not last long. After Purim, however, they embraced these fasts fully.

All this reflects the principle that Ayin, 'exclusive transcendence' or no-thing-ness, must precede a revelation of the deeper essence of Yesh. Only through fasting, detaching from cravings, and letting go of habitual reliance on external sources of satisfaction, can our feasting, our re-engagement with the body, become truly happy, nobl,e and grounded in the Source of the body, the Essence of Yesh.

THE ESSENCE OF JOY & ESSENCE AND JOY

Purim is rooted in *Etzem* / Essence, and thus Purim is not merely a time to feel or express joy, but awaken to the Essence of joy, and consciously embody the joy of Essence. It is not just a physical or spiritual 'high', it is a realization of the essential 'depth' of Being.

In stark contrast to all other Yamim Tovim, where the celebration is structured and the happiness measured, the joy of Purim knows no bounds. On other Yamim Tovim, we are commanded to rejoice, but that joy is calibrated. We drink a designated measure of wine, a glass of four ounces perhaps, to fulfill the Mitzvah of Simchah. On other Yamim Tovim, once the cup is emptied, the requirement has been met, and there is no real value in indulging in more. This type of joy is contained within form and framework. Purim is of a different order. It shatters all containment. Its joy is boundless, its celebration immeasurable. Even the act of drinking is figuratively limitless. Why is there such an emphasis on unrestrained ecstasy and joy? And why is there a necessity to feel this in the body?

Purim is an experience of our essence unifying with the Essence of All of Life. This radically deep state was awakened by the *Mesiras Nefesh* / self-surrender of the Jewish People in the time of Haman, in their unwavering devotion above all reason. As a result of this self-transcendence, "Their salvation was for all eternity" — this unshakable, unbreakable essence-to-Essence connection with Hashem will always reside within us and in all future generations. To consciously relive that awakening, however, we too must transcend ourselves. We must drink not to escape reality, but rather to pass through its surface and reach a consciousness that is beyond the Yesh of knowing and doing. When we realize we are not the knower of experience, nor the doer of actions, we are Ayin, so to speak. And in and through this state, we can access our essence, our own *'Yesh Amiti'* / true existence, which is one with the Ultimate Essence at all times. The greatest of all joys arises when we are one with our true self, our deepest identity, at one with the One.

All of the Yamim Tovim are expressions of the four letters of the Divine Name, channeling a particular revelation, a facet of the Name. Purim, though, is different, for in the Megilah, the Name of Hashem is not mentioned explicitly. This is not an 'omission' or absence, rather an expression of the fact that the Megilah is about Essence.

Purim is not the expression of a letter of the Name, not even the 'highest' letter, the Yud. Purim, rather, is like the point atop the Yud, the 'source' of the Yud, and the original essence expressed within every letter, within every expression of Light. Every letter of the Aleph-Beis has at least one small Yud-like form on top, and this Yud is itself topped by a tiny point called the *Kotzo Shel Yud*

/ the 'thorn' of the Yud. This point represents the essence of every letter, and thus even the 'essence' of the Divine Name, so to speak. In this way, Purim touches the very core of the Name, beyond articulation and form. Purim is the joy of Essence itself, prior to the Divine Name, as it were. Purim is the deepest, most boundless joy, a joy not rooted in the 'letters' of revelation, but in What Is.

FIVE LEVELS OF JOY

There are five primary types of joy, corresponding to five matrices in time when we are specifically commanded by the Torah or the Sages to rejoice in a manner that is beyond the Mitzvah to be joyful at all times.[*] The five times are: every Shabbos, every Yom

---

[*] "Serve Hashem with joy": *Tehilim*, 100:2. And since we need to serve Hashem always, at all times, we need to always be joyful. Certainly, this is true when we are performing an actual Mitzvah: Rambam, *Hilchos Lulav*, 8:1. An allusion to this idea is that the word *Simchah* / שמחה is an acronym for שמחת מצוה חיוב הוא / joy in Mitzvah is an obligation: Chida, *Avodas haKodesh*, Tziporen Shamir, 11:161. All the rebukes in the Torah, says the Arizal, are תחת אשר לא עבדת את ה' א-להיך בשמחה ובטוב לבב / "because you did not serve Hashem your G-d with joy and gladness of heart": *Devarim*, 28:47. The Arizal himself merited the revelation of the deeper levels of Torah specifically because of his level of serving Hashem with joy: *Sefer haChareidim*, Hakdamah l'Mitzvos 4. Chida, *Avodas haKodesh*, Moreh b'Etzba, 10:327. *Lev Dovid*, 4:3. *Torah Ohr*, Toldos, p. 20a. *Sefer haBris*, 2:12:4. *Toldos Yaakov Yosef*, Re'eh. *Sheivet haMussar*, 20:8. *Mishnah Berurah*, Orach Chayim 669:11. When a person performs a Mitzvah with joy, the joy enhances and beautifies the Mitzvah: *Sefer haIkarim*, 3:33. In truth, a person should constantly strive to be in a state of joy, as the *Tanya* (chapter 26) states, one must serve Hashem at every moment, and joy is what gives a person the strength to overcome their inner struggles and serve effectively. Joy, in fact, literally contributes to a person's health: *Orchos Tzadikim*, Sha'ar Simchah. Moreover, the Baal Shem Tov revealed that not only do we need to perform the Mitzvos with joy, but joy itself is a Mitzvah: *Keser Shem Tov*, Addenda, Sec. 159. "It is a great Mitzvah to always be joyful": *Likutei Moharan* 2, 24. Or, as Rebbe Aharon of Karlin said, "It is true that there is no explicit positive Mitzvah to be joyful, and no explicit prohibition against melancholy. However, the levels that joy can elevate a person to, no single

Tov, specifically the Yom Tov of Sukkos, *Simchas Beis haSho'eivah* / "The Joy of the House of Water Drawing" / the nights of rejoicing on the intermediate days of Sukkos, and the month of Adar, especially on Purim. These times align with five types of joy: physical joy, emotional joy, intellectual joy, spiritual joy, and essential joy.

Physical joy is joy experienced through the body and is therefore felt bodily. Emotional joy is the feeling of love that one feels toward others or when others express love toward them. Intellectual joy comes in the form of a new understanding, a fresh perspective, or the discovery of a new concept. Spiritual joy is when a person's inner being expands and elevates, when one feels connected to something far greater than themselves. Essence joy, the joy of being.

Four of these joys correspond to the four letters of Hashem's name, Yud-Hei-Vav-Hei, and the fifth level corresponds to the crown above the Yud. They also correspond to the five levels of the soul: Nefesh, the sense of action, physical consciousness. Ruach, the sense of emotion, emotional consciousness. Neshamah, the sense of thought, intellectual consciousness. Chayah, the spiritual sense, transcendental consciousness. Yechidah, the sense of oneness and essence, unity consciousness.

Mitzvah can achieve that. And the depths to which sadness can bring a person, no sin can drag them so low." In the deepest way, the 'Mitzvah' to "serve Hashem with joy" means that being joyous is itself serving Hashem: the Yid haKadosh, *Kedushas haYehudi*, Simchah.

Matrix in Time	Type of Joy	Level of Soul	Letter of Name
Shabbos	Physical	Nefesh	Lower Hei
Yom Tov	Emotional	Ruach	Vav
Sukkos	Intellectual	Neshamah	Upper Hei
Simchas Beis haSho'eivah	Spiritual	Chayah	Yud
Adar / Purim	Essential	Yechidah	Tip of Yud

Physical Joy: Physical joy corresponds to Shabbos and the final or 'lower' Hei of Hashem's name. The lower Hei represents the Sefirah of Malchus, or 'nobility'. On Shabbos, we celebrate the completion of creation by resting from certain creative activities. The Torah says, "On the days of Simchah, on your designated holidays" (*Bamidbar*, 10:10), and according to our Sages (*Sifri*, 10:10), this refers to Shabbos (The Bahag rules there is an obligation to be happy on Shabbos. See also Radbaz, *Metzudas David*, Mitzvah 91. *Manhig*, Tefilos Shabbos. *Shibolei haLeket*, 82. *Beis Yoseph*, Orach Chayim, 281. And see also *Ya'aros Devash*, 2, Derush 10. *Shu'T Chasam Sofer*, Orach Chayim, 168. We do not make the special Seuda of Purim on Shabbos: Yerushalmi, *Megilah*,1:4, so as not to mix the Simchah of Purim with the Simchah of Shabbos: *Pri Chadash*, Orach Chayim, 688. See, however, *Magen Avraham,* Orach Chayim, 529:4. *Shu'T Rebbe Akiva* Eiger, Hashmatos 1. *Me'iri*, Moed Katan, 8b. *Tosefos*, Moed Katan, 23b. The language of the Alter Rebbe regarding Simchah on Shabbos is לכך נהגו להרבות במיני מאכלים ביו"ט יותר מבשבת שלא נאמר בה שמחה: *Orach Chayim*, 529:7. Hence, there is a type of Simchah on Shabbos, just a little different from Yom Tov: *Likutei Sichos* 33, p. 62-70. Perhaps Simchah is included within the Mitzvah of Oneg Shabbos: *Likutei Sichos* 4, p. 1090).

The joy of Shabbos is a joy in which the entire physical self is invited to participate. It is a day of rest from exertion and physical delight, such as festive meals, intimate connection, and even an extra nap in the afternoon. This form of joy is deeply connected with the restoration of the often overworked body. Shabbos joy is associated with the final, 'lower' Hei of the Divine Name. Hei, often silent, symbolizes rest, receptivity, and containment. On Shabbos, the body is not bypassed, but rather honored as the home and vessel for our soul.

Emotional Joy: Emotional joy corresponds to the inner experience of each Yom Tov, and is associated with the Vav of Hashem's Name, the channel of connection, and the level of Ruach, our emotional and relational reality. The Torah declares, "You shall rejoice on your festival... and you shall be only joyous" (*Devarim*, 16:14-15). On Yom Tov, if we are attuned, we can sense a heightened resonance of Divine emotion, so to speak, a revelation of one of the seven emotional Sefiros, as explored earlier. For instance, on Pesach, as we celebrate Hashem taking us out of Egypt, we can feel the embrace of our Heavenly Parent lifting us from our personal *Mitzrayim* / constrictions, limitations, fears, and inner bondage. Each Yom Tov is a celebration of a unique revelation of Divine affection, a moment in time when Hashem's love for Klal Yisrael shines more openly. Such awareness that we are cherished and held by our Creator awakens a profound emotional joy, the joy of being loved.

Intellectual Joy: Intellectual joy is particularly connected with the Yom Tov of Sukkos, and corresponds to the 'upper' Hei of Hashem's Name, the realm of Neshamah, or expanded mental awareness. This is the joy born of a breakthrough in understanding, when confusion is resolved, when a question finds its answer, when the mind becomes clear, and we have proper awareness. "There is no joy like the resolution of doubt" (*Metzudas Dovid*, Mishlei, 15:30. *Mish-*

betzos Zahav, Siman 682:1). As the Rama writes, "One has not tasted joy until he tastes the resolution of intellectual doubts" (*Toras haOlah*, 1:6). This is a type of intellectual joy of the mind. This is the joy of Da'as, a deep, stable, and clear knowing.

While there is a general Mitzvah to rejoice on every Yom Tov, the Torah singles out Sukkos with an extraordinary emphasis on joy, commanding us three separate times to be joyous during this Yom Tov (*Yalkut Shimoni*, Emor 247:654). The Torah says, "You shall dwell in Sukkos for seven days... so that your generations will know that I caused the Children of Israel to dwell in booths when I brought them out of Egypt" (*Vayikra*, 23:42-43). The word *Yeid'u* / 'shall know', highlights the central role of Da'as on Sukkos. Without this knowing, the Mitzvah of sitting in a Sukkah is not fulfilled at all (*Bach*, Orach Chayim, 625. *Bikurei Yaakov* 625:3). Unlike many other Mitzvos, where the role of intention is debated whether a person who performed a Mitzvah without intention has fulfilled their obligation or not, in the Sukkah, conscious awareness is essential (*Berachos*, 13a. *Eiruvin*, 95b. *Pesachim*, 113b. *Tosefos*, Sukkah, 39a. *Tosefos*, Pesachim, 7b. *Orach Chayim*, 60, Magen Avraham. *Beis Yoseph*, ibid., 489).

Sukkos, then, is a Yom Tov of Da'as, just as Purim is the celebration of *Lo Yada*, transcendence of Da'as. On Sukkos, we become aware, with clarity and depth, that just as Hashem sheltered us in Clouds of Glory or physical booths in the Desert, so too He continues to protect and guide us through all the days of our lives. This awareness, this Da'as, becomes the source of a higher, deeper, and more secure joy: the joy of knowing and clarity.

Spiritual Joy: Spiritual joy arises from the awareness of being connected with something greater than oneself, an elevated sense of unity with the Divine. This form of joy was most powerfully expressed during the nights of *Chol haMo'ed Sukkos* / the intermediate days of Sukkos in the Beis haMikdash, through the extraordinary celebration known as the *Simchas Beis haSho'eivah*, the Joy of the House of Water Drawing. This festive gathering, filled with song, dance, and even acrobatics, accompanied the ritual drawing of water at night, which was then poured as a libation upon the altar during the day. Though the act of drawing water was simple, its spiritual depth and connection to Divine service inspired a joy so intense that the Sages declared: "One who did not see the joy of Simchas Beis haSho'eivah did not see joy in his life" (*Sukkah*, 51a).

At first glance, it would seem that the joy of this time was primarily connected with the actual drawing of the water. Yet, writing about this festive event, the Rambam begins (*Hilchos Shofar v'Sukkah v'Lulav*, 8:12) by writing, "Although we are required to rejoice on all festivals, there was special rejoicing in the Beis haMikdash during the Sukkos festival, as it is written, "You shall rejoice before Hashem your G-d (meaning, in the Beis haMikdash) seven days" (*Vayikra*, 23:40). It is clear from the Rambam's words that the celebration of Simchas Beis haSho'eivah is not merely an independent event, connected with the water drawing, but rather flows directly from, and is inseparable from, the Mitzvah of rejoicing on Yom Tov, and most especially on Sukkos. In our context, this means that this celebration and its joy are rooted in Da'as, and even the higher Da'as of prophetic insight, Ruach haKodesh (Rashi writes that Da'as means רוח הקודש / *Ruach haKodesh*: Rashi, *Shemos*, 31:3).

Clearly, beyond the ritual act of just drawing the water for libation, there is an emphasis on the state of one's cultivated consciousness in relation to the event. Tosefos (*Sukkah*, 50b) writes in the name of the Yerushalmi that the word *Sho'eivah* / drawing, alludes to the fact that the participants who celebrated on these special nights would 'draw' down *Ruach haKodesh* / Divine intuition and flow, as they dance with ecstatic joy through the night.

On these powerful nights, the Sages of old would enter elevated states of consciousness and Divine inspiration, drawing down Ruach haKodesh through their ecstatic joy. We, too, are called to access this, each on our own level.

The joy that comes through Da'as, through deep knowing, becomes a gateway to an even higher state of awareness. This transcendent joy corresponds to the letter Yud of Hashem's Name, associated with Chochmah, higher wisdom and intuitive insight. It also reflects the inner dimension of Chayah, the level of spiritual consciousness that transcends ego and touches the infinite. This is spiritual joy, a joy of expansive, elevated awareness, the soul's delight in being connected with something far beyond itself and experiencing expanded states of consciousness.

Essential Joy: The Joy of the Essence of Being is related to Purim, and associated with the crown Above the Yud in Hashem's Name. The level of Yechidah, our existential and fullness of self, and a joy that is connected with the entire month of Adar, as our Sages say, "When Adar enters we increase in joy" (*Ta'anis*, 29a).[*]

[*] Neither the Rambam nor the Shulchan Aruch discusses the theme or quotes the idea that "When Adar enters, we increase in joy." The Rambam does, however, mention the opposite quote: "When Av enters, we decrease in joy." The reason could be that being joyous is a 'non-doing' Mitzvah; it is a feeling in the heart, rather than a positive activity. In Av, the Mitzvah to 'decrease in joy' is active, since it involves actively refraining from certain activities and foods. See also *Shu'T Chasam Sofer*, Orach Chayim, Siman 170. *Nimukei Orach Chayim*, Siman 686.

This is the highest and most all-encompassing joy imaginable. Existential joy is not merely the joy of immanence, of inhabiting the fullness of self and body, nor is it limited to emotional or intellectual delight, or even to transcendent ecstasy. Rather, it is a joy of the harmonious embrace of all these dimensions at once, full integration of all levels of being.

Our Nefesh-Ruach-Neshamah comprises the wholeness of our finite self: our actions, our feelings, and our thoughts, the tapestry of our embodied experience. This is the self that lives, feels, and thinks. Our Chayah is the transcendent self, our infinite self, the one who witnesses life from beyond, the observer behind the scenes, beyond the experiences themselves, beyond the actions, emotions, and even the thoughts. It is the expansive field of awareness itself. Yet beyond both the finite self and infinite self is our Yechidah, the essence of who we are, our deepest uniqueness. Our Yechidah is deeper than both our finite and infinite selves, and it also includes them as well. Yechidah is our very uniqueness, our unique way of being in the world, and yet it is utterly transcendent of any experience-based definition.

Yechidah is one with the *Yechidah Shel Olam* / the Unique One of the World; it is the essence of our being that is one with the Essence of All. The joy that flows from this place is the Joy of Essence. It includes everything, transcends everything, and is the deepest expression of who we truly are.

The crown atop the Yud, a tiny dot perched on the tip of the smallest and most elevated letter, symbolizes a level of utter transcendence. Yet paradoxically, it also represents the primordial 'point' from which all letters, forms, and manifestations emerge. This is the secret joy of Purim. The joy of Purim is of Lo Yada, a state beyond knowing, yet it is also the very source from which all Da'as, all awareness and all joy, flow. Lo Yada is not simply the absence or negation of knowledge; it is the fountainhead of knowledge, intuitive wisdom, and inspired decision-making. It is at once light and grounded, sacred uncertainty and sacred clarity. This is a joy that transcends, yet does not escape; it soars beyond the mind while remaining fully embodied. It is a state of elevation that is also deeply present, both beyond and within the body.

The crown that rests above the Yud hovers beyond the four letters of Hashem's Name and alludes to a level that transcends all articulation and form. With regards to Yom Kippur, the Torah says ...*Lifnei Hashem Tit'haru* / "Before Hashem you shall be purified" (*Vaykira*, 16:30). The words *Lifnei Hashem* can be translated as 'before Hashem' in the sense of 'beyond Hashem', beyond the Name, beyond the revealed will and expression of the Divine. On Yom Kippur, we are elevated to a pristine and transcendent inner space that reaches into the Essence of HaKadosh Baruch Hu, beyond even the manifestations of His Name. It is from this essential place, symbolized by the crown above the Yud, that Teshuvah and *Tikun* / rectification becomes possible, even for that which has damaged, so to speak, the very Name of Hashem. Purim, too, shares this quality. Like Yom Kippur, Purim transports us to a realm beyond all Names, all garments, all Divine masks.*

---

* In the Torah, Yom Kippur is called *Yom haKipurim*, thus *Ki-Purim*, 'like Purim' (*Tikunei Zohar*, Tikun 21). Tellingly, we feast on Purim to make up for our lack of food and drink on Yom Kippur, as the Gra on this passage writes. Similarly, Rav Yitzchak Chaver (from the school of the Gra) writes that before Purim, there is a fast day to make up for the day before Yom Kippur when we feast. On a deeper level, as explored earlier, Purim is connected with an even higher, deeper reality.

Purim draws us into contact with the infinite Essence Itself.

In other words, on Yom Kippur, we ascend the external world and ascend into the inner, Penimiyus realm that is beyond sin and even the possibility of sin. On Purim, the Penimiyus of Klal Yisrael, the level of צהלי ורני יושבת ציון כי־גדול בקרבך קדוש ישראל / "O shout for joy, You who dwell in Tziyon (ציון / *Tziyon* refers to the essence of the Neshamah), for the Great One in your midst, the holy one, Yisrael" (*Yeshayahu*, 12:6), which is also the level of קדוש ישראל / "Holy, Yisrael," is revealed in the body. In this revelation, the body and external self are also holy.

Both within us and Above us, there exists a *Chitzoniyus* / external and outer world of masks, Names, and definitions. On Yom Kippur, we withdraw from the external world, refraining from food, drink, work, and physicality, and in this withdrawal, we enter the inner world, the Penimiyus, where our innate purity and perfection shine unobscured. On Purim, the opposite movement occurs. The inner essence, the Penimiyus of Klal Yisrael, bursts forth into the outer world, into the realm of masks, garments, and the full vibrancy of physical life, food, and drink. The Penimiyus of Klal Yisrael, which is the Penimiyus of Hashem's Light, is revealed within the concealments themselves, within the body, within the seeming chaos, within the very fabric of external manifestation (Through Mordechai, who is the Yesod of Abba, the *Tov* / point of goodness and light that exists within *Amo* / "His People," which is the weakest definition of Klal Yisrael, becomes revealed. As the Megilah concludes, דרש טוב לעמו (creatively translated as) "Mordechai sought the *Nekudah* / point of goodness within his people").

מלא כל הארץ כבודו / "The entire world is filled with Your glory and honor" (*Yeshayahu*, 6:3). The word כבוד / *Kavod*, say our Sages, refers to a person's garments (רבי יוחנן קרי למאניה מכבדותא: *Shabbos*, 113b). In other words, Hashem fills the universe in a way that is enclothed within the many garments of Creation, as the Maggid of Mezritch teaches, "The Holy One, blessed be He, enclothes Himself in this world" (*Likutim Yekarim*, 222). Purim, however, transports us beyond all garments, beyond every Divine mask (hence, the deeper reason for masks on Purim), where we are granted a glimpse of Etzem, the very Essence of *Elokus* / Divinity.

"The Etzem of the day (Yom Kippur) brings acquittal...." This is because Yom Kippur touches the Etzem of the Divine, and therefore unlocks the power of return, of renewal, of reestablishing a revealed connection when the connection has been severed. The essence of the day reveals the essence of a Yid, whose essence is one with the Essence of Hashem (so to speak), and no sin or negative act can sever this connection. Thus, there is a total atonement.

On this day, the essence of the day reveals the essence of a Jew, that in the realm of pure essence, our core is one with the very Essence of Hashem. At this level, no sin, no act of separation, can truly sever the connection. From this place of indivisible unity, forgiveness flows naturally, and atonement is complete. Purim as well is connected to our Etzem, the level of soul called Yechidah, and to the Etzem of Hashem. This is why the joy of Purim is unlike any other, as it is the perfect joy of Etzem. Just as the Essence of Hashem is, so to speak, one with our own essence, and from this unity flows complete atonement, so too, the very Etzem of the *Hashpa'ah* / Divine outpouring from Above, the *Chayus* / vitality of this world, is an expression of Divine Love and Joy (See *Toldos Yaakov Yoseph*, Eikev, 630. *Zohar Chai*, Medrash haNe'elam, Vayera, 119. *Baal Shem Tov*

Al haTorah, Bereishis, 25). On Purim, we connect to that Essence, the Essence of all Life, and therefore the result is not merely that there is joy *on* the Yom Tov, but that the Yom Tov *itself* is joy. Purim is defined as יום משתה ושמחה / "a day of feasting and rejoicing." The joy is not an accessory to the day, and added dimension, it is the day's very essence (In the name of the Griz it is written (*Emek haBeracha*, Seudas Purim, p. 126. *Birchas Refael*, Purim, p. 223) that Purim is different from all other Yamim Tovim in that on Purim there is a Mitzvah to drink excessively, Ad d'Lo Yada. Why? The Griz answers because in all other Yamim Tovim the Mitzvah is to be *Mesameach* / joyful with Hashem, and the eating of meat and drinking of wine are only a means to awaken that joy and bring one into that state, thus they are only a means to an end. However, the Megilah calls Purim ימי משתה ושמחה / "days of feasting and joy." This reveals that the joy is not merely a vehicle to reach something higher, but rather is the *Tachlis* / end, in itself. The celebration, feasting, drinking, and Simchah are the very purpose of the day. Unlike other Yamim Tovim, here the Simchah is not a means; it is the end).

The joy of Purim flows from *Radla* / the Unknowable Head, the Keser of all Kesarim, the Crown of all Crowns, where all opposites dissolve, and every definition falls away. All other forms of joy exist in relation to their opposite; joy measured against grief, delight emerging from loss, elation contrasted with sorrow. We know the joy of finding what was lost, of union after long separation, of holding a child after years of heartbreak, depth of pain magnifying the height of gladness. These are all joys within the realm of duality, not a joy of Essence, of the One. The joy of Purim is of another order entirely. It cannot be quantified, bound, or even contained within the notion of 'unlimited'; it is the joy of Essence itself, joy without contrast, joy without external cause, the pure delight of Being. And yet, in its all-encompassing radiance, it embraces and elevates every other form of joy, gathering them all into its boundless light.

The joy of Purim is paradoxically beyond joy, and yet, even the phrase "beyond descriptions" falls short, for the joy of Purim is not only transcendent, but also the very root from which all four kinds of joy emerge. It encompasses them all, even as it surpasses them and functions on a plane beyond dualities and opposites.

This existential joy is accessed through עד דלא ידע / *Ad d'Lo Yada* / "until one does not know," a state that transcends ordinary conceptions of what is known as joy. Yet, hidden within this phrase is a deeper teaching: the first letters of the three words עד דלא ידע spell ידע / *Yada* / 'knows'. This reveals the paradox of Purim: its un-knowing is not a void, but a fullness. It contains and elevates every form of knowing and joy. Lo Yada is not the absence of awareness, but the overflowing of a deeper, truer knowing, one that dances beyond opposites, and celebrates the mystery at the heart of all things.

THE WORLD OF *ETZEM* VS. THE WORLD OF *GILUYIM*

There exists a world of *Giluyim* / revelations and manifestations of Light, and a world of Etzem, the innermost essential core beyond all expressions and Lights, the Luminary in Itself. All the Yamim Tovim, with the exception of Purim, are rooted in the world of Giluyim. Each one reveals a particular Divine Attribute in powerful, awe-inspiring ways. Pesach is a revelation of Chesed, Divine kindness, as Hashem performed open miracles to redeem us from Egypt. Shavuos unveils Tiferes, beauty and harmony, through the Giving of the Torah. These are manifestations, illuminations of the Infinite Light as filtered through these *Sefiros* / attributes, vessels, or prisms.

On Purim, there are no overt Giluyim. The miracles are hidden within the natural order. There is no suspension of nature; rather, the Etzem, the Divine *Anochi* / 'I', is simply Present within nature, within history, and within the seemingly coincidental events of our lives. This is why Purim is celebrated in the immediacy of our bodies. On Purim, there is a revelation (so to speak) of what can never truly be revealed, for it simply Is: the Essence itself.

Our body, in relation to our soul, represents our Etzem, our essential core, whereas the soul is our Giluy, the revealed channel to the Ohr Ein Sof, the Infinite Light. This is because it is specifically the bodies of Klal Yisrael that *Atzmus* / the Divine Essence, "chooses," as explained in Tanya (ch. 49). Since the Essence chooses the body, the body itself becomes the truest expression of our essence (See Rebbe Rashab, *Toras Shalom*, 120. See also *Torah Ohr*, 73b. *Likkutei Torah*, Tzav, 15c).

This is why our Sages teach that in the Era of Mashiach, when even loftiest revelations will be unveiled, all the Yamim Tovim will be 'nullified' or rendered superfluous, except Purim. For when higher, brighter light is being revealed, all the less intense Giluyim become obsolete and unnoticeable, as a "candle (trying to) shine in daylight" (*Chulin*, 60b). Purim (and Yom Kippur) is not a light among lights; rather, it is Etzem, and Etzem is always and everywhere.

BEYOND THE NEED TO GO BEYOND KNOWING

One of the leading *Poskim* / Halachic authorities of our generation, Rav Shlomo Zalman Auerbach, once offered a remarkable ruling regarding Purim (*Kovetz Mevakshei Torah*, Vol. 3, addition 13. *Moadim l'Simchah*, Adar, Siman 14, Note 5). He argued that although Purim as a whole will endure eternally and never be nullified, one particular aspect will no longer apply in the future: the obligation to drink Ad d'Lo Yada. There is a technical Halachic rationale for this position, yet beneath the surface lies a profound spiritual truth.

In our current reality of existential, outward and inward *Galus* / exile, disconnection, alienation, concealment, and hardship, we must often step outside ourselves to connect with something deeper within and access deep joy. On Purim, we drink to transcend our ordinary consciousness, to rise above pain, limitation, and the inner burdens of exile, and to momentarily touch the deepest realm of Keser, Above and within. We drink not merely for joy, but to forget, to forget sorrow, fear, constriction, and to remember a deeper truth, a hidden wholeness.

However, in the Era of Mashiach, joy will flow naturally and continuously. We will live from a place of Etzem within our personal consciousness, effortlessly embracing paradox. There will no longer be a need to lose ourselves in order to access transcendence, though one may drink, or not. The seeming tension between knowledge and unknowing will be harmonized within our very being.

In the world we inhabit today, the world of Galus, a realm of exile, struggle, and fatigue, we need Lo Yada. We need to step beyond ourselves, beyond our usual patterns of thought and perception, in order to access true joy. This often requires us to leave behind the rigid structures of our rational mind (Though in truth, the highest level of Keser, Radla, or, in this context, Etzem, already encompasses and permeates our everyday reality; we are simply not always conscious of it, nor do we consistently live in alignment with it). In the Era of Mashiach, the Era of Essence, our own deepest truth and Etzem will be revealed, and with that revelation, joy will become our natural state. In truth, joy *is* our natural state. The essential condition of all Creation is one of quiet, radiant joy, the simple joy of being. In the natural world, there is no dissonance between identity and action. A tree 'trees', a lion 'lions'; their being and doing are one. They express themselves without conflict or hesitation. There is no friction between who they are and what they do. Only human beings, endowed with self-awareness and the capacity for free choice, can experience fragmentation, a disconnect between who we are and how we live, and it is from this inner rift that dichotomy and thus sadness emerges. Purim, 'a Mashiach Yom Tov', comes to dissolve that divide.

On Purim, and ideally in every moment of conscious living, we are invited to return to our natural state of joy. We are invited to release tension, to remember who we are beneath the masks, to rediscover the effortless joy of simply being. This is the deepest joy: not the joy of achievement or excitement, but the serene, essential joy that flows when we are no longer at odds with ourselves, when we are simply whole, aligned, and free.

THE FOURTEENTH & FIFTEENTH DAYS

Now to the issue of timing, the day of the month on which Purim is celebrated. In our current reality, most of world Jewry, living in the Diaspora or in non-walled cities, celebrates Purim on the Fourteenth of Adar, while in Shushan and in ancient walled cities, Purim is observed on the Fifteenth.

On the surface, this distinction is purely historical: the miracle of salvation occurred on the Fourteenth for most of the Jewish People living throughout the kingdom of Achashverosh, while in

Shushan, the battle continued into the Fifteenth. Yet, nothing is incidental or a coincidence; certainly, issues related to the Torah. Every detail is Divinely orchestrated. There must be a deeper metaphysical significance to the numbers fourteen and fifteen, and the particular days chosen for celebrating Purim.

Pesach and Sukkos both begin on the fifteenth of their month, the Fifteenth of Nissan and the Fifteenth of Tishrei (the third, Shavuos, is connected and a continuation of Pesach, hence, fifty days after the first day of Pesach). Months follow the lunar cycle. At the start of the month, the moon is hidden from view. Slowly it waxes, becoming more visible, until it reaches its fullness on the fifteenth. Spiritually, the fifteenth of the month symbolizes fullness, revelation, clarity, and *Giluy*. The fifteenth is the midpoint, the essence of the month, when light reaches its peak. Fittingly, Pesach and Sukkos are days of open miracles, of Divine light made manifest in the world. Their celebrations align with the full moon, the full expression of spiritual revelation.

Purim, however, is not celebrated on the Fifteenth of Adar by most; it falls on the Fourteenth, just before the moon's fullness. This is not arbitrary. The miracle of Purim was woven into the *Hester* of the natural order. It was not a supernatural disruption of reality, but a sublime orchestration of events, people in the right place at the right time, each piece perfectly aligned, yet cloaked in the garments of coincidence.

The Fourteenth represents that liminal space, almost full, almost revealed. Fourteen is a number that reaches toward Giluy but stops just short, reflecting the nature of Purim itself: a miracle concealed in the folds of history, perceptible only to those attuned to the deeper rhythms of Divine Providence.

In Shushan, where the miracle extended into an additional day and became more overt, Purim is observed on the Fifteenth, corresponding to a more revealed Divine Hand. But for most of us, Purim remains on the Fourteenth, a celebration of hidden light, a day that whispers its miracles rather than shouting them (King Dovid is connected with the number 14 and the one who actually builds the Beis haMikdash, King Shlomo is connected with the full moon and the fifteenth: *Medrash Rabbah*, Shemos, 15:26. *Pri Eitz Chayim*, Purim, 6).

In Hebrew, every letter communicates via both a sound and a numerical value. The letter Yud represents the number ten, and Dalet the number four, together forming fourteen (י״ד). The number fifteen, by contrast, is composed of Yud and Hei (ט״ו), ten and five. These combinations contain profound spiritual significance, both in their numerical value and in their form, their actual shape.

The Yud is a simple point, a seed, the source and origin. The Yud symbolizes the *Mashpia* / giver, the initiator, the one who bestows. The Hei, expansive vertically and horizontally, and open, represents the *Mekabel* / receiver, the vessel that receives and absorbs the flow. Together, Yud-Hei forms a union (and also a Divine Name in itself), representing the dynamic interplay between giving and receiving, influence and absorption. Yud and Hei is a model of a genuine relationship, where two distinct identities merge into a unit, yet do so without losing their individuality and uniqueness.

This interplay is reflected in the Yamim Tovim. On Pesach and Sukkos, which begin on the fifteenth of their respective months, at the peak of the moon's fullness — the Divine giving (Yud) is met with full human reception (Hei). Open miracles from Above are clearly perceived Below. There is perfect harmony between giver and receiver. The miracle is not hidden, nor is it lost upon its recipient. Furthermore, the Giver Above does not overwhelm the receiver, Below, and the receiver does not reduce what was given. An open miracle perceived and recognized by man, without either man or the miracle, the Below or the Above being diminished in the process.

Purim, by contrast, is celebrated by most on the fourteenth, י"ד. The Yud, the Divine flow, the miracle, is fully present and revealed. Yet, the Dalet, which represents the receiver (*Shabbos*, 104a), is in a state of 'Dalet' or *Dalus*, from the root דל / *Dal*, meaning poor or destitute, in a diminished state of reception. The hand of Hashem is there, orchestrating every detail within nature, but it may be hidden from the perception of the receiver. The receiver may still be in a state of constriction, of spiritual poverty, and see the events unfold, but cannot fully comprehend their magnitude and miraculous nature. True, he or she may sense a miraculous twist of events tangled up within the natural unfolding of the story, but they fail to realize that on Purim the deepest, most sublime miracle occurred, a miracle so deep and penetrating that it was able to unfold within nature, as the Essence, which is 'Above' miracle and nature.

On other Yamim Tovim, the roles of Mekabel and Mashpia both exist very clearly. There is a miracle from Above, and human beings appreciating it below; there is a clear Yud and a clear Hei (י"ה). On the Fourteenth of Adar, the arousal from Above is there (the Yud), it is just that man below may not sense it (as man is on the level of Dalet). Yet, the beauty of Purim is precisely that it invites us to awaken. The purpose of Purim is to help us become aware, to open our eyes to the hidden Divine Hand, and thereby to transform our Dalet-consciousness into Hei-consciousness (Symbolically, the letter Hei/ה is a Dalet/ד with a (an extended) י as its left, suspended leg. Yud/י corresponds to Chochmah. ד/Dalet to Malchus. On Purim, the Light of Chochmah (Yesod Abba) is revealed in Malchus. ה/Hei is when the Yud of Chochmah becomes fully integrated into the Dalet, thus becoming the letter Hei. Yud-Dalet / 14 is the day of Purim for the Diaspora and unwalled cities (in exile, where Malchus is still in a state of poverty, Dalus), and Yud-Hei (15) is the day of Purim in Shushan and the walled cities).

Intriguingly, when you combine the letters Yud and Dalet, inserting the proper vowel, you also spell the word *Yud* itself. In this sense, the Dalet is not separate from the Yud; it is a necessary part of it, contained within it, waiting to be vocalized, brought to life.

Moreover, the word *Yad* / יד / hand is formed from the same two letters, Yud and Dalet. On Purim, there is but *one* Hand, not the hands of the Giver and the receiver as 'separate' entities, but a single, unified gesture: Essence touching Essence.

This is the secret of Purim. On its outer level, it may appear to be a 'lesser' miracle, and even a 'lower' form of Yom Tov, and a Yom Tov that is celebrated on the Fourteenth rather than the Fifteenth, being without any open wonders or supernatural displays of miracles. Yet, in truth, Purim is the most profound of all Yamim Tovim.

Purim is a time of *Atzmus* / Essence, where the apparent duality of giver and receiver dissolves. There is no longer a miracle from Above and a witness below who perceives the miracles, as there is no separation between heaven and earth. There are no 'greater' and 'lesser' miracles. There is only Oneness.

And yet, as deep as this Oneness goes, the outer forms of distinctions, identities, and the reality of Yesh, remain intact. The world does not collapse into abstraction; rather, Essence merges with essence *within* the reality of form and Yesh. That is the paradox and the power of Purim: not that the One replaces the 'two', but that the One is fully present within the 'two'. Indeed, Purim is a glimpse into what always is and what will be 'revealed' in the times of Mashiach; a revelation that there is no two, only One; the One is reflected and refracted into the many, while nonetheless remaining One.

PURIM IS CONNECTED WITH THE NAME ADO-NOI

In earlier times, the Megilah could be read as early as the Eleventh of Adar, with the latest permissible day being the Fifteenth. The Name of Hashem, Yud-Hei-Vav-Hei (י-ה-ו-ה), also referred to as Havayah, can be divided into two separate names, the Yud-Hei, as in the Name י״ה, which numerically is fifteen, and the second two letters, the Vav-Hei, which equal eleven. Due to our current spiritual condition, the Name Havayah is considered ineffable; though it is fully written in the text, it is never pronounced as such. Instead, we read it as *Ado-noi*, a name that represents a more constricted, accessible revelation. In essence, the Name of the Giver, "Hashem," is fully and openly presented on the page, but the 'receiver', the human being reading and animating the Name, lacks the spiritual capacity to absorb its full brilliance. Therefore, it is received and read through the lower name, Ado-noi.

The structure of the Name Havayah illustrates a spiritual process: The Yud symbolizes a point of origin, the One Above, the Ultimate Giver. The upper Hei expands this point into understanding and insight, the higher level of receiver. The Vav represents the drawing down of this light, much like the line-shaped letter Vav. And finally, the lower Hei signifies the lower receiver, us, and us in a state of integrating the light in our lived consciousness.

A true revelation of the Name of Hashem implies that this entire flow, from the highest Infinite Light to human consciousness, is realized and absorbed. There is a revealing of the Above, the Giver, to the Below, the receiver, and the receiver is equipped to receive the Light of Above. On Purim, the Giver is fully present; in fact, the Essence beyond the Infinite Light is there. However, in terms of Giluyim, or revealed light, this presence is hidden within nature, cloaked and concealed. What is revealed in terms of human perception is only the Name Ado-noi, the accessible interface of the Divine, the Name of judgment and concealment (The letters of Ado-noi spell the words *Aleph Din* / the 'judgment' or concealment of the Aleph, the One).

This mystery is further reflected in the range of days for reading the Megilah: 11+12+13+14+15 equals 65, the exact numerical value of Ado-noi (10=י, 05=נ, 4=ד, 1=א). The Mishnah teaches, מגילה נקראת בי״א בי״ב בי״ג בי״ד בט״ו, לא פחות ולא יותר / "The Megilah is read on the 11th, 12th, 13th, 14th or 15th, not earlier and not later." The phrase "not less and not more" alludes to this precise alignment with the Name Ado-noi. Not less: not on the 10th. Not more: not on the 16th. Together, these two 'bookends' equal 26, the numerical value of the Name Hashem. Purim is precisely connected with Ado-noi, and not the revelation of the Name of Hashem. As explained, Purim is connected with *Lifnei Hashem* / 'Prior to the Name'; beyond, so to speak, the Name or expression of Hashem (26), for Purim, on the deepest level is connected with the Essence Itself.

ANOTHER CONNECTION
BETWEEN THE FOURTEENTH AND PURIM

Beyond historical happenstance, the fact that Purim, at least in the Diaspora, falls on the Yud-Dalet, the fourteenth day of the month, carries profound symbolic meaning. The letters Yud and Dalet spell the word יד / *Yad* / hand. This concept of the Hand is deeply connected with Amalek, of whom Haman is the embodiment. And the Megilah reading, central to Purim, is in essence the erasure of Amalek (*Megilah*, 7a. Yerushalmi, *Megilah*, 1:5).

Who is Amalek, what does Amalek represent, and what is the connection to *Yad* / hand?

When the Torah speaks about the war that will continue until the final erasure of Amalek, it says, כי יד על־כס י-ה מלחמה לי-ה-ו-ה בעמלק מדר דר / "Because Hashem (has sworn with His) Hand upon His Throne that Hashem has a war with Amalek from generation to generation" (*Shemos*, 17:16). Clearly, there is a connection between the Divine Hand and the war of Amalek (יד is numerically 14, so is Haman in small numerical volume: 5+4+5=המן). Who is Amalek? And what do they represent?

THE HISTORICAL & FIRST EMBODIMENT OF AMALEK

As Klal Yisrael left Egypt and were journeying to the Promised Land, the ראשית גוים / *Reishis Goyim* / 'the first of the nations' to attack and wage war upon them, was Amalek (*Bamidbar*, 24:20). Amalek did not go to war with Klal Yisrael in order to protect their own land, nor a preemptive strike out of fear of being overwhelmed in their land (as the Egyptians potentially feared, or said they feared). Klal Yisrael posed no immediate threat. Nor was Amalek's war one of expansion, as Klal Yisrael were still landless and journeying through the Desert. Amalek's only motivation was simple hate. This hate was not rational, national, or existential. The war of Amalek was completely unjustified, waged purely out of hatred for the sake of hatred. They felt the very existence of Klal Yisrael to be repulsive, an insult.

Overall, there are two types of potentially 'justifiable' enemies, so to speak: an *Oyev* / enemy and a *Soneh* / foe. The Pasuk says, ויפצו איביך וינסו משנאיך / "May Your enemies (*Oy'vecha*) be scattered and may Your foes (*Son'echa*) flee before You" (*Bamidbar*, 10:35). What is the difference between an Oyev and a Soneh? And why is the blessing that our 'enemies' be scattered and our 'foes' flee?

Rashi tells us that your 'enemies' are those who are massed for battle, whereas 'foes' are those who are actively pursuing you. In other words, an 'enemy' is an adversary that is sitting in its own land and massing an army for battle so that if it is invaded, it can attack. An 'enemy' may feel frightened, whether by a real or assumed threat, and there is some type of justification for their armament and readying for battle. A 'foe' pursues another; they are aggressive, often wishing to expand their own territory, gain spoils, or destroy someone out of revenge or out of ideological hatred. They are not protecting their homeland, nor do they specifically feel the threat of being conquered or overwhelmed. They attack out of aggression.

Throughout the millennia, there have been nations and cultures that felt threatened by the existence of a powerful Klal Yisrael; whether they perceive us as an external threat or as a 'fifth column' that could join their other enemies, or even as a saboteur from within. These perceptions are of an *Oyev*. Other groups despise the Jewish People due to long-standing prejudices, past grievances, or theological opposition, and they actively pursue to hurt (Heaven forbid) Klal Yisrael. This is seeing us as a Soneh.

Expulsion and persecution have tragically punctuated Jewish history, and this is a great, filthy stain on the perpetrators. The worst offense is attempting to annihilate us, not simply removing Jews from their country, but aspiring to eradicate Jews everywhere. This is, in fact, the *Kelipah* / destructive force of Amalek. Anyone who embodies Kelipas Amalek, no matter their national, religious, or cultural identity, is dedicated to this genocidal hatred and intolerance and actively seeks to remove the Jewish People from existence.

While Amalek was once a specific nation, they now represent a recurring archetype, a metaphysical, diabolical force that resurfaces across societies and epochs. Amalek is the ideology that views the Jew as an existential threat to their *Metziyus* / existence and a mortal threat to the world. They believe that if a Jew is alive, they cannot live; this is an absolute 'us or them' worldview. They are convinced that they must inflict Jewish individuals and groups with physical and political violence wherever they may be found throughout the world. In this way, Amalek is both an Oyev and a Soneh (as the Rambam writes, שאסור לשכח איבתו ושנאתו / "It is forbidden to forget their enmity (*Oyev*) and hatred (*Soneh*)": Rambam, *Hilchos Melachim*, 5:5).

This dedication to enmity and hatred is not based on generational trauma, oppression, or poverty, or even maleducation and prejudicial religious training. The Kelipah of Amalek is a spiritual force that is actively chosen and nurtured. As a demonstration of this, some individuals have been able to renounce and disentangle themselves from Amalekite cults, turn their lives around, and sincerely support the Jewish People. When they do so, it is a small foretaste of the future, when Amalek will be "wiped out from beneath the Heavens."

AMALEK IS THE ANTITHESIS OF EVERYTHING HOLY, DIVINE, AND GOOD

Amalek is the antithesis of the Jew. The war that Amalek wages is fundamentally against all that is holy and Divine. It is a mortal struggle against everything Hashem and His Torah and People represent: the belief that Creation has a purpose, that history is moving toward a culmination of complete, universal goodness, and that every human being is born with a *Tzelem Elokim* / a Divine image, and is therefore inherently worthy of dignity and honor.

Amalek cannot tolerate the existence of hope, compassion, or righteousness. In this way, Amalek is not only the existential enemy of Klal Yisrael, but it is so of all humanity and all living beings. Ultimately, Amalek is 'at war' with the revelation of Hashem in this world. Amalek is the embodiment of opposition to everything a Jew stands for. As a Jew is Hashem's witness in this world, Amalek is against everything that Hashem Himself stands for, as it were. As Chazal teach, כל זמן שזרעו של עמלק בעולם, לא השם שלם, ולא הכסא שלם. אבד זרעו של עמלק, השם שלם והכסא שלם / "As long as the seed of Amalek exists in the world, the Name (of Hashem) is not whole, and the Throne is not whole. Once the seed of Amalek is lost to existence, the Name is whole and the Throne is whole" (Rashi, *Shemos*, 17:16. *Medrash Tanchumah*: שעומד כנגד ישראל כאילו עומד כנגד הקב"ה / "One who stands in opposition to Klal Yisrael is as if he stands in opposition to the Holy One, Blessed be He": Rashi, *Bamidbar*, 31:3. אמר משה רבון העולם, אם היינו ערלים או עובדי ע"ז או כופרים במצוות, לא היו שונאים אותנו, ולא רודפים (אחרינו) [אותנו]. אלא בשביל תורה שנתת לנו. לכך הנקמה [היא] שלך: *Tanchuma*, Matos, 3).

The Rambam writes in *Igeres Teiman,* his letter to the suffering Jewish community of Yemen, that the enemies of Israel ultimately seek to fight Hashem Himself, but since they cannot, they turn their fury toward Klal Yisrael, who bear His Name and mission in the world.

Amalek is the embodiment of cruelty, cynicism, coldness, and the rejection of meaning. Amalek stands in existential opposition to the very principles of moral clarity, compassion, covenant, and commitment, against goodness, holiness, and the vision of redemption. He rejects the nobility of Creation, the belief that the world is purposeful and progressing in meaningful ways. He denies the higher status of humanity, that man is created in the Divine image. And he negates the nobility of existence itself, that there is a Creator who imbues all things with significance. Therefore, the very existence of a Jewish person is a direct 'affront' to Amalek and to his world view. He declares, "I cannot truly exist if this Jew exists."

The wars against the Jewish People that we are witnessing today, throughout the entire world, are very much wars between the force of Divine Goodness and the force of meaninglessness and evil. They are a desperate struggle between life and death, between humanity and brutality, between holiness and desecration, between hope and nihilism. This world war against kindness and civility, progress and possibility, prayer and redemption, may seem to give the upper hand to the cults of death, chaos, to the cheapening of life, unconcealed evil, pessimism, and despair. This *Milchamah b'Amalek* / war with Amalek may sometimes seem to be destroying the world and everything of value in it, yet the truth is, Amalek is destined to lose and to disappear.

PURPOSELESSNESS LEADS TO NIHILISM, WHICH LEADS TO DEATH

Amalek is called *Reishis Goyim*, the first nation to attack the new-born Nation of Yisrael; however, Klal Yisrael is also called a ראשית / *Reishis* / beginning. Rashi teaches that the opening word of the Torah, בראשית / *B'Reishis*, does not just mean "In the beginning…" but 'for the *sake of* the beginning', meaning, בשביל התורה ובשביל ישראל / "for the purpose of Torah and Klal Yisrael." The world was created with intention, for the sake of Torah and for the sake of Yisrael.

Yisrael are the *Reishis* / ראשית of Hashem, as it is written (*Yirmeyahu*, 2:3): קודש ישראל לה׳ ראשית תבואתה / "Yisrael is holy to Hashem, the ראשית / beginning of His harvest." And the Torah, too, is called ראשית, as it is written ה׳ קנני ראשית דרכו / "Hashem created me as the beginning of His way" (*Mishlei*, 8:22). Klal Yisrael therefore represents 'purposefulness' itself, the conviction that all existence and all of Creation has an end-goal, a תכלית / *Tachlis* / ultimate purpose. Torah, the blueprint of Creation, and Yisrael with their Divine mission, embody the very meaning behind Creation.

Amalek is a different type of Reishis: ראשית גוים עמלק ואחריתו עדי אבד / "Amalek is the Reishis first of nations, *but his end is utter destruction*." The *Reishis* / ראשית of Amalek leads only to emptiness and annihilation, for when life is stripped of purpose, it collapses. This is not just a prediction of Amalek's historical fate; it is also a truth about the very essence of purposelessness. A purposeless 'beginning' without any end, a 'first' without a goal, must eventually collapse into non-being.

When one's life is stripped of meaning, one's life cannot endure. Nihilism, by its very nature, consumes itself. An individual, culture, or nation without a Tachlis, without an orientation and sense of progression toward a greater future, becomes unsustainable.

Amalek's אחרית / end is obliteration (אחרית in numerical value is 619. The phrase המן בן המדתא האגגי / "Haman son of Hamdasa the Agagi" is also 619). It cannot be otherwise. A seed that has no inner telos rots in the ground. A journey with no destination wanders into nothingness. The ultimate fruit of purposelessness is cynicism, and cynicism is death.

When a society loses its sense of purpose, its individuals feel an arbitrariness about their lives. Without a guiding principle and positive core value, souls hunger for meaning but taste only bitter or numbing emptiness. Into that emptiness creeps cynicism, a defense mechanism against the void. Cynics mock idealism because they cannot believe in anything. Cynics sneer at sincerity because sincerity exposes their hollowness. At first, cynicism presents itself as cleverness, as a sharp eye that 'sees through' illusions, but soon it corrodes the very possibilities of hope, striving, and transcendence.

The endpoint of such cynicism is death. This is not necessarily physical death, but a kind of spiritual death while the body is still alive: a deadening of the heart, a suffocation of the imagination, or a paralysis of the will. Without feeling, vision, and will, a soul loses its vitality and becomes a slow march toward complete nihilism.

Amalek promotes this purposelessness, plants doubt, drains conviction, and mocks any possibility of higher meaning. This is why the Torah tells us that Amalek's end "is utter destruction" (אחריתו עדי אבד). A life-force that is fundamentally rooted in emptiness can only end in ugly self-obsolescence and self-obliteration.

A beginning infused with meaning, the 'Reishis' of Yisrael points toward a *Tachlis* / purpose and an ultimate fullness. Amalek begins in vanity and ends in oblivion. Yisrael begins with intention and ends in the fulfillment of Hashem's will, the beautiful integrity of true Tachlis.

Where Amalek is cynicism, Klal Yisrael is faith.

Where Amalek is emptiness, Klal Yisrael is fullness.

Whereas Amalek ends in death, Klal Yisrael carries the seed of eternal life.

AMALEK IS APATHY AND COLDNESS

Amalek is, in fact, a force that is much deeper than 'enmity'. At its core, Amalek is the force of *Kar* / 'coldness' (עשה אותך קר כמים / "He (Amalek) made you cold like water": *Pesikta Rabbasi*, 12), the chill of spiritual apathy that turns on others to cool their passion and dull their faith. Amalek seeks to extinguish the flame of the soul in others, by whatever means. Thus, Amalek is likened both to cold water that douses the fire of inspiration, and to the 'heat' of wasting seed (Keri), a mode of misdirecting one's vital energy into emptiness (כתיב הכא אשר קרך וכתיב התם כי יהיה בך איש אשר לא יהיה טהור מקרה לילה: *Zohar* 2, 195a). Amalek will use whatever it can, sometimes the icy grip of cynicism or doubt, and other times the feverish lure of base desire, so long as it can cool or disconnect all fervor for *Kedushah* / holiness and meaning.

AMALEK IS COLDNESS AND APATHY TO ANYTHING HOLY AND MEANINGFUL

Amalek embodies the force of Kelipah, the negative, destructive energy whose purpose is to infect the hearts of Klal Yisrael with doubt in Hashem's Omnipotence and Omnipresence, and doubt in their sacred mission to make this world a "dwelling place for Hashem."

Our Sages liken Amalek's historical attack to a tub of scalding water into which no one dares enter, until another person leaps in before them. Though it badly burns him, Amalek jumps in first (*Reishis*), thereby cooling the water enough for others to follow (*Medrash Tanchuma*, Ki Teitzei, 9). When Klal Yisrael left Egypt and passed through the split Sea, they were ablaze with certainty and faith, in Hashem, in themselves, and in their mission. They knew where they had come from, where they were going, and what they were meant to accomplish in this world. They felt fully worthy to serve as conduits for the revelation of Hashem's Presence. Their identity was clear, their purpose unwavering, and their hearts burned with a fiery commitment to be ambassadors of Hashem's light on earth. Then Amalek came. Their physical attack was not only an act of war, but it was a calculated assault on the heart of Klal Yisrael. Amalek sought to diminish this heat of holiness, to cool the passion and spiritual fervor that had carried the people forward. Klal Yisrael still "knew" their higher purpose intellectually and could articulate their mission conceptually, but something had shifted.

The fire in their hearts was diminished, their enthusiasm muted. A subtle but disturbing separation had been introduced between the cool clarity of their minds and the blazing passion of their hearts.

ראשית גוים עמלק / "Amalek was the first of the nations..." (*Bamidbar*, 24:20). The first letters of these three words spell the word רגע / *Rega* / moment. In conversational Hebrew, the word *Rega* means 'Wait a moment.' Amalek whispers, 'Wait a minute, cool it, why are you getting so excited and passionate right now? Hold your horses, slow down, get real.'

Describing Amalek's first assault on Klal Yisrael, the Torah states: "Remember what Amalek did to you on your journey, after you left Egypt, אשר קרך בדרך / when he chanced upon you on the way when you were famished and weary, and cut down all the stragglers..." (*Devarim*, 25:17-18). The word קרך / *Karcha* / 'chanced' upon, denotes happenstance, a sense of randomness. This is the essence of Amalek: the belief that life is governed by coincidence, that nothing has purpose, nothing is sacred or truly meaningful. The Rambam writes that we should not, observing what is occurring in our life, simply say, נקרה נקרית / "This was merely happenstance" (*Hilchos Ta'anis,* 1:3). This is the way of Amalek, and is, as the Rambam adds, a "cruel" and an 'indifferent' way to look at life. To view the world as random is to deny the presence of Divine providence, of purpose and destiny, and it is to reduce life to a hollow carousel, spinning without direction, without redemption.

For this reason, every time Klal Yisrael prepares to build a Mikdash, a sacred, intentional space dedicated to revealing the Presence of HaKadosh Baruch Hu in this world, Amalek rises to attack. A

Mikdash proclaims that there is holiness in this world and that Creation has a definite purpose, and this is the greatest denial of Amalek's ideology of chaos and happenstance.

Amalek attacked Klal Yisrael when we were preparing to build the Mishkan in the wilderness, and he rose again in the days of King Shaul, right before they built the First Beis haMikdash. In the Purim story, Haman, a descendant and embodiment of Amalek, attempted to annihilate us just prior to the building (or completion) of the Second Beis haMikdash.

This pattern has tragically repeated itself in our times, with the Amalek of the 20th Century, and the Amalek of the 21st Century, may their names be blotted out, who unleashed unspeakable horrors upon our people, just before the dawn of the rebuilding of the Third Beis haMikdash, may it be built speedily in our days.

AMALEK IS DOUBT

The Jew as an individual and the Jewish People as a whole embody eternal hope, unwavering belief in possibility, in future, and in redemption. We are palpably charged with the sacred mission of revealing the inner goodness and light within life, to reveal the Divine Providence that stands behind Creation, flowing within even apparently random events. Amalek is the illusion of randomness, and thus cold apathy towards anything hopeful. When a person is filled with enthusiasm and clarity of purpose, Amalek appears and attempts to sell them a thought of corrosive doubt: 'Is it really possible? You are destined to fail. Why even try?'

This inner voice of doubt and uncertainty is paralyzing when purchased, preventing growth, stalling momentum, and distancing one from living with meaning, conviction, and *Simchah* / joy. Inwardly, every time a person feels ignited by a new project or a higher calling, the manipulative voice of Amalek tells them to douse the flames.

Just as Amalek attacks the individual, it targets the collective as well. Amalek aims to unravel the shared sense of mission within Klal Yisrael and to sow cynicism and indifference, and to replace forward movement with doubt, apathy, and conflict.

Amalek and the word *Safek* / doubt have the same numerical value (240). Amalek is thus *Makom haSafek* / "the place of doubt" (The Mishnah teaches, "The fittest of butchers is a partner of Amalek": *Kidushin* 82a. Rashi explains: ספיקי טריפות באות לידו... / "Doubts regarding unkosher foods come into his hand...." In other words, his trade inevitably exposes him to frequent uncertainty (Safek) in matters of Kashrus. From here, we see a deep connection between Amalek and Safek. The *Kelev* / wild dog is also symbolically linked to Safek: there is a debate ('doubt') in the Mishnah as to what type of animal a Kelev is, כלב מין חיה רבי מאיר אומר, מין בהמה / "'Is the dog a type of wild animal?' Rebbe Meir says, 'It is a domesticated animal'": Mishnah, *Kelayim*, 8:6. The very identity of the dog is subject to doubt. Furthermore, the Kelev is described as being insatiable: "And the dogs are greedy, they never know satiation" (*Yeshayahu*, 56:11). They are never certain whether they have eaten enough. And Amalek is likened to a *Kelev*... כך היה לוהט אחר עמלק אחר ישראל ככלב / "Amalek chased after Klal Yisrael like a dog": *Tanchuma*, Ki Teitzei, 9. "Amalek is like a Kelev": *Megaleh Amukos*, VaEschanan, 140).

Moshe commands Yehoshua, "Choose men for us, and go out to battle with Amalek, tomorrow, I will station myself on top of the hill" (*Shemos*, 17:9). Our Sages tell us that the word "tomorrow" is one of the five words in the Torah on which there is a *Safek* / doubt regarding where the word should be placed (*Yuma*, 52b). In other words, there is a doubt whether the Pasuk should read, 'Choose men for us, and go out to battle with Amalek *tomorrow*. I will station myself on top of the hill,' or, 'Choose men for us, and go out to battle with Amalek. *Tomorrow* I will station myself on top of the hill.' This grammatical ambiguity is not incidental; it reflects the very nature of the battle with Amalek. Amalek thrives by creating doubt and confusion. The entire confrontation with Amalek is shrouded in uncertainty, beginning with Moshe's command to Yehoshua, which is itself steeped in ambiguity.

HANDS LOWERED REPRESENTS NON-INTENTIONAL ACTIONS, HAPPENSTANCE

When the Torah describes Amalek's attack on Klal Yisrael, it states, ויבא עמלק וילחם עם־ישראל ברפידם / "Amalek came and fought with Klal Yisrael at Rephidim" (*Shemos*, 17:8). Why does the Torah emphasize the location of the battle? Chazal explain that the name 'Rephidim' hints at the inner cause of the attack: רפו ידיהם / their 'hands weakened' in fulfilling Torah and Mitzvos (*Tanchumah*, Yisro, 3:3. Note, the word רפו / *Rafu* and פור / *Pur* have the same letters). When Klal Yisrael's spiritual enthusiasm faltered, Amalek saw an opening and struck.

When a person's hands are left 'hanging', meaning they are not uplifted to the 'head' and not connected to Da'as, then the principle of ידיים עסקניות הן / "their hands are busy" applies. That is, hands left to their own devices naturally tend to come into contact with dirt or impure things (*Shabbos*, 14a. Rashi, *ad loc.*). "Busy hands" implies a kind of haphazard, unfocused activity, a state of restless motion lacking conscious direction or intentionality. This is a kind of disconnect between the mind and the body (Hence, the root letters of

Amalek are מלק, which are also the root letters of מליקה, a type of offering performed in the Beis haMikdash in which the head of a bird was detached from its body by the nail of the Cohen's thumb. Similarly, Amalek severs the 'head,' the intellect, from the rest of the body; thus, the "hands" act on their own without Da'as. Parenthetically, Haman in small numerical value is 14, as the word Yad, Hand. *Machberes haKodesh*, Sha'ar Purim).

As such, Moshe needed to create a Tikun for Klal Yisrael's weakened hands, and thus he waged battle with Amalek through his hands. The Torah tells us והיה כאשר ירים משה ידו וגבר ישראל / "And it was, whenever Moshe held up his hands, Israel prevailed" (Shemos, 17:11). Moshe lifted his hands upwards, near his head, the place of Da'as, and beyond, and when Klal Yisrael looked upwards, through Moshe's hands directing them to the Divine Presence Above, so to speak (Mishnah, end of *Rosh Hashanah*), Amalek could not prevail.

Similarly, the goal of Purim is to break the spell of Amalek, the worldview of happenstance, randomness, and disconnection. Purim lifts up our יד / *Yad* / hand (14/י"ד), upward toward Heaven. Hence, Purim (in most of the world) takes place on the Fourteenth of Adar, the Yad, the Hand raised to the level of Da'as, directing focus upwards to Heaven (What is more, it says that during the entire battle with Amalek, ויהי ידיו אמונה / "and his hands were steadfast": Shemos, 17:12. Moshe needs ידיו / his hands to be אמונה / *Emunah* / 'steadfast' to battle Amalek. Amalek is Safek, doubt, Moshe's praying and his hands uplifted created a world of ודאי / certainty, to counter the uncertainty of Amalek. The word ידיו / his hand, plus the letter Aleph / א for Emunah (אמונה) creates the word ודאי / certain).

On an even deeper level, Purim lifts our hands beyond Da'as, beyond mere 'conscious awareness', to a place where even the autopilot functioning of our body is holy, noble, and aligned with our soul.

Purim not only reconnects our hands to Da'as, but it also elevates them beyond Da'as, where our automatic and unconscious movements and actions come into sync with deep truth and Divine purpose. Here, the hands no longer need the supervision of the intellect, because they instinctively move toward the good and the holy. No longer are our hands עסקניות / busy in the negative sense, wandering aimlessly into impurity through 'random' motion. Instead, the hands and the body itself are revealed as vessels naturally inclined toward positivity and Mitzvos. Acts of holiness and kindness now emerge effortlessly, almost as if randomly, but from a place of inner alignment. This is the deeper meaning of *VeNahafoch Hu* / "It was turned around." There is a complete reversal: our hands, once instruments of distraction and randomness, are now instruments of purpose and meaning, conduits of Divine Providence.

The ultimate victory over Amalek is not merely when we act with conscious Da'as, but when even our unconscious actions align seamlessly with the soul, when holiness and goodness flow naturally through our body into the world, as if by second nature (although on the deepest level, as will be explored, it is the body's 'first nature').

This 'reversal' on Purim is hinted at in the Halacha, כל מי שפושט ידו ליטול נותנים לו / "We give to whomever extends their hand to receive." This statement reflects a generosity that transcends all judgment and evaluation, indiscriminate, spontaneous giving, what might appear to be 'random' acts of kindness. This is a revelation of a higher order, in which the human hand itself becomes a 'chariot' or instrument of the Divine will, and thus the true will of the soul.

As the Tanya (Chap. 23) describes it, the hand becomes a יד המחלק
צדקה / "a hand that distributes charity." The hand gives, not as a
conscious decision of Da'as, but as a natural outflow of its deepest
identity.*

THE MITZVOS / PRACTICES OF PURIM

There are four core Mitzvos uniquely associated with Purim:
1) reading the Megilah, 2) *Mishloach Manos* / sending portions of
food to a friend, 3) Distributing *Matanos laEvyonim* / gifts to the
poor, and 4) celebrating *Seudas Purim* / the festive Purim meal.

These four Mitzvos correspond to the four letters in Hashem's
Name. The two Heis represent the two acts of giving and receiving,
as Hei is a feminine letter, symbolizing the receiver. The higher Hei
of Hashem's Name is Mishloach Manos, which is enacted with a
receiver who may have enough to eat on their own but who behaves,
in this context, as a receiver. The lower Hei is Matanos laEvyonim,
a transaction with an actually poor receiver. Vav (ו) is like a pipe, a
channel transmitting a flow of energy. The Vav of Hashem's Name
is the Megilah reading, which begins with the letter Vav (ויהי) and
ends with a letter Vav (זרעו), reflecting the continuity and connec-

---

* As the word 'hand'/ יד has the numerical value of 14, it alludes to the Fourteenth of Adar,
when Purim is celebrated in unwalled cities. By contrast, the upper Name of Hashem י-ה
equals 15, corresponding to the Fifteenth of Adar, when Purim is celebrated in Shushan
and other ancient walled cities. On the Fifteenth, a deeper annihilation of Amalek took
place, with the eradication of Haman's extended family and the Amalekites that were
living in the capital itself. Yet even this was not the full revelation of Hashem's Name.
The complete Name Yud-Hei-Vav-Hei (numerically 26) will only be fully manifest when
Amalek is entirely erased from the world, and Divine Oneness is universally recognized.
Note that the name דוד / Dovid, as in King David, is also 14. The true kingdom belongs to
the house of Dovid, and there are three Mitzvos that we needed to do when we entered
the Land: to anoint a king and then to eradicate Amalek. See Rambam, *Hilchos Melachim*,
1.

tive narrative of Divine Providence throughout the story. Yud is the smallest letter, like a hand (Yad) pointing upwards. The Yud in Hashem's Name is Seudas Purim, the feast which directs us to the supra-rational joy of Ad d'Lo Yada, a joy that transcends Da'as. The joy of Purim soars beyond the mind into the realm of absolute Emunah, the realm of Chochmah, and even Keser, the crown above all comprehension.*

---

* Alternatively, the four Mitzvos of Purim mirror the four letters of the Divine Name, Yud-Hei-Vav-Hei in the following way (*Machshevos Charutz*, 6): *Megilah* corresponds to the letter Yud, the point of Chochmah, Torah, and Higher Mind. *Matanos laEvyonim* corresponds to the upper Hei, Binah and understanding, the expansive act of giving and bringing a little 'freedom' to those in need. Hei is numerically five, alluding to the open hand with its five fingers, giving to another whose hand opens with five fingers to receive. *Mishloach Manos* corresponds to the Vav, the channel of the six emotional attributes, an expression of love, connection (as Vav is connection), and heart. *Seudas Purim* corresponds to the final Hei, Malchus, the realm of action and embodiment, joy expressed in the body. Beyond these four stands the higher calling of Purim of *Ad d'Lo Yada* / transcending reasoning, corresponding to the Kotzo Shel Yud, the crown above the letters, the level of Keser, 'beyond mind'.

The four Mitzvos also parallel the four expressions in the Megilah (8:6), "Light, happiness, joy, and glory." Chazal teach (*Megilah*, 16b) that "light" refers to Torah, "happiness" to Yom Tov, "joy" to *Bris Milah* / circumcision, and "glory" to Tefilin.

Torah is Light and the letter Yud (Chochmah). Happiness is Yom Tov, the upper Hei, the expanded consciousness we experience on Yom Tov (the idea of Yom Tov is Binah and Da'as, as explained). Joy is the Mitzvah of Bris Milah, connected with the lined letter Vav, the procreative body part of Yesod. Glory is the Mitzvah of Tefilin, the final Hei, Malchus, that also becomes the 'crown' over all lower realms. Tefilin is our crown and the 'signet' of the King that we bear.

Additionally, it can be said that since the evil decree was להשמיד להרג ולאבד את־כל־היהודים ושללם לבוז... / "to destroy (spiritual destruction) massacre (physical destruction), and exterminate all the Jews (their remembrance)... and to plunder their possessions" (even the memory of what they owned) (3:13), there are four Mitzvos to counter those four evil acts:

• The Seudah is to counter the decreed physical destruction.

• Reading the Megilah (Torah) counters the decree of spiritual destruction.

MEGILAH READING

With the onset of Purim, on Purim Eve, the very first Mitzvah we fulfill is the Megilah reading. Although the daytime reading is considered the primary fulfillment of the Mitzvah (*Tosefos*, Megilah 4a. S*hu'T Noda b'Yehudah*, Orach Chayim, 41), the nighttime reading remains essential. According to some opinions, the Shehecheyanu blessing is recited only during the nighttime reading, as it marks the beginning of the Purim observances (The Mechaber writes that we do not recite Shehecheyanu by day, while the Rama that rules we do: וביום אינו חוזר ומברך שהחיינו: (הגה) וי"א אף ביום מברך שהחיינו. Even though the Alter Rebbe rules in the Siddur like the Mechaber, the Tzemach Tzedek rules like the Rama).

The Yamim Tovim are not merely nostalgic celebrations of monumental moments in our national history. They are each eternally relevant, illuminating every person in every time and place. Also, if we were to celebrate every miraculous event in Jewish history, our calendar would be overflowing with Yamim Tovim. Clearly, then, we have enshrined as Yamim Tovim only those events whose spiritual resonance continues to echo into the present, those whose breakthroughs recur each year. Take Pesach, for example, although the Exodus occurred thousands of years ago, we continue to celebrate it on the night of the Exodus because the very same force of liberation that was revealed then becomes accessible again each year on that same date. Likewise, Purim is not only a retelling of a past miracle; rather, it is a portal into the redemptive energies that were revealed then and are once again available now (*Kedushas Levi*,

• Mishloach Manos, bonding with others of Klal Yisrael, counters negation of our remembrance and connects us to the *Nitzchiyus* / eternity of Klal Yisrael.

• Matanos laEvyomim demonstrates our ownership of our material things, so much so that we can give them away to another.

Kedushah Rishonah, Chanukah). Although the literal events of the past are not reenacted each year, as there is not always a Haman or a Queen Esther in the physical sense, yet on a deeper, metaphysical plane, the very same *Hashpa'os* / the spiritual influences and transmissions are present and just as real in our time as they were in the original stories.

The conduit for these transmissions is the Torah itself, the inner structure and blueprint of Creation. When we read the story of Purim from a Megilah, we do not merely recall the events intellectually; we draw down the very power that enabled those events. The act of remembering through the reading reawakens the original channels of miracle and redemption. The Chozeh of Lublin taught that when we read and recite the narrative of the Exodus from Egypt and the attendant miracles and wonders that occurred, we too will experience a personal Exodus from all of our constrictions. In his words, "Through the recitation of the letters in the Torah that speak about the miracle, we awaken the source of the miracle itself" (*Zos Zikaron*, Beshalach).

When the Torah describes the Splitting of the Sea, the Going out of Egypt, or the miraculous appearance of the Manna, for example, the Torah is not merely describing the events that occurred physically. Rather, the Torah is articulating and invoking the spiritual Source of the event, and because there is a spiritual arousal of the event Above, there is also a correlating effect Below. For this reason, reading the Torah's description of Klal Yisrael going out of Egypt gives us the strength to go out of our own personal 'Egypts', and draws down redemptive potentials to be redeemed from all forms of inner and outer oppression and limitation (*Chasam Sofer Al haTorah*, Eikev, 7:17).

Parenthetically, this spiritual dynamic can also work in reverse, to counteract negativity. For example, if a person struggles with inappropriate desire, he can visualize the words of the Torah "You shall not covet," as if they were inscribed on the screen of his inner vision, and repeat these words aloud (*Ohr haGanuz LaTzadikim*, Parshas Yisro. *Darchei Tzedek*, 1:11). Through the visualization and verbalization of these words, the power to overcome the impulse is drawn down.

So too, when we recall the events of Purim through the Megilah reading, the revelation is not just remembered, it is re-lived. The same spiritual influence that once brought about redemption is reawakened and made present. "These days of Purim," says the Megilah, are meant to be נזכרים ונעשים / "remembered and performed" (9:28). This is because through "remembering" (reading the Megilah), those original days of Purim are reactivated, re-achieved, and thus "performed" in the present. The act of commemoration brings about acts of celebration, and the same powers are reactivated every year, anew (*Kedushas Levi*, Kedushah Rishonah).

THE GRAGGER

At times, peripheral elements or objects, details that seem secondary, take on a symbolic weight that far surpasses the central event itself. When most people, certainly young people, think of Purim, the imagery that comes to mind is that of masks and Graggers, the iconic noisemakers used to blot out the name of Haman during the Megilah reading.

There are no accidents. In fact, the very essence of the Purim story teaches us that nothing is coincidental. Everything is orchestrated by Divine Providence, even when it appears as a random sequence of natural events. This is, in fact, the core revelation of Purim. Behind the mask of chance and outer circumstances lies the ever-guiding Hand of Hashem.

With this in mind, we can explore the Gragger more deeply, not just as a festive toy, but as a vessel of meaning and even a mystical symbol. The Gragger consists of a thin handle, usually made of wood or plastic, which supports a broader structure at its top. When twirled, it produces a whirring, rattling sound, aggressive, almost defiant. Viewed symbolically, the physical form of the Gragger reflects one of the deepest themes of Purim, as explored earlier, the drawing down of the Makif, the encompassing, transcendent light, into the Pnimi, the inner and integrated. The broader, upper part that twirls represents the expansive, transcendent realm, the surrounding or encircling Light. The narrow, stationary stick below represents the defined and directed channel through which the higher reality enters the lower reality. The energy of the circular movement above descends into the stationary stick, pointed downwards, and held in the hand of the receiver. The flow trickles downward, penetrating its truth on all levels of reality.

And yet, the stick is held in the hand of the one turning the noisemaking element above, symbolizing that the activation of the descent of the Makif begins with an awakening from below. As the movement of the Gragger is produced by the hand below, the Purim miracle was initiated by an awakening of human beings, below. We became inspired and awakened to transform ourselves, and as a result, we 'moved the Heavens', transforming the negative decree to a Yom Tov of joy and celebration. This is the deeper truth of Purim: unlike miracles that descend from Heaven unprompted, the miracle of Purim was initiated by us, through our Teshuvah, fasting, prayer, and courageous inner transformation. The movement of the Gragger is set in motion by the human hand, teaching us that the redemptive flow of Divine energy was drawn down through our own spiritual arousal below.

Each time we hear Haman's name and spin the Gragger, we affirm the defeat of Amalek and his chaos, undoing all evil decrees. Haman sought to access the Makif in its raw, unstructured form, a place beyond moral order where good and evil are blurred. But the miracle of Purim was the redirection of that very force into a redemptive channel, for the good. The Makif was internalized and brought into Penimi, overturning impending tragedy and despair, and turning them into triumphant ecstasy.

This brings us to another fascinating contrast, the Gragger on Purim with the other known traditional 'toy', the Dreidel of Chanukah. On the surface, these seem similar. They are both spinning toys connected with a Yom Tov. Yet a closer look reveals a meaningful symbolic inversion.

The Gragger is held below and it spins above, only the top spinning, while the handle remains stationary. In contrast, the Dreidel is held by a 'stick' and spun from above, and its entire body spins. These differences mirror the nature of the respective Yamim Tovim.

Chanukah was a miracle from Above, an open, supernatural, and visibly transcendent miracle. The laws of nature were suspended, the laws of nature were cast aside so that a small group of fighters were able to defeat a large army, and that a tiny jug of oil, barely able to last for one night, lasted eight nights. Accordingly, the

Dreidel is held from above and spins completely, the above and the below. Everything is in motion. Heaven touches earth in a revealed way, and nature itself spins in a miraculous, new way.

Purim was a miracle within nature. Nothing overtly supernatural occurred. The events unfolded through human actions, coincidences, and political intrigue. Mordechai overheard a plot. Esther became queen. The king couldn't sleep. And the hidden Divine orchestration became clear only in retrospect. The miracle was embedded in nature. Thus, in the Gragger, only the top spins, and it is held from below. The bottom remains still, as nothing really changes in nature. On the surface, all appears normal, unchanged. Yet, from above, a hidden motion stirs everything.

The central theme of Purim is that while life may at times appear chaotic and random, each event seemingly disconnected from the next, in truth, everything is interwoven and Divinely orchestrated. There are two ways of seeing: from the 'lower', limited perspective, life appears fragmented and unmoored, devoid of a single unifying thread, yet, from the 'higher' level of perception, every moment is guided by precise Divine providence. This duality is beautifully illustrated in the simple act of holding a Gragger: the upper piece spins in rapid motion, circling from east to north, to west, to south, linking every point until, at a certain speed, all movement seems to vanish. What was seen to be turning from one distinct direction to another now merges into a single blur, encompassing every direction at once, revealing the hidden Unity that was there all along.

SQUARES & CIRCLES

The top part of the Gragger, the part that spins, is a rectangle

— conceptually a square. If this 'square' were to be spun from the bottom extremely quickly, what was once 'square' would blur into the appearance of a circle.

A circle has no beginning or end, no corners or distinct points; it flows endlessly, representing continuity and unity. A square is defined by its sides and corners. Each side has a clear beginning and end, and each corner marks a distinct direction in space. The square, then, is marked by separation and structure, with multiple definable points along its perimeter. The circle resists definition by nature. No point on its circumference can truly stand apart or be isolated, for any point is part of the same continuous flow, the same whole.

In this way, the square symbolizes the finite and definition, boundaries, and limitations. The circle symbolizes the infinite and undefinable, or the breaking of boundaries and the transcendence of limitation. On Purim, we dissolve the rigid limitations of 'square-consciousness' and transform them into the paradigm of the circle. By 'spinning ourselves' in joy on Purim, we break through the confines of our identification with rigid form and lose ourselves in a boundless realm of joy, identifying only with unity and essence. The effect of this is a 'blotting out' of Amalek's name and influence.

PROSE VS. POETRY

The square represents prose, the linear, structured, and objective narrative of our lives. The circle, by contrast, evokes poetry, the non-linear, fluid, and deeply subjective experience that pulses beneath the surface.

Law and strict order is square or linear, whereas music and poetry are more circular. The objectively true law of the Written Torah is absolute and linear, and yet the Written Torah is also called a *Shirah* / song, and *Shir* means 'song' and 'circle'. The Pasuk says, ועתה כתבו לכם את־השירה הזאת / "And now, write down this Shirah" (*Devarim*, 31:19). This is the Mitzvah to write the entire Torah, not just the particular poem or song expressed in that Torah reading (Rashi), but to write the entire Torah (Rambam, *Hilchos Tefilin, Mezuzah v'Sefer Torah*, 7:1 (*Sanhedrin*, 21b). See *Tzafnas Paneach*, ad loc. ע"כ כונת התורה דצריך. לכתוב התורה כולה ונ"מ אם בלתה התורה ונשתיירה השירה אם יצא: *Sha'agas Aryeh*, Siman 34. Shir means 'circle'... כשיר מהו: *Baba Metziya*, 25a. The word *Shir* in Hebrew and Aramaic means 'a piece of round jewelry' like a bracelet: *Yeshayahu*, 3:19. *Targum*, Bereishis, 24:22. Mishnah, *Shabbos*, 51b: וסוס בשיר וכל בעלי השיר יוצאין בשיר ונמשכין בשיר).

In this sense, the entire Torah is called a Shirah, a song, even though its primary form is not poetic verse, but rather law and instruction. The word Torah itself derives from Hora'ah, meaning guidance or directive. This guidance is expressed through clarity, structure, and law, an absolute and objective framework. Law is fixed, impersonal, and linear; its path is straight, its boundaries defined. Song, music, and poetry, by contrast, are fluid and subjective. They move in circles, not lines, personal, expressive, and open-ended. Thus, the Torah holds both dimensions: it is at once a legal document and a living song; a structure of truth and a flow of spirit, binding and liberating, all at once.

TOP DOWN VS. BOTTOM UP

In a more specific way, the Written Torah is primarily associated with the line or square, structured, defined, and linear, while *Torah*

She-b'Al Peh / the Oral Torah corresponds to the circle; it is fluid, expansive, and ever-evolving. The Written Torah reflects a top-down paradigm; Divine revelation descending into the world in clear, immutable form. The Oral Torah, however, emerges through a bottom-up process, human engagement, questioning, interpretation, and response. As will be further explained, this bottom-up movement naturally aligns with the mode of 'circles'.

The Written Torah, which we accept with humility and reverence, is imposed from on High, and one is obligated to follow it. Yet, the Oral Torah, teachings that originate in the hearts and minds of the Sages 'Below', ultimately loop back into the top-down revelation from 'Above'. As explored earlier, these teachings become recognized as part of the Divine transmission that began at Sinai. In this way, the Oral Torah blurs the line between past and present, much like a circle that has no beginning or end.

Perhaps the most profound expression of 'Circle Torah' is found in the collective poetry of Klal Yisrael, as enacted through our *Minhagim* / sacred customs. These inspired practices, our heartfelt embellishments, the nuanced ways we choose to celebrate our Yiddishkeit and express our identity as servants of the Eternal, arise organically from Below, yet they too loop back, retroactively, into the original revelation at Mount Sinai. In this way, Minhagim complete the circle of Torah, weaving present devotion into the eternal tapestry of Divine revelation.

Minhagim rise up from within our collective, deepest, holy subconsciousness. Klal Yisrael possesses a 'collective prophetic soul', an unconscious spiritual intuition that channels Divine will into lived expression (אם אין נביאים הן בני נביאים הן / "If they are not prophets, they are the children of prophets": *Pesachim*, 66a). Hence, when an authentic Minhag arises, it is not merely a cultural expression, but rather an expression of Torah from Sinai (note Rambam, *Hilchos Mamrim*, 1:2). In the words of the Rishonim, מנהג ישראל תורה היא / "A custom of Yisrael *is* Torah."* This statement does not specify 'a Minhag of the Sages or learned people'; rather, it means the customs of the collective K'neses Yisrael, the People of Yisrael. For within the 'collective prophetic soul' of the nation lies a wellspring of prophecy, and what the People, in their holy sincerity, choose to do in service of Hashem, carries within it the resonance of revelation.

CIRCLES AND MINHAG

From deep within the prophetic imagination of the Jewish soul, the Circle Reality emerges most vividly through the realm of popular customs. There are two fully Rabbinic Yamim Tovim: Purim and Chanukah. Yet another celebration has emerged, not through formal Rabbinic enactment, but through the collective spiritual instinct of the People, and that is Simchas Torah (Though it is not technically a Rabbinic Yom Tov and deserving of its own blessings, Simchas Torah is mentioned in the Zohar and recorded by the Geonim over a millennium ago). Strikingly, the customs on these special days, Purim, Chanukah, and Simchas Torah, are all centered around the symbolic act of making circles around squares or converting squares into circles.

---

* Tosefos, on *Menachos*, 20b, write: ומנהג אבותינו תורה היא / "The custom of our ancestors (*Tosefos* refers to the French Ashkenaz Sages) is Torah." See Ritva on *Pesachim*, 105a. Rosh on *Pesachim*, 10:13. *Tur*, Orach Chayim, 591 (The Ramban writes [*Pesachim*, 7b], regarding the customs of the morning blessings: ומנהג ישראל תורה היא / "and the custom of Yisrael is Torah"). For hundreds of years now, a popular version of this statement is מנהג ישראל תורה היא / "The custom of Yisrael is Torah." This does not say 'the custom of our ancestors', i.e., in the context of Tosefos, this particularly refers to the customs of Ashkenaz, rather, 'the custom of Klal Yisrael', all of Klal Yisrael.

Squares, like lines, are associated with routine and obligations, the things we *must* do. Circles, the non-linear pulsing of the heart, represent the things we *want* to do, like spontaneous gestures of love. You may joyfully choose to cook a beautiful meal, but then comes the clean-up, the obligatory follow-through. Torah She-b'Al Peh, and even more pointedly, Minhag, the cherished customs of our people, represent the offerings we relish giving to our Beloved, our Creator. We offer these not because we are 'obligated', but because we yearn to do so. These customs are born not of duty, but of joy and devotion. Minhagim, moreover, sustain and uplift our experiences of our obligatory deeds. They infuse even the most structured aspects of Torah with inspiration, vitality, and joy, transforming what we *have* to do into what we *love* to do.

Parenthetically, this is also the deeper reason why Purim is so rich with customs, such as dressing up, putting on Purim plays, or centuries ago, a custom of jumping over fire pits or burning effigies of Haman (The Avudraham writes, כתוב בערוך שמנהג שמנהג בבבל ועילם כל הבחורים עושים צורה בדמות המן קודם פורים ותולין אותה על גגותיהם ימים ובימי הפורים עושין מדורה ותולין אותה הצור' לתוכה ועומדין סביבה ומזמרין ויש להם טבעת תלויה בתוך האש שתולין בה הצורה וקופצין מצד האש לצד האחר: *Avudraham*, Purim, 25. The Gemara speaks of a fire pit and jumping over the pit on Purim ...משוורתא דפוריא: *Sanhedrin*, 64b, Rashi. Regarding dressing up, see *Shu'T Mahari Mintz*, 16. Rama, Orach Chayim, 690:17. *Elyah Rabbah*, 696. Although, regarding Maseches Purim, see *Shu'T Devar Shmuel*, 193. *Ba'eir Heitiv*, Orach Chayim, 696:13).

On Purim, we re-accepted the Torah, yet this time not under coercion, as at Sinai with the mountain suspended over our heads, but out of love, joy, and willing devotion. And love is most fully expressed not in doing just what is formally commanded, but in taking upon ourselves additional voluntary acts. A Mitzvah fulfills an obligation; a Minhag overflows from the heart. Customs are the intimate gestures of the relationship between us and HaKadosh Baruch Hu, acts and gestures that are not strictly required, yet are cherished precisely because they arise from love. Thus, Purim, as the festival of love-filled acceptance, naturally abounds with customs, each one a spontaneous expression of love and joy.

DREIDEL, HAKAFOS, GRAGGER

On Chanukah, there is a beloved informal Minhag of playing with a Dreidel. Though it is certainly not a Rabbinic Mitzvah, this custom holds deep meaning and significance. The Dreidel, a four-sided spinning top, begins as a square. But when it is set into joyful motion and spins rapidly, its rigid shape blurs, transforming into a 'circle'. In that moment, we turn a square into a circle, structure into flow, obligation into delight.

Simchas Torah also has a very pronounced theme of circling connected with squares. Simchas Torah is steeped in the profound symbolism of circling the square. The Bimah in the Shul is traditionally shaped as a square, like the *Mizbe'ach* / Altar in the Beis haMikdash. This is also where the Written Torah, from the world of lines or squares, is read. By dancing in circles around the Bimah, we encompass a square with circles. Our 'poetry', so to speak, is revealed as the *Makif* / encompassing light around the linear 'prose' of the Written Law. Dancing with a rolled-up, closed Torah scroll is also a way of making lines and squares into circles. The *Kesav* / script of the Torah is laid out in pre-indented, precise, horizontal lines on the parchment, called *Sirtut*, etched upon rectangular parchments. Sirtutim are etched into the parchments in order to ensure that all the letters stay aligned; it is of utmost importance for the letters of the Torah to be 'in line'. When Torah is open and being read, one sees lines on a rectangle. On Simchas Torah, when we are dancing with the Torah scroll rolled up, the horizontal lines that once stretched across the page are coiled into tight spirals. The straight lines become curves. The rectangle becomes a scroll. The square becomes a circle. We dance in a circle around a square Bimah, carrying a closed Torah scroll, whose lines are now circles. In this sacred circling, we reveal a deeper truth: that even within structure lies Infinite flow, and that the heart of Torah is not only to be read and intellectually understood, but to be danced and lived in real life.

And of course, there is the Gragger, a joyful expression of the theme of circularity that infuses all of Purim. From the wine that causes a loss of balance, to the loosening of the rigid boundaries of reason, to Mishloach Manos, where we send gifts of food to one another, in a 'cycle' of giving and receiving, all 'linear' forms of giving are becoming circles.

Even the Megilah, which recounts the Purim story in the form of a text, carries this quality. The Megilah tells a linear narrative, yet the Megilah is called an *Igeres* / a letter and is rolled and closed into a tight spiral. The narrative actually has circular properties, as well, such as a 'loop' mentioned before: Achashverosh listens to the advice of his counselor (Haman) and decides to execute his wife (Vashti). Then he listens to the advice of his wife (Esther) and decides to execute his counselor (Haman). When Haman built a gallows for Mordechai, he thought it would bring the 'linear' result he wanted, but it turned back upon his head, and he was executed on the same gallows. When the Jewish People made *Teshuvah* /

'returned' to the Torah, they changed their linear trajectory, which would have led to their destruction, and instead circled back to who they really are, and came around to a fresh start with a 'new Matan Torah'.

WINE VS. OIL

Beyond the simple imagery of the Dreidel on Chanukah and the Gragger on Purim, these two Yamim Tovim also express their contrasting themes through the very substances most closely associated with them, oil and wine respectively. On Chanukah, the miracle was wrought through oil. Oil enough to burn for only a single night endured for eight nights, illuminating the darkness with an otherworldly light. For this reason, the ideal way to fulfill the Mitzvah of lighting the Menorah is specifically with oil. Accordingly, all of Chanukah is deeply bound with oil, not only in the Menorah, but also in its customs and celebrations, as reflected in the traditional foods of the Yom Tov, such as latkes and donuts, all of which echo this central theme of oil. Purim, by contrast, is intimately bound with wine; the meals in the story of the Megilah revolve around wine, and one of the central Mitzvos of the day is to drink wine until reaching the state of Ad d'Lo Yada.

The difference between these two fluids is striking. Oil naturally rises, always floating above, pointing Heavenward, signifying transcendence and ascent, and the world of miracles, Above. Wine, however, like most liquids, flows downward, seeking the lowest point. Yet on Purim, this downward movement is not a descent in the negative sense. We are not to drink wine in a way that debases, depresses, or endarkens us. Wine penetrates and saturates, its effects reaching into the Tachton, the lower realms within us, and the natural world, transforming them, opening their wellsprings of joy and making their inner, essential Light shine: *LaYehudim Haysa Orah v'Simchah... /* "For the Jews there was Light and joy...."

MISHLOACH MANOS: OFFERING FOODS TO FRIENDS

During the course of the day we fulfill two beautiful Mitzvos of connection: *Mishloach Manos /* gifts of foods to a friend or friends, and *Matanos laEvyonim /* gifts to the poor. Both of these acts are expressions of the very essence of Purim, revealing the oneness of Klal Yisrael, that we are *Am Echad /* one people.

Haman says, ישנו עם־אחד / "There is a certain people scattered and dispersed..." (*Esther*, 3:8). The term ישנו / *Yeshno /* "There is" can also be read as *Yashnu*, meaning 'asleep'. Haman was subtly referencing not only the Jewish People's dormancy, as they were asleep from performing Mitzvos (ישנו מן המצוות: *Megilah*, 13b. Maharsha, ad loc. Note Maharal, *Ohr Chadash* 3:8), but also, as the Medrash teaches אלקיהם של אלו ישן הוא / "The G-d of these people *Yashen /* is asleep" (see *Esther Rabbah*, 7:12). The Ohr haChayim haKadosh revealed that these Pesukim can be read as a dialogue and conversation between Haman and haKadosh Baruch Hu (*Rishon l'Tziyon*, ad loc.). Haman says, ישנו / 'There is, there is a people asleep, with their G-d asleep,' and Hashem answers, 'No, עם־אחד / *Am Echad /* they are one people, connected to the One (Haman says, מפזר ומפרד בין העמים / 'They are spread out among the nations.' And Hashem says, 'No, בכל מדינות מלכותך / in all their lands and dwellings that are always connected to the King of the world.' This way of reading the Megilah continues. The Ohr haChayim writes that he heard the basic idea from the Heavenly Academy. The *Kesem Ofir*, 3:8, expands on this idea).

Beyond Am Echad, we are a *Goy Echad* / a singular nation (*Shmuel* 2, 7:23). The word *Goy* shares a root with the word *G'viyah* / body, as in, "Nothing remains before my Lord, except גויתנו / our bodies..." (*Bereishis*, 47:18). Indeed, Klal Yisrael is like one Guf, one body. In the words of the Ritva, כל ישראל ערבין זה לזה וכלם כגוף אחד / "All of Klal Yisrael are responsible for each other, and all of them are like one body" (Ritva, *Rosh Hashanah*, 29a. Klal Yisrael is like a *Guf Echad* / single body with one *Nefesh* / soul, *Mechilta,* Rashbi, Yisro, 19:6. Maharal, *Nesivos Olam*, Nesivos haTochacha, 2. When speaking about the Mitzvah not to take revenge, our Sages use the analogy of one hand of a person doing something negative, and the other hand absurdly slapping it for doing so: Yerushalmi, *Nedarim*, 9:4. Klal Yisrael is likened to a sheep, similar to a sheep when one part of the body hurts the entire body hurts: *Medrash Rabbah*, Vayikra, 4:6.

Klal Yisrael is like a Guf Echad, especially once they went into the "One Land," Eretz Yisrael. *Shu'T Avnei Neizer*, Yoreh De'ah, 126:4. *Shu'T Tzefnas Paneach* 1, 143:2. Maharal, *ibid.*, *Nesiv haTzedakah*, 6. Note the opinion of the Noda b'Yehudah, *Tzlach*, Berachos, 20b, that Kohanim do not have *Arvus* / responsibility to Yisraelim, perhaps because Kohanim do not have a portion in Eretz Yisrael, and Arvus is connected with living in one land).

Just as a singular body is composed of multiple limbs, so too Klal Yisrael is made up of many individuals, each with their own role, personality, and place in the world. Hence, our celebration of Purim reflects this unity-in-diversity; some observe it on the Fourteenth of Adar, and others on the Fifteenth. When Haman approached Achashverosh with his wicked plot, he declared: "There is a nation that is, *Mefuzar u'Meforad* / scattered and dispersed" (3:8). His accusation was not only that the Jews were different, but that they were divided, they were splintered as a people. In his mind, their lack of physical and internal cohesion meant they were spiritually weak.

Yet the truth is precisely the opposite: though the Jewish People may be "dispersed" across the globe, "scattered" across different lands and cultures, at our core we remain one indivisible essence, a single living body. The very acts of Purim, seeking out a friend to send food to, or a poor person to assist, are not merely acts of kindness; they are affirmations of our shared identity. These acts reveal the threads that weave us into a single, unified body. Even the word *Manah* / מנה (portion), the singular of *Manos*, contains a hidden message, as it shares the same letters as Haman / המן. By giving two Manos to a friend, we symbolically overturn Haman's claim that we are fundamentally disconnected. We show our unity and replace Haman's conception of disunity with an outpouring of unity and love.

While Mishloach Manos speaks of unity, the term *Matanos laEvyonim* underscores this point further. If what is given to the poor is 'charity', the Megilah should have said *Tzedakah laEvyonim* / 'charity to the poor', but it uses the word *Matanos* / gifts instead. There is a marked distinction between giving a gift and giving Tzedakah.

Actually, the word *Tzedakah* is more precisely translated as 'righteousness'. The Mitzvah of Tzedakah is also to give to the poor, but not out of kindness, rather just because it is the 'right' thing to do. For all intents and purposes, money given to the poor actually belongs to the poor. It is merely that you were chosen as the conduit for the other person's blessings, and as a custodian of their money until it reaches them, the 'rightful' owner. Giving a present, on the other hand, is an act of pure kindness, reaffirming the unity, and showing a desire to reach out to another and help them. Giving presents to the poor on Purim, and not merely Tzedakah, we go beyond justice to express a deeper truth: we are one. Their joy is our joy; their lack is our lack, and in that giving, the illusion of separation fades. In doing this Mitzvah we step into the essence of Purim, where disunity is overturned, and we are revealed once more as *Goy Echad* / one people, like one body with one heart (This is a subtle comparison with Matan Torah, where we received the Torah because we were "like one person with one heart." On Purim we again reveal our oneness, and we joyfully re-receive the Torah).

A DEEPER KAVANAH FOR MATANOS LAEVYONIM & MISHLOACH MANOS

Let us now explore more deeply the Penimiyus, the inner dimension of these extraordinary Mitzvos of Purim, beginning with words from *Kisvei Arizal* / The Writings of the Arizal (*Pri Eitz Chayim*, Sha'ar Rosh Chodesh, Chanukah Purim, 6. This is not from the Arizal himself, rather it is deduced from his teachings. עד כאן הגיעו דרושי הרב זלה"ה וענין משלוח מנות איש לרעהו לא נתבארו מפי הרב ז"ל: *Sh'ar haKavanos*, Derushei Chag haPurim).

Here is the holy Arizal's teaching in its literal translation: "The Sages said that one is required to give two מנות / *Manos* / portions to one person and two מתנות / *Matanos* / gifts to two poor individuals. Why this distinction? And why is it that the word *Manos* (portions) contains only one letter Tav (מנות), whereas *Matanos* (gifts) is spelled with two Tavs (מתנות)? It is known that the attribute of Yesod is called *Ish* / man (as it is a masculine position of giving and transmission), and the essence of Purim is the revelation of the Yesod of Abba (Father / Masculine / Chochmah), when clothed within the Yesod of Ima (Mother / Feminine / Binah). Therefore, *Manos* contains only one Tav, as Tav is associated with *Nukva* / feminine (Tav is connected with Malchus, the receiver, which is feminine), in the way of two portions (as Malchus has two levels, the upper level of Leah and the lower level of Rochel)... And it says, איש לרעהו / "A man (gives) to his fellow," symbolizing the Yesod of Abba reaching towards the Yesod of Ze'ir Anpin, and although Abba is greater, when descending to an even lower level, the level of the Yesod of Ze'ir Anpin, it becomes referred to as "his fellow" (an equal). Whereas מתנות לאביונים / "gifts to the poor" is the drawing down of the level of Ima (mother, Binah), and thus there are two Tavs (in *Matanos*). It is the feminine side, expressing the double aspect of the feminine (receiver), and there are two gifts to two poor people. These two gifts are given to two poor individuals, who correspond to the lower Sefiros of Netzach and Hod, who (in comparison to the higher Sefiros) are poor" ענין משלוח מנות - אמרו רז"ל

שתי מנות לאיש א' וב' מתנות לשני האביונים. גם יש לדעת, למה ברעהו אמר מנות בתי"ו אחד, ומתנות לאביונים בב' תוי"ן. אמנם כבר ידעת, כי היסוד נקרא איש, ועיקר הארה יום זה, הוא גלוי יסוד אבא, והוא זכר בהיותו מלובש תוך היסוד דאמא, לכן אמר מנות בתי"ו אחד לבד, כי תי"ו הוא מצד הנוקבא, באופן שהם ב' מנות... ואמר איש לרעהו, איש שהוא יסוד אבא, לרעהו שהוא יסוד ז"א, כי אם היות אבא גדול, בהיותו יורד למקום היסוד ז"א נקרא רעהו...ומתנות לאביונים שהם מצד אמא, ולכן הם בב' תוי"ן, כי הם מצד הנוקבא, והם ב' מתנות לשני אביונים, שהם נצח הוד, שהם אביונים).

Let us now unpack this idea and give a practical *Kavanah* / intention for giving Mishloach Manos and Matanos laEvyonim on Purim. In the writings of the Arizal, the giver of Tzedakah on Purim, and in particular the Gabai Tzedakah, the one entrusted with collecting and distributing funds to the poor on Purim, is portrayed as the Mashpia, the channel of bestowal. More precisely, he is associated with the attribute of Yesod of Ze'ir Anpin, the masculine, transmitting force. In the moment of giving, he channels blessing and abundance downward, bestowing it upon Malchus, the feminine, receptive dimension, embodied by the poor person.

In every single interaction with the world around us, this dynamic of Yesod and Malchus is at play. Yesod is the giver, the one who extends and transmits, while Malchus is the receiver, the one who accepts and integrates. For example, in a conversation between two people, when one speaks, that person embodies Yesod, while the listener becomes Malchus. When the roles reverse, and the other person speaks, the former speaker now becomes Malchus, receiving from the other's Yesod. The same is true in countless subtle ways. When you touch an object, you are Yesod, imprinting upon it through contact, while the object itself is Malchus, receiving that touch. Conversely, when something impresses itself upon you, when you listen, are moved, or are affected by an experience, you become Malchus, receiving from the Yesod of the world around you.

All acts of giving that we perform on Purim contribute to the overall rectification of the relationship between the Yesod and Malchus in this world, and the Avodah that we do below is reflected Above, in the Yesod and Malchus in the Upper Worlds.

MATANOS LAEVYONIM: GIVING GIFTS TO THE POOR

In general, it is essential for the Mashpia to be discerning about to whom they give and how they give. This is because Malchus, being merely a vessel, can be vulnerable and susceptible to *Yenikah l'Chitzonim* / a "siphoning" or leakage to external, negative forces. In such a state, the flow intended for holiness and connection can be diverted and drawn into unholy vessels, causing what is given to be misdirected or diminished.

In fact, unfocused or misdirected giving not only squanders what is bestowed, but also drains the vitality and life-force of the giver. This occurs when the Yesod energy of the Mashpia is diverted into an unproductive vessel, rather than being received and internalized in holiness and connectivity. The result is twofold: the intended recipient is left with nothing of substance, and the giver emerges feeling empty and depleted.

Moreover, even when the gift reaches a proper recipient, if the act of giving is motivated by self-centered reasons, whether subtle, concealed, or overt, it will lead to a profound state of inner depletion. This is because in such a case, there is no genuine exchange of Chayus, no living flow between giver and receiver. Nothing returns to replenish the giver, and the act of giving, rather than generating vitality, leaves behind a sense of exhaustion and loss.

When a Mashpia gives in the proper way, to a fitting recipient who is able to fully receive what is given and truly benefit from it, responding with presence, gratitude, and attentiveness, the Mashpia in turn receives an even greater Light through the act itself, reflected back through the receiver. In this way, giving is transformed into a form of receiving as well. Through authentic reception, the receiver naturally transmits energy back to the giver, completing the circuit. This reciprocal exchange of *Chayus* / life-force creates an energetic loop that nourishes both sides.

This is not merely a mystical concept; there is a tangible experience of satisfaction that arises when your giving is willingly received and appreciated. Conversely, a sensitive person can feel a sense of emptiness when what he gave was not properly received, valued, or utilized.

We must always be mindful, in our giving, to ensure there is no Yenikah l'Chitzonim, no leakage of energy to negative or external forces. On Purim, however, this concern does not exist, and therefore, "To whoever stretches out their hand we give." The root of Purim's giving flows from the Yesod of Abba, the world of Chochmah, whose Light is so overwhelming and all-encompassing that it illuminates the Yesod of Ima. This immense radiance then empowers the receiver to align completely with the giver, ensuring that every act of giving is received in purity and wholeness. In this state, there can be no leakage, no misdirection, only perfect flow, from giver to receiver and then reciprocated back.*

We sometimes see a small reflection of this even in ordinary life, when you give with such passion, joy, and enthusiasm, the sheer energy of the giver is contagious. Even if, under other circumstances, the receiver might have squandered or misused what was given, the force of the giver's light inspires them to receive properly and use it well.

---

* In other words, the Yesod of Abba builds Nukva / Malchus. The reading of the Megilah draws down Yesod d'Abba into Malchus. Hence, certain Mekubalim had the practice of giving Matanos laEvyonim before reading the Megilah in the morning, as first Nukva needs to be built properly and only then can Yesod d'Abba be drawn into Nukva: *Shemen Sason*, 24. *Kol Yaakov Siddur*, Kavanos Purim. This is not the common practice, certainly since the Berachos for the Megilah are also for all four Mitzvos of Purim. Besides, the general drawing down, on an internal level, occurs already with the Tefilos of Purim, beginning with Ma'ariv on the eve of Purim.

On Purim, this principle is magnified infinitely; every gift carries within it such overwhelming Light that it uplifts the receiver into perfect alignment with the giver.

What is more, (though not directly related to Matanos laEvyonim per se), the Arizal explains, as we explored earlier, that during and after the Purim story, the light of *Ima* / Binah shines directly into Malchus. During the Purim story, in the depths of exile, there was a *Nesirah* / severing between Ze'ir Anpin and Malchus, shifting them from *Achor b'Achor* / back-to-back to *Panim el Panim* / face-to-face. In that transitional state, Malchus no longer draws life and light from Ze'ir Anpin, as Ze'ir Anpin is severed. Instead, in order for Malchus to exist (if Malchus were to cease to exist, so would our world), Malchus was sustained and enlivened directly from beyond Ze'ir Anpin, receiving its vitality from Ima. This happened during the Purim story, the Arizal further reveals that this is the great Chidush, the novelty of Purim is that even after the Nesirah and after Ze'ir Anpin being in a face-to-face relationship with Malchus, Malchus still receives vitality from Ima. In this way, on Purim, even Malchus becomes suffused with the light of Yesod d'Abba (via Ima). In this exalted state, there is no concern for Yenikah l'Chitzonim; all giving is pure and perfectly aligned. On Purim, Yesod of Chochmah is revealed and reaches all the way down to the lowest level of Malchus, to Rochel herself. This is the essence of Purim, the Highest spilling over into the lowest, the infinite with the finite, the soul with and within the body.

KAVANAH FOR MATANOS LAEVYONIM

Here is a simplified *Kavanah* / intention to hold in mind when giving Matanos laEvyonim. It is rooted in the flow from Yesod d'Abba (like everything on Purim), but most prominently, what is being revealed is the Yesod d'Ima. In this *Nukvah* / feminine energy (*Ima* / Mother), there are two levels: Leah and Rochel, hence the two Tavs, and therefore there are two gifts to the poor. These gifts are given to (at least) two poor people. These two people represent the lower and 'poor' Sefiros of Netzach and Hod, and as they receive these gifts, they are the Malchus, the receivers of all the above.

When giving Matanos laEvyonim think the following:

I am a Mashpia, a giver.

I am using my Seichel, my understanding, my Binah, to give to those in need, and I am doing so through my inner attribute of Yesod, which, as the Baal Shem Tov teaches, is pleasure.

I delight in giving. I love giving money to help others, and it brings me great pleasure.

I give freely. I give to anyone who stretches out their hand, because if they are asking, it is a sign that they are in need (whether literally or emotionally and mentally), and that I have been blessed with the ability to help them.

It fills my heart with happiness to share my resources freely, without judgment or boundary, embracing all who seek assistance.

My giving knows no boundaries; it is open to all who seek help.

And now I turn to You, Hashem:

Master of the Universe, just as I give with love and pleasure to any-

one who asks, so too, may You, our compassionate Father in Heaven, in Your boundless love and infinite joy and delight, give to us; sustain Your children with Your endless goodness.

Here I stand, humbled as Malchus before You. I stretch out my hand to You, and I ask: Please, Abba, fill my cup with overflowing blessings, both material and spiritual, with all that is truly good, and may it endure forever, and culminate in the ultimate good, the revelation of Mashiach Tzidkeinu, speedily in our days.

KAVANAH FOR MISHLOACH MANOS

We give Mishloach Manos איש לרעהו / "a man to his friend." This symbolizes the Yesod of Abba reaching towards and lowering itself towards the Yesod of Ze'ir Anpin, which is akin to friends bonding. Yet, since Yesod of Abba flows through Yesod of Ima, the Feminine, therefore, there are two Manos, as the feminine has two levels, as mentioned.

Unlike Matanos laEvyonim, where you are giving to the poor, in Mishloach Manos you are giving to your 'friend', your equal. Giving Manos to your friend is more like giving to another 'giver'. The Higher giver is Yesod of Abba, and the receiver of this giving is Yesod of Ze'ir Anpin, also the attribute of Yesod, 'the Lower Giver'. In other words, through the act of Mishloach Manos, you are *Mashpia* / giving for the purpose of the other person being a Mashpia as well.

Furthermore, in Mishloach Manos, I am not only sharing my physical possessions with my friend, but also my spirituality. The Ramdu explains that ordinarily, every Tzadik, and indeed every person, the potential Tzadik, has their own unique spiritual state. Each is said to be "burned" by the *Chupa* / canopy of another, meaning that the spiritual level and achievements of one Tzadik may be beyond the grasp or comprehension of another (*Baba Basra*, 75a). Mishloach Manos, however, embodies a different dynamic: it symbolizes Tzadikim sharing their states and spiritual attainments with one another. Through this mutual exchange, no one is "burned" by another's greatness; rather, each contributes from their own level to their peers, and all are enriched by receiving from the spiritual levels and understanding of others.

When we can live without jealousy and purely seek the best interest in our fellow man, we are experiencing a glimmer of the World to Come (ובאותו הזמן לא יהיה שם... ולא קנאה: Rambam, *Hilchos Melachim*, 12:5. Although, see ibid., *Baba Basra*). This is the deeper reason why the words מנות איש לרעהו / "gifts from one to his friend" have the same numerical value as שמע ישראל ה' אלקינו ה' אחד / *Shema Yisrael, Hashem Elokeinu, Hashem Echad* / "Listen Yisrael, Hashem is our G-d, Hashem is One" (*Kesem Ofir*, 10:19*). When will Hashem be truly *Echad* / One? When the entire world recognizes the Oneness of Hashem and lives with a sense of oneness and unity with our fellows.

---

* The words ה' אלקינו ה' / *Hashem Elokeinu Hashem* are comprised of fourteen letters. This number is deeply significant, for it is associated with the eradication of Amalek, a process tied, as discussed, to *Yad* / hand, whose numerical value is fourteen. This same meaning is reflected in time as well: the Fourteenth day of Adar, the day on which Purim is celebrated in the Diaspora and in unwalled cities.

Here is a simplified Kavanah, intention based on the above. When giving Mishloch Manos, think the following:

I am a Mashpia, a giver; I desire to share all that I have, both physically and spiritually, with my friends.

My giving comes from a place of understanding, compassion, and profound joy, for there is no greater pleasure than being a channel for goodness in this world.

And now, I turn my heart to You, Hashem:

Master of the Universe, I want to give selflessly, with all my being, for my deepest desire is to bring more kindness, more giving, and more light into Your world. So too, I ask You, Hashem, to share Your boundless Reality with me and the world. Share with us Your infinite level of השפעה */ giving and bounty. For I know that You, our compassionate Creator, desire nothing more than to bring an even greater flow of* Shefa */ abundance and countless blessings into Your world, and ultimately draw down the ultimate goodness, the revelation of Mashiach Tzidkeinu.*

SEUDAS PURIM: THE FESTIVE MEAL & WINE

The highlight of Purim, and the note on which we conclude the day, is the festive meal, a time of joy, celebration, and, yes, to have a drink or two until we "do not know the difference between 'cursed is Haman' and 'blessed is Mordechai.'" Whether this is the actual Halachah, and whether it is meant literally or figuratively, is a matter of debate. Some say it means to drink just enough to grow drowsy and fall asleep, thus becoming unable to differentiate. Others interpret it as drinking until one can no longer calculate that the numerical values of "cursed is Haman" and "blessed is Mordechai" are equal (*Agudah*. Quoted in the *Darkei Moshe*, the *Bach*, and the *Magen Avraham*, Orach Chayim, 695). But the deeper question remains: why would there be a Mitzvah to 'lose one's mind' in any which way; either falling asleep, not being able to calculate, or literally not knowing? Is a state of clarity and knowing not the ideal? Is not Da'as, conscious awareness, the goal of our Avodah in this world? Since when is "not knowing" even a desired goal, let alone on one of the most holy days of the year?

The answer lies in understanding the inner dynamics of wine. The Hebrew word *Yayin* / wine has the same numerical value as the word *Sod* / secret. The connection is that "When wine enters, secrets come out." A good, healthy drink, taken in the right spirit, in the right context and mindset, often lowers one's guard. The external 'masks' people often wear, the protective layers of the ego or the socially-imposed personas that people assume upon themselves, many times begin to dissolve, whereas the more authentic, inner layers of self have an easier chance to burst forth.

When approached with the right intention, Purim drinking is not about dulling the mind but about quieting the surface mind, letting go of the superficial self, the external protective mind, so that the deeper, truer self of the soul, of transcendence can shine through. It is the temporary suspension of the outer form in order to reveal a higher form within.

At times, a complete concealment of the outer, external flight or fight self is necessary for the sake of birthing and revealing the more authentic self. Radical transformation often requires the veiling of the surface in order for the deeper identity to emerge. In the sacred joy of Purim, even the wine, taken in holiness and within the context of Yom Tov and as a Mitzvah, can become a tool for this inner unveiling, allowing the truest self to step forth from behind the mask, as the masks are peeled away.

DRINKING WINE

The central feature of Achashverosh's feast was wine. והשתיה כדת אין אנס / "The drinking was according to the law, without coercion." And then a little later, כטוב לב-המלך ביין / "When the king's heart was merry with wine," he called for his wife Vashti, but she did not appear. The king became angry with her, killed her, and thus Esther became the queen.

The entire event revolved around wine.

Yet, the Arizal teaches (*Mishnas Chasidim*, Maseches Adar, 3) that the wine at Achashverosh's feast reawakened the *Cheit Eitz haDaas* / the primordial sin of eating fruit from the Tree of Knowledge, which, according to one opinion in Chazal (*Berachos*, 40a), was a grape, i.e., wine. That drink of Adam and Chava was the first 'drunkenness' in history, leading to a fall into an extreme, unhealthy 'self-aware' state, which is the source of all types of depravity and negativity. This negative Da'as is vain ego-consciousness and self-absorption.

Accordingly, the Tikkun for the Cheit Eitz haDaas is to again drink wine, but not in a way that drags us *below* Da'as, and into self-centeredness and unholiness, but to drink in a way that carries us *above* and beyond Da'as, transcending self-consciousness, and reaching a state of expansive awareness in which we choose goodness, light, generosity, and joy.

The Hebrew word for wine, *Gefen* can be read as *Gimel* (which is the number 3) plus the word *Pan* / turn, hinting at the three possible "turns" one can take with drinking wine: 1) To the left, to *Gevurah* / restriction, concealment, harmful behavior, such as the angry drunk who wounds others, 2) To the right, to the *Chesed* / kindness, openness, and warmth of the 'good drunk,' yet in a way that makes them slip into irresponsibility, foolishness, or even licentiousness, or 3) *Tiferes* / balance, the golden 'middle path', which includes the benefits of Chesed and Gevurah but without their potential detriments. Balanced drinking, such as in the Kiddush of Shabbos and Yom Tov, serves to open the heart without leading to a loss of intentionality.

In essence, *Kav haChesed* / the path of Chesed with regards to wine drinking, taken to excess, leads to overexposure and moral looseness. *Kav haGevurah* / the path of Gevurah with regards to wine drinking, taken to excess, leads to aggression and harm, hurting self or worse, hurting others (רבא אמר אל תרא יין כי יתאדם אל תרא יין שאחריתו דם / "Rava says, 'Look not upon wine that reddens,' means: 'Look not upon wine, as it leads to *Dam* / (red) bloodshed'" *Sanhedrin*, 70a). The *Kav haEmtza'i* / middle path is just the right measure, releasing joy and inner goodness while keeping the soul, mind, heart, and body aligned.

Wine can either raise a person up, making them a *Rosh* / head or crown, uplifting and ennobling them, or it can drag them down, leaving them *Rash* / impoverished and diminished. Wine can gladden the heart with true joy, or unsettle the mind and even drive a person to madness (זכה נעשה ראש, לא זכה נעשה רש. זכה משמחו, לא זכה משממהו: *Sanhedrin*, ibid.).

AD D'LO YADA: WHAT DO WE REALLY KNOW?

The idea of Lo Yada can at first glance seem like an immature or inferior state of mind. In our celebrated culture, to admit that something is beyond our grasp is often seen as a weakness. "Knowledge is power," people say, and by implication, the one who does not know is powerless. Yet how much do we truly know? Of course, a person should strive for understanding, not remain in ignorance, to learn, to inquire, to probe the depths of life. But can everything really be known? Even in the realm of science, suppose humanity were to discover a "unified theory," would that mark the end of knowledge or science as some have predicted? Or would there still remain endless layers to explore? Perhaps what we currently know of this vast universe is but the tip of the iceberg. Perhaps our discoveries of even the basic properties of the universe are like those of a small child playing on the seashore, while the great ocean of truth lies undiscovered before us.

And yet, this is only within the realm of limited knowledge, the finite wisdom of the physical universe, what the Zohar calls *Chochmah Tata'ah* / the lower wisdom. How much more so when it comes to the Infinite knowing, the *Chochmah Ila'ah* / upper wisdom of the Torah, of which it is said (*Pesikta d'Rebbe Kahana,* 12:20), מפני מה ניתנה במדבר סיני... מה המדבר אין לו סוף, כך היא התורה אין לה סוף, שנ' ארוכה מדה ורחבה מני ים / "Why was the Torah given in the wilderness of Sinai? Just as the wilderness has no end, so too the Torah has no end, as it is written (*Iyov,* 11:9) 'Longer than the earth is its measure, and broader than the sea.'"

It is axiomatic that the Creator's infinitude transcends all definition and all human tools of grasp. If the finite universe and its
wisdom appear infinite to us, how much more so that which is truly
without end. How, then, can one tap into this boundless wisdom?
How can we drink from that limitless well? If you recognize that
you do not yet know, and that it can never be intellectually known,
you are open to so much more that can be known and perhaps
through this awareness you get to 'experience' the Unknown (of the
level of known), or at least get a 'taste' of it (although, the Ultimate
will remain forever Unknown).

There is a saying repeated by Rishonim: תכלית הידיעה שלא נדע /
"The ultimate *Tachlis* / extent (or purpose) of knowing, is not to
know," or 'The deepest knowing is not knowing' (The original version
in the Rishonim is תכלית הידיעה, שנדע שלא נדעך / "The ultimate extent (or purpose) of knowing, is to know that we cannot know *You*": *Bechinos Olam*, 13:4. Yet,
the above version is the way Chasidic sources and later writings quote the statement). This is not the "not knowing" of ignorance, nor the absence
of Da'as through deficiency. Quite the contrary, it is the awareness
that comes precisely from deep knowledge, the knowing that there
is a reality infinitely beyond our present knowing and beyond all
knowing. It is the humble, expansive realization that what we do
not yet grasp points to the boundless possibility of what can be
known. We know that we do not know.

Again, the phrase is 'The deepest knowing is not knowing.' They
did not say the ultimate in a person, or the noblest of people, is one
that acknowledges that there are great depths that are unknown.
Nor did they say that the ultimate knowledge is not known. What
they did say is that the peak of human knowledge, the ultimate

form of human knowing, is *not* to know, to know that one has reached the limit of what can be known. To know that you do not know is, if you will, a way to experience or at least touch the Unknowable.

ANSWERS LEAD TO DEEPER QUESTIONS

The unknown of yesterday becomes the known of today. Yet with each day, we encounter a deeper unknown, a hiddenness that lies beyond our present grasp.

As the destination itself is Infinite, so too is the journey toward it. Knowledge, especially Divine wisdom, is without end. Every question calls forth an answer, yet each answer is but a stepping stone to a greater question. Questions give birth to answers, and answers give rise to new questions. Every thesis carries its own antithesis, which calls forth a greater synthesis until that synthesis itself becomes the basis of the thesis on a higher level. As the Baal Shem Tov would say, for every answer he could find a deeper question, and for every question a deeper answer, and this can continue *ad infinitum*. Each summit we reach opens a broader horizon. Such is the course of human intellectual development: a dance of tension and resolution. What satisfies the mind today should not, indeed must not, satisfy it tomorrow.

Remarkably, even in the realm of 'lower wisdom', the willingness to question, to challenge the status quo, and to say 'I don't know' is the catalyst for true breakthroughs. This is why younger minds, still supple and unencumbered by rigid patterns, are often more innovative and prone to true *Chidushim* / novel ideas. In both Torah and (*LeHavdil* / 'to separate between holy and mundane') the sciences, many of the most transformative discoveries have come from younger scholars (or young at heart), those who still retain openness, wonder, and the humility to question. First comes the state of not-knowing, and from it flows greater creativity and deeper understanding. How much more so when our quest is to draw from the Infinite fountain of wisdom, the 'upper wisdom' that is beyond the linear, the conventional, and the bounded. To ascend, we must release, we must embrace Lo Yada so that we can climb beyond, and even 'beyond the beyond'. In doing so, we draw from a higher Makif, a surrounding transcendence, and then integrate that reality until it becomes our Penimi, our inner reality, our understanding.

Hashem is *Ein Sof* / Infinite. To truly know the Infinite is an endless quest. Whatever we grasp of the Ein Sof remains finite, and beyond it lies an even deeper hiddenness. Purim reveals this truth through Esther, whose very name evokes *Hester* / concealment. Behind all that is revealed stands the Hidden One, the Essence of HaKadosh Baruch Hu that is forever hidden. No matter what is known, the Essence remains concealed. Purim connects us directly to that Infinite hiddenness which can never be revealed (see Alter Rebbe, *Torah Ohr*, Megilas Esther, 90d). This hiddenness is not a deficiency in our ability to apprehend what is revealed; it is simply that 'revelation' is not Essence; manifestation is not the Manifester. To let go of our knowing and of our attachment to what we think we know allows us to unite with the infinite mystery of the Ultimate Unknowable.

Paradoxically, the deeper one delves into the hidden chambers of Torah, the more one discovers that knowledge itself is but a mirage, a flickering banner luring us toward the horizon, only to dissolve in the light of an even greater mystery. For the ultimate truth is 'I do not know.' Hashem is the Infinite Unknowable, and thus all that flows from Him is ultimately unknowable. To learn, then, is to arrive at the shore of wonder, where knowing bows to mystery, and the highest wisdom whispers, 'The deepest knowledge is not knowing.'

The path forward to such 'not-knowing knowing' begins with surrender, acknowledging the limits of intellect and the left brain, and accepting that the binary apparatus of the brain can only process what is linear and defined, contextualized and measured. This is the inner meaning of the call to attain Lo Yada, to open ourselves to ever-higher, ever-deeper levels of experiences that are beyond normative understanding, and knowing that we will never know, yet despite not knowing, we choose to live with faith, committed and radical dedication to Torah and Mitzvos.

AMALEK AND THE TRANSFORMATION OF DOUBT TO HOLY DOUBT

Part of the Avodah, the inner and spiritual work of the state of Lo Yada is to live with a deeper level of 'not knowing' or, what can be called *Safek d'Kedushah* / 'holy doubt'.

Amalek, as explored, is the place of Safek, crippling doubt, uncertainty, cynicism, nihilism, and the cooling down of any passions for growth or anything good. Haman was a descendant and embodiment of this archetype of all the 'enemies' of Israel and its mission, but just as there is unholy, negative, crippling doubt, there is also holy, positive, freeing doubt.

Holy doubt is rooted in Radla. The letters of *Adar* form an acronym for **Reisha D'Lo Is'yada** / 'the Unknowable Head' or 'the head that does not know', usually called by its acronym, *Radla*. This refers to the deepest level within the Divine Self, so to speak, the highest of the three levels within Keser, the metaphorical crown that sits above Hashem's Head, the Keser of all Kesarim, as explored. Although inexpressible, for our purposes, Radla can be thought of as Divine 'doubt', a place where all is possible, for no-thing is yet to be defined (ואלה הם הספיקות של רדל״א. והענין כי כל מה שמסתפקים בה, אינו שאפשר שלא יהיה, הכל יש אלא אדרבא: *Adir BaMarom*, Pelugta d'Sa'arei, Chap. 13). 'Below' Radla there is a level called *Galgalta* / skull, which is the meta-source of all defined masculine qualities. Below that, in turn, there is *Mochin Stima* / hidden 'brains' or mind, which is the meta-source of all defined feminine qualities. The level of Radla is so transcendent, it cannot be known by any living being or angel, nor even by itself, so to speak. In Radla, it is as if the Everpresence is hiding from Itself.* This is the paradox of paradoxes, the ultimate reality, *Etzem* / Essence.

In contrast, Amalek, the *Reishis Goyim* / 'head' of all the nations, is the head or *Keser* / crown of all the enemies of Klal Yisrael. In this way, Amalek symbolizes and embodies the destructive and negative side of holy 'doubt' and 'not-knowing' of Keser, the negative shadowside of Radla. When this negative force of Amalek

---

* There is a phrase found in Chasidus, quoted in the name of the Arizal: פנימיות אבא הוא פנימיות עתיק / the inner essence of Chochmah is the inner essence of Atik, the level of Keser. See *Kuntres Limud haChasidus*, p. 6, the Hagaha of the Rebbe, for the source of this 'idea' in the writings of the Arizal. Rebbe Chayim Vital writes concerning what this means, and why it is this way, ולא ידעתי הטעם / "I do not know the reason." Regarding these words, לא ידעתי הטעם, the Alter Rebbe teaches: it is not that he does not know the reason, rather, it is rooted in Atik, which is a place beyond reason, that of 'not-knowing': *Pelach haRimon*, Bereishis, Toldos, p. 156. Tzemach Tzedek, *Ohr Torah*, Bamidbar 2, p. 699.

attacks us, it attempts to create pessimism in the place of optimism, cynicism in the place of enthusiasm, and coldness and indifference in the place of passion and engagement.

Klal Yisrael represents the world of truth and holiness, of life and light. Its eternal archenemy, Amalek, represents the world of lies, uncertainties, death and spiritual, ethical, and moral ambiguity. There are two primary ways that a foe can oppose the truth. One is to fabricate a counterfeit, an impostor, a lie, and present it as truth. Once two supposed 'truths' are set against one another, the outcome is unpredictable. The second way, the way of Amalek, is subtler and far more insidious. Rather than confronting truth with an alternative claim, an allure of all the -*isms* throughout history, Amalek merely plants the seed of doubt. This quiet skepticism can cool the warmth of conviction and drain the heart of its fire.

For example, imagine you are filled with passion for Tzedakah and Chesed, or you approach Tefilah with deep fervor and meditative joy. Amalek's voice whispers: "What you are doing is admirable, but shouldn't you also be focusing on other priorities? Wouldn't it be better to spend less time in prayer and more time studying Torah? You linger over the Amidah, but did you even finish this week's Parsha? Who do you think you are?" Notice, this is not a direct assault on the act itself. The words may even sound pious or reasonable. Yet beneath the surface, they carry a single intention: to puncture enthusiasm, to dilute passion, to replace burning clarity with tepid 'realism' and measured 'responsibility' or even 'righteousness'.

NEGATIVE DA'AS

Haman, who embodies the quality of Amalek, is a manifestation of the *Kelipah* / negative side of *Da'as* / knowing, connectivity (Arizal, *Likutei Torah*: 'Balak (Amalek and Bilam) are Da'as of Kelipah. Da'as that is *Bala* / swallowed up. *Eitz Chayim*, Sha'ar 8:4. Bilam (Bala) draws power from the letters קר, *Megaleh Amukos*, Ki Tisa, Derush 3:3, and *Kar* / cold is the quality of Amalek, as discussed). On one level, 'Da'as of Kelipah' implies the idea of waging war on Da'as itself, an attack on *knowing* and by extension on the All Knowing One (*Derech Mitzvosecha*, Mitzvas Zechiras uMechiyas Amalek, 1).

On a deeper level, Amalek's claim is that there is nothing truly worth knowing, and ultimately, there is nothing at all to know. Everything labors under the world of *Safek* / doubt; hence, everything is relative, and all of life is devoid of any meaning or purpose.

This is one dimension of the Kelipah of Da'as. On a deeper level, since Kelipah denotes concealment and negativity, Da'as of Kelipah can be understood as negative 'knowing', a presumed knowing about not-knowing. It is, in essence, a small-minded 'certainty' regarding the uncertainty of existence, a conviction that nothing can truly be known. This is Da'as of Safek, a knowing rooted in doubt, a stubborn attachment to the belief, "I do not know, and I can never know, for there is nothing real to be known." It is a mindset that clings to not-knowing as an end in itself: a perpetual state of doubt without any drive to seek resolution, where relativism becomes the only absolute, and nihilism reigns supreme.

AMALEK AND THE SNAKE

Amalek, and later, his embodiment in Haman, is linked to the Nachash, the primordial serpent in the Garden of Eden who sowed doubt in Chavah's mind about what was truly good and bad (והא כמה ערבובין אנון בישין בעירן וחיוון. אבל אית ערבוביא מסטרא דנחש.... ואית ערבוביא מסטרא דמזיקין דנשמתן דחייביא אנון מזיקין דעלמא ממש. ואית ערבוביא דשדים ורוחין ולילין וכלא מעורבבין בישראל. ולא אית בכלהו לטייא כעמלק דאיהו חויא בישא אל אחר / "Various impurities are mingled in the composition of Klal Yisrael like animals among men. One kind is from the side of the serpent...another from the side of *Mazikim* / malevolent spirits, for the souls of the wicked are literally the Mazikim of the world, and there is an impurity from the side of the demons and evil spirits. And there is none so cursed among them as Amalek, who is the evil serpent, the 'foreign deity'": *Zohar*, 1, 28b. Indeed, Eisav, who is the grandfather of Amalek, had engraved the image of a snake on his thigh: *Sefer Tziyoni*, Toldos, p. 44. Shaloh haKadosh, *Torah She-b'Kesav*, Tzon Yoseph, 12).

Our Sages tell us that the *Nachash* / snake is associated with *Zuhama* / זוהמא / spiritual filth and impurity (*Shabbos*, 146a. Zuhama is *Tumah* / stagnant impurity in the language of Gemara: *Resisei Layla*, 19). The word זוהמא can be read as a Hebrew word, and further broken down into the words זו מה היא / This, what is it? (*Pirush haSulam*, Zohar 1:17). This is the voice of corrosive doubt, reducing the sacred, the holy, the noble, the ethical to a question mark. Like the serpent, Amalek seeks to inject the Tumah of skepticism into the heart. "So you prayed with focus and devotion, but what is it really worth? Yes, you helped someone in need, but how did you really help in the grand scheme of things? Probably nothing."

This is Amalek's venom: not a direct denial of good, but the subtle erosion of its value through incessant questioning and doubt. The nature of the snake is to operate in the hidden, in the places of 'doubt', so to speak, as the Primordial Snake did in the Garden of Eden. The snake does not confront its prey in open battle; it does not roar, nor does it charge like a lion or a wolf. The way of a snake is far more insidious; it waits, silent, hidden in the dense thicket, coiled within the underbrush, unseen, unnoticed, and then, when least expected, it strikes. There is no warning, no clash, no visible enemy to defend against, and by the time a person is aware of it, it has already bitten. This is the essence of the snake, and the essence of doubt. Doubt rarely arrives as an open denial or a clear opposition to what you want to do; rather, it creeps in quietly. Doubt is not a loud and *Vadai* / certain 'No,' but a quiet and gnawing *She'ma* / 'Maybe....'

In contrast, the not-knowing of Kedushah is liberating. It opens us to ever-deeper levels of understanding and inspires an unending search for meaning. The *Taharah* / purity of 'holy doubt' leads to a life of infinitely renewable purpose, continually refreshed by a living commitment to goodness. Paradoxically, it moves us to greater acts of kindness and Mitzvos than any static, fixed "knowing" ever could. This holy not-knowing might begin as an intellectual or existential question that yields an answer, which in turn gives rise to an even deeper question, leading to deeper answers, and finally, to more impactful and elevated action.

In the realm of holy intellect, our not-knowing is rooted in a place beyond not-knowing, the Keser of all Kesarim. It is the same sublime plane where, so to speak, HaKadosh Baruch Hu freely chooses the righteous, as explored earlier. And when we exercise our own free choice from that place, we are moved only toward optimism, enthusiasm, and passion for Mitzvos, because in that transcendent place, HaKadosh Baruch Hu chooses goodness, purpose, and meaning.

Torah and Mitzvos, Tzedakah and Chesed, all stand beyond the ordinary categories of certainty, Da'as, and uncertainty beyond Da'as. When we connect to this higher transcendence, we connect to our deepest self in its Source. In doing so, we draw upon the energies of Radla, the "Divine uncertainty," as will be explored, to open our minds and hearts to radical new possibilities in life.

This life-giving form of doubt does not weaken us; it frees us. It awakens a perception of untapped possibilities, inspiring us to pursue unexplored answers and to plunge into unknown depths of optimism. Far from making us indifferent, it ignites our passion. Instead of becoming passive, we become more proactive, engaged, and dynamic. This is the quality hinted at in the fact that "Moshe Rabbeinu was born in Adar." Adar is the month of coming alive, of truly beginning to exist, through humility (symbolized by the humblest of men, Moshe) and surrender to ever-higher visions of what is possible. One life-affirming choice opens the door to more life-affirming choices, each infused with expanding confidence and trust in Hashem and His Creation.

Here lies the deeper reason: Safek in the form of an 'openness to possibility' brings us to a deeper commitment to a firmer *P'sak* / ruling or 'certainty' (ספק / *Safek* and פסק / *P'sak* have the same letters but in a different order). When a P'sak Din that is confirmed is rooted in the freshness and openness of Safek (in Radla) that P'sak is crystal clear, yet still remains vibrant and brimming with life and possibilities of applications (Rebbe Chayim Vital writes of the various *Sefeikos* / doubts regarding levels within Keser, how they function, what they reveal and draw down, from where they draw their source, and so forth. The deeper reason for these Sefeikos is that sometimes they are revealed one way, and other times another way, depending on the situation: *K'lach Pischei Chochmah*, 86. The Magid of Koznitz also adds that it depends on the level of the generation and the people who are tapping into these levels).

Da'as of Kelipah is the small-minded stubbornness that clings to what one thinks one knows, and to the belief that nothing beyond this can be known. This stuckness in thought is a form of death.

Mordechai tries to convince Esther to go to the king and ask him to annul the decree against the Jewish People: ומי יודע אם־לעת כזאת הגעת למלכות / "And who knows, perhaps you have attained a royal position for the sake of a crisis such as this" (*Esther*, 4:14). Why does he say, ומי יודע / "And who knows?" Why does he not speak with conviction? Why not tell her plainly, "It is *clear* to me that the whole reason you are queen is to help save the Jewish People." Because the essence of Purim is Lo Yada, releasing the need to know, or to cling to what one thinks one knows, and refusing to be trapped in the Kelipah of Da'as.

SAFEK & FLUIDITY IN AVODAS HASHEM

In our Avodas Hashem, we must continually free ourselves from becoming trapped in fixed patterns of behavior, even those that appear positive or have served us well in the past. What once uplifted us may no longer be the path we need today. We must be willing to release ideas, habits, and methods of service that no longer breathe life into our living and present connection with Hashem. The wise Rebbe, Reb Bunim of Peshischa, taught, "The principle in Avodas Hashem is that there are no principles...and even *this* principle does not exist!" In Yiddish, דער כלל איז, אז לגבי עבודת ה' איז נישט דא קיין כללים, און אפי' די כלל איז אויך נישט דא.

"You shall *not do so* to Hashem, your G-d" / לא תעשון כן לה' אלקיכם (*Devarim*, 12:4). The phrase "not do so" means not to perform the idolatrous actions the Torah had described just prior to this verse (Rashi, *ad loc.*). Yet, the early Chasidic Rebbes offered a deeper, reread interpretation, "You shall not do 'כן / like this' to Hashem your G-d." In other words, do not turn your service of Hashem into a rigid 'this is how it is done' formula, repeated mechanically and without renewal. To serve Hashem in the exact same way, day after day, without openness to fresh inspiration, is itself a subtle form of idolatry, worshipping the old, the form rather than the Living connection with the Living G-d. True Avodas Hashem is alive and dynamic. We must resist turning it into a fixed כן, a single, unchanging mode, and instead remain ready to discover new pathways in our connection and Avodah (the Chozeh of Lublin, *Hagadah Shel Pesach Mar'eh Yechezkel*, p. 25).

Even in the realm of positive spiritual *Hanhagos* / personal practices and disciplines, we must remain attuned to their inner effect. We need to quietly sense which practices are genuinely expanding us, deepening our awareness, and drawing us closer to HaKadosh Baruch Hu, and which have grown stale, reduced to habit and empty routine. The Chozeh of Lublin, after detailing the many uplifting customs he had undertaken, adds with characteristic humility, "All of the above practices have many, infinite branches and details, and yet, ולפעמים צריך להתנהג להפך / sometimes a person has to act exactly the opposite" (*Zos Zikaron*, p. 4).

While this is true throughout all the days of the year, the 'headquarters' of this idea is Purim. Purim embodies the awareness that 'you never know' or, in the words of the Megilah, "Who knows?" By stepping beyond the confines of what we think we know, we open ourselves to possibilities far greater than our present vision, and to an ever-deepening Avodas Hashem.

AMALEK SAYS THERE IS NO TOMORROW

Amalek embodies the negative form of doubt, the shadow-side (Kelipah) of the holy reality of Keser. This most destructive of all Kelipah cripples a person with suffocating uncertainty and even moral paralysis, whispering, "You cannot do anything, because there is really nothing to be done."

In Amalek's doubt-ridden and pessimistic worldview, there is no tomorrow, there is no true future, and by extension, there is no real reason to take responsibility for the present. Everything is locked in a perpetual fog of existential doubt, where even the possibility of a brighter horizon is questioned. Gradually, sometimes so subtly as to go unnoticed, a person can come to believe that there has never been, and never will be, any real progress, hope, or redemption, for history, for civilization, or for the self. In this darkened vision, there is no tomorrow, neither for the individual nor for the world. There is no hope and no tomorrow.

Concerning Amalek, the Torah says, "Go and wage battle with Amalek *tomorrow*" (*Shemos*, 17:9). This is not merely a historical charge, but an ongoing call to confront, with vigor and passion, the most corrosive Kelipah of all, Amalek's denial of tomorrow. Indeed, later on in history, Dovid haMelech also wages battle with Amalek, and as the Torah tells us (*Shmuel 1*, 30:17), ‏ויכם דוד מהנשף ועד־‏ ‏הערב למחרתם‏ / "Dovid attacked them from before dawn until the evening of the next day." Says Rashi, ‏למודים הם עמלקים ללקות ביום מחר‏ / "The Amalekites are accustomed to being defeated on the second day (tomorrow)."

In the words of the Medrash, ‏אין מפלתו של עמלק אלא למחר‏ / "The downfall of Amalek is also connected with a tomorrow" (*Yalkut Shimoni*, Esther, 1096).

It is not enough to rid the world of evil people who raise a banner of destruction and wish upon us genocide, *Chalilah* / Heaven forbid. The Torah calls us to a deeper and more enduring battle, the war against destructive ideologies. We must wage battle against Amalek's mindset, against ‏מחשבת המן‏ / Haman's thoughts (*Esther*, 8:5), the worldview and inner logic that denies meaning, dismisses purpose, and reduces tomorrow to nothing more than a weary repetition of today and yesterday (Olam haTohu (Eisav, Amalek) is called '*Esmol* / yesterday': *Adir BaMarom*, Olam haNikudim, Sheviras haKeilim, Chap. 6).

For this reason, when Queen Esther begins to formulate the downfall of Haman-Amalek, she tells Achshveirosh and Haman during the first meal she prepared for them ‏יבוא המלך והמן אל־המשתה‏ ‏אשר אעשה להם ומחר אעשה כדבר המלך‏ / "Let Your Majesty and Haman come to the feast which I will prepare for them; and tomorrow I will do Your Majesty's bidding." As the downfall of Amalek is on the tomorrow, and tomorrow she will reveal to the king the diabolical nature of Haman. And indeed, when the story finally turns around, and the king informs Esther of what is occurring throughout the lands, Esther, who wishes to completely defeat Haman and Amalek, says, ותאמר אסתר אם־על־המלך טוב ינתן גם־מחר ליהודים אשר בשושן לעשות כדת היום / "If it please Your Majesty, let the Jews in Shushan be permitted to act tomorrow as well" (*Esther*, 9:13). This is a battle against the idea that there is no real tomorrow; thus, the downfall of Amalek is on tomorrow.

This is a worldview that corrodes all hope and possibility. An ideology that denies meaning, dismisses Divine purpose, and insists that life is nothing more than a closed loop, today and tomorrow being but the same as yesterday, without true change, progress, or redemption. Such thinking breeds spiritual stagnation and moral and ethical paralysis, convincing a person that nothing they do matters.

The Bnei Yissaschar (Adar, Ma'amar 4, 10) says that the 30 days from Purim until Pesach are about overcoming and defeating Amalek. There are 720 hours in these 30 days. The numerical value of *Amalek* is 240. Three times 240 is 720. Therefore, there are three levels of Amalek with which we must struggle and overcome during this period: doubt in thought, in speech, and in action.

To defeat Amalek is not only to dismantle the forces of physical destruction, the Amalek who acts, but also to uproot the subtler, more insidious forms, such as the 'Amalek' that infiltrates the minds of people with corrosive doubt, and the Amalek that shapes the words that people use into the language of cynicism and hopelessness. True victory comes when we replace these with a mindset and speech that affirm faith, meaning, and purpose, restoring within ourselves and the world at large, the certainty that tomorrow can be new and radiant, and filled with the light of the future Redemption.

AMALEK REPRESENTS INEVITABILITY & ABSENCE OF HOPE

The inner, doubting Amalek whispers to a person, "There is no need to act, no action can truly change anything." In its most insidious form, Amalek implants the crushing belief that you have sunk so deeply into negative or addictive patterns that these patterns have become the very fabric of your being. It paints the illusion that this state of negativity is a מחוייב המציאות / 'necessary existence', that there is no alternative, no way out. It declares the situation absolute, and absolutely hopeless (Chas v'Shalom).

But is there truly a level of impurity so deep, of a stuckness so solidified, that those bound to it can never change? Can there exist a state where evil is a מחוייב המציאות / a necessary existence, with no alternative and no possibility for goodness, no opening for transformation?

The structure of our world answers this question. The dimensions of Creation correspond to the number seven, as in the seven days of Creation, and the fullest expression of this world is 49, seven sub-levels within each of the seven dimensions. In fact, the word *Midah* / measurement has the numerical value of 49 (*Sefer Rokeach*, Hilchos Pesach, 294. *Megaleh Amukos*, Parshas Behar). For this reason, as the light of Torah 'descends' into creation, it refracts into 49 possible ways of *Isur* / prohibition and 49 possible ways of *Heter* / allowance (*Medrash Tehilim*, 12); 49 ways of purity and 49 ways of impurity (Yerushalmi, *Sanhedrin*, 4:2. See also *Eiruvin*, 13b; Ritva, *ad loc.*).

This 'world of 49' is the world of opposites, the binary, and therefore the realm of choice. The higher a person ascends on the 49 rungs of Kedushah, the more they are aligned with purity, clarity, and transparency to the Divine. The lower they descend on the 49 rungs of impurity, the more they are bound in negativity, distortion, and spiritual stagnation.

Yet, at any of these 98 rungs, whether in the 49 of purity or in the 49 of impurity, there is always the possibility to choose the other path. This is why the Torah speaks of the 98 *Kelalos* / curses (in Ki Savo, see Rashi, *Bamidbar*, 29:18), for each rung has its opposite. Any level of goodness within the 49 rungs of holiness is called an אפשרי המציאות / 'possible existence'. One can remain in purity, but it is also 'possible' to fall. And conversely, even from the depths of impurity, it is always 'possible' to rise.

On both scales, there seems to exist a fiftieth level. In the realm of Kedushah, this 50th level is called *Yovel* / Jubilee, a state of complete freedom, even a freedom from the Yetzer haRa, the negative inclination, and even from death itself (*Medrash Rabbah*, Shemos, 41). Here, goodness exists without an opposite; it stands entirely beyond the binary paradigm of impurity or prohibition. At this height, purity becomes a מחוייב המציאות / necessary existence, unchangeable and absolute. There is no alternative, no possibility of descent or fall. Purity at this level is endless, unassailable, and everlasting. The question remains, however: does there also exist a 50th level on the side of *Ra* / evil, negativity, and impurity, that is equally absolute and without end?

Many post-Zohar and post-Arizal Kabbalistic sources (although not found in the 'regular' Zohar, nor in the teachings of the Arizal) speak about a 50th level of *Tumah* / impurity, on which negativity seems absolute. As such, just as one can become endlessly free on the 50th level of Kedushah, it seems one can become so removed from the *Yetzer Tov* / positive inclination that there is no longer even a possibility of doing good. On the 50th level of Tumah, the capacity for goodness no longer exists (*Shaloh haKadosh. Alshich. Siddur Reb Shabtai. Chayei Adam* (in their respective Hagados, on "Matzah Zu"). *Chesed l'Avraham*, 2:56. The Ramdu, *Eis LeChen'nah. Ohr haChayim*, Shemos, 3:8. The *Beis haLevi*, Derush 2, and many places in Chasidus). Yet, other sources write that there is, in fact, no 50th level of Tumah; there is no place where negativity and darkness are absolute (Gra, *Mishlei*, 16:4).

As we explored earlier, Haman constructed a wooden gallows fifty Amos high, intending to hang the righteous Mordechai upon it. Symbolically, it appears that Haman sought to tap into a realm where evil is final and irreversible, a supposed 50th level of impurity. This might seem to suggest that such a level exists.

To reconcile this, it could be argued that there is, in reality, no true 50th level of Tumah. No soul can ever fall so low that the possibility of ascent is gone. As our Sages teach, nothing stands in the way of Teshuvah, no barrier can prevent genuine return and transformation (*Zohar* 2, 106a. Yerushalmi, *Pe'ah*, 1:1). "There is no misdeed that cannot be mended through Teshuvah" (*Tanya*, Igeres haTeshuvah, 4 and 11. *Ohr Hashem*, Ma'amar 3, Klal 2:2. Me'iri, *Chibur haTeshuvah*, Meishiv Nefesh, Ma'amar 1:3. "The doors of Teshuva are forever open." *Pesikta d'Rebbe Kahana*, 45:8). The very idea of an absolute, inescapable evil is itself a deception, the central lie of Amalek, to convince you that all hope

is lost, that there is a realm where negativity is a מחוייב המציאות /
"necessary existence."

In erecting his fifty-Amah gallows, Haman was making a statement: "There is a place where evil is permanent, a place where
evil is a מחוייב המציאות / necessary existence, and that is where you,
Mordechai, and all of Klal Yisrael are now dwelling. You are so lost,
so entrenched in impurity, that your downfall is inevitable. You and
Klal Yisrael have sunk so low, there is no getting up. Tomorrow will
only be a repetition of today, and today you are doomed to death,
and so it will be. There is no possibility of Teshuvah, of movement,
of progress, of redemption. You are irredeemable."

AMALEK & THE DESCENDANTS OF ROCHEL

"Moshe said to Yehoshua, 'Pick men for us, and go out to do
battle with Amalek'" (*Shemos*, 17:9). Moshe specifically chooses
Yehoshua, who is a descendant of the matriarch Rochel, to wage
battle against Amalek because, "Amalek can only be destroyed
through the descendants of Rochel" (Medrash, *Pesikta Rabbasi*, 13, as
Yehoshua and Mordechai. והיה בית־יעקב אש ובית יוסף להבה ובית עשו לקש :*Ovadia*, 1:18).
Later in *Sefer Shoftim* / 'The Book of Judges', we read, מני אפרים
שרשם בעמלק / "Out of Ephrayim, came those whose roots are in
Amalek" (5:14). Ephrayim, grandson of Rochel, carries the spiritual
power through which Amalek will be vanquished (This is an allusion
to Yehoshua specifically, as Rashi writes, and a general allusion to the tribe of
Ephrayim: מן אפרים יצא שורש יהושע בן נון, לרדות בעמלק לחלש אותו לפי חרב). But what
is this unique power of Rochel's descendants that makes them the
antidote to Amalek?

Amalek's essence is the denial of tomorrow, the claim that there is no better future to long for. The word *Amalek* is numerically 240, similar to the Hebrew word פעמים / *Pa'amayim* / twice, repetition. Amalek's strength lies in fostering the illusion that nothing will ever change, that life is but an endless repetition of what has been before, that yearning is pointless, and hope is irrelevant.

The descendants of Rochel possess the precise spiritual weapon to counter this illusion. Among Yaakov's two primary wives, Leah bore many children, while Rochel, for years, remained childless. Her longing for children was fierce and unrelenting. She lived in a state of boundless *Tzima'on* / an infinite thirst, to build her family. This longing burned so deeply that she cried out to Yaakov: "Give me children, and if not, I am dead" (*Bereishis*, 30:1). Rochel's legacy is an unquenchable yearning, a soul-force that refuses to accept a static reality. It is the power to envision, to ache, and to strive for a better tomorrow, and in so doing, to shatter Amalek's spell of repetition and despair.

Rochel's very life is bound to this constant longing for more. When she finally gives birth, she names her son, Yoseph, saying, "May Hashem grant me yet another son" (30:24). Her yearning did not end with the blessing received; it only deepened, with a yearning for another child. This same quality flows into Yoseph, as reflected in his very name, and into her other son, Binyamin, whose tribe longed to be the dwelling place of the Divine Presence (*Zevachim*, 53b. *Megilah*, 26a).

When Klal Yisrael was exiled from Eretz Yisrael after the destruction of the first Beis haMikdash, it is our mother Rochel who weeps for her children and "refuses to be comforted for her children, who are gone." Hashem's reply to her was, "Restrain your voice from weeping, and your eyes from shedding tears; for there is a reward for your labor... and there is תקוה / hope לאחריתך / for your future" (*Yirmeyahu*, 31:16-18). Rochel's tears, her relentless longing for redemption, are met with Divine assurance; her yearning will bear fruit, her hope will not be in vain.

Amalek's mission is to extinguish yearning and declare hope pointless. Rochel and her descendants embody the exact opposite: a spiritual desire, passionate longing, and the unshakable conviction that the world can be healed and transformed, even against all odds. Amalek's attempt to exterminate yearning and hope is powerfully countered by Rochel and her descendants' yearning (*Resisei Layla*, 52).

The descendants of Rochel, which is all of Klal Yisrael, called the Bnei Yoseph, children of Yoseph, stand as living refutations of Amalek's cynicism, carrying within the eternal promise that, ויש־ תקוה לאחריתך / "There is hope for your future..." (*Yirmeyahu*, 31:17). Indeed, there will be an *Acharis* / אחרית / end when history reaches its culmination, when all wounds are healed, and righteousness shines in its full perfection. For this, we yearn with our *Kol*, our entire being.

Amalek also has an *Acharis* / אחרית / end, but not one that is filled with healing and hope, quite the opposite. ראשית גוים עמלק ואחריתו עדי אבד / "Amalek was the first of the nations, and his fate shall be *everlasting destruction*" (*Bamidbar*, 24:20). Since Amalek rejects hope and denies redemption, clinging instead to destruction as its creed, its own end is in fact destruction. Amalek will simply end and disappear forever. Hashem has קֵץ שָׂם לַחֹשֶׁךְ / "placed an 'end' to darkness" (Iyov, 28:3, as interpreted by the Rebbe Rayatz in *Reishis Goyim Amalek*). As such, there is no such thing as absolute evil or endless evil. All injustice has an endpoint; all darkness will fade.

When we live fully rooted in the present, yet with our eyes and hearts fixed on the coming of Mashiach, no force of negativity can ensnare us. The schemes of Amalek, and of every Haman in history, inevitably collapse upon their own heads, fulfilling their own prophecy of ruin, destruction, and hopelessness, while Klal Yisrael moves steadily toward the radiant light of redemption.

MOVING TOWARDS A TOMORROW

There are *RaMaCH* / 248 positive Mitzvos in the Torah (Reish/200, Mem/40, Ches/8). The letters of *RaMaCH* can form the words *Machar* / 'tomorrow' or *Rechem* / 'womb'. The Torah and its Mitzvos call us to live fully in *haYom* / today, to be deeply present in this moment, while holding a profound awareness that the present is the womb from which the future is born. Every thought, word, and action we choose today shapes the contours of tomorrow. With even a single good deed or kind word, each of us has the power to "tip the scales for himself and the entire world toward the side of merit, and to bring about his own salvation and that of the whole world" (Rambam, *Hilchos Teshuvah*, 3:4).

In the paradigm of Kedushah, where there is a revealed connection to the *Ohr Ein Sof* / Infinite light of Hashem and a place for 'holy doubt', everything is possible, and everything is imbued with meaning. The future redemption is felt so vividly that its light reverberates into the present. In the paradigm of Amalek, by contrast, nothing feels possible or meaningful. There is a flat denial of the Creator's existence and thus of any purpose, intentionality, and direction for creation, and certainly there is no future salvation.

"Hashem's Name will not be complete until Amalek is completely eradicated" (*Tanchuma*, Ki Teitzei. Rashi, *Shemos*, 17:16). Amalek's war against hope, growth, and meaning is, in truth, a war against Hashem Himself, the very Source of hope, progress, and purpose. For if there is a Creator and the creation was created within intention, then there is a purpose, and if there is a purpose, then there is direction; and if there is a direction and an end game, then there is a path toward that redemption. As Klal Yisrael are the living witnesses and ambassadors of this truth in the world, the eternal people of hope, Amalek's attack is directed at them specifically.

As explained earlier, Amalek, "the *Reishis* / head of all the nations," is rooted in the head or Keser of Kelipah, which manifests as a corrosive and paralyzing doubt. Klal Yisrael, however, is rooted in an even higher Source, *Radla* / the Unknowable Head, which manifests liberating, empowering, holy doubt.

Negative doubt constricts and immobilizes. It leaves us feeling powerless, draining us of strength, and leaving us convinced that nothing matters and nothing can be done. Holy doubt, by contrast, opens and expands. It frees us from the illusion of fixed limitations, offering us a fresh vantage point from which we can choose new life and renewed possibility.

This is the inner reason why the Yom Tov of Purim, celebrating Klal Yisrael's triumph over Haman and Amalek, is named for the

Pur, the lottery, which on the surface symbolizes randomness and uncertainty. Logic would suggest naming it after the salvation, perhaps "Yom Esther" or "Yom Shushan." Why name it after the very instrument of the decree? Because Adar and Purim are bound to the deepest level of Keser: Radla, the place of seeming randomness and "not-knowing" that, in truth, is the womb from which all conscious knowing, mindful choice, and ultimate meaning emerges.

HAMAN-AMALEK: NO MEMORY & NO HISTORY. NO PAST, THUS NO FUTURE

Without memory, there is no history, and without history, there is no future.

The consciousness of Amalek is steeped in doubt, cynicism, and a corrosive uncertainty. In its worldview, everything is mere happenstance, devoid of purpose, direction, or intention. If nothing has meaning, there is no destiny, no tomorrow, and no redemption to anticipate. Life becomes a closed, stagnant cycle, aimlessly repeating itself. Life is cyclical and coincidental, and because of that, directionless and random.

Amalek denies the possibility of *Tikkun* / correction because it denies both past and future, reducing time to an endless loop where nothing significant has happened and nothing significant ever will. If all events are random, memory loses its value. There are no soul-searching questions, nor any enduring commitments drawn from past experiences, only shallow and trivial recollections, facile answers, and a general refusal to engage in any form of meaningful change, as it is not possible in an Amalek state of mind.

This is the essence of Amalek, a rejection of the very notion that creation has a purpose and is steadily moving toward redemption. If there is no past, there can be no future. The arc of history is flattened and certainly not moving forward and upward. More deeply still, Amalek is committed to believing in nothing, resolutely and with Da'as, a willful allegiance to non-commitment, to doubt, to chaos, and to the empty relativity of meaninglessness.

The Torah's command is decisive: "Remember what Amalek did to you...You shall blot out the memory of Amalek from under Heaven" (*Devarim*, 25:17-19). At first glance, this is paradoxical; to blot out Amalek's memory seems to mean forgetting them entirely, yet we are commanded to remember them. How can we do both? The answer is we blot out Amalek precisely *through* remembering them.

Amalek thrives in forgetfulness. To remember, actively and meaningfully, is to defeat them. Memory connects past to future, revealing the trajectory of history and allowing us to live with purpose (The letters of the name עמלק stand for קהת ,לוי, משה ,עמרם. This means Moshe's father was Amram, his grandfather was Kehos, and his great-grandfather was Levi. Reminding us that Moshe's own mission to battle Amalek was rooted in a living chain of memory). Cultivating memory and using its meaningful lessons to move forward into a more fulfilled destiny allows us to eradicate Amalek and what Amalek represents. Recording sacred history becomes a weapon against Amalek. This is the reason Esther asked that the story of Haman, the Amalek of her generation, be written down and canonized in *Tanach* / Torah: "Write me for future generations." Esther knew that to truly eradicate Amalek and its embodiment in Haman required memorializing the past as a guide for our future. Thus, the story of Purim became the third time in Tanach where Amalek is remembered and blotted out ("Esther sent to the Sages: 'Write me the story of Purim for future generations and canonize the book of Esther into the Tanach.' They sent her an argument: It is written (*Mishlei*, 22:20), 'Have I not already written for you three times?'" They meant that the story of Amalek is already mentioned three times in Tanach: Shemos, Devarim, and Shmuel 1: "See, it says three times, and not four times!" The Sages did not accede to Esther's request until they found a verse written in the Torah: כתב זאת זכרון בספר ושים באזני יהושע / "Write this for a memorial in the Book, and rehearse it in the ears of Yehoshua, that I will utterly blot out the remembrance of Amalek from under the Heavens" (*Shemos*, 17:14). "Write this," the Sages realized, refers to that which is written in the Torah here, in Shemos. And in Devarim, the phrase 'a memorial' refers to that which is written in the Prophets. 'In the book' then refers to that which is *written* (eternally) in the Megilah. Thus, the Megilah is in fact the required third mention of Amalek, and not an extraneous fourth": *Megilah*, 7a. ויהיה סמך למקרא מגילה מן התורה: Ramban, *Devarim*, 25:17. The Medrash, *Toras Kohanim*, Bechukosai, teaches, זכור את אשר עשה לך עמלק יכול בלבך כשהוא אומר לא תשכח, הרי שכחת הלב אמורה. הא מה אני מקיים זכור שתהא שונה בפיך. Regarding this the Ra'avad writes, זכרון עמלק שתהא שונה בפיך הלכות מגילה).

Purim needs to be remembered not only as an oral memory; an oral memory can be altered through transmission and the passage of time. Esther recognized that oral memory alone is fragile, vulnerable to distortion over time and transmission. She therefore ensured that the Purim story would be permanently inscribed, its message unaltered, in the sacred canon. The blotting out of Amalek must be done through reading aloud certain passages in the Torah (Torah law demands that we remember Amalek by reading the Parsha of Amalek from an actual Sefer Torah: *HaEshkol*, Hilchos Chanukah v'Purim, 10. *Bach*, Orach Chayim, 685. *Mishnah Berurah*, ibid., 7:14. Although the Minchas Chinuch [Mitzvah 603] argues that reading Parshas Zachor is only a *Mitzvah m'deRabanan* / from the Sages). Blotting out Amalek requires both the *telling* of the story and its *inscription* in writing. But it could not remain as a mere historical chronicle; it had to be woven into the eternal fabric of Torah itself. For the memory to endure for all time, it needed to be embedded in all three divisions of Tanach: the *Torah* / Five Books of Moshe, the *Nevi'im* / Prophets, and the *Kesuvim* / Writings. In the Torah, the story of Amalek is recorded in Shemos, and its repetition in Devarim. In the books of the Nevi'im, the story of the descendants of Amalek is recorded in the Book of Shmuel. And now it is also inscribed in the books of Kesuvim, in Megilas Esther (*Yerushalmi*, Megilah, 1:5). In this way, the remembrance and eradication of Amalek are assured for every generation and through every medium of Tanach.

Moreover, the Yerushalmi teaches that even the Oral Torah itself enshrines this memory: the very existence of *Maseches Megilah* is to prevent Amalek from being forgotten. The Yerushalmi writes that the reason why there is a particular *Maseches* / tractate in the Mishnah and Talmud for Purim called *Maseches Megilah*, is that it will help us to *not* forget Amalek: "And the memory of them shall never perish among their descendants" (*Esther*, 9:28). "From this verse, our Sages understood to establish a Maseches" (*Yerushalmi*, 2:4). In other words, Amalek must be inscribed not only in all three divisions of the Written Torah, but also within the living, breathing flow of the Oral Torah, in Mishnah and Gemara, preserved in the vibrant, ever-renewed transmission of Torah from mouth to ear, from heart to heart.

This, then, is the meaning of כתב זאת זכרון בספר ושים באזני יהושע / "Write this as a 'remembrance' in the Book, and place it in the ears of Yehoshua" (*Shemos*, 17:14). To blot out Amalek, to "Write this," the story needs to be remembered and written down in all forms of Torah, all books of Tanach, and even a full volume of Talmud. Furthermore, "and place it in the ears," means that it needs to be frequently read and re-read, "in the ears," in the living tradition of Klal Yisrael. It needs to be written down, repeatedly recited, heard, and deeply listened to, as a living, relevant memory. This threefold act of remembering ensures that Amalek and everything that Amalek represents is completely eradicated. By inscribing, speaking, and internalizing this memory, we dismantle Amalek's ideology of forgetfulness. And in doing so, we move history itself closer to the day when Amalek's name, and all it represents, will be utterly erased.

ERADICATING AMALEK & WAR

This insight, that erasing Amalek requires a living, accurate sense of history, illuminates a puzzling episode the next time Klal Yisrael confronted Amalek, in the days of King Shaul.

In Sefer Shmuel, we read that Shaul haMelech / King Saul was commanded by Shmuel haNavi, the prophet, to wage war against Amalek and utterly destroy them. Shaul went to battle and emerged victorious, yet he spared the life of Agag, the king of Amalek. After the battle, Shmuel rebuked Shaul for this failure. The Pasuk then records that Shmuel said to Agag, "As your sword has bereaved women, so will your mother be bereaved among women" (*Shmuel 1*, 15:33), and Shmuel himself killed him. The question is obvious: why does Shmuel justify Agag's execution on the grounds that he was a murderer, when the Torah commands the eradication of Amalek regardless?

The Brisker Rav brings down in the name of his father, Rebbe Chayim (*Reshimas Talmidim*, Nach, *Shmuel 1*), that the Mitzvah to erase Amalek applies specifically in the context of battle, as alluded to in the Pasuk that says, מלחמה לה׳ בעמלק / "a war for Hashem against Amalek" (*Shemos*, 17:16). Once the battle had concluded, Shmuel could no longer kill Agag by virtue of that Mitzvah alone. Therefore, he executed him on the basis of his crimes as a murderer, not because of the Mitzvah to erase Amalek.

But why should the Mitzvah to eradicate Amalek be limited to a formal war? If they are an enemy bent on destroying us, why not eliminate them by any means, even covertly? If an enemy is intending to kill you, it is permissible to preempt them and kill them first, whether by assassination or battle.

The answer is that Amalek is not merely a physical enemy; it is an ideology. Amalek is the antithesis of everything Klal Yisrael and the Torah stand for: purpose, meaning, memory, and redemption. The real battle is against the mindset of Amalek, not merely its people (Amalek is more than a people, it is also an ideology. According to the Rambam, a person born an Amalekite can throw off his beliefs and accept the universal Torah laws for all mankind, and no longer be considered 'from Amalek': Rambam, *Hilchos Melachim u'Milchamos*, 6:4, as the *Kesef Mishneh* explains). Therefore, to truly erase Amalek, we need more than simply 'to kill them off'; we need to erase the entire ideology of Amalek. To accomplish this requires that we do so in a 'battle'.

The difference between battle and assassination, for example, is that battle is waged in the open, and there are *Halachos* / laws of war. The Halachos of battle ensure that a war is methodically defined, organized, and delineated; and that it occurs out in the open, which allows it to be properly recorded and monitored. The Torah tells us about a "Book of the Wars for Hashem": עַל־כֵּן יֵאָמַר בְּסֵפֶר מִלְחֲמֹת ה׳ / "Concerning this it is told in the Book of the Wars of Hashem..." (*Bamidbar*, 21:14). The Even Ezra (*ibid.*) writes that there was such a book which described all the wars Hashem fought on behalf of those who fear Him, and it is possible that this book already existed in the time of Avraham. The Rambam (*ibid.*) likewise notes that in every generation, the wise took care to record the details of great battles, preserving them for posterity.

This is precisely why Amalek must be defeated on a battlefield, publicly, formally, and in a way that is recorded for posterity. The story of Amalek must be recorded and written down in "The Book of Wars." In such a battle, they are countered physically *and* their ideology is discredited and written into history as a failed, futile, defeated force. Only in this way can Amalek's memory be blotted out both in body and in idea, erased from the world and from the human story.

HAMAN / AMALEK: HAPPENSTANCE

Without a sense of history, destiny, and purpose, life dissolves into randomness and, ultimately, meaninglessness. When describing Amalek's first assault on Klal Yisrael, the Torah says, "Remember what Amalek did to you on your journey, after you left Egypt. אֲשֶׁר קָרְךָ בַּדֶּרֶךְ / *He chanced upon you on the way*, when you were famished and weary, and cut down all the stragglers in your rear..." (*Devarim*, 25:17-18). The word *Karcha* / קָרְךָ / chanced upon, conveys the essence of Amalek's worldview: happenstance, randomness, the absence of design. The Rambam warns that we must never look at the events of life and dismiss them as mere coincidence, simply saying, נקרה נקרית / "This was merely happenstance" (*Hilchos Ta'anis,* 1:3). This is the way of Amalek, and is, as the Rambam adds, a "cruel" way to look at life. To view the world as unplanned and undirected is to strip it of holiness, meaning, and destiny, reducing life to a ceaseless merry-go-round with no progress, no movement toward redemption.

It is for this reason that Amalek always appears and attacks when Klal Yisrael is on the verge of building a Mikdash, a place intentionally dedicated to the service of HaKadosh Baruch Hu. A Mikdash is the ultimate affirmation of purpose and sanctity, and therefore the ultimate affront to Amalek's creed and cruel ideology of happenstance.

Amalek thus attacked when we were about to build the Mishkan in the Desert, as we read just before the Torah portion of Terumah, prior to the laws of building the Mishkan. Amalek attacked again in the times of King Shaul, before the building of the First Beis haMikdash. Haman, the descendant of Amalek, was struck during the Purim story, before the building (or the completion of the building) of the Second Beis haMikdash. And, tragically, in our own times, the Amalek of the 20th Century, the Nazis, *Yimach Shemam* / may their names be erased, and, in the 21st Century, Hamas and other radical Islamic forces, Yimach Shemam, have risen in defiance before the dawn of the era that will usher in the Third Beis haMikdash, to be built with the coming of Mashiach, speedily in our days.

Amalek's lens on reality is *Mikra* / "It (just) happened." Tellingly, this is the exact same term Haman uses when he tells his wife and family כל־אשר קרהו / "everything that 'happened' to him" (*Esther*, 6:13). He was a descendant of Amalek and thus viewed everything as mere happenstance. He embodied this philosophy of randomness. The story of Purim unmasks this delusion, revealing that what seems coincidental is in truth Divinely woven. Indeed, upon these words in the Megilah, *Chazal* / our Sages say, ויגד לו מרדכי את כל אשר קרהו, אמר להתך לך אמר לה בן בנו של קרהו בא עליכם, הדא הוא דכתיב אשר קרך בדרך / "And Mordechai told him everything that happened to him." Mordechai told Hasach, Go and tell her (Esther), the grandson of קרהו / 'Happened' has come upon us, as it says, regarding Amalek, אשר קרך בדרך / "He chanced upon you on the way" (*Esther Rabbah*, 8:5).

But there is a deeper layer still. Recognizing that nothing is truly a chance is one level of insight. A higher level is perceiving the holy side of happenstance. Just as there is a 'holy doubt' that expands the mind to possibilities we had not imagined, so too there is a holy form of surprise, moments of unexpected blessing that awaken wonder and gratitude. The ultimate *v'Nahafoch-Hu* / reversal of Mikrah into something positive in itself.

The great reversal is not simply the replacement of darkness with light, but the transformation of darkness into light. A transformation of doubt into certainty is not an actual reversal, but rather a replacement with its opposite. Complete reversal means turning negative doubt into positive doubt. The same is true with the phenomenon of *Karcha* / happenstance. Negative happenstance is not merely replaced by predictability and order; it is elevated into a holy happenstance, where the 'unexpected' becomes a vessel for a life of intentionality.

The very name of Purim is a testament to this truth. The lot, seemingly devoid of intention and completely dictated by happenstance, revealed the hidden, 'unexpected' deeper intention of the Creator. Even in what appears random, Hashem is present, waiting to be recognized.

When blessings arrive unanticipated, without prior expectation, they carry a special freshness, a thrill born of surprise. To live open to Divine "happenstance" is to dwell in a state of constant aliveness and holy spontaneity, ready to be surprised at any moment. In such a life, everything that comes your way is received as a delightful revelation, a precious gift placed in your hands suddenly and unexpectedly.

Just as "positive doubt" propels us to engage more deeply in discerning our purpose, so too a positive sense of "happenstance" awakens in us a heightened appreciation for all of life, enabling us to greet every Mitzvah, every encounter, every opportunity to do good or offer thanks, with freshness, wonder, and a sense of precious surprise. Thus, when the Megilah describes the final reversal of events and the salvation of Klal Yisrael, it employs a telling word. At the story's climax, we read: "For the Jews it was a time of light, joy, gladness, and יקר / *Yekar* / glory" (*Esther*, 8:16). This Yekar signifies a holy, life-affirming sense of astonishment, the capacity to see every aspect of existence as radiant and precious. It was precisely through the unexpected turn of events that they came to perceive that everything which arises is, in truth, infinitely Yakar beyond measure in worth. This is the ultimate *v'Nahafoch-Hu* / reversal of קרי / *Keri* / happenstance (*Vayikra*, 26:21) into יקר / *Yakar* / precious surprise (יקר and קרי have the same letters).

BEYOND KNOWING: REACHING A POINT OF 'MAYBE'

On Purim, we are called to enter a state of joy that transcends Da'as, knowledge, and certainty, Ad d'Lo Yada. Ordinarily, we live and choose through Da'as, making decisions with clarity and discernment. But Purim invites us higher still, to Lo Yada, to touch Radla, the 'unknowable' point beyond knowing, where choice flows from our Etzem, our very essence, unbound by coercion, condition, or self-imposed limitation. Here, the horizon of possibility is truly endless.

When confined to Da'as alone, one may be rich in answers yet closed to deeper questions. In the opposite extreme, negative lack of Da'as, the Safek of cynicism, everything is thrown into doubt, but without direction. Such doubt leaves us paralyzed, with unanswerable questions, drained of vitality, unable to act with passion or resolve.

On Purim, however, we taste the holy form of "not knowing," the essence-consciousness of Lo Yada, above and beyond Da'as. In this space, our indestructible faith in infinite possibility is revealed through our oneness with the Source of All. Here, answers are fluid and alive, giving birth to deeper questions, which in turn lead to higher answers. This dynamic, ever-ascending exchange of question and answer is itself a Nahafoch Hu, a turning of all states, our victory over Haman's narrowing doubt.

Simply transforming negative Safek into ודאי / *Vadai*, doubt into certainty, does not yet reach the full alchemy of Purim. The deeper 'Nahafoch Hu' happens when even paralyzing, cynical questions, questions born of the void, are themselves transfigured into living, holy questions, inner explorations that open us to what lies beyond our current knowing. For this reason, the word *Purim* in numerical value is 336 (Pei/80, Vav/6, Reish/200, Yud/10, Mem/40 = 336), the same numerical value as *Sha'alah* / question (Shin/300, Aleph/1, Lamed/30, Hei/5 = 336).

Imagine you feel a passionate pull to create something holy, for example, a skill, a project, or a public offering that could truly benefit others. Yet alongside your excitement, a whisper of self-doubt creeps in: 'I'm not formally trained. Others are more authoritative, more skilled. Who am I to do this?' Still, you muster the courage to learn as you go, to seek guidance, and to launch your vision. Now picture this: a presumed authority figure confronts you with questions that land squarely on your most vulnerable point: 'Is this a joke? Who do you think you are, presenting yourself as a resource to others?'

The full Nahafoch Hu, the complete inner reversal, does not come from flipping instantly from *Safek* / self-doubt to *Vadai* / certainty, simply replacing the questions with affirmations. Rather, it comes from engaging with the questions more deeply, allowing them to reveal unexpected answers that transform their very nature.

If someone says, 'Is this a joke?' without defensiveness, ask yourself honestly: 'Is there indeed a part of me that treats this as a joke? Am I, in some corner of my heart, fooling myself or acting irresponsibly?' If the answer is no, if you find that, while you may be taking a risk, you are deeply committed to learning, growing, and helping others, then own that truth. Then you could ask the same question from the standpoint of truth: 'Is this a joke? Is helping others, even in a small way, a joke? Not at all!' The cynical question has now become a holy one, refining your clarity and deepening your commitment, and perhaps taking you beyond your previous level of Da'as.

If someone says, 'Who do you think you are, presenting yourself as a resource to others?' turn the question of doubt inward: 'Yes, am I overestimating my abilities? Am I willing to refer people elsewhere when I meet something beyond my scope? Am I prepared to say, "I don't know" when appropriate?' And more profoundly: 'Who, indeed, do I think I am? Do I secretly think I'm incapable, unlovable, or unworthy? Or do I recognize that I was created with a purpose, that perhaps I am in this very position to fulfill part of that purpose? Do I understand that my yearning to do good is from Hashem, and that, in truth, I am one with Hashem, the ultimate Source of all?'

Notice how it feels when you transform negative, stifling questions into sacred, life-giving ones. Do you feel lighter, freer, more fluid? Or more grounded, stable, and assured?

This is the inner work of Purim, to convert cynical, paralyzing questions into holy Lo Yada, wholesome not-knowing. 'I don't know, and therefore I can learn more, rise higher, and be open to the surprises Hashem has prepared for me, beyond what I can see or know today.'

LEARN TO LOVE THE QUESTIONS AND THE MAYBES OF LIFE

Our Sages tell us אהב את השמא / "Love the *maybe*" (*Derech Eretz Zuta*, 1. *Kalah Rabsi*, 3). On a simple level, this can mean being cautious in where you walk and what you do (*Sefer Chasidim*. See also *Peleh Yoetz*,

31). But more profoundly, it can mean being open; open with love to infinite possibilities, and thereby open to the Infinite Unknown of HaKadosh Baruch Hu (The *Paneach Raza*, on Bereishis, 1:1, writes that the first letter of the Torah, Beis can be transmuted into the word שמא / *She'ma* / 'maybe'. As the world came into being as the infinite possibilities of maybe combinations came in front of HaKadosh Baruch Hu, and the Creator formed a certain formation from these letters and created specific realites: פתח התורה בבי"ת בעבור כי במלואה בצירוף חילוף אותיותיה בא"ת ב"ש שהוא שמ"א יעלה בין הכל תשנ"ג כמספר אורים ותומים כי בכל המקרא תומים שאצל אורים חסר ו' רמז כי האירו ועלו האותיות לפניו ית' איך ומה לבראת כל דבר ודבר ע"ד משפט אורים ותומים שבחושן. In other words, the *She'ma* state of not knowing connects us with the Creator and the letters in their infinite potential).

Purim acquaints us with this holy openness, with the positive dimension of Lo Yada, the "not-knowing" that emerges from genuine questions. Such questions lead us to deeper answers, which in turn give rise to even more profound and authentic questions, an endless unfolding. True questions are not asked to provoke uncertainty for its own sake, nor to challenge authority or undermine the status quo. They are not like the playful questions of a child who seeks only to stump a parent by asking, "Why is the sky blue?" Rather, true questions yearn for a deeper truth, reaching beyond what is presently known, engaging us in a humbling, mind-opening dialectic. Yet, beyond the answers, which represent certainties, the highest revelation of Purim is learning to dwell in the question itself, to embrace holy doubt, the sacred realm of 'maybe'.

Ordinarily, one might think that the antidote to doubt, to Amalek, to uncertainty, would be mustering up great *Vadai* / certainty. And in fact, one of the Names of Hashem is called *Vadai*, as we say in the *Nusach haTefilah* / liturgy of prayer, *haVadai Shemo* / "His name is Certainty." Yet, Purim is named after the Pur which means a lottery, an image of uncertainty. Moreover, as mentioned, the numerical value of Purim equals the value of *Sha'alah* / question. Purim teaches us that the true response to the unholy doubt of Amalek is not simply absolute certainty. Rather, it is the transformation of negative doubt into holy doubt, a profound openness brimming with unrevealed potential.*

Just as there is a Divine Name 'Vadai', one of the names of the Shechinah is אולי / *Ulai* / 'Maybe' (*Tikunei Zohar*, Tikun 69. *Koheles Yaakov*, Erech Aleph). This is the dimension of Lo Yada, the holy not-knowing. In this spirit, Mordechai tells Esther, *Mi Yodea* / 'Who knows! Are we so certain in our judgments about this predicament? *Ulai*, maybe there is another way. Maybe we are called to remain open to other possibilities. Who knows, perhaps it is precisely for this moment that you have attained your position, to bring forth salvation for our people.'

Remarkably, the very river that encircled the ancient city of Shushan, where the Purim story unfolded, was called אולי / *Ulai* (*Doniel*, 8:2. ואראה בחזון ויהי בראתי ואני בשושן הבירה... ואראה בחזון ואני הייתי על־אובל אולי

---

*The Pasuk says with regards to the battle with Amalek: והיה כאשר ירים משה ידו וגבר ישראל / "And when Moshe lifted his hands, Klal Yisrael was victorious." On the one hand, this means that by lifting his hands with *Emunah* / faith, as the Pasuk also says, ויהי ידיו אמונה / and hands were steadfast" (*Shemos*, 17:12), he created a world of ודאי / certainty, to counter the uncertainty of Amalek. Thus, as mentioned earlier, the word ידו / his hand, plus the letter Aleph / א for Emunah (אמונה) creates the word ודאי / certain. Yet, on a deeper level, raising both hands upwards means as follows. The concept of doubt arises when a person is faced with two options before him and does not know which one to choose, and thus, the doubt is cripplin,g and he chooses nothing. Moshe Rabbeinu lifted both of his hands, thereby indicating that there is no need to choose one over the other and that one can make use of both. In this way, he weakened the power of Amalek, which is negative doubt, for Moshe Rabbeinu demonstrated that there is, in fact, no crippling doubt here, since both possibilities can coexist together.

/ "I saw in the vision — at the time I saw it I was in the fortress of Shushan…I saw in the vision that I was beside the Ulai River"). The life-giving waters of this holy 'maybe', this profound not-knowing, served as a Sovev, a surrounding and transcendent light, encircling and framing the story of Purim. Likewise, it encircles the story of each of our own lives, inviting us to recognize that Hashem is ever-present, hidden within every twist and turn, in every place we may think 'maybe' no here and 'maybe' not now.

Purim is singular among all the other Yamim Tovim in that its highest aim is to enter the state of Ulai, of Lo Yada. Take Sukkos, for example. The principal Mitzvah of the Yom Tov is bound to Da'as, knowledge: "You shall dwell in booths for seven days… so that future generations may *know* that I caused Israel to dwell in booths when I brought them out of Egypt" (*Vayikra*, 23:42-43). On Sukkos, Da'as is indispensable; if one sits in the Sukkah without knowing its reason, the Mitzvah itself has not been fulfilled (the Bach, based on the words of the *Tur, Orach Chayim*, 625. *Bikurei Yaakov*, 625:3). But Purim reverses the pattern. On Purim we drink wine, literally and metaphorically, until we transcend Da'as, until we move beyond discernment between blessing and curse. Purim draws us instead into the flowing waters of Ulai, into the mystery of *Reisha d'Lo Isyada* / the Divine Head that does not know, the source of true freedom, true knowing and truly life-affirming possibilities.

This transformation, from doubt to holy uncertainty and beyond, unfolds dramatically in the Megilah. What began in trembling doubt, with an ominous decree threatening annihilation, was overturned completely. The decree was radically transformed to such an extent that Haman was hanged on the same gallows that he had prepared for Mordechai. The experience of uncertainty regarding their fate ultimately brought out within them a positive kind of uncertainty. This opened them to a deeper commitment to their faith and a radical re-acceptance of the Torah. In this way, their uncertainty brought about an even deeper sense of possibility, conviction, and commitment.

A WORLD BEYOND DUALITY AND POLARITIES; THE BODY KNOWS

The drinking of wine bestows on the individual the ability "to elevate the *Nitzutz* / spark of Holiness and Divinity that is trapped in the lower realms of Kelipah" (Arizal, *Shaar haKavanos*, Purim, Derush 1). The sage Rava says, "A person is obligated to become inebriated on Purim until he doesn't know the difference between 'blessed is Mordechai' and 'cursed is Haman.'" He does not say, "...until one does not know the difference between cursed is Mordechai and blessed is Haman." In other words, we are not drinking in order to *confuse* good and evil, but to go beyond the paradigm of binary and polarity. Hence, even when we rise above Da'as and do not distinguish or articulate the difference, still, we naturally choose and confirm that 'Blessed is Mordechai', the good and the holy, and 'cursed is Haman' the unholy and evil.

For this reason, even in our state of "inebriation" on Purim, we trust that the deeper wisdom of the body-consciousness will instinctively incline toward the good. This is a place that lies *beyond* the free choice of deliberate, mindful Da'as. Here, goodness is not something external that must be weighed, deliberated, and consciously chosen, it is simply who we are. On this level, we do not require Da'as to instruct us in what is right or wrong.

On some level, our body, in relation to our soul, represents our Etzem, our essence, whereas the soul is our *Giluy* / revealed connection to the Ohr Ein Sof, the Infinite Light. This is because the Divine *Bechirah* / choice in Klal Yisrael is the choice of our bodies (as explained in Tanya, 49), and since it is the Essence of HaKadosh Baruch Hu (*Kiviyachol* / so to speak) that chooses us, chooses our bodies, thus our bodies are one with the Essence. In essence, the body is therefore holy and because of this, in its deepest level of choosing, the body always chooses HaKadosh Baruch Hu ("The bodies of the upright are holy": *Zohar* 3, p. 70b. "The body is like the parchment upon which the Torah scroll is written": Ramban, *Moed Katan*, 25a. Ramban, *Toras haAdam*, Inyan Keriah).

Our drinking on Purim becomes a Tikun for the drinking of Achashverosh. His intoxication led him to folly and cruelty, even to the point of murdering his wife. In contrast, our drinking carries us beyond the narrow confines of rationality into life-giving expansiveness. In that state we express love and kindness instinctively, toward our spouse, our family, our friends, and toward every fellow being, through Mishloach Manos, Matanos laEvyonim, and Seudas Purim.

The "not-knowing" of Purim allows us to act from instinct, from the primal, childlike vitality of the body in its full and raw purity. We drink, dress up, laugh, and play, like children unburdened by self-conscious restraint. We lose our Da'as, the distinctions that divide one thing and one person from another, and so we give without measure, to "anyone who stretches out a hand." And yet, even in our not-knowing, we instinctively affirm "Blessed is Mordechai and cursed is Haman."

Living beyond Da'as is like tasting from the fruit of the Tree of Life, a state to be entered only at certain times and under specific conditions. For most of the year, a person requires mindful Da'as in order to choose rightly and to ascend. This is why the Sages of the Purim generation were initially hesitant to include the Megilah among the *Kisvei haKodesh* / Holy Writings, even when Esther urged them to do so (*Megilah,* 7a). Its sanctity and its Avodah, the spiritual work it summons, are not immediately apparent to be holy and thus wholesome. Yet that is precisely the point, that the intense holiness of Purim is hidden, subtle, and veiled, masked in the trappings of the seemingly mundane and even unholy. And this, in truth, is the very essence of the 'whole Megilah', the point of Purim.

DRINKING AS 'FRAGRANCE'

When our Sages instruct us to drink wine on Purim until becoming inebriated, they employ the term *l'Besumei* from the same root as *Besamim* / botanical fragrances, alluding to the sense of smell (There is also a type of wine that is called מבשם יין / fragrant (cooked) wine: *Shulchan Aruch,* Choshen Mishpat, 230:10. *Baba Basra,* 98a). This choice of words is deeply significant. Of all the human senses, only the sense of smell remained untouched by the primordial transgression of the Cheit Eitz haDa'as, the sin of eating from the Tree of Knowledge. The Torah describes how Adam and Chavah saw, heard, touched, and ultimately tasted of the fruit, but nowhere is it written that they smelled it. This was the one sense, among the five senses, that was not (as much) damaged in this cosmic event. As a result, the sense of smell retains a purity, a direct line to the innocence of Gan Eden before the sin. To become *l'Besumei* on Purim, then, is not merely to lose oneself in intoxication, but to awaken the fragrant, Edenic dimension within, the state of consciousness prior to duality, prior to the split between good and evil. It is to touch a space beyond the calculating mind of Da'as, a realm of innocence and unity beyond all binary, the Edenic state beyond rational knowing.

Indeed, Mordechai and Esther are connected with a pleasurable fragrance (*Chulin*, 139b, regarding Mordechai. *Megilah*, 13a, regarding Esther / Hadassah. Haman is also connected with the sense of smell, but connected with the foul scent of the Chelbana: Arizal. *Shaloh*, Parshas Zachor. See also *Kesem Ofir*, Esther 3:1. *Haman* and *Chelb'nah* are both numerically 95. "The Chelb'nah has a foul odor...": *Kerisus*, 6b The eleven ingredients of the Ketores correspond to Haman and his ten sons. As the decree was one of total annihilation, Klal Yisrael responded with total Mesiras Nefesh for HaKadosh Baruch Hu. As the Alter Rebbe explains in *Torah Ohr* on Megilas Esther (91b, 97a, 99b), this self-transcending devotion annulled the decree. For this reason, Purim is connected to the Avodah of Ketores, which signifies absolute unity and bonding with Hashem. As the Zohar teaches, בחד קטירא אתקטרנא ביה בקוב"ה / "With one bond, I am bound to the Holy One, blessed be He": *Zohar* 3, 288a).

By contrast, a person 'smells bad' when they live inauthentically, trying to impress or manipulate others. The Baal Shem Tov once made *Aliyas haNeshamah* / a soul-ascent, and met the spirit of a person who had a foul odor. The Baal Shem asked him, "Why do you smell so bad?" "Because," he responded, "I performed Mitzvos on earth with *Peniyos* / ulterior purposes."

In an Edenic state, beyond Da'as, choices are no longer weighed, debated, or forced. They flow effortlessly and naturally, as instinctive as not placing one's hand on burning coal. In a state of Lo Yada, beyond knowing, goodness arises without deliberation, not as a product of conscious Da'as decision-making, but as a spontaneous emanation of the soul. It is not so much that you choose the good, but that the good chooses through you. It is a non-choice choice.

Ultimately, in Lo Yada, we enter a state in which the Divine chooses with us and through us. At Mount Sinai, the Torah recounts that *Kafa Aleihem Har* / "Hashem held the Mountain above their heads," declaring that if Klal Yisrael would not accept the Torah, it would become their grave. In that moment, the acceptance of Torah was not their choice, but Hashem's choice alone.

Yet before this seeming coercion, Klal Yisrael had already declared *Na'aseh veNishma* / We will do, and only afterward will we understand" (Tosefos, *Shabbos*, 88a. כפה עליהן הר כגיגית ואע"פ שכבר הקדימו נעשה לנשמע). By this, they chose to surrender their Da'as, to enter into a covenant of action and faith even prior to comprehension. They were choosing to submit their Da'as and live according to the directives of the Torah, and only later would their minds understand and accept it intellectually. It was their conscious decision to step into a space beyond decision, to embrace choicelessness by choice.

Purim integrates these two modes, choice and choicelessness, and reveals a third:

Choice: Na'aseh veNishma, the willing submission of mind.

Choicelessness: The coercion of Sinai, where Hashem alone chooses.

Choiceless Choosing: The Ad d'Lo Yada of Purim, where human and Divine choosing merge seamlessly.

This dynamic is reflected in the turning point of the Megilah:

"The king was unable to sleep that night...and the chronicles of the king were read in front of him" (6:1). The text does not state who read the chronicles, only that "they were read." The Zohar explains that whenever Scripture omits the agent, it hints that Hashem Himself is acting. Hashem Himself read the chronicles to Achashverosh.

So too in the state of Lo Yada: our actions and choices are no longer merely ours, but transparent channels of Divine will. This is not a descent below Da'as, but an ascent beyond Da'as. In that Edenic realm, HaKadosh Baruch Hu chooses through us.

Da'as, conscious, discursive awareness is what separates us from the raw immediacy of experience. Da'as places a reflective layer between ourselves and life, allowing us to measure, analyze, and choose. When we suspend or surrender Da'as, that separation dissolves, and experience flows as one seamless stream. Picture a child eating ice cream. The child is not self-conscious, not analyzing the act or weighing its significance. They are wholly absorbed in the taste, free of calculation or reflection, immersed in a state of pure, unmediated flow. This is the innocence we are invited into on Purim, to become again like children in Eden, before eating from the fruit of the Tree of Da'as, when existence was experienced without fragmentation, without inner division.

Yet this state, as exalted as it is, carries a great danger when misunderstood or misapplied. If one confuses escapism or self-indulgence with transcendence, Lo Yada can become an excuse for irresponsibility. One might claim, "I am beyond thinking, guided only by being," as a way of justifying harmful choices. Without true alignment, what is meant to be a state of Edenic innocence can collapse into self-deception. This is why Chazal frame the Avodah of Ad d'Lo Yada, the Avodah that is beyond Avodah, as a once-a-year reality. On Purim, we taste, for a brief moment, the World to Come, a time when this fragrant innocence will be restored, when separation will be healed, when, as explained earlier, every day will be Purim. Until then, this state remains a holy exception: a gift granted once a year, to lift us beyond Da'as, to remind us of who we are, and to give us a foretaste of a redeemed world.

DRINKING & KNOWING THE 'NO' OF LIFE AS ONE WITH THE 'YES' OF LIFE

Purim is profoundly connected with the sense of smell. The Gemara asks: Where is Mordechai hinted to in the Torah? It answers with the Pasuk "*Mor D'ror* / flowing myrrh," which the Aramaic translation renders as *Mira Dachya*, the very same letters as *Mordechai* (*Chulin*, 139b). *Mor* is a spice (The *Tur*, on Orach Chaim 216, explains that Mor originates from an impure source, it is produced from the coagulated blood of a non-kosher animal which later dries and becomes Mor. Because of this, some authorities caution against eating it: הואיל ואתא לידן נימא ביה מילתא י"א שהוא זיעת חיה והנכון בעיני שחיה ידועה היא ויש לה כמין חטוטרות בצוארה ומתקבץ שם תחלה כמין דם ואח"כ מתייבש ונעשה ממנו המור והרמ"ה היה אוסר לאכלו משום חשש דם וה"ר יונה כתב שאפשר ליתן בו טעם להתירו דפירשא בעלמא הוא אע"ג דתחלתו היה דם דבתר השתא אזלינן). Esther, the other central figure of the Purim story, is also linked to fragrance. At times she is called Esther and at times Hadassah. The Gemara (*Megilah*, 13a) states that while her true given name was Esther, she was called Hadassah in reference to the righteous, who are likened to (fragrant) myrtles. Thus, both Mordechai and Esther are associated with fragrance and the sense of smell. Even the calendar reflects this connection. The word ריח / *Rei'ach* / smell has a numerical value of 218, which is equal to ג"י אדר / "the Thirteenth of Adar," the day of Ta'anis Esther. When including the word itself (*Rei'ach* = 219), it equals ד"י אדר / "the Fourteenth of Adar," the day of Purim in the Diaspora, and the beginning of Purim in Eretz Yisrael. In fact, according to Sefer Yetzirah, the month of Adar corresponds to the organ of the nose which is the sense of smell.

From all the senses, it is smell that most directly delights the soul (*Berachos,* 43b). In Eden, every sense was entangled in the eating of the Tree of Knowledge: sight, touch, taste, and hearing — all except smell. "The woman saw... she took... ate... they heard." Each sense descended into polarity, save for smell, which remained untouched, forever linked with the Tree of Life, the Eitz haChayim, with unity beyond duality, beyond the polarity of good and evil. For this reason, from all other senses, the sense of smell awakens our past most acutely. Smell is also the most evocative sense of memory. Other senses register us within the present, but smell uniquely transports us back into the past, bypassing the distance of time. The past is separated from the present by the flow of time, which suggests duality, the "Tree of Opposites." Thus, it is the sense of smell over all the other senses that can recapture for us a memory of the past most vividly, piercing the veils of time to evoke the past with startling immediacy. This is because the sense of smell is still more connected with the primordial condition of the brain and the Tree of Life.

Smell is linked to the deepest and most primordial regions of the brain and the deeper states of unified consciousness. Thus, when a person faints, smelling salts are offered to revive them, as the soul takes pleasure in smell, and the smell awakens vitality at the root of life itself, Tree of Life, beyond the tree of opposites and beyond the world of faint, 'death' and therefore, fatigue.

Purim, then, becomes a sanctuary in time, a passage into a deeper dimension both within and without, dimensions which are in truth one. On Purim, we are called to reach a level of Lo Yada, beyond Da'as, beyond knowing, this does not mean ignorance, but rather rising above duality, beyond the opposites of cursed and blessed, into a consciousness of unity where only Divine goodness exists.

Ad d'Lo Yada may be read homiletically: 'Until you know, not,' meaning, until you come to know the *no*'s of life as well as the *yes*'s, meaning to recognize Hashem not only in blessings, but also in concealments, the places of apparent absence. To "know *not*" is to know the deeper truth within a 'not', a 'no'; to discover the Divine Goodness and Life affirmation, even within negation, and to perceive the hidden light within what seems dark. And this is the rectification of the *Cheit Eitz haDa'as* / the transgression of the Tree of Knowledge. By entering the state of Lo Yada, knowing the 'not', we transcend the binary paradigm of good and evil and reenter the consciousness of the Tree of Life, where all is unified, and we can see even within a 'no' the 'yes', the Divine goodness.

One definition of *Nahafoch Hu* is 'the transformation of Da'as into a higher, deeper form of Da'as'. In the place of the lower Da'as, which is cut off from the Tree of Life, one experiences reality as binary, an either/or, either good and life-affirming and thus the place where the Holy rests, or the opposite. The higher, deeper level of Da'as is a Da'as that is not exclusive, rather inclusive, and the recognition that even in the place of an apparent 'no' of life, a place that seems dark and devoid of Divinity, that there is Only One, and Hashem is there just as much as anywhere else. In the language of one of the students of the Alter Rebbe, Reb Aaron Strasheler, ועיקר שלימות הדעת הוא כשיכול לסבול היפוכו, כשיש היפוך ממנו והוא סובל אותו אז נקרא שלימות החכמה, שלימות הדעת״ / "And the essence of the perfection of Da'as is when it can tolerate its opposite. When there is something contrary to it, and it is able to bear it, then it is called the perfection of Chochmah, the perfection of Da'as" (*Avodas haLevi*, Derushim l'Shabbos, p. 92d).

Even the word פור / *Pur* / lot, the root of Purim, reflects this truth. *Pur* in numerical value is 287 (counting the word itself), which is precisely the value of טוב / *Tov* / good (17) and the word רע / *Ra* / bad (270), combined. The essence of Purim is the realization that all is One. As such, Purim grants us the power to ascend beyond the fragmentation of the Tree of Knowledge and to taste, if only for a day, the seamless reality of the Tree of Life, where even 'death' is *Tov Meod* / very good (והנה טוב מאד, והנה טוב מות: *Medrash Rabbah*, Bereishis, 9:5).

TRANSFORMING THE NEGATIVE

In the seemingly unbalanced state of Lo Yada, one can no longer distinguish between the accursed Haman and the blessed Mordechai. Yet from this higher vantage point, the very energy of curse is transformed into blessing.

A *Gematriya* / numerical value, reveals this secret: *"Arur Haman* / cursed is Haman" and *"Baruch* / blessed is Mordechai" both equal 502. *Arur* (Aleph/1, Reish/200, Vav/6, Reish/200) equals 407. *Haman* (Hei/5, Mem/40, Nun/50) equals 95. Together, these equal 502.

Similarly, *Baruch* (Beis/2, Reish/200, Vav/6, Chaf/20) equals 228. *Morde-chai* (Mem/40, Reish/200, Dalet/4, Chaf/20, Yud/10) equals 274. Together, these equal 502.

This shared value is not incidental. In Torah, numerical correspondences reveal hidden unity. The number 502 itself reduces to seven (5+0+2), alluding to the seven fundamental *Midos* / traits. Both Haman and Mordechai embody the full spectrum of these seven qualities, their destructive and redemptive expressions.

The reason why numerical correspondences reveal hidden unity is that *Lashon haKodesh* / ancient Hebrew is not a conventional language but a Divine medium of creation. As Sefer Yetzirah teaches, the letters are the channels through which Divine energy flows to animate reality. Unlike English, where the word 'table' has no inherent link to an actual table, in Lashon haKodesh, the very letters *Shulchan* ('table' in Lashon haKodesh) serve as vessels for the life-force that sustains the table. Words are not arbitrary; rather, they are conduits of being. Therefore, when two words share a numerical equivalence, it is not a mere coincidence but testimony to an inner bond. "Blessed is Mordechai" and "cursed is Haman" may stand as opposites, yet at their core, they are interwoven. Even what appears as utterly negative contains sparks of the Divine, created with a purpose, and ultimately it too will be, through the work we do in this world, elevated, returned to its Source, and its purpose revealed.

This is the essence of Lo Yada: to surrender one mode of comprehension and ascend to a space beyond duality, where concealment dissolves, and the Divine is revealed in all. Practically, this means the acknowledgment of Hashem Light even within the *Lo* / the 'no's of life. Our task, as co-creators, then, is not passive acceptance of the world's fractures, nor resignation before negativity or running away from it. Rather, we are called to be co-creators with the Divine, to confront darkness, to fight the darkness with light and draw out its hidden Sparks and purpose for good. To transform the power of Haman and make them the strength of Mordechai, to harness even the raw, brute forces of existence and channel them for transcendent, altruistic purposes.

This is the labor of unity, of living from a place of Yichud, where there is no waste, and everything can be included (albeit, sometimes the release of the Holy Sparks is through avoidance and friction, and not engagement and inclusion). To live with Yichud, unity is to live not in opposition, but in integration. To reveal that within every curse lies the seed of blessing, and that the ultimate destiny of all creation is harmony and the revelation of Hashem's Oneness.

TAKING FROM CREATION
OR BEING PART OF CREATION

The root of all sin, descent, and inner negativity in the world, as alluded to earlier, lies in the primordial act of eating from the Tree of Knowledge of Good and Evil. The Zohar (*Zohar Chadash*, Eicha, 91b) teaches that when the Pasuk says they ate מפריו / *m'Piryo* / "from the fruit" (*Bereishis*, 3:6), the Satan seized the letter מ / Mem from the word *m'Piryo*, and through this, מות / *Maves* / death entered the world (*Maves* / death also begins with the letter Mem).

What is the meaning of this? The prefix Mem denotes 'from'. By eating *m'Piryo* / "from the fruit," they introduced the very notion of 'from-ness' or separation. Instead of receiving reality as an undivided whole, they took "from" it, carving out a fragment of 'something' from the 'Everything'. Their act of taking fractured their perception of the seamless flow of Oneness. It turned life into a game of possession, a world of unity into a world of ego and separation. Hence, once separation was born, the Satanic force could transform that rupture into death itself, the ultimate separation, the severing of body and soul. Purim is a Tikkun for the primordial sin of eating from the Tree of Knowledge, and for this reason, Purim uniquely celebrates the body (Moreover, the ultimate Nahafoch Hu, the complete reversal, is the transformation of the very concept of separation itself. Fittingly, the Tikun for the Cheit thus comes about through a person whose name starts with a Mem, Mordechai. Incidentally, the Geulah from Egypt was also initiated by a person whose name starts with Mem, Moshe, so is the Geulah in the Chanukah story, Mattisyahu, and so is the final Geulah, Mashiach).

On Purim, life is not approached from a place of taking "from," of מ / Mem / 'm'. Our eating and drinking are not about 'me' and 'mine', personal consumption and ego, the world of separation, and thus waste. Instead, the Avodah of Purim is in giving, in giving gifts of food and drink to friends, and charity to those in need, freely, without calculation of who deserves or needs what. On Purim, we give Mishloach Manos and Matanos LaEvyonim; both Mishloach and Matanos begin with a מ / Mem, transforming our taking from life, m'Piryo / from the fruit, into a posture of giving, Mishloach Manos and Matanos LaEvyonim. Even our drinking of wine is not for self-gratification, but a way to serve Hashem and thus a way to transcend the bounds of Da'as, rational calculation, and spread joy and laughter to others.

In truth, the Shefa, the infinite outpouring of Divine love that descends upon us on Purim, is too vast for us to contain. We have no vessel large enough to hold it. All we can do is open ourselves, receive it with joy, delight in its sweetness, and extend it outward by giving generously to others.

DRINKING: THE REDEMPTION OF IMAGINATION

There is another important point to highlight about drinking a little more than usual on Purim, and how this relates to the transformative quality of the day. Purim, as our Sages note, is parallel to Yom Kippur, Yom Kippurim, a day 'like Purim'. Both days are about *Teshuvah* / returning to center, realigning with our truest self, the Divine point within. Yet, Purim is 'higher', as Yom Kippur is called *Ki-Purim* / 'like Purim', not the other way around (Alter Rebbe, *Torah Ohr*, Megilas Esther, 95d). Purim contains this great power of transformation, the power to create a new image of oneself and step into a new reality, even through feasting, not fasting, and thus "taking the edge off" with a bit of extra wine, which can serve as a medium to facilitate this transformational process.

During the Seudas Purim, the festive meal when people, and often entire families, gather together as the Megilah states, משפחה ומשפחה / "families" (9:28), and as Rashi explains, "Families gather together to feast and to drink," it is customary to partake of a bit more wine than usual. There are many settings in which shared experience unites people into partners. When people study together, they become partners in *mind*. When they pray together, they become partners in *heart*. When they sing together, they become partners in *voice*. When they meditate together, they become partners in *silence*. And those who drink together become partners in *imagination*.

A drink, within a holy conducive context, has the power to loosen the rigid image one carries of oneself, to break the chains of old stories and binding narratives. It becomes a window opening to new horizons, where one can glimpse an alternative, elevated vision of who they might yet become. One lifts a cup, says *l'Chayim*, and in blessing another, blesses themselves as well. In that instant, the weight of the past, its heaviness, its shadows, whether real or imagined, can be lifted. One becomes unburdened, free to aspire, to soar, to dream of greatness. In that moment of release, they may envision themselves no longer confined by struggle, but living from the deepest truth of their being, the inner Tzaddik, the whole, luminous, expansive self, a self that even now glimmers within, and which, at the end of days, will shine forth in its full clarity and radiance.

From the perspective of smallness, the constricted ego-self, life can appear like a narrow and terrifying path: a tightrope stretched from birth to death, suspended over the abyss. Every step is fraught with fear, trials, and the trauma of mere existence. But from the perspective of largeness, from the soul's more expansive vision, everything shifts. "The whole world is filled with Your glory." Life does not feel any longer like a nightmare but rather as a vast, rich, and saturated reality, brimming with Divine goodness, a goodness that permeates even in its darkest corners. What appears like refuse is, in truth, Hashem's Garden of Delight. Purim, with its lightness, joy, and laughter, calls us into this broader vision. Purim teaches us to see not only what is lacking, and the realness of lack, but also to connect with the Fullness hidden within the absence, and the Beauty masked in the ugliness. Not neglecting the realness of your reality, but deepening it.

There is a childlike quality to Purim. The costumes, the playfulness, the reaching of Ad d'Lo Yada, not knowing. Like children, we are invited into radical wonder, into awe of the miracle of creation and its Creator. A child does not live weighed down by regret or ruminations. A child lives in the immediacy of discovery and majesty of amazement.

This is the difference between Yom Kippur and Purim. Both are days of cleansing, purifying, and returning. But Yom Kippur's Teshuvah is more about *Charatah* / regret, remorse, and the labor of rectifying the past with tears and supplications. Purim's Teshuvah, by contrast, is more about *Kabbalah* / acceptance for the future and doing so with joy. It is the Teshuvah of one who suddenly discovers their deepest, truest self. Here, the past is not dwelled upon or consciously regretted, but uplifted in the radical transformation of the present moment (the Kabbalah *creates* the Charatah). It is not about becoming someone new by erasing what was, but about reimagining and thus proclaiming the real "you" so powerfully that past, present, and future are all redeemed together.

In a sense, Purim completes Yom Kippur and Yom Kippur completes Purim. Every Yom Tov carries a dual rhythm, *laHashem* / devotion directed wholly toward Hashem, as well as *Lachem* / for yourself, joy and delight within the human realm. Yom Kippur inclines toward Hashem: a day of fasting, prayer, and withdrawal from the material, human world. Purim, by contrast, leans toward

Lachem: a day of feasting, drinking, and rejoicing. Together they form a perfect whole, the solemn return of Yom Kippur and the past, and the joyous return of Purim and the future, two distinct yet harmonious pathways, each guiding us in the present moment, back to our Source.

MASKS & LO YADA

Just as the Gragger has become a familiar emblem of Purim, so too has the custom of masks and costumes. The popular image is of a child in costume, Gragger in hand, joyously embodying the spirit of the day. On the surface, dressing up is a way of concealing one's identity, mirroring the hiddenness of the Purim miracle. But on a deeper level, Purim invites us to step beyond all dualities, to leave behind the fragmented world of *Pirud* / separateness and enter the higher realm of *Yichud* / unity.

Wearing clothing that is otherwise foreign to us becomes an expression of Lo Yada, similar to the 'beyond knowing' that we taste through drinking more than usual. To assume another form is to suspend, even briefly, the patterns, temperaments, and habits that define us. In doing so, we allow something deeper, more essential, to emerge. A Purim mask not only conceals but also reveals. Hiding your face gives permission for another 'personality' to surface, a face beneath your face. The mask frees you from the tyranny of your own self-image, from the persona you have learned to wear each day, the one shaped by expectation, habit, and fear. When one dons a mask, one is freed from the rigid lines of identity. Old boundaries soften, new possibilities appear. The shy may become bold, the cautious, playful, the rigid, spontaneous. In this way, Purim's costume becomes a spiritual practice of Lo Yada, entering a space beyond all fixed definitions and assumed personas.

MASKS & THE QUEST FOR AUTHENTICITY

When we look closely, we begin to notice that each of us already wears a mask, the persona we present to the world. Yet more often than not, this mask was never freely chosen. It was fastened upon us by parents, shaped by teachers, reinforced by peers, or pressed upon us by circumstance. For this reason, so much of adolescence is spent in a restless rebellion against these inherited coverings. But tragically, the rebellion often leads not to freedom, but merely to substitution: discarding one inauthentic mask only to adopt another, borrowed wholesale from the surrounding culture, absorbed unconsciously like a "social virus." Adolescence thus becomes a battlefield of masks, a constant exchange of borrowed identities. One tears away the parental mask, only to don the mask of friends, of fleeting trends, of subcultures promising belonging. What is mistaken for liberation is often just another layer of disguise. Rebellion is confused with freedom, performance with authenticity, expression with essence.

And yet, there is no cause for despair, for this struggle itself is totally real and wholly authentic. The struggle reveals a deeper yearning, the longing to find an authentic voice, a truer self-expression, beneath and beyond all masks. The very act of resisting, of tearing at the layers that do not belong, reveals a deeper yearning: the soul's cry to find its authentic voice, its truer self-expression that exists beneath and beyond every mask. The rebellion, the dissatisfaction, is itself a holy spark, an intimation that there is something real beneath the borrowed costumes, something of one's own essence waiting to be revealed.

Clothing, like a mask, can conceal as much as it reveals. A person's garments may reflect their role or profession, yet clothing can also tell a lie. Indeed, the Hebrew word for garment, *Beged*, shares its root with *Bagad* / betray. Clothing can signal identity and position, but it can just as easily distort or deceive (ותנח בגדו אצלה, ולא לבושו, בבגדו בה כיון שבגד :*Kidushin*, 18b. Note, *Zohar* 3, Ki Teitzei :אלא בגדו, לישנא דבוגדים בגדו בה שוב אין רשאי למוכרה. Or as in, אוי לי בגדים בגדו ובגד בוגדים בגדו / "Woe is me! The treacherous have dealt treacherously; yea, the treacherous have dealt very treacherously": *Yeshayahu*, 24:16). Tellingly, through the mystical letter-substitution system known as *A"T Ba"Sh*, where the first letter of the Aleph-Beis, Aleph, is changed to the last letter, Tav, and the second letter, Beis, is changed to the second to last letter, Shin, and so on, the word *Beged* / בגד transforms into *Sheker* / שקר / falsehood. The Beis becomes a Shin, the Gimel a Reish, and the Dalet a Kuf. This transformation hints that clothing, while necessary, is also vulnerable to misuse; it can conceal truth as much as it reveals.

While Purim may appear to be a more lighthearted Yom Tov, in truth, it is also profoundly serious, deeply introspective, and perhaps one of the most spiritually demanding days of the year. Like Yom Kippur, Purim is a time of Teshuvah, of turning inward, of peeling away our superficial images in search of the soul beneath. Sometimes that means shedding false forms altogether; other times, it means refining or reshaping them.

The act of donning a mask on Purim carries within it a subtle but profound message. Whether you wear one yourself or behold others in disguise, the mask whispers: you may imagine yourself a rabbi, a teacher, a scholar, a doctor, a lawyer, a businessperson, but that is only what you do, not who you truly are.

Parenthetically, so it is as well with body and soul. You are not a body that happens to house a soul; you are a soul, luminous and eternal, temporarily entrusted with a body.

The costume, in its playful disruption of self-image, serves as a gentle reminder not to cling too tightly to the identities we project. Yes, you must take others seriously, honoring their dignity, their roles, and the image they hold of themselves. But when it comes to your own self-image, you are invited to hold it more lightly: to wear it with grace, yet without rigidity. Purim whispers this paradoxical truth: take life seriously, but take yourself lightly.

Within each of us, there are many layers of selfhood. There is an outer 'self', the 'face' we present to the world, and there is an inner self or face, which is how we feel and imagine ourselves within. Our deepest face is rooted in the soul, who we truly are, not shaped by circumstances, feelings, or imagination. For some people, some of the time, these three 'faces' are one and the same, and for others, less so. At times, for some people, these layers align and appear as one. At other times, they are fragmented, even at odds with one another. On Purim, by dressing up and placing yet another layer over your more external image, you are symbolically making light of your projected image, assuming that it is inconsistent with your innermost face. Thus, you are demonstrating to yourself that your projected identities are not ultimate, that they are but external garments which can be exchanged for something more authentic. Of course, this is not an invitation to dismiss life, to evade responsibility, or to disregard others. On the contrary, we must take others with the utmost seriousness, and we must take our own lives and responsibilities with sincerity and care. But when it comes to the fragile 'external image' of self we may carry, Purim invites us to smile at it, to loosen its grip on us, and to remember that our essence lies far deeper than any mask or costume we could ever wear.

This lightness is woven into the very fabric of Purim. The story itself is a Divine comedy, so to speak, a tapestry of reversals. A queen from a royal lineage (Vashti) is dethroned, and a common orphan (Esther) replaces her. The mighty minister (Haman) is humiliated, and the condemned nation is redeemed. Everything is turned on its head. The month of Adar, as explored earlier, is connected with laughter and comedy. Comedy emerges from incongruity, from the collapse of expectation into surprise. That is precisely the rhythm of the Megilah, and the lesson of life gleaned from the Purim story, that nothing is ever fixed, all is in flux, certainly our assumed and external self-image is not set in stone. Indeed, what appears absolute today can be overturned and completely transformed for the better, tomorrow. In this way, we should never despair and never give up hope in ourselves.

Hence, dressing up on Purim is not only playful but transformative. On one level, it frees us from the superficial self, helping us touch a deeper self. On another, it trains us not to treat the ego's mask as final, not to get stuck in a single external image.

Costumes and masks open us to growth, change, and possibility. For how could we ever expand, evolve, or deepen if we believed that our outermost image is the finished product, that there was nothing beyond it, nothing truer within? Purim reminds us that there is always more, always deeper, always beyond.

This, too, is part of the Teshuvah dynamic of Purim. As the Sefer haChinuch writes, "The heart follows the actions." Often, one must first act a certain way before truly becoming it. Sometimes, we must pretend before we can embody. Be authentically inauthentic to become a little more authentic. On Purim, perhaps, we (or our children or friends) may dress as our ultimate self, as 'Mordechai the Tzadik', and in doing so, we begin to live from that place. As the Mishnah (*Peah*, 8:9) teaches, one who feigns poverty will not leave this world before tasting poverty (וכל מי שאינו לא חגר, ולא סומא, ולא פסח, ועושה עצמו כאחד מהם, אינו מת מן הזקנה עד שיהיה כאחד מהם / "Anyone who is not lame or blind but pretends to be as one of these, he will not die of old age before he actually becomes one of these." There is also a Mishnah that speaks of actually getting dressed up: המכריך סמרטוטין על עיניו ועל שוקיו ואומר תנו לסומא למוכה שחין זה סוף שהוא אומר לאמתו / "One who wraps rags around his eyes and around his thighs, and says, 'Give to this blind man, to this boil-infected man,' in the end his words will come true": *Avos d'Rebbe Nasan*, 3:1).

If dressing in the negative, as lame, blind, or afflicted, is a reality that is not truly ours, not now, and G-d willing will never be, and yet the very act of donning such a guise can draw that state toward us, how much more so is this true in the positive. When we clothe ourselves in the image of who we long to become, the perfected Tzadik that, in the end of days and across all incarnations, we are destined to embody (for ultimately, all will return in Teshuvah), we set the stage for that destiny to unfold more swiftly. By adorning ourselves in the garments of our higher self, we draw that future closer, allowing the eventual reality to begin revealing itself within us even now.

As such, there are many ways to 'wear' Purim. We may dress as the very image that holds us back, and laugh at it until it loses its grip. A person plagued by anger might dress as a raging fire, only to see how absurd and pitiful it looks. Another who suffers from self-righteousness may dress as a holy man to expose the ridiculousness of his own smugness. Or we may dress as the self we long to become, embodying that vision even before it fully flowers. Or, of course, we may simply dress to enter the spirit of Purim's joy.

In all cases, the mask is not about concealment alone, but revelation. It is a way of loosening the hold of the false and external self; the self driven by fear, bound to fight-or-flight. The masks allow us to laugh at our own illusions and dare us to step into truer possibilities.

Purim invites us to wear our masks lightly, so that one day, we may finally stand unmasked, soul revealed, essence shining.

MASKS: HIDING THE HIDDEN

The root of every idea is in Torah, and within Torah itself, the root of an idea is where the Torah alludes to it directly. When we think of masks in Torah, the image that comes most immediately to mind is the מסוה / *Masveh*, the covering Moshe Rabbeinu placed over his radiant face. When Moshe descended from Har Sinai, his face shone with such brilliance that the people could not bear to look at him. Therefore, whenever he was not engaged in teaching Torah to the people, or in direct communion with Hashem, he would place upon his face a *Masveh* / veil (*Shemos*, 34:33).

A mask is commonly thought of as something that hides. Yet, paradoxically, concealment can be revelation. In our ordinary encounters, we tend to relate to others through surface impressions, their clothing, facial features, mannerisms, or the persona they present. All of these belong to the outer layer of self. A mask interrupts this automatic reliance on externals. By obscuring the familiar face, it forces a shift of perception; the gaze is redirected from the surface toward the depth, from the external form toward the essence that lies within.

In this way, when Moshe was in communion with Hashem, or transmitting Torah to the people, no mask was necessary. In those moments, he was encountered in complete transparency, essence meeting essence. Hashem, of course, "saw" Moshe as he truly was, and even Klal Yisrael perceived him not merely as a man, but as a vessel of living Torah, glowing with Divine light. But in the realm of the everyday, when Moshe would go about his ordinary comings and goings, there was a danger that people might confuse his form with his essence. They might see only a human figure (which he also was) and reduce Moshe to external categories, overlooking the truth of who Moshe was. Here, the mask assumed its higher role, not (merely) as a concealment, but as an invitation to see deeper. The mask Moshe wore drew people away from being fixated on Moshe's outer image and compelled them to encounter him more deeply, to sense the mystery beyond the visible.

THE MASVEH AND THE DIVINE NAMES

Masveh / מסוה numerically equals 112 (Mem/40, Samach/60, Vav/6, Hei/5 with the word itself 112). The number one twelve is the sum total of the higher or 'deeper' Names of Hashem: *Ehe'ye* / "I will be" = 21. *Havaya* / Hashem = 26 and *Ado-noi* / Master = 65 in total = 112. All these Divine names represent the Infinite Transcendence.

Ehe'yeh is a Divine Name connected with the state of becoming, a future. Ehe'yeh Asher Ehe'yeh, which is the Name revealed to Moshe at the Burning Bush, means "I am who I am" or "I will be with them now and I will be with them in the future…" It is the world of *Keser* / Crown which gives rise to all becoming.

'Havayah' / Hashem represents Infinity. The Name of Hashem is composed of four letters: Yud, Hei, Vav, Hei. These four letters can be rearranged to spell the words Ha**y**ah / 'was', the past, **H**oveh / 'is', the present, **V**'Yi'**H**iyeh / 'and will be', the future. In other words, all of time, past, present, and future. The Name thus suggests an aspect of Infinity, encompassing past, present, and future as one, the world of Eternity, the Eternal.

The Name 'Ado-noi' is the garment or tool through which the Name Havayah, the Infinite One is pronounced and thus contextualized. In simple language, we pronounce the Name of Havaya as Ado-noi.

By contrast, finite Creation emerges through the Name Elokim: *Bereishis Bara Elokim* / "In the beginning, Elokim created" (*Bereishis*, 1:1). Elokim is the Divine Name related to concealment, to nature, to structure, the vessel that veils the Infinite within the created order. Because human cognition is built on binary distinctions such as light-dark, past-future, and self-other, our experience of multiplicity is rooted in this Name (hence, Elokim is in the plural).

Humanity itself is described as created *b'Tzelem Elokim* / "in the Image of Elokim," with the Divine-like creative power to steward and further Creation. And yet, when Moshe donned the Masveh, he concealed his level of Elokim, concealing the concealment itself, and thereby revealed the Names of Transcendence, the Infinite hidden within. In other words, he covered his image to uncover his Essence.*

GARMENTS OF KELIPAH & THE EGO

This points to two types of masks: a holy, wholesome, healthy mask hides the 'hider' in order to reveal something deeper, as with Moshe's veil. And an unholy, unwholesome mask, the mask of Kelipah, simply conceals in order to obscure its 'true self', concealing the fact that it is really empty and nothing inside.

---

* Hence, *Masveh* is also the numerical value of the Name of Hashem = 26, and Elokim = 86. 26+86 = 112. The word כבוד / *Kavod*, say our Sages, refers to garments. מלא כל הארץ כבודו / "The world is filled with Your glory and honor." This means that Hashem fills the finite universe, and the Infinite One is enclothed within the many garments of Creation and of physical nature. The Holy One, blessed be He, clothes Himself in this very world of concealment and nature: *Likutei Yekarim,* 222. On Purim, wearing masks serves as a profound symbol: they conceal the ordinary garments of nature (*Elokim* is numerically 86, the same as the word *haTeva* / 'the natural'), yet at the same time point beyond them, revealing the possibility of touching the Essence of Elokus, of Divinity itself, that lies beyond and within all the garments of the world. In other words, through the Name Hashem, there is a mitigation and a sweetening of the name Elokim.

The numerical value of *Purim* is 336, *Hashem* is 26, *Elokim* is 86. Three times 26 = 78. Three is the fullness of an idea, the three dimensions. Three times 86 = 258, and 78 plus 258 = 336. On Purim, there is a Hamtaka of *Din* / Elokim, through the Name of Hashem (Although, the root of the word *Purim, Pur,* is 286, which is only the world of Din. *Elokim* equals 200 *b'Ribuah* / squared, as such, Aleph=1. Aleph, Lamed = 31. Aleph, Lamed, Hei = 36. Aleph, Lamed, Hei, Yud = 46. Aleph, Lamed, Hei, Yud, Mem = 86. 1+31+36+46+86 = 200. And the name Elokim itself is 86, hence 286. Similarly, Chazal say, מרדכי מן התורה מנין דכתיב מר דרור ומתרגמינן מירא דכיא, מירא דכיא / "...The name Mordechai is rooted in the words *Mira Dachya*," meaning flowing myrrh, which in numerical value is 286: *Likutei Levi Yitzchak,* Vol. 3, pp. 96-99).

On Purim, we wear masks of the first kind. By covering the surface self, we gesture to the Infinite depth within, reminding ourselves that the image is not the essence.

This duality of the different types of masks is reflected in the Purim story itself. Our Sages relate that at Achashverosh's banquet, the king demanded that Vashti appear unclothed (*Megilah*, 12b). She refused and did not show up. Says the Baal Shem Tov (*Moreh b'Omek*, Megilas Esther, p.197. *Baal Shem Tov Al haTorah*, Megilas Esther), the reason is that without garments, Vashti, who represents Kelipah, the ego, the unholy, the unwholesome, there is no Vashti. Exploitation, ego, and falsehood have no true substance; their whole reality is concealment. Remove their garments, and there is nothing beneath. Kelipah is the emperor with no clothes, and when the coverings are gone, the emperor itself is gone.

Kelipah has no true or independent existence of its own. Kelipah's entire function is concealment, like a mirage or phantom; it appears real only in the way it obscures and distorts the truth of what reality is, and who we are. When called upon to reveal itself 'without garments', Kelipah cannot comply. For at its core, it is nothing more than a mask. When the King of the World demands that Kelipah come forth without a veil, without the garments of illusion, Kelipah must refuse, for without the mask, there is nothing left. Kelipah's very existence is the veil itself, and so when stripped of that cover, it dissolves into nothingness.

On a cosmic level, the very definition of Kelipah is concealment, a mask, a covering that hides the Divine unity and Light. Just as a shadow has no reality of its own apart from the light it blocks, so too Kelipah has no essence apart from the 'garments' it wears. Without garments, without the story, Kelipah simply disappears.

Inwardly, this Kelipah of concealment and garments is a reference to the ego. The ego does not simply protect; in fact, for the most part, it actually spins stories, weaves 'garments', fashions, false narratives, about who we are and how reality must be approached. These narratives are not neutral; they are self-tailored to preserve the ego's illusion of control. Indeed, the default script it leans upon is one of *fight or flight*: resist, defend, attack, or escape. The ego clings to familiar roles and stories, even false ones, to avoid the terror of the unknown Self, the greater wholeness within us. Much of what we call 'ego' is a survival system; when the nervous system senses threat, it locks us into fight, flight, freeze, or fawn. These responses are protective, but they also become a prison when we mistake them for our true identity and refuse to live with the deepest self that the Creator calls us to be. Instead of embracing our vastness, we collapse into smaller narratives, stories of victimhood and endless conflict.

At its root, then, the ego is not afraid of our weakness; it is afraid of our greatness. To live from the deeper self means to live vulnerably, expansively, with openness to love, creativity, and Divine Presence. This mode of being cannot be controlled, cannot be contained. It makes the ego lose its claim to supreme importance. And so, the ego continually invents false garments, stories of threat, of competition, of being 'right' or 'wrong', because these keep the spotlight on itself. The ego, the Kelipah side of self, fears nothing more than dissolution in the vastness of who we truly are.

Clearly, the ego shrinks reality into manageable dramas, fabricating a world of winners and losers, allies and enemies, so that it can remain master of the house. But this endless 'fight or flight' story keeps us small, circling in cycles of fear, anger, and avoidance. All the while, it conceals the radiant truth that our essence is not fragile, but boundless; not threatened, but eternal.

On a very simple level, inwardly, Vashti, i.e. the ego, means the garments, the excuses that the ego fabricates to protect itself. No one says, 'I did wrong for no reason.' There is always a justification, always a story.

These are the 'garments' of Vashti that are masking the cosmic and microcosmic truth. Still, it should be pointed out that the inner work of Purim, and of all days, is not to destroy the garments, the ego and its stories, but to wear them lightly, to recognize them as tools, not identity. When the false coverings are seen for what they are, the deeper self can begin to shine.

KELIPAH / VASHTI IS ALWAYS *SHTEI* / TWO

On a practical level, thinking of Vashti herself as a person and what she embodies and is an archetype of, there are two dimensions to consider. First, there is Vashti as she is in herself, the actual human being created by Hashem, prior to any narrative or story connected with her, unrelated to people's impressions of her, or her impressions of herself from others. This dimension is not defined by how others perceive her or how she projects herself outwardly, but rather her essential existence as a creature created by Hashem. In that sense, she is pure, as all of Hashem's creations are.

The second dimension is how Vashti appears, how she projects herself outward, and how others interpret or project onto her. This is the realm of garments, her projections of self, the external garments and the 'inner garments', her thoughts, words, actions, and impressions that mediate between self and world (*Tanya*, 3). These garments carry narratives, stories of temptation, allure, and negative attraction. Thus, what is Kelipah in Vashti, as in any other person or thing, is not her being, but the way she presents herself, her garments, the way she thinks, speaks, and acts, thus the way others perceive her through these garments.

Negative beauty is precisely this dynamic. Beauty in itself, like any aspect of Hashem's Creation, is inherently neutral and ultimately holy and simply beautiful. But when a person projects beauty outward as a means to attract inappropriate attention to self, or when it is received by an observer through distorted garments of perception and desire, it becomes negative and Kelipah. It is not the thing itself that is negative; it never is, rather it is the story we attach to it. As Rebbe Bunim once quipped, "A horse is merely a horse." The horse itself is not the problem; it is what the person imagines about the horse that can become corrupt (of course, the 'horse' is a metaphor for what may be tempting).

Kelipah is always dual, *Shtei* / two (alluded to in the very root of the name Va**shti**). On the one hand, there is the object in and of itself, which, as a creation of Hashe,m is holy and pure. On the other hand, there is the additional layer, the narrative, the projection, the garments through which one relates to it, that can distort and make it appear negative.

The thing itself is always from Kedushah, for Hashem created it. What becomes Kelipah is not the essence of the object, but the *Shtei*, the second layer, the garments, the stories, the relationships people may construct around it. A fantasy, for example, is never about the bare thing itself; the object is neutral. It is the story people weave around the object, the meaning and projections people attach to it, that turn it into something negative.

This is the nature of garments. They are the interface through which we encounter the world. Every interaction involves both the garments of the one presenting and the garments of the one perceiving. In Vashti's case, when the King commands her to appear "without garments," she cannot comply. For Kelipah cannot exist without the veil of projection and narrative. Strip away the garments, and there is no story, no temptation, there is only the pure creation, which in truth is no longer 'Vashti' as Kelipah, but rather is actually Esther, the opposite of concealment, the revelation of inner Light and Holiness.

Esther embodies Kedushah. Her very name (Esther from the word *Hester* / concealment) signals hiddenness, but her hiddenness is only a vessel for revelation. Thus, when Esther finally removes her mask before the King and declares her true essence, "for I am a Jew," she reveals not emptiness or disappears, rather she reveals the Divine Presence shining through her. And through that act, she brought life and salvation to the Jewish People.

Esther is the embodiment of the Light of the Shechinah hidden within nature. Thus, when her mask is lifted, there is *Gilui Elokus* / a revelation of Divinity within the world and within nature.

True beauty, Kedushah, is inwardly directed; it is not divided into two, self and projection, but whole and one, the world of *Echad* / One, not *Shtei* / two. This is the beauty of Esther, whose very name means 'hidden'. Chazal tell us that Esther was exceedingly beautiful, yet her beauty was regal and dignified, not a lure for external desire. Her beauty was not meant to seduce, project, or attract, but simply and effortlessly expressed *Tzniyus* / inwardness, hiddenness, depth, essence, and inner majesty.

The Megilah itself begins and ends with garments. At the opening, Achashverosh adorns himself in deceptive garments, robes of the Cohen Gadol, though he is no Cohen Gadol. This is an act of arrogance and betrayal, garments used to project power and mask emptiness. Likewise, Vashti cannot appear without her garments, for without the veil of external projection, there is nothing left. These are garments of falseness, ego, seduction, and deception, the world of 'two', of object / subject narratives. Yet, the story of Purim gradually transforms garments from false coverings into true expressions. Mordechai first tears away pretense, dressing in sackcloth and ashes. Only then is he clothed in Royal Garments, not of falsehood but of authenticity, garments that reflect the King of Kings and Mordechai as His ambassador in this world of deception. Esther also dresses up in royal garments, but only after concealing her identity. She projects her inner hiddenness outward, using the mask of concealment itself as holy service to save Klal Yisrael.

Indeed, false garments conceal essence; true garments effortlessly reveal it. And so it is with us. On Purim, we wear masks and costumes, but these masks are not for a deceptive concealment of

Self; they are means of revelation. By covering the outer, we invite the inner to shine. Hiddenness becomes the doorway to essence. In the joy of Purim, we taste a deep truth, that everything in Creation is pure and holy, once stripped of the false narratives and garments of illusion.

The masks of Purim are not child's play, although they are child-like; they are playful, mystical mirrors of reality. Concealment itself can be the path to revelation. This is the secret of Radla, "the Head that is not known." The hiddenness of Purim, the garments and the masks, do not obscure but disclose. They allow the soul to shine forth, revealing that beneath it all, in essence, all is pure and all is holy. And beyond Mordechai and even Haman, there is only blessing and the Oneness of Hashem.

THE OVERARCHING THEME OF THE MITZVOS OF PURIM

All the Mitzvos of Purim carry their own profound spiritual meaning, as explained, yet together they share a unifying theme, a single golden thread weaving them into one tapestry.

Earlier, the giving of the Torah at Mount Sinai with the re-acceptance of Torah in the days of Purim was contrasted and explored. At Sinai, we stood overwhelmed, "a mountain suspended overhead," compelled by a revelation too awesome to resist. In the Purim era, however, we embraced the Torah freely and joyfully; we confirmed by our own volition what we had previously received by 'force'. Actions performed under compulsion may be dutiful, but they rarely inspire joy. By contrast, what is done out of love is never 'enough'; love always longs to give more, to go beyond the minimum. An employee bound by obligation counts the hours until the workday ends, but the artist or musician or a person who truly enjoys what they are doing is never finished, and is never content and always seeking to do more.

So it is with Purim. All its Mitzvos embody this spirit of going beyond, of exceeding measure: Torah is read publicly throughout the year, in fact, every three days, yet Purim adds an extra layer with both the reading of the Torah on Purim and the unique Mitzvah of reading the Megilah. Similarly, acts of kindness are always encouraged, yet on Purim, we are called not merely to be kind, but to actively seek out friends and send them Mishloach Manos. Charity, as well, is a constant Mitzvah, but on Purim we must go further, not just giving to the poor, but pursuing the poor and ensuring that all receive Matanos laEvyonim. Purim trains us to be exceedingly sensitive to the needs of the poor, seeking them out, and finding a poor person to offer gifts. Seudas Purim, as well, where families gather together in joy and friendship, is a similar theme, especially if it includes assisting the poor, as that is the ultimate, pure, holy joy, as the Rambam explains and discussed previously.

All in all, the theme of Purim is unity, connection, camaraderie, and equality. The Mitzvos bind people together: friend with friend, rich with poor, family with family.

This quality of equality is also the seed of new beginnings. When a person rests in an inner state of existential equality, they stand on ground that is always fresh, always open to renewal. True beginnings are possible only in the present, when one is fully here, unencumbered by the weight of past failures or even past triumphs. Where there is equality, no path predetermined, no destiny fixed, there arises the freedom of the now, and with it, the possibility of choosing anew. In this way, Purim and Yom Kippur meet in their shared essence as days of renewal and new beginnings. On the surface, they appear as opposites, one a day of fasting, awe, and solemn return; the other a day of feasting, joy, and overflowing celebration. Yet at their core, both are bound by the mystery of the Lottery, the space of radical equality where all possibilities stand open. Purim draws its very name from the Pur, the lot cast by Haman, and Yom Kippur is marked by sacred lots in the Beis haMikdash, where one goat is chosen for sacrifice and the other sent into the wilderness. From this ground of indeterminacy, where nothing is fixed and all is potential, emerges the power of true choice, and with it, the possibility of beginning anew.

Both Purim and Yom Kippur draw their power from a dimension that is beyond

Names, beyond dualities and binaries. Of Yom Kippur it is written, *Lifnei Hashem Titharu* / "Before Hashem you shall be purified." The mystics explain this as not only "before Hashem," but also 'before' or beyond the very Name of Hashem, touching the Divine Essence that transcends all distinctions and reveals the absolute Unity. So too with Purim. The Megilah is remarkable in that the Name of Hashem is never explicitly mentioned. This is not an absence but a profound presence: it gestures to a level that is beyond all names and articulations, to the hidden Essence itself. From this place of radical equality and equanimity, where all is held in oneness, the possibility of true choice emerges, the freedom to choose the good, not out of compulsion, but from the depth of the soul's connection to the Infinite.

EQUALITY AND UNITY, NOT SAMENESS & UNIFORMITY

Equality is not sameness. Sameness flattens and stifles individuality, while equality affirms and empowers it, granting voice, value, and dignity to each unique soul. Appropriately, Purim itself stands apart from every other Yom Tov, for it is the only Yom Tov not celebrated on a single day by all. Most communities observe it on the Fourteenth of Adar, while those in Shushan and ancient walled cities celebrate on the Fifteenth. This very divergence embodies the truth: genuine unity is not when everyone does the same thing, but when each honors the other in their distinct expression. When those who celebrate on the Fifteenth can look with respect and joy upon those who celebrate on the Fourteenth, and vice versa, then individuality is not erased but embraced, and from that arises true equality and true unity.

This interplay between unity and disunity is central to the Purim story itself. Haman's plot was born of division, and he declared, "There is a certain people scattered and dispersed…," a people fragmented, disunited, and therefore vulnerable. His accusation was not only that the Jews were different, but that they were divided, they were splintered as a people. "Scattered" refers to geographically, in different locations. "Dispersed" means internally, even where they live physically together, they are disunified (*Manos HeLevi*, ad loc.). Esther's response to Mordechai was the opposite: "Go, *gather* together all the Jews." Unity became the remedy. Their salvation was born in the act of coming together, in fasting, in prayer, in courage, and later in victory, as the Megilah proclaims: "The Jews gathered themselves together in their cities…to lay hands upon those who sought their harm." The miracle of Purim was drawn forth by the power of *Achdus* / unity.

In fact, from the Divine perspective, the very reason Hashem allowed Haman's decree to be set in motion was to awaken and deepen the unity of Klal Yisrael. Throughout Jewish history, we see this pattern: times of persecution and antisemitism, though painful and terribly tragic, have consistently driven us to stand closer together in unity. This is, so to speak, the Divine intention, the *Tachlis* / purpose behind 'why' such events are allowed to unfold. They are sometimes needed in order to draw the scattered sparks of our people back into unity. And this is exactly what happened in the days of Purim. Haman's decree, intended to annihilate us, instead ignited within us a profound solidarity and unity, a renewed sense of shared destiny and belonging, and it was from this place and because of this unity that redemption emerged.

Fascinatingly, Haman is called the *Tzorer haYehudim* / צורר היהודים (*Esther*, 3:10), the enemy of the Jews." The root צרר / *Tzorer* carries the sense of *Tzar* / distress, and *Hatzara* / constriction (as in *Meitzar* / strait, narrow passage), as well as hostility, and in this case actively seeking to cause pain and suffering to Klal Yisrael. Yet strikingly, the very same root also means a bundle, as in צרור הכסף / *Tz'ror haKesef* / "bundle of money" (*Bereishis*, 42:35, Rashi). In other words, Haman rose to destroy us, yet through נהפוך הוא / *Nahafoch Hu* / "It (the decree) was reversed," through the Divine Power that transforms negativity into positivity, Haman himself was destroyed. Not only that, but he caused us to become one 'bundle', making Klal Yisrael more unified than ever before.

Yet, this unification of Klal Yisrael on Purim was (and is) not a unity of 'sameness', rather, it is a unity within diversity. This is illustrated by the fact that different communities within Klal Yisrael celebrated the victory on different days. Those in unwalled cities rested and celebrated on the Fourteenth of Adar, while those in the walled city of Shushan celebrated on the Fifteenth. True unity embraces difference, weaving diversity into a single, unbreakable whole.

So too, in our celebration of Purim, we do not merely commemorate, we reawaken, this *Koach* / power of Achdus. The Mitzvos of the day are each designed to foster connection, as they are acts of friendship, generosity, mutual responsibility, and shared joy. Though we may dwell in different places, separated by geography and circumstance, as Haman cynically observed, we remain one people, a unified people, bound to one Torah, serving one Hashem. Our unity is not despite our differences but through them.

Haman sought to draw from the realm of Makif, that transcendent place beyond all distinctions, even beyond the division of good and evil. What he failed to grasp, as explored previously, is that in the "beyond beyond," the choice is always for the good. For the highest level of Makif does not remain abstract and untethered, rather its Light descends into Penimi, into the inner, dimensional reality of distinctions (Thus, after a *Hekef* / cycle of eight days, which is 180 hours (Kuf=100, Pei=80), a child enters the covenant of Bris Milah, as the Makif is drawn into the Penimi, into the body, and the line within the body: *Megaleh Amukos,* Toldos). In striking irony and Nahafoch Hu, Chazal teach that the descendants of Haman became Torah scholars in Bnei Brak, among them the great teacher of children, Rebbe Shmuel bar Shilat (*Sanhedrin*, 96b, Ayin Yaakov. *Gittin*, 57b˙). The very image of a child united with a teacher, distinct, unequal, yet bound together in a living exchange of wisdom and transmission of Torah, becomes the Tikkun for Haman's distortion. Teacher and student are unified in a perfect dance and embrace, and even learn from each other, yet they are not the 'same', one is the teacher and the other the student. Haman desired the detached infinity of Makif, but the true rectification is the harmony that arises when transcendence enters relationship, when unity is revealed not as sameness but as the weaving together of distinct voices into a single, indivisible song.

To truly absorb Torah, the Divine wisdom, the fountain of life rooted in ultimate Oneness, we too must become one. Achdus is not an accessory to receiving Torah but a prerequisite. At Mount Sinai, the Torah was given only when the nation stood "as one person with one heart." Only through inner harmony and outward unity can the Divine unity flow into us. Torah was first given at Sinai, yet it was only fully embraced during the days of Purim. Just as Sinai demanded unity, so too the completion of receiving Torah in the Purim era was possible only through Achdus.

---

* Although, principally, converts are not accepted from Amalek: *Mechilta*, end of Beshalach. *Tanchuma*, end of Ki Teitzei. Yet, the Rambam holds that even someone from Amalek (not during wartime) can convert: *Hilchos Melachim,* 6:4. See also *Hilchos Isurei Bi'ah,* 12:17. See *Shu'T Avnei Nezer,* Orach Chayim, 508:3, for the source of this Rambam. Perhaps also, since there was a mixing of the nations, and so when one of them came to convert, the *Beis Din* / court did not realize that they were descendants of Amalek and converted them: See *Chazon Ish,* Yoreh De'ah, 157:5 (For other answers, see *Shu'T Maharsham,* 3, Siman 272. *Pri Tzadik,* Purim, 2. *Likutei Amarim,* 16). This answer, on a deeper level, could mean that on the level of Da'as, conscious awareness and Avodah, it is impossible to elevate any sparks within Amalek. Thus, ובבזה לא שלחו את־ידם / "And they did not lay hands on the spoils" (*Esther,* 9:15), yet, on a level of Lo Yada, beyond knowing, beyond normal Avodah, sparks within Haman and Amalek can indeed be elevated, and this is 'higher than Avodah', the Avodah of Purim on the level of the 'head' and beyond, רישיה דעשו...בגו עטפיה דיצחק / "The head of Esav is within the embrace of Yitzchak": *Targum Yonason,* Bereishis, 50:13.

Fittingly, all four Mitzvos of Purim begin with the letter Mem, whose numerical value is 40, a number deeply bound with Torah and to Moshe, the receiver of Torah, as his name begins with a Mem. The Mitzvos of Purim are *Mikra Megilah* / the Megilah reading, Mishloach Manos, Matanos laEvyonim, and *Mishteh v'Simchah* / feasting and joy. The symbolism is striking. Moshe ascended the mountain for forty days to receive Torah, and it takes forty years to truly grasp its depth (*Avodah Zarah*, 5b). The Oral Torah (Mishnah) itself begins with the letter Mem: *Me'eimasai...* / "'From when' do we read the Shema...." The Mem thus also signals transition and maturity: from written to oral, from prophecy to wisdom, from revelation to interpretation. Purim embodies this shift. It is the point where Torah is no longer only a gift descending from above, but a living wisdom that arises from within, innovated and intuited from Below.

In this way, the miracle and Mitzvos of Purim are all expressions of unity within our own diversity. Through generosity, friendship, shared joy, and communal gathering, we weave ourselves together into a vessel capable of receiving Torah's essence. Only when we unify within ourselves and with each other can we truly absorb the oneness of reality, and draw the Divine wisdom that continues to flow into the world.

CHAPTER 7

THE UNIQUENESS OF PURIM EXPLAINED:

Questions and Answers

H *aving examined Purim from multiple directions and dimensions,* we are now in a position to address the enigma of this most mysterious and concealed Yom Tov. Earlier, twenty-one distinctive features of Purim were outlined and expanded upon. On the basis of the foundations established throughout the text, it now becomes apparent why Purim possesses these singular qualities.

What follows is a concise summary of the questions and their respective answers. For a full appreciation of each, one can return to the earlier chapters where they are discussed in detail.

1. *Question*: All other Yamim Tovim are designated by Hebrew names, yet *Purim* comes from the Persian *Pur*, 'lot'. Why is it not called by the Hebrew word for 'lot', *Goral*?

   Answer: The essence of Purim is the recognition of the Divine Hand within the ordinary and the concealed. By employing the Persian term, the Yom Tov itself conveys the fact that Divinity, goodness, and holiness is not limited to sacred language or overtly spiritual settings. The Divine Presence must be discerned within exile, within everyday reality, and within the languages and expressions of the mundane world. This is an essential meaning of the story of Purim.

2. *Question*: All other Yamim Tovim are named after the *miracle* they commemorate. Why is Purim named after the Pur that Haman threw in order to plan the date of Klal Yisrael's annihilation?

   Answer: The name *Purim* highlights a profound truth: nothing in existence is truly random. What appears as chance or mere coincidence is in truth an instrument in the subtle, guiding hand of Divine Providence, directing history. On Purim, we celebrate not the open miracles but rather the hidden miracle within the 'Pur', the seemingly natural unfolding of events.

   On a deeper level, the Pur represents that which is 'beyond' natural cause and effect and logic, namely the dimension of Keser. It represents even that which is 'beyond the beyond': the Keser of Keser, meaning the deepest, most inscrutable desire of the Creator. It is from this place of all-transcendent desire that our miraculous redemption and transformation manifested. In this way, we are victorious over Haman not due to any cause or 'reason', but simply because such is Hashem's deepest desire. And this is why Purim is actually the perfect name for this day. It conveys the fact that even when 'random' events seem to threaten us, those same events will be revealed as instruments of Divine love and redemption.

3. *Question*: All other Yamim Tovim are marked by open and revealed miracles, such as splitting seas and clouds of glory. Yet the story of Purim contains no such wonders. Why is this day celebrated as a Yom Tov?

   Answer: Actually, that is precisely the point of Purim. This day reveals that even in exile, and even within ordinary, 'mundane' life, every moment is truly miraculous. Purim teaches us to recognize the hidden miracles woven into nature and history and the subtle presence of Divine Providence guiding every event and every movement. This is the revelation of the Essence of Hashem, so to speak, that is present always and everywhere, not only in the extraordinary and supernatural, but within the ordinary and natural as well.

4. *Question*: Pesach and Sukkos, two of the major Yamim Tovim, both begin on the Fifteenth of the month, the time of the full moon. Purim, however, is celebrated in most places on the Fourteenth of Adar. Why this distinction?

   Answer: The Fifteenth day, when the moon is full, symbolizes the state in which the moon, the receiver, the 'Below', perfectly reflects the light of the sun, the Giver 'Above'. When a miracle descends from Above to Below and is revealed openly within nature as a miracle from Above, the day of celebration is the Fifteenth. It is a moment of fullness and completion, exemplified by the full, complete moon. Purim, however, is the story of the Below, of us, the receivers, struggling and striving upward toward the Above. The miracle of Purim is hidden, arising within nature itself, through human initiative and Divine concealment. Therefore, its celebration is set on the Fourteenth of the month, *before* the moon has reached fullness, since it represents the journey of the Below reaching Upward.

5. *Question*: Every Yom Tov is celebrated on the same date, regardless of where one lives. Purim, however, is unique in that it is celebrated on two different days depending on one's location. Why this distinction?

Answer: The essence of Purim is the revelation of Divine Providence within the particulars and details of dualistic existence, not only in the grand, sweeping general Providence. Purim is connected with the Ohr Makif, the transcendent Infinite Light that permeates the Penimi, the inner reality of distinctions. To reveal this truth, Purim is not marked with 'sameness' but with 'difference'. This affirms that individuality has a place within the collective, that the Divine Hand is found not only in the vast and universal but also in the intimate and personal. True peace is not flattening distinctions into sameness, but rather the deeper harmony born when the many are embraced within the One, while remaining distinct.

6. *Question*: On every Yom Tov, the Mitzvos are performed on the day itself. Yet, uniquely, the Megilah reading may, under certain circumstances, be read even up to three days before Purim. Why is this so?

Answer: The nature of Purim is that the higher Light does not descend all at once, in one moment, in one day, but is gradually drawn down and integrated into the lower realms. Its radiance extends beyond the strict boundary of the day, allowing the Light of Purim to be received, appreciated, and assimilated according to the capacity of each community and each individual vessel. See also the previous answer.

7. *Question*: The central figures of most Yamim Tovim are male. On Purim, the heroic figure is a woman, Queen Esther. Why is this so?

Answer: All other Yamim Tovim represent a 'top-down' movement, a revelation of Light from Above that breaks and shatters the natural order below, manifesting itself as a miracle beyond nature. In this symbolism, the masculine corresponds to the giver, the initiator, the force that descends from the higher, the Above, to the lower, the Below. Purim, however, is unique as it unfolds from within nature itself, within the Below. The miracle of Purim is not an open shattering of the world and nature, but a hidden transformation from within. Fittingly, it is embodied in the feminine, in Queen Esther, the receiver who reveals the Divine indwelling within nature and a redemption that emerges not from Above in the form of an open miracle, but rather from within the very fabric of life.

8. *Question*: All of the Torah-rooted Yamim Tovim are associated with a male transmitter, for example, the Torah of Moshe. Purim is the exception, where the canonical text is named *Megilas Esther*, the scroll of Esther. Why is this so?

Answer: Purim embodies the dynamic of the Below rising Upward, as noted in the previous answers. It is therefore aligned with the feminine, the quality of receptivity. This is also the essence of *Torah Sheba'al Peh* / the Oral Torah, through which Divine wisdom from on High is disclosed not as a one-way descent from Above, but predominantly through the active participation and articulation of those below. Thus *Megilas Esther* bears the name of the feminine voice through which this truth is revealed.

9. *Question*: On most Yamim Tovim, women are exempt from many of the time-bound Mitzvos connected with the Yamim Tovim. Yet on Purim (and Chanukah), women are equally obligated as men to perform the Mitzvos of the day. Why is this so?

Answer: The Mitzvos established by our Sages, such as those of Purim (and Chanukah) reflect the spiritual quality of the cosmic feminine dynamic. These days are not given to us by the masculine Divine Giver in the manner of the Yamim Tovim of the Torah; rather, they are sanctified and initiated through the righteous dedication and innovation of the Sages. This 'feminine' act of revealing hidden light within the world is mirrored in women's equal obligation to enact the Mitzvos of Purim.

Beyond this symbolic explanation, Chazal also teach the more direct reason: אַף הֵן הָיוּ בְּאוֹתוֹ הַנֵּס / "They too were part of the miracle." This can be understood in two ways. On the simple level, the decrees of annihilation were directed against women as well as men, and so women are *included* in the obligations of Purim. On a deeper level, the salvation came specifically through the agency of a woman, Queen Esther (similar to Yehudis in the Chanukah story), making the feminine role *central* to the redemption. This implies that women have a special responsibility and empowerment to perform the Mitzvos of Purim, and a special ability to activate and awaken the redemption of Purim within our times.

10. *Question*: Most Yamim Tovim mark the beginning of new cycles: Rosh Hashanah is the 'dawning' of the 'year of days', and Pesach is the first full moon of the 'year of months', the lunar year. Chanukah is a 'late' Yom Tov, starting at the end of the month of Kislev, but Kislev is only the ninth month. Purim falls in the final, twelfth month of the lunar year, Adar. What does this distinction imply?

    Answer: Purim represents the closing of an old paradigm, the end of open miracles, and the final curtain call of the Prophetic age. This is one deeper reason that it falls out in the final month of the year. Yet Purim is also the beginning of something new, a new relationship with Hashem born through human initiative, creativity, and love. On Purim, the Torah was re-accepted not from awe and compulsion, but from joy and choice. It is the end of one modality and the birth of another. Indeed, the redemption of Purim is a kind of 'preparation' for the redemption of Pesach, which is the first Yom Tov in the first month.

11. *Question*: What makes Purim so special that it is considered an eternal Yom Tov, never to become superfluous, and that it is a model of how all the Yamim Tovim will manifest in the future?

Answer: This is because Purim was the first Yom Tov established after the destruction of the First Beis haMikdash, in the time when prophecy had ceased. Purim arose in exile, without open miracles, and precisely for this reason, it is a Yom Tov that can and will accompany us in every exile, in every fall, and every place of darkness and trouble. Also, Purim carries within it a potent seed of redemption, planted deep within exile, which will one day break through the surface of world consciousness and blossom as eternal redemption, as we sing exultantly on Purim (*Shoshanas Ya'akov*, sung after the Megilah reading): *Teshu'asam Hayisa laNetzach, v'Tikvasam b'Chol Dor vaDor* / "Their salvation was for eternity and their hope is for every generation!"

12. *Question*: All the Yamim Tovim trace their roots back to *Matan Torah* / the Giving of the Torah at Mount Sinai. Purim is the re-acceptance of the same Torah, yet it is also considered a *Chidush* / a novelty. What does this mean?

Answer: The Chidush of Purim is the re-acceptance of Torah from love, not compulsion. This love is expressed in the four Mitzvos of Purim. These Mitzvos are in the pattern of the Mitzvos of the Torah of Sinai, yet they are done in a novel way: by reading the Megilah (Torah study), enjoying a festive meal (rejoicing in the Divine Presence), Mishloach Manos (expressing Ahavas Yisrael), and Matanos laEvyonim (giving Tzedakah). On Purim, we take the observance of these basic Mitzvos further, doing them with elated joy, unrestrained abundance, and enthusiastic alacrity. This is the novelty: practicing Judaism not from mere 'obedience', but with the open hand and overflowing gestures of one who is spiritually in love.

13. *Question*: While most Yamim Tovim are connected with Moshe, as they are rooted within the Torah that was transmitted by Moshe, Purim is more closely linked with Yehoshua, his student. What is the connection?

Answer: Moshe, the perfect conduit to reveal what is Above to the Below, the highest prophet, is similar to the Sun Light, the ultimate transmitter of Torah, the origin of the Light. Yeshosua represents the 'next generation', not the generation of the Exodus, not the generation that lived off miracles, off the *Mon* / Manna rather, a generation that needs to wage battle, needs to plow the land to eat, as such, Yehoshua represents the Moon Light, reflective light, not generating it, as the moon has no light of its own (*Baba Basra*, 75a). Moshe is Above, Yeshoshua Below (*Zohar* 2, 65b. With regards to the war with Amalek, אמר משה, אנא אזמין גרמי לההוא קרבא דלעילא, ואנת יהושע זמין גרמך לקרבא דלתתא). Purim belongs to this movement from Below to Above, embodying the reflective light of Yehoshua, the moonlight that shines even in exile's night.

14. *Question*: The events celebrated on other Yamim Tovim took place either in Eretz Yisrael itself, like Chanukah, or on the way there, during our journey through the Desert after the Exodus from Egypt. Purim, however, commemorates events that unfolded outside of Eretz Yisrael, in the lands of Persia. What does this symbolize?

Answer: Purim teaches us that even the seemingly random, mundane flow of profane history is not outside of Divine Providence. Nothing is mere happenstance or chance. Even in exile in Persia, Hashem is present and guiding events, although not through prophecy or open miracles, but through the hiddenness of nature. Purim is a Yom Tov that reveals the apparently concealed, uncovering the hidden within, and recognizing that Hashem is always with us, even in the darkest corners of our collective or even personal estrangement, alienation, and exile.

15. *Question*: All other Yamim Tovim are either rooted in the Torah itself or commemorate events that took place when the Beis haMikdash still stood. Purim, however, occurred outside of Eretz Yisrael and at a time when the Beis haMikdash lay in ruins or at least when the second Beis haMikdash was not yet rebuilt. What is the significance?

Answer: Purim reveals that Hashem is with us always, not only in the Beis haMikdash, not only in Eretz Yisrael, but everywhere and forever, even in exile, even in hiddenness. The other Yamim Tovim shine with the light of prophecy, open miracles, and the sanctity of the Beis haMikdash or

Mishkan. Purim, by contrast, unfolded in the shadow of exile, in Persia, far from the holiness of Yerushalayim, with no Beis haMikdash and no prophecy. On the surface, everything appeared political, random, and driven by human schemes. Yet it is precisely here that we learn the deepest truth: Hashem is with us always.

The very name Esther means "concealment," teaching us that even when Hashem's Face is veiled, the Divine Hand guides history. The miracle of Purim was not the splitting of seas or the falling of Mon from Heaven, but the quiet weaving together of ordinary events until they revealed extraordinary meaning. In this way, Purim becomes 'the Yom Tov of exile', showing us that even in the darkest places, Hashem is present, faithful, and near.

16. *Question*: On the other Yamim Tovim, ordinary weekday activities are prohibited, yet on Purim, all work is technically permitted, as we did not accept upon ourselves that it should be a full Yom Tov, where no work is allowed. What is the difference?

    Answer: When a Yom Tov commemorates a miracle revealed from Above, a moment that shattered or suspended the laws of nature, it is marked by stepping out of the mundane and ordinary rhythms of life. We refrain from everyday tasks to mirror that transcendence, separating from the ordinary in honor of the holy. On a deeper level, we are not merely recalling past miracles, but they recur each year during the Yom Tov. Each year, at the very time in the calendar when those miracles first occurred, their spiritual power returns. To connect with miracles that transcend nature, we too must rise above nature and refrain from work.

Purim, however, is different. The miracle of Purim is hidden within nature, clothed in what appears to be ordinary events. Nothing overtly supernatural occurred, and yet everything was guided by the Divine Hand. Therefore, Purim is celebrated not by withdrawing from the everyday, but by sanctifying it, rejoicing, feasting, giving, and even in the midst of life's seemingly trivial and mundane acts, discovering that holiness dwells there too.

17. *Question*: Each Yom Tov carries with it a directive, to become aware of its meaning, to enter its consciousness with mindfulness, with Da'as (especially Sukkos). On Purim, however, the opposite seems true: the Mitzvah is to reach a state of *Ad d'Lo Yada* / until one does not know." Why is this the pinnacle of Purim?

Answer: All other Yamim Tovim are rooted either in the journey toward Eretz Yisrael or within the Land itself, in the days when the Beis haMikdash still stood. They commemorate open miracles, the splitting of the sea, or a single cruse of oil burning for eight days. Purim, by contrast, is a Yom Tov of exile. Its story unfolded in Persia, and even right after its redemption, the Jewish People, for the most part, remained scattered and under foreign rule.

When we live in the mode of ordinary awareness and consciousness, we are then constantly making distinctions, distinctions between blessings and curses, exile and redemption, nature and miracle. As the Chasam Sofer explains (*Derashos,* Purim, p. 392), when one drinks, that discriminating quality is blurred and fuzzy. On Purim, this blurring becomes a holy act. By transcending the world of hard distinctions, at least for a few moments, we get to taste a deeper truth, and that is that Hashem is with us always. In blessings and in what seems like curses, in exile and in redemption, in the natural and the miraculous, always and forever.

18. *Question*: On the Yamim Tovim during which wine is imbibed to fulfill the Mitzvah to be joyful by drinking wine, there is a very specific measurement of wine that needs to be consumed. On Purim, however, we are specifically instructed to drink without measurement. Why this difference?

    Answer: Ordinarily, being conscious, aware, and able to choose rightly is the essence of living as a Torah-committed and civilized human being. Consciousness and discernment are indispensable to a life of holiness. Yet on Purim, for a few brief hours, we are asked to step beyond control, to suspend the grip of our rational awareness, and to admit the limits of what we truly know, for what do we truly know?

    Of course, just as every Yom Tov carries an element that extends into all the days of the year, with each day containing a trace of Pesach, a touch of Yom Kippur, or even an echo of Tisha b'Av, so too, Purim resonates within every day. Each day we are called to recall that תכלית הידיעה שלא נדע / "The Tachlis, ultimate knowledge is to know that we do not know";

that the deepest knowing lies beyond knowing. Yet Purim is distinct, for it stands as the headquarters, the central portal through which this truth pours forth into the fabric of our daily lives.

Moreover, in the language of Rashi, as mentioned, עבודה שאתה עובד בשכרות קרויה חול / "(When a Cohen performs a holy) Avodah in the Beis haMikdash, if he is drunk, it is (nevertheless) considered a *Chol* / mundane act" (*Zevachim*, 17b). Yet, this is precisely the Avodah, the holy work that needs to be performed on Purim: to reveal Divine Presence and Light even within the mundane.

19. *Question*: Unlike the other Rabbinic Yom Tov, Chanukah, when we are not commanded to hold a festive meal (according to most opinions, with the exception of the Rambam), on Purim, there *is* a specific Mitzvah to partake in a lavish feast. Why is this so?

Answer: Purim is 'the Yom Tov of the body'. The decree of Haman was not merely against Jewish practice or spiritual observance, as in the story of Chanukah, where the decrees targeted Torah study, Mitzvos, and the sacred rituals of the Beis Hamikdah. Rather, the Purim decree was directed against the existence of Jewish bodies, to annihilate the Jews physically. The *Nahafoch Hu*, the great reversal, was that this decree was transformed; hence, the miracle of Purim unfolded not in the open suspension of nature, but clothed within nature itself, in the "body" of the world, so to speak. If Chanukah, as all other Yamim Tovim, highlights the 'soul of the world', the transcendent Divine light that breaks through nature in revealed miracles, Purim reveals the hidden miracles within nature, within the garments and 'body' of the world. Therefore, we celebrate Purim not only with spirit but with the physical, with food, with drink, with embodied joy. The Mitzvah of the Purim feast ensures that the miracle and joy of Purim permeates not only the soul but the body, which was endangered by the decree of Haman. In this way, Purim is the most 'embodied' among all the Yamim Tovim.

20. *Question*: On all Yamim Tovim, the norm is to dress in dignified and respectable attire in honor of the Yom Tov. In contrast, Purim is marked by children, and perhaps even adults, wearing masks, costumes, and playful disguises. Why this departure?

    Answer: The miracle of Purim was concealed within the ordinary workings of nature. Nothing appeared openly supernatural, yet hidden within the veil of events was the guiding hand of Hashem. In reflection of this, we ourselves conceal our usual appearance, dressing in garments that mask our external identity.

    On a deeper level, Purim is about peeling back facades to reveal Essence. Nature itself is a garment, a covering that seems to obscure the Divine. Yet Purim reveals that beneath the concealment, at the core of all things, lies Divine providence and presence of Hashem. By donning costumes and covering our external selves, we train our vision to look past appearances, to sharpen our awareness of the inner reality, and to uncover the truth beneath the masks of the world.

21. *Question*: On all other Yamim Tovim, there is a Mitzvah to rejoice, to be b'Simchah, and on Sukkos, this joy is even heightened to a state of *Simchah Yeseira* / added, overflowing joy. Yet it is only with Purim that the very month itself becomes transformed into a season of gladness, "When Adar enters, we are to increase in joy." Each day of Adar calls us to deepen our rejoicing. Why is this? Why does Purim generate a joy that surpasses even the exalted joy of Sukkos?

Answer: The joy of Purim is unique because it is one born not from a revelation from on High, but from within a place of concealment. Other Yamim Tovim commemorate open miracles, revelations that lift us beyond ourselves. Such miracles awaken joy, yet it is a joy sparked by what was experienced from Above. Purim, however, celebrates miracles hidden within nature, redemptions veiled in ordinary events. Purim tells us that even within darkness, exile, and concealment, Hashem is always present. The joy of Purim, therefore, is not dependent on revelation, but on the recognition that the Infinite is found even in the most finite, that Hashem's love embraces us even in disguise. This is the deepest and most enduring joy, the joy of Essence, hence, a joy that no concealment can obscure, and no exile can diminish.

These twenty-one points offer but a glimpse into the many dimensions that distinguish Purim from all other Yamim Tovim, with their reasons only briefly captured here. To truly grasp their depth, one must return and explore the preceding chapters in full.

May your Purim shine with a radiant light,
a joy unbound and unbroken.

May clarity emerge from within concealment,
and may you experience a true Nahafoch Hu,
darkness transfigured into light, sorrow into celebration,
hiddenness unveiled into revelation.

And may we, together, behold the ultimate Nahafoch Hu,
with the dawning of redemption
and the revelation of Mashiach, swiftly, in our days.

Other Books by Rav Pinson

Rav Pinson on the Torah

Awakenings:

Drawing Life from the Weekly Torah Reading

The deeper teachings of the Torah reveal to us that the weekly Torah reading is connected to the unique energetic properties of that week. Every Torah portion, and thus every week, radiates with a particular quality, a distinct energy that, when understood and received, can bring tremendous guidance and assistance to every facet of our lives.

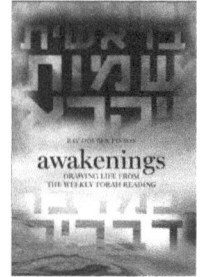

Delving into the weekly Torah reading and uncovering its overarching theme allows us to apply the power available on that week in our practical life.

We can learn how to harness the Ko'ach, power, of each unique Torah reading to expand consciousness, overcome challenges, gain control of our lives, and come to learn how to serve Hashem, self and others more mindfully, productively and effectively.

Weaving together the various facets of Torah interpretation, from the most esoteric (Kabbalah) and mystical (Chassidus) to the straightforward literal meaning (Peshat), this book is a multi-dimensional tapestry of practical, allegorical, philosophical, and mystical ideas and implications.

Rav Pinson on the Life Cycle

A BOND FOR ETERNITY
Understanding the Bris Milah

What is the Bris Milah – the covenant of circumcision? What does it represent, symbolize and signify? This book provides an in depth and sensitive review of this fundamental Mitzvah. In this little masterpiece of wisdom – profound yet accessible —the deeper meaning of this essential rite of passage and its eternal link to the Jewish people, is revealed and explored.

UPSHERNISH: THE FIRST HAIRCUT
Exploring the Laws, Customs & Meanings
of a Boy's First Haircut

What is the meaning of Upsherin, the traditional celebration of a boy's first haircut at the age of three? Why is a boy's hair allowed to grow freely for his first three years? What is the deeper import of hair in all its lengths and varieties? What is the meaning of hair coverings? Includes a guide to conducting an Upsherin ceremony.

THE JEWISH WEDDING:
A Guide to the Rituals and Traditions
of the Wedding Ceremony

The Jewish Wedding: A Guide to the Rituals and Traditions of the Wedding Ceremony.

This guide is based on the teachings of Torah, Talmud, Medrash, Zohar, Halacha, Poskim, Kabbalah and Chassidus. By quoting these teachings, we actively draw down the 'presence' of these holy souls who revealed these teachings, thus extending blessings to the bride and groom and all in attendance at the Chupa.

THE MYSTERY OF KADDISH
Understanding the Mourner's Kaddish

The Mystery of Kaddish is an in-depth exploration into the Mourner's Prayer. Throughout Jewish history, there have been many rites and rituals associated with loss and mourning, yet none have prevailed quite like the Mourner's Kaddish Prayer, which has become the definitive ritual of mourning. The book explores the source of this prayer and deconstructs the meaning to better understand the grieving process and how the Kaddish prayer supports and uplifts the bereaved through their own personal journey to healing.

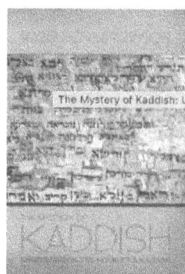

THE BOOK OF LIFE AFTER LIFE

What is a soul?
What happens to us after we physically die?
What is consciousness, and can it survive without a physical brain?
Can we remember our past lives?
Do near-death experiences prove immortality?
What is Gan Eden? Resurrection?

Exploring the possibility of surviving death, the near-death experience and a glimpse into what awaits us after this life.

(This book is an updated and expanded version of the book; Jewish Wisdom of the Afterlife)

Rav Pinson on Kabbalah

REINCARNATION AND JUDAISM
The Journey of the Soul

A fascinating analysis of the concept of Gilgul / Reincarnation. Dipping into the fountain of ancient wisdom and modern understanding, this book addresses and answers such basic questions as: What is reincarnation? Why does it occur? And how does it affect us personally?

INNER RHYTHMS
The Kabbalah of Music

Exploring the inner dimension of sound and music, and particularly, how music permeates all aspects of life. The topics range from Deveikus/Unity and Yichudim/Unifications, to the more personal issues, such as Simcha/Happiness and Marirus/ sadness.

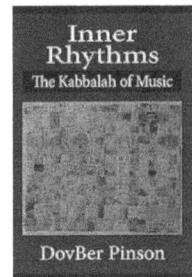

THIRTY–TWO GATES OF WISDOM
Into the Heart of Kabbalah & Chassidus

What is Kabbalah? And what are the differences between the theoretical, meditative, magical and personal Kabbalistic teachings? What are the four paths of interpreting the teachings

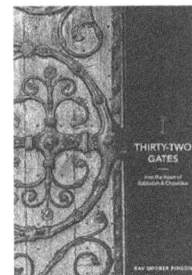

of the ARIzal? What did Chassidus teach? These are some of the fundamental issues expanded upon in this text. And then, more specifically, why are there so many names of G-d and what do they represent? What are the key concepts of these deeper teachings?

The book explores the grand narrative of the great chain of reality, how there was and is a movement from the Infinite Oneness of Hashem to a world of (apparent) duality and multiplicity.

———————

PASSPORT TO KABBALAH
A Journey of Inner Transformation

Life is a journey full of ups and downs, inside-outs, and unexpected detours. There are times when we think we know exactly where we want to be headed, and other times when we are so lost we don't even know where we are. This slim book provides readers with a passport of sorts to help them through any obstacles along their path of self-refinement, reflection, and self-transformation.

———————

THE SEVEN PRINCIPLES:
Towards a Life of Meaning and Purpose
A book on the Seven Mitzvos of Noach

These seven principles will open you up to a new and empowering way of thinking and being in this world.

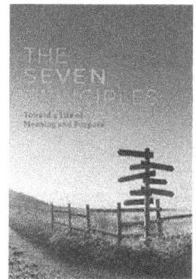

It will inspire you to engage in life proactively with openness, care, clarity of consciousness and attachment to the Source of life and fulfillment. Overflowing with thought provoking insights, Divine guidance and practical exercises, The Seven Principles is a manual to leading a life of purpose and joy.

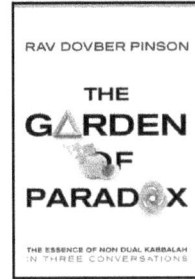

THE GARDEN OF PARADOX:
The Essence of Non - Dual Kabbalah

This book is a Primer on the Essential Philosophy of Kabbalah presented as a series of 3 conversations, revealing the mysteries of Creator, Creation and Consciousness. With three representational students, embodying respectively, the philosopher, the activist and the mystic, the book tackles the larger questions of life. Who is G-d? Who am I? Why do I exist? What is my purpose in this life? Written in clear and concise prose, the text, gently guides the reader towards making sense of life's paradoxes and living meaningfully.

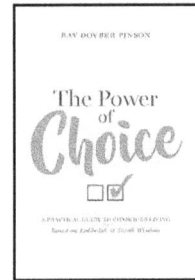

THE POWER OF CHOICE:
A Practical Guide to Conscious Living

It is the essential premise of this book that we hold the key to unlock many of the gates that seem closed to us and keep us from living our fullest life. That key we all hold is the power to choose. The Power of Choice is the primary tool that we have at our disposal to impact the world and effect change within our own lives. We often give up this power to outside forces such as the market, media, politicians or peer pressure; or to internal forces that often function beyond our conscious control such as ego, anger, lust, greed or jealousy. Making conscious, compassionate and creative decisions is the cornerstone of living a mature and meaningful life.

MYSTIC TALES FROM THE EMEK HAMELECH

Mystic Tales of the Emek HaMelech, is a wondrous and inspiring collection of stories culled from the Emek HaMelech. Emek HaMelech, from which these stories have been taken, (as well as its author) is a bit of a mystery. But like all good mysteries, it is one worth investigating. In this spirit the present volume is being offered to the general public in the merit and memory of its saintly author, as well as in the hopes of introducing a vital voice of deeper Torah teaching and tradition to a contemporary English speaking audience

---

Rav Pinson on Meditation

MEDITATION AND JUDAISM
Exploring the Jewish Meditative Paths

A comprehensive work encompassing the entire spectrum of Jewish thought, from the sages of the Talmud and the early Kabbalists to the modern philosophers and Chassidic masters. This book is both a scholarly, in-depth study of meditative practices, and a practical, easy to follow guide for any person interested in meditating the Jewish way.

TOWARD THE INFINITE

A book focusing exclusively on the Chassidic approach to meditation known as Hisbonenus. Encompassing the entire meditative experience, it takes the reader on a comprehensive and engaging journey through this unique practice. The book explores the various states of consciousness that a person encounters in the course of the meditation, beginning at a level of extreme self-awareness and concluding with a state of total non-awareness.

BREATHING & QUIETING THE MIND

Achieving a sense of self-mastery and inner freedom demands that we gain a measure of hegemony over our thoughts. We learn to choose out thoughts so that we are not at the mercy of whatever belches up to the mind. Through quieting the mind and conscious breathing we can slow the onrush of anxious, scattered thinking and come to a deeper awareness of the interconnectedness of all of life.

Source texts are included in translation, with how-to-guides for the various practices.

SOUND AND VIBRATION:
Tuning into the Echoes of Creation

Through our perception of sound and vibration we internalize the world around us. What we hear, and how we process that hearing, has a profound impact on how we experience life. What we hear can empower us or harm us. A defining human capacity is to harness the power sound -- through speech, dialogue, and song,

and through listening to others. Hearing is primary dimension of our existence. In fact, as a fetus our ears were the first fully operating sensory organs to develop.

This book will guide you in methods of utilizing the power of sound and vibration to heal and maintain mental, emotional and spiritual health, to fine-tune your Midos and even to guide you into deeper levels of Deveikus / conscious unity with Hashem. The vibratory patterns of the Aleph-Beis are particularly useful portals into our deeper conscious selves. Through chanting and deep listening, we can use the letters and sounds to shift our very mindset, to induce us into a state of presence and spiritual elevation.

VISUALIZATION AND IMAGERY:
Harnessing the Power of our Mind's Eye

We assume that what we see with our eyes is absolute. Yet, beyond our ability to choose what we see, we have the ability to choose how we see. This directly translates into how we experience life. In a world saturated with visual imagery, our senses are continuously assaulted with Kelipa/empty/fantasy imagery that we would not necessarily choose. These images can negatively affect our relationship with ourselves, with the world around us, and with the Divine. This volume seeks to show us how we can alter that which we observe through harnessing the power of our mind's eye, the inner sanctum of our imagination. We thus create a new way to see and experience the world. This book teaches us how to utilize visualization and imagery as a way to develop our spiritual sensitivity and higher intuition, and ultimately achieve Deveikus/Unity with Hashem.

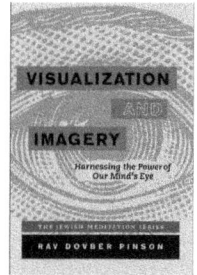

CONTEMPLATING AND TRANSCENDING MIND

Hisbonenus: The Meditative Path of Chabad

What is Hisbonenus / meditative contemplation? And how is it actually practiced? The illustrious first Rebbe of Chabad, the Alter Rebbe, aimed for the deepest teachings of the Torah and Chassidus to be internalized and deeply contemplated.Hisbonenus, the process of focused contemplation, begins by training your mind to dwell, for example, on the unity of Hashem, for extended periods. This practice engages the entire spectrum of your intellect-your Chochmah (wisdom or spark of intuition), Binah (analysis and understanding), and Da'as (knowledge and integration). As you progress, your thoughts will naturally stir your heart and emotions. When your mind contemplates lofty concepts such as the unity of the Creator with all of Creation, emotions of profound love for Hashem and a deep sense of wonder will arise. These emotions become more refined and subtle as you delve deeper, eventually leading to Ayin (transparency of self) and Deveikus ('conscious' unity with the Divine).

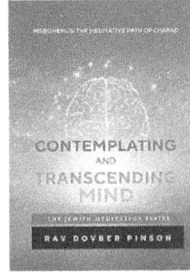

When the mind reaches its full potential for concentration and contemplation, it may 'implode' from exhaustion, so to speak, leading to a state of Ayin. This phenomenon shows that we don't have to circumvent or invalidate the intellect to transcend it. Rather, we can use the mind itself as a bridge to the Beyond.

Achieving 'intellectual exhaustion' allows us to transition into a state of Ayin-consciousness and mystical union more easily than trying to leap over the mind or stop thinking entirely. This advanced stage of Hisbonenus involves moving from Binah (understanding) back to Chochmah (supra-rational wisdom), and beyond.

Rav Pinson on The Holidays

THE HAGGADAH:
Pathways to Pesach and the Haggadah

"In every generation a person must regard oneself as having gone out of Mitzrayim / Egypt." This means that when recalling the Exodus, which occurred thousands of years ago, we also need to envision ourselves as being taken out of Mitzrayim and freed from enslavement.

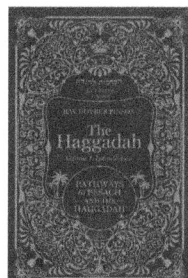

Introducing the Haggadah and the themes of Pesach, this book delves into the greater context of the Festival and the Seder, allowing us to tap into the profound inspiration and Koach / power that Pesach and Seder Night offers.

EIGHT LIGHTS
8 Meditations for Chanukah

What is the meaning and message of Chanukah? What is the spiritual significance of the Lights of the Menorah? What are the Lights telling us? What is the deeper dimension of the Dreidel? Rav Pinson, with his trademark deep learning and spiritual sensitivity guides us through eight meditations relating to the Lights of the Menorah, the eight days of Chanukah, and a fascinating exploration of the symbolism and structure of the Dreidel. Includes a detailed how-to guide for lighting the Chanukah Menorah.

THE PURIM READER
The Holiday of Purim Explored

With a Persian name, a masquerade dress code and a woman as the heroine, Purim is certainly unusual amongst the Jewish holidays. Most people are very familiar with the costumes, Megilah and revelry, but are mystified by their significance. This book offers a glimpse into the hidden world of Purim, uncovering these mysteries and offering a deeper understanding of this unique holiday. (This is the original pamphlet. This book covers the larger scope.)

The High Holiday Series:

A CALL TO MAJESTY:
The Mysteries of Shofar & Rosh Hashanah

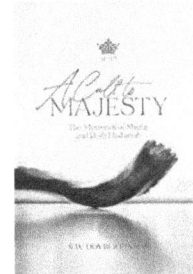

The Shofar is the preeminent symbol of Rosh Hashanah, waking us up to a time of deep introspection and celebration. But why do we blow the Shofar on this most special of days? While the Torah decrees that the Shofar must be blown, it does not provide a reason. On the deepest level, the Shofar is of course beyond reason altogether, and yet, from within its shape, sound and story, a constellation of "reasons" emerge. Rebirth. Responsibility. Radical Amazement. On a primal vibrational level, the Shofar calls each of us to a place of deeper consciousness and community as we crown the King of All Creation.

A CALL TO MAJESTY delves deeply into the world of Rosh Hashanah and its primary Mitzvah, the sound of the Shofar. Weaving together a multi-dimensional tapestry of practical, allegorical, philosophical, and mystical ideas and implications, the teachings collected herein empower us all to answer the higher calling of the Shofar.

A LIGHTNESS OF BEING:
Your Guide to Yom Kippur

Yom Kippur is unabashedly transformative; the power of the day beckons us to work toward fundamental transformation and Teshuvah / return to who we really are. Often, the word Teshuvah is unfortunately translated as 'repentance'. It is more accurately rendered as 'return', meaning both a return 'from' our states of spiritual alienation and exile, as well as a 'turning to' experiencing our deepest selves. Yom Kippur empowers us to return to our essence, reclaim who we truly are, and live from that place.

A LIGHTNESS OF BEING delves into the powerful and transformative day of Yom Kippur. Weaving together a multi-dimensional tapestry of practical, allegorical, philosophical and mystical ideas and implications, the teachings gathered herein empower us all to enter Yom Kippur and truly feel enlightened, elevated, lighter and transformed.

EMBRACED IN DIVINE SPACE:
The Festivals of Sukkos, Hoshana Rabba & Simchas Torah

From among all the Yamim Tovim, Sukkos stands out as one of the most elusive and mysterious. While Sukkos is called "the Season of our Joy" - and it is a very joyful time indeed, replete with singing, celebrating, and dancing - it may not be so clear what we are celebrating and why joy is so central to the Yom Tov. Weaving together the various threads of Torah interpretation, from the most esoteric and mystical (Sod / Kabbalah / Chassidus) to the straightforward literal meaning (Peshat), as well as the allegorical (Remez) and homiletical (Derush), this book is a multi-dimensional tapestry of practical, philosophical, and mystical ideas and implications. The graceful interaction of all these elements reveals profound insights which will greatly enrich one's experience of Sukkos.

THE FOUR SPECIES
The Symbolism of the Lulav & Esrog

The Four Species have inspired countless commentaries and traditions and intrigued scholars and mystics alike. In this little masterpiece of wisdom both profound and practical - the deep symbolic roots and nature of the Four Species are explored. The Na'anuim, or ritual of the Lulav movement, is meticulously detailed and Kavanos,, are offered for use with the practice. Includes an illustrated guide to the Lulav Movements.

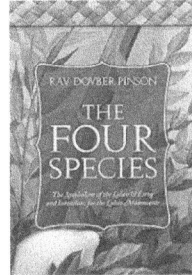

Rav Pinson on Prayer

INNER WORLDS OF JEWISH PRAYER
A Guide to Develop and Deepen
the Prayer Experience

While much attention has been paid to the poetry, history, theology and contextual meaning of the prayers, the intention of this work is to provide a guide to finding meaning and effecting transformation through the prayer experience itself.

Explore: *What happens when we pray? *How do we enter the mind-state of prayer? *Learning to incorporate the body into the prayers. *Discover techniques to enhance and deepen prayer and make it a transformative experience.

This empowering and inspiring text, demonstrates how through proper mindset, preparation and dedication, the experience of prayer can be deeply transformative and ultimately, life-altering.

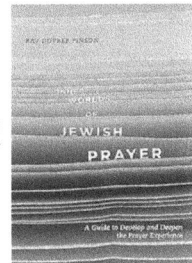

ILLUMINATED SOUND:
The Baal Shem Tov on Prayer

In the year 1698 a great light was revealed to the world with the descent of the holy soul of the Baal Shem Tov. In time, the Baal Shem Tov became one of the most important and influential teachers of Torah in all of history, and the founder of Chassidus.

Amongst the vast repository of profound and revolutionary teachings of the holy Baal Shem Tov, the teachings on the path of Tefilah / Prayer are the most elaborate. The teachings of the Baal Shem Tov on Tefilah include some of his most innovative expressions, or Chidushim. Tefilah is the essential and central tenet from which all other teachings flow.

In this masterful and practical text, Rav Pinson revives the awe-inspiring and transformational teachings of the Baal Shem Tov, and illuminates his unique path to Tefilah.

Rav Pinson on Jewish Practice

RECLAIMING THE SELF
The Way of Teshuvah

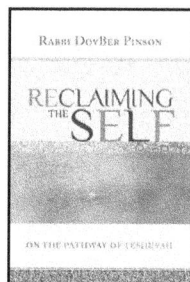

Teshuvah is one of the great gifts of life. It speaks of a hope for a better today and empowers us to choose a brighter tomorrow. But what exactly is Teshuvah? How does it work? How can we undo our past and how do we deal with guilt? And what is healthy regret without eroding our self-esteem? In this fascinating and empowering book, the path for genuine transformation and a way to include all of our past in the powerful moment of the now, is explored and demonstrated.

WRAPPED IN MAJESTY
Tefillin - Exploring the Mystery

Tefillin, the black boxes and leather straps that are worn during prayer, are curiously powerful and mysterious. Within the inky black boxes lie untold secrets. In this profound, passionate and thought-provoking text, the multi-dimensional perspectives of Tefillin are explored and revealed. Magically weaving together all levels of Torah including the Peshat (literal observation), to Remez (allegorical), to Derush, (homiletic), to Sod (hidden) into one beautiful tapestry. Inspirational and instructive, Wrapped in Majesty: Tefillin, will make putting on the Tefillin more meaningful and inspiring.

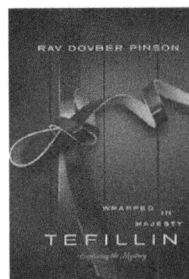

SECRETS OF THE MIKVAH:
Waters of Transformation

A Mikvah is a pool of water used for the purpose of ritual immersion; a place where one moves from a state of Tumah; impurity, blockage and death— to a place of Teharah; purity, fluidity and life.

In SECRETS OF THE MIKVAH, Rav Pinson delves into the transformative powers of the Mikvah with his trademark all-encompassing perspective that ranges from the literal, Pshat observation and Halachic implications of the texts, to the allegorical, the philosophical, and finally, to the deep secrets of the Mikvah as revealed by Kabbalah and Chassidus.

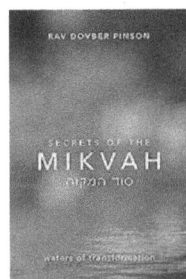

This insightful and inspirational text demonstrates how immersion in a Mikvah can be a transformative and life-altering practice, and includes various Kavanos—deep intentions—for all people, through various stages of life, that empower and enrich the immersion experience.

THE MYSTERY OF SHABBOS
Shabbat Rediscovered

Delving into the transformative power of Shabbos. With an all-encompassing perspective that ranges from the literal, Pshat observation and Halachic implications of the texts, to the allegorical, the philosophical, and finally, to the deeper secrets as revealed by Kabbalah and Chassidus, creating an elegant tapestry of thought and experience. THE MYSTERY OF SHABBOS is a profound meditation on the meaning of Shabbos and demonstrates the physical, emotional, mental and spiritual possibilities available and given to us with the gift of Shabbos. Studying and contemplating this inspired text on the depths of Shabbos will unveil a redemptive light in your experience of the Seventh Day -- and by extension, every day of your life.

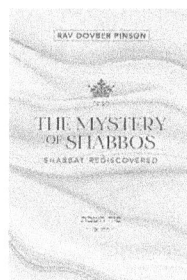

THE SPIRAL OF TIME:
A 12 Part Series on the Months of the Year

VOL 1: THE SPIRAL OF TIME:
Unraveling the Yearly Cycle

Many centuries ago, the Sages of Israel were the foremost authority in the fields of both astronomical calculation and astrological wisdom, including the deeper interpretations of the cycles and seasons. Over time, this wisdom became hidden within the esoteric teachings of the Torah, and as a result was known only to students and scholars of the deepest depths of the tradition. More recently, the great teachers, from R. Yitzchak Luria (the Arizal) to the Baal Shem Tov, taught that as the world approaches the Era of Redemption, it is a Mitzvah / spiritual obligation to broadly reveal this wisdom.

"The Spiral of Time" is volume 1 in a series of 12 books, and serves as an introductory book to the basic concepts and nature of the Hebrew calendar and explores the special day of Rosh Chodesh.

VOL 2: THE MONTH OF NISAN:
Miraculous Awakenings from Above

The month of NISAN is the first month of the lunar cycle of the year, a month that brings in the spring and a month of redemption. Spring represents a time of plenty, abundance, sunshine, hope, and possibility. Redemption, on whatever level, feels palpable and accessible. In spring, the world is redeemed from the cold winter,

the flower is redeemed from the tree, the grass from the earth, and we too feel that redemption is possible. A whole complex of ideas, including newness, redemption, going out of Egypt, and being freed from slavery, is intricately bound with the idea of Aviv / spring and the powerful month of Nisan.

VOL 3: THE MONTH OF IYYAR: EVOLVING THE SELF
& The Holiday of LAG B'OMER

The month of IYYAR is the second month of the spring, a month that connects the Redemption from Egypt in Nissan with the Revelation of Torah in Sivan. The Chai/ Eighteenth day of the Month is the day we celebrate the Rashbi (Rabbi Shimon Bar Yochai) and the revealing of the hidden aspects of the Torah. This is the 'Holiday' of Lag b'Omer. The book explores the unique quality of this special month, a month that has a Mitzvah of counting the Omer every day. In addition, the book explores the roots and significance of the mystical 'holiday' of Lag b'Omer. Including the customs & Practices of Lag b'Omer, such as, bonfires, bows & arrows, parades, Upsherin, and more.

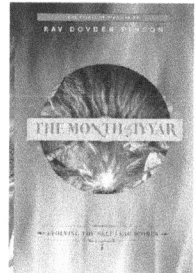

VOL 4: THE MONTH OF SIVAN:
The Art of Receiving:
Shavuos and Matan Torah

Sivan is the third month of the lunar cycle. One is a singularity. Two is division. Three is harmony, a unity that synthesizes individuality and multiplicity, Heaven and Earth, Spirituality and Physicality. During this month we celebrate Shavuos and the giving of the Torah, the ultimate expression of the unity of the

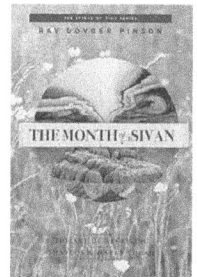

Above and Below and we aspire to connect with the Keser/Crown of Torah that Transcends and yet includes all Worlds. Learning how to truly receive Higher wisdom in our Lower faculties is the mental, emotional, and spiritual exercise of the month.

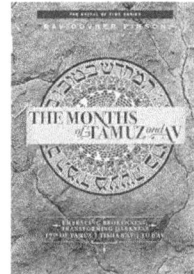

———————

VOL 5: THE MONTHS OF TAMUZ AND AV:
Embracing Brokenness -
17th of Tamuz, Tisha B'Av, & Tu B'Av

Each month and season of the year, radiates with distinct Divine qualities and unique opportunities for growth and Tikkun.

The summer month of Tamuz and Av contain the longest and hottest days of the year. The raised temperature is indicative of a corresponding spiritual heat, a time of harsher judgement and potential destruction, such as the destructions of the first and second Beis HaMikdash, which began on the 17th of Tamuz and culminated on the 9th and 10th of Av.

A few days later, on Tu b'Av, the darkness is transformed and reveals the greatest light and possibility for new life. During these summer months of Tamuz and Av we embrace our brokenness so that we can heal and transform darkness into light.

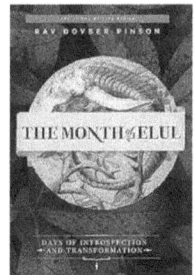

———————

VOL 6: THE MONTH OF ELUL:
Days of Introspection and Transformation

Each month of the year radiates with a distinct quality and provides unique opportunities for growth and personal transformation. Elul, as the final month of the spring/summer season is connected to endings. Elul gives us the strength to be able to finish strong, to end well. Elul also serves as a month of preparation for the New Year/Rosh Hashanah.

We inhale our past year, ending with wisdom and then we also gain the wisdom to begin anew and exhale a positive year into being. The mental, emotional, and spiritual objective of this month is introspection and the reclaiming of our inner purity and wholeness.

VOL 7: THE MONTH OF TISHREI:
A Time of Rebirth & Upward Movement

Each month of the year radiates with distinct Divine qualities and unique opportunities for growth and spiritual illumination. As Tishrei begins the new yearly cycle, it is an appropriate month to introspect, reflect and resolve to move forward and preserve moving forward into the more inward months of the winter. This month creates the space to unburden ourselves from our negativities, and enter a more sacred, grounded sacred space. In Tishrei we are given the gift of forgiveness and then the ability to truly regain our space and inner joy.

VOL 8: THE MONTH OF CHESHVAN:
Navigating Transitions, Elevating the Fall

Directly on the heels of the inspiring and holiday-filled month of Tishrei, Cheshvan is a month that is quiet and devoid of holidays. In the month of Cheshvan we use the stored up energies of the previous months to self-generate our inspiration and creativity and provide ourselves with the strength to rise up after a fall. In Cheshvan we are entering into a stormier, wetter and colder season. It is a month of transition. The mental,

emotional and spiritual objective of this month is to weather the transitions, learn to self-generate and stand tall. And if we do fall, we use the quality of this month to get back up and do so with more conviction, strength, wisdom and clarity.

VOL 9: THE MONTH OF KISLEV:
Rekindling Hope, Dreams and Trust

Kislev is the final month of the fall. Throughout this month, daylight progressively shortens, and the temperatures drop. Towards the end of the month, at the darkest hour, the winter solstice arrives and we begin the celebration of Chanukah. We commemorate the miracle of a small jug of oil that burned for eight nights, and as we celebrate, daylight expands. In the month of Kislev-despite the darkness, or perhaps because of it-we have the ability to tap into the Ohr HaGanuz, the hidden light of hope that rekindles our dreams and aspirations.

VOL 10: THE MONTH OF TEVES:
Refining Relationships, Elevating the Body

The quality of Teves is generally harsh—much like its counterpart Tamuz in the summer, thus the tendency for many is to hunker down, retract, curl up and wait for the month to pass by, only to reemerge when the harshness has dissipated. Think for a moment about the 'easier' months of the year, which, like gentle waves in the ocean, carry us where we want to go. We can ride these energies easily and they can propel us forward effortlessly, we just need to go with the overall flow, so to speak. The harsher months, on the other hand, can be compared to the more powerful waves that emanate from the belly of the ocean,which come forcefully crashing down and can easily drown a person before they even realize what has happened. However, those who want to uti-

lize the momentum of the powerful energy that is available during such times can, with caution and creativity, harness these intense waves and ride them higher and farther than other, more gentle circumstances may allow. However, harnessing the power of Tohu, the raw energy of the body, does in fact need to be approached with great care and attention.

VOL 11: THE MONTH OF SHEVAT: ELEVATING EATING
& The Holiday of Tu b'Shevat

Each month of the year radiates with a distinct Divine energy and thus unique opportunities for growth, *Tikkun* and illumination. According to the deeper teachings of the Torah, all of these distinct qualities, opportunities and natural phenomena correspond to a certain data set. That is, the nature of each month is elucidated by a specific letter of the Aleph Beis, a tribe, verse, human sense, and so forth. The month of Shevat is particularly connected to food and our relationship to bodily intake. During this month we celebrate Tu b'Shevat, the New Year of the Tree, and aspire to create a proper and physically/emotionally/spiritually healthy relationship with food.

VOL 12: THE MONTH OF ADAR:
Transformation Through Laughter & Holy Doubt

Each month of the year radiates with distinct Divine qualities and unique opportunities for growth and spiritual illumination. As Adar concludes the monthly cycle of the year, as well as the solar phenomena of the winter, it is an appropriate month to think about our essential identity, before moving out to meet the world come spring. This month we strive to create a healthy relation-

ship with holy humor, unbounded joy, and a general sense of lightness of being. Through the work of Adar we transform negative, crippling doubt and uncertainties into radical wonderment and openness.

PROCESS AND PRESENCE
Life in Balance

In the world of process, the self and the world are broken,
and we ambitiously strive to improve and to better.
In presence reality, all is now, everything is perfect, and
there is
nowhere to progress and certainly no reason to fight or strive.
This book offers the gift of a balanced life, wherein the path of process and the pathless path of presence are lived in unison.

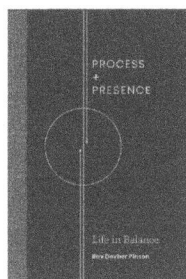

New Release!

MARRIAGE:
The Microcosmic Dance of Creation

The book invites the reader to approach marriage as a living sanctuary, nurtured through the Five Keys named in the wedding blessings: joy, love, kinship, peace, and friendship. A good marriage echoes the great rhythm of Creation: from Infinite Oneness, to separation and yearning, and finally to reunion in love. Just as the Creator made space for the world to be, spouses learn to make space for one another—through listening, patience, humility, and gentleness. And just as the Creator sustains the world moment by moment, the couple learns to renew the bond each day. Marriage is the reunion of two souls that were once one. Yet this reunion does not erase the uniqueness of either. Each arrives whole, stands face-to-face, and co-creates intimacy with intention and devotion, moving from longing to a deep and abiding oneness that continues to unfold, ever widening, ever deepening, without end.